The Transition to Sustainability
The Politics of Agenda 21 in Europe

Edited by

Tim O'Riordan

and

Heather Voisey

Earthscan Publications Ltd, London

First published in the UK in 1998 by
Earthscan Publications Limited

A catalogue record for this book is available from the British Library

ISBN: 1 85383 468 8
ISBN: 1 85383 469 6

Typesetting and page design by PCS Mapping & DTP, Newcastle upon Tyne
Printed and bound by Biddles Ltd, Guildford and Kings Lynn
Cover design by John Gosling

The content of this publication is the sole responsibility of the authors and in no way represents the views of the Commission or its services.

For a full list of publications please contact:

Earthscan Publications Limited
120 Pentonville Road
London N1 9JN
Tel: (0171) 278 0433
Fax: (0171) 278 1142
Email: earthinfo@earthscan.co.uk
http://www.earthscan.co.uk

Earthscan is an editorially independent subsidiary of Kogan Page Limited and publishes in association with WWF-UK and the International Institute for Environment and Development.

This book is printed on elemental chlorine free paper from sustainably managed forests.

CONTENTS

List of Contributors

Tim O'Riordan is Associate Director of the Centre for Social and Economic Research on the Global Environment and Professor of Environmental Sciences at the University of East Anglia, Norwich NR4 7TJ.
E-mail: t.oriordan@uea.ac.uk

Heather Voisey is a Senior Research Associate in the Centre for Social and Economic Research on the Global Environment at the University of East Anglia. E-mail: h.voisey@uea.ac.uk

Nigel Haigh is the former Director of the Institute for European Environmental Policy, London, Dean Bradley House, 52 Horseferry Road, London SW1P 2AG. E-mail: kpartridge@ieeplondon.org.uk

Martin Hession is Lecturer in Environmental Law at the Centre for Environment and Technology, Imperial College London, 48 Prince's Gardens, London SW7 2PE. E-mail: m.hession@ic.ac.uk

Richard Macrory is Professor of Environmental Law at the Centre for Environment and Technology, Imperial College London, 48 Prince's Gardens, London SW7 2PE. E-mail: r.macrory@ic.ac.uk

David Wilkinson is Senior Fellow at the Institute for European Environmental Policy, London, Dean Bradley House, 52 Horseferry Road, London SW1P 2AG. E-mail: dwilkinson@ieeplondon.org.uk

Clare Coffey is Research Officer at the Institute for European Environmental Policy, London, Dean Bradley House, 52 Horseferry Road, London SW1P 2AG. E-mail: ccoffey@ieeplondon.org.uk

Christiane Beuermann and **Bernhard Burdick** are Research Associates at the Wuppertal Institute for Climate, Environment and Energy, Döppersberg 19, D–42 103 Wuppertal, Germany.
E-mail: christiane.beuermann@wupperinst.org

Liv Astrid Sverdrup has previously worked as a Research Associate at the Fridtjof Nansen Institute, N–1324 Lysaker, Norway. Since January 1997, she has worked as a Senior Executive Officer at the Ministry of Defence in Norway.

Teresa Ribeiro, formerly a Senior Policy Analyst at CEEETA (Centro de Estudos em Economia da Energia, dos Transportes e do Ambiente) (see below), is currently in charge of Environmental Scenarios and Policy Instruments at the European Environment Agency, Kongens Nytorv 6, DK–1050 Copenhagen, Denmark. E-mail: teresa.ribeiro@eea.eu.int

Valdemar Rodrigues is a Senior Research Associate at CEEETA, Rua Gustavo de Matos Sequeira, 28, 1: Dto, 1200 Lisbon, Portugal. E-mail: vjrodrigues@mail.telepac.pt

Panos Fousekis is a Researcher in the National Foundation for Agricultural Research, Institute of Mountainous Agriculture, 2nd Km Karpenisiou-Lamias, Karpenision 36100, Greece. E-mail: ioaok@athena.compulink.gr

Joseph Lekakis is Associate Professor in the Department of Economics, University of Crete, Rethimno 74100, Crete, Greece. E-mail: lekakis@fortezza.cc.ucr.gr

List of Tables, Figures, Boxes and Appendices

Tables

Figures

BOXES

APPENDICES

Acronyms and Abbreviations

A21	Agenda 21
ACE	Action by the Community relating to the Environment
ACNAT	Action by the Community Relating to Nature Conservation
AIDS	Acquired Immune Deficiency Syndrome
BMBau	Federal Ministry for Regional Planning, Building and Urban Development (Germany)
BMBFT	Federal Ministry for Education, Science, Research and Technology (Germany)
BMU	Federal Ministry for the Environment (Germany)
BMZ	Federal Ministry of Economic Cooperation and Development (Germany)
BSE	Bovine Spongiform Encephalopathy ('mad cow disease')
BUKO	Bundeskongress Agrarkoordination (agriculture and development NGO) (Germany)
BUND	Bund für Umweltund Naturschutz Deutschland (Friends of the Earth, Germany)
CAP	Common Agricultural Policy
CCT	Compulsory Competitive Tendering (England)
CEC	Commission of the European Communities
CEETA	Centro de Estudos Economia da Energia, dos Transportes e do Ambiente (Portugal)
CFC	chlorofluorocarbons
CITES	Convention on International Trade in Endangered Species
CNA	National Commission for the Environment (Portugal)
CO_2	carbon dioxide
COM	European Union communications to the Council
CSD	(United Nations) Commission on Sustainable Development
CSERGE	Centre for Social and Economic Research on the Global Environment (UK)
DEM	deutschmark
DETR	Department of the Environment, Transport and the Regions (UK)
DG	Directorate-General
DG XI	Directorate-General for Environment, Consumer Protection and Nuclear Security
DGB	Deutscher Gewerkschaftsbund (German Trade Union Federation)
DNR	Deutscher Naturschutzring (umbrella group of German environmental organisations)
DoE	Department of the Environment (UK)
Dst	Association of German Cities (Deutscher Städtetag) (Germany)
DStGb	Deutscher Städte und Gemeindebund (Germany)
EAGGF	European Agriculture Guidance and Guarantee Fund

EBA	Environmental Basic Act (Portugal)
EC	European Community
ECJ	European Court of Justice
ECOSOC	UN Economic and Social Development Committee
ECU	European currency unit
EDE	Ministerial Committee on the Environment
EEB	European Environmental Bureau
EEC	European Economic Community
EIA	environment impact assessment
EKA	Athens Centre for Workers (Greece)
EMAS	Environmental Management System
EPA	Environmental Protection Association (Portugal)
EPA	Environmental Protection Agency (US)
EPAA	Environmental Protection Associations Act (Portugal)
EPLL	environmental protection at the local level (Norway)
ERDF	European Regional Development Fund
ESF	European Social Fund
EU	European Union
FCCC	Framework Convention on Climate Change
FIFG	Financial Instrument for Fisheries Guidance
FoE	Friends of the Earth
FONE	Forum for Norwegian Ecomunicipalities (Norway)
GATT	General Agreement on Tariffs and Trade
GDP	gross domestic product
GEF	Global Environment Facility
GEOTA	Group for Studies on Landuse Planning and the Environment (Portugal)
GFG	Going For Green (UK)
GNP	gross national product
GSEE	General Confederation of Greek Workers (Greece)
Habitat II	Second UN Conference on Human Settlements
HOLSCSD	House of Lords Select Committee on Sustainable Development
ICLEI	International Council for Local Environmental Initiatives
IGC	Intergovernmental Conference
IIED	International Institute for Environment and Development
IPAMB	Institute of Environmental Protection (Portugal)
ISEW	index of sustainable economic welfare
ISO	International Standards Organisation
JNICT	National Council for Scientific Research (Portugal)
KPE	Centre for Environmental Education (Greece)
KS	Norwegian association of local and regional authorities (Norway)
LA21	Local Agenda 21
LGA	Local Government Association (UK)
LGMB	Local Government Management Board (UK)
LIFE	L'Instrument Financier pour l'Environnement (France)
LO	landfill operator

LPN	League for the Protection of Nature (Portugal)
MAFF	Ministry of Agriculture, Fisheries and Food (UK)
MECU	million European currency units
MENR	Ministry of Environment and Natural Resources (Portugal)
MEP	Member of the European Parliament
MoE	Ministry of the Environment (Norway)
MPAT	Ministry of Planning and Territory Administration (Portugal)
NEPP	National Environmental Policy Plan (Portugal)
NEF	New Economics Foundation
NGO	non-governmental organisation
NOK	Norwegian krone
NO_x	nitrous oxides
OECD	Organisation for Economic Cooperation and Development
OFGAS	Office of the Regulator of the Gas Industry (UK)
OJC	Official Journal of the EC
ONS	Office of National Statistics (UK)
PCSD	President's Council on Sustainable Development (US)
PPG	planning policy guidance
PTE	Portuguese escudos
QUERCUS	National Association for Nature Conservation (Portugal)
ROAST	resist, observe, accommodate, seize, transcend
RTS	Reclaim the Streets (UK)
SEA	strategic environmental assessment
SEA	State Department for the Environment (Portugal)
SEARN	Secretariat for the Environment and Natural Resources (Portugal)
SEB	Association of Greek Industrialists (Greece)
SO_x	sulphur oxides
SRU	German Council of Environmental Experts (Germany)
TEN	Trans-European Network
UK	United Kingdom
UN	United Nations
UNCED	United Nations Conference on Environment and Development
UNEP	United Nations Environment Programme
UNGASS	United Nations General Assembly Special Session on the Environment
VAT	value-added tax
VOCs	volatile organic compounds
WCED	World Commission on Environment and Development
WEED	World Economy, Ecology and Development NGO (Germany)
WTO	World Trade Organisation
WWF	Worldwide Fund for Nature
YPEHODE	Ministry for the Environment, Physical Planning and Public Works (Greece)
YVET	Ministry of Industry, Energy and Technology (Greece)
5EAP	Fifth Environmental Action Programme
£/p	Pound/pence (UK)
$	Dollar

ACKNOWLEDGEMENTS

A book of this complexity requires coordinated and supportive effort. We were enormously helped by the responsiveness and enthusiasm of all the authors. They took to our strictures and guidance with great good grace and remarkable equanimity. The consequence was a happy band of people who learned much from each other and felt the better for it.

A study like this also needs cash and patronage. The latter was supplied by Andrew Sors and Angela Liberatore, the former by their Directorate-General XII of the Commission of the European Communities. This funding was provided under the auspices of the Socio-Economic Research line of DG XII. All of us are very grateful to the Directorate and to Drs Sors and Liberatore for making this research possible.

Equally important was the final production of the manuscript. For this we thank Ann Dixon of CSERGE Norwich for patiently coping with a seemingly endless stream of manuscripts and corrections. We also thank Rowan Davies of Earthscan who sat patiently while the manuscript was transformed from a series of promises to final delivery.

Tim O'Riordan, Heather Voisey
Norwich
January 1998

PREFACE

Tim O'Riordan and Heather Voisey

The pages that follow are the result of a collaborative study examining how various parts of the European Union (EU) are coming to grips with Agenda 21 (A21), the framework agreed at the United Nations Conference on Environment and Development (UNCED), held in Rio de Janeiro in June 1992, for implementing sustainable development. It details how all nations on the planet are repositioning their economies, their societies and their collective purpose to maintain all life on Earth, peacefully, healthily, equitably and with sufficient wealth to ensure that all are content in their survival. These are fine words and similar sentiments have been expressed by philosophers, monarchs, politicians and activists since the dawn of humanity.

Specifically for this project, funded by Directorate-General XII of the European Commission, the aim was to develop a fuller understanding of the political dynamics associated with the organising focus that is sustainable development. To do this, the project team examined a number of indicators of both policy shift, including policy integration, and structural or positional adjustment in the pattern of forces guiding and coordinating policy. These organisational and procedural modulations are associated with a host of actors and agencies including government departments, non-departmental public bodies, regulatory agencies, business, local government, the voluntary sector, communities and citizens.

Throughout our assessment we were influenced by the conclusions of the climate politics study undertaken by O'Riordan and Jäger (1996, pp351–360). These observations suggested that the following themes should be addressed in any future analysis of institutional dynamics in response to global environmental change initiatives:

- institutional adjustment takes place in a number of policy arenas, which may work cooperatively, but not necessarily with the same set of political triggers. Response to sustainable development, therefore, can and should come in a number of guises;
- robust institutional adjustment has to be backed by economic ministries and economic policy strategies. Tackling the roots of macro-economic philosophy with an environmental agenda will fail, unless the two approaches can be made to reinforce one another; and
- because policy networks are constantly coalescing and fissuring, the most

successful institutional adjustments require linkages of policy coalitions – fresh groupings of interests whose cooperative support buttresses a number of policy innovators and executors at a variety of levels. For sustainable development to occur, such coalitions have to shape a common political space and combine economic, social and environmental interests.

Therefore, the project team approached this task by searching for policy indicators that might herald a shift towards a more sustainable pattern of economic development and social welfare. The study was influenced by a trio of conditions that the research team believe underpins any serious analysis of sustainable development. These are:

- *continuation, durability and reliability of economic performance,* not undermined by avoidable costs of environmental restoration or resource substitution, and where the precautionary principle applies to the maintenance of 'global commons' life-support processes;
- *stewardship, trusteeship and a duty of care towards vulnerable ecosystems and peoples,* especially where non-sustainable activities increase susceptibility to catastrophe and undermine inbuilt resilience, *and to future generations*, whose vulnerability to environmental and social change, and economic globalisation, is unknown; and
- *localism, democratic innovation, and greater self-reliance* in communities in the face of environmental, economic and social insecurities, as a measure of collective defence against threat.

The project team regards these three powerful shaping forces as both sequential and synergistic. They are sequential in the sense that only when politicians perceive that sustainable development guarantees reliability and resilience in wealth and job creation can they embrace a wider set of principles on stewardship and empowerment. Synergism, however, is equally vital. Small shifts in policy and social experience in the crucial areas of stewardship and empowerment are essential to persuade economic innovators that these are necessary conditions for durability in economic performance. This implies a radical notion that elements, and possibly whole chunks, of standard neo-classical political theory may have to be reconstructed to incorporate ecological and social equity considerations, precaution, and the interests of future generations. This accounts for the interest in green accounting and ecotaxation – two significant indicators of a transforming economic practice.

Sustainable development is a deliberately ambiguous concept; this is its strength. Its organising focus is ecological and human–sensitive accounting, the application of a precautionary duty of care, and the scope for civic activism at local level. This provides it with a distinctive role in the evolution of human and natural wellbeing. Institutional innovation is a permanent feature of the human condition. What is relevant here is the relationship between various general trends in institutional change, promoted by a host of factors: laws, treaties, intervention, communication, value change and civic protest. Such change is, by definition, continuous and unpredictable. Then there is the specific change promoted by sustainable development. Here the picture is more variable, with some very distinct moves in the form of policy integration, indicators and targets, and local initiatives. The contradictions between open markets and social democratic principles which favour the protection of individual and natural rights become more sharply defined. This is the area in which the next phase of sustainable development will evolve. For that to be effective, the mood of the body politic will have to favour greater local autonomy and greater collective responsibilities in order to protect the interests of both the vulnerable and future generations. The law will follow this attitude shift, but it need not be far behind. The key lies in the juxtaposition of the basic principles of growth and development with the flowering of stewardship, and the demand for greater local control over our futures. It is possible that this ideal juxtaposition will occur in the next decade. If so, it will be due to the institutional innovation spurred by sustainable development that we record here.

Sustainable development starts from various points on the economic and social compass and will surely end in a huge variety of outcomes at many levels. We must not lose sight of the fact that there is no template for the transition to sustainability. Nevertheless, there is a direction and there are principles, both are extensively analysed in Chapter 2. For those interested in reading the basic summary of our findings, before grappling with the text as a whole, the objectives of the research can be found on pp31–32, and the principal conclusion on pp44–56. The editorial introductions to each section are designed to provide a sense of perspective. The richness and the diversity of the responses to the A21 initiative should excite rather than overwhelm us. The great quality of any eco-phenomenon lies in diversity, cooperation, and comparative advantage together. We hope that we have shone a little light on the beginnings of an almost imperceptible revolution, whose outcome our grandchildren will be best placed to assess.

Part I

Setting the Scene

Chapter 1

THE POLITICAL ECONOMY OF THE SUSTAINABILITY TRANSITION

Tim O'Riordan and Heather Voisey

The sustainability transition is just what it suggests and more. It is not just a change from our present society to another form; it is the endless quest for a permanent and habitable planet on which life evolves with reliability and dignity. Sustainability is like democracy and justice. It is a moral ideal, a universally acknowledged goal to strive for, a shared basis for directing the creative and restorative energies that constitute life on Earth, and is notably resplendent in the human condition. Sustainability has that ring of universal desirability about it: no one is prepared to fundamentally challenge its precepts, no matter how vague these are, simply because there is an almost holistic human wish for a viable future for this unique planet and its inhabitants. It is not surprising that sustainability, democracy and justice are seen as composite and comprehensive human ideals. The grinding progress of transition is of itself permanent precisely because sustainability can never actually be attained, or at least cannot be envisioned by people because of the immense and fundamental changes in our society that it entails. We cannot comprehend a completely sustainable future, nor the quality of life that would follow. We understand the human condition a little better simply by striving to attain that elusive, and mystifyingly ambiguous, goal.

The sustainability transition, therefore, is the process of coming to terms with sustainability in all its deeply rich ecological, social, ethical and economic dimensions. The transition is as much about new ways of knowing, of being differently human in a threatened but cooperating world, as it is about management and innovation of procedures and products. As a species, we have barely begun to imagine how to think sustainably, though we suspect much of this will have to do with the adjuncts of justice and democracy. These include loving and caring, listening and sharing, revealing and rewarding, and fully sensing the history and future of the creative evolution that is life on Earth. The transition is, above all, a participatory and spiritual process of welcoming the purpose of human and personal existence on this planet.

That is why the sustainability transition is forever part of our lives; and so, it will surely become the very essence of the human condition in the next millennium. We may learn to love it or to hate it, to fear it or to be energised by it, but no one will be able to ignore it. The ultimate political economy of the sustainability transition is inside our heads and our hearts: it is as much a personal exploration as it is a societal quest. The political bickering that accompanies international and national responses to the call for sustainable development (discussed at the end of this chapter) is a sign that this personal exploration has not yet manifested itself in political behaviour. This is hardly surprising since humanity is neither culturally nor organisationally structured to cope with the transition. This is the heart of the dilemma. To move forward involves relative and responsive shifts in a host of institutions – in the way we think, the manner in which we judge, and in the structures and legal arrangements of our governance. These shifts cannot be random, nor can any single dimensional change move too far or too fast in relation to other single dimensional adjustments; an element of balance is required.

More to the point, as we shall illustrate throughout this text, the institutional arrangements that need to be readjusted in order to embrace the sustainability transition actually thrive on, and endure in, a non-sustainable world. The innate logic of these institutions encourages them to vary marginally the status quo, though never more than is suboptimally tolerable. However, this may cripple interactive innovations in institutional behaviour and organisational positioning that are an essential part of the transition. No wonder sustainable development is taking time to be credibly articulated in policy and in day-to-day behaviour. Realistically, there may not be much noticeable change even within a generation – unless the information economy lives up to its promise and releases us from the tyranny of our non-sustainable history. We return to this point in Chapter 16.

We shall refer in Chapter 2 to ecological tax reform, one of the economic lubricants of the sustainability transition. But ecological tax reform will be resisted if it jumps the gun of industrial competitiveness, revenue hypothecation (predetermined earmarking), or administrative competence in order to collect and disburse the income. This example demonstrates that the sustainability transition requires dynamic, flexible and influential strategic vision and accompanying participatory procedures that have not been devised in a modern polity. This is a tough number. It is no wonder that politicians shy away from the notion of sustainable development and long to carve it up into bite-sized, fragmented programmes for action.

ON DEFINING SUSTAINABILITY

Andrew Basiago (1995, pp110–112) and Keith Pezzoli (1997) have done the academic world a service by attempting to define sustainability in an ordered way. Figure 1.1 and Box 1.1 summarise and extend their perspective. The text that follows uses their analysis as a jumping-off point from which to explore a large canvas of ideas. Basiago notes (p110) that the sustainability concept is

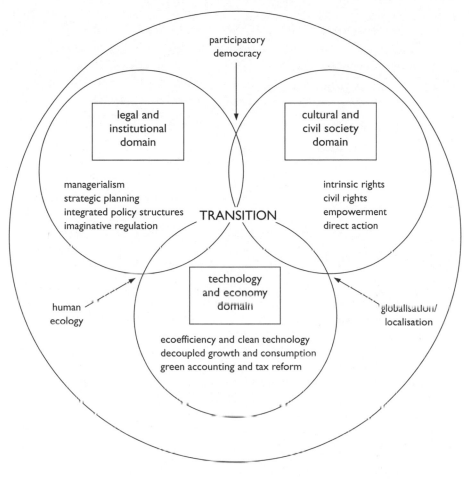

Source: based on Pezzoli, 1997, p555

Figure 1.1: The domains of sustainability

'spoken of in reverence, as if it were a new emancipating philosophy'. Lurking always in the background of the debate is a dark veil of planetary chaos detrimental to the human race – the ecological version of the Christian hell; damnation for humanity's failure of stewardship. The medieval view of damnation helped to keep societies in order when poverty, disease and military destruction were commonplace. Indeed, for many people they are still commonplace today. However, the modern version of damnation is of global calamity, the curse of bequeathing to future offspring a once-avoidable termination of their livelihood and, possibly, lives. If people really believed that such a spectre of preventable holocaust was the inevitable outcome of their present profligacy or poverty, the sustainability transition would surely spurt onwards. Right now, that lurking fear remains shrouded in doubt, self-deceit and optimistic imaginings. The human race still believes that current practices of

5

Economic and social improvement that is:
- continuous and permanent
- durable and reliable
- protective and just
- enterprising and sharing

Governed by three principles:
- maintain and protect essential life-support processes of the planet
- utilise renewable resources to the point of precautionary replenishment
- price the cost of living according to its natural burdens and social disruption

Implemented through:
- international agreements around the safeguard of life support
- compensatory transfers to recognise the legitimate needs of the sacrificers and the vulnerable
- national integrative policies coupled to formal duties of environmental care
- comparative economic performance and regulatory equal treatment
- local commitment via formal and informal community democracy

Figure 1.2: Sustainable development is…

economic growth can bequeath protection and security from this scenario and its present symptoms. So the transition stutters even in its initial phases.

At the heart of sustainability is self-regeneration – of the soul as well as of economy, polity and society. Self-regeneration is the vitality of the planet. According to the gaian theorists led by the redoubtable Jim Lovelock (1992), the Earth is a self-regulating organism with an inherent capacity to accommodate and adjust its life-support processes so that life itself, in whatever form, is genuinely permanent. Only solar radiative energy is required to trigger and maintain this extraordinary process: the rest is apparently self-generating and -adjusting. That is the ultimate in sustainability – a planetary totality that guarantees its own survival. No particular locality need be self-regenerating, nor is any particular species necessary for the viability of the Earth itself.

According to Basiago, the origins of sustainability lay in the first global analysis of *Limits of Growth* (Meadows et al, 1972) and *Blueprint for Survival* (Goldsmith, 1972). However, initially more relevant is the assessment of the American historian Sam Hays (1959, pp260–277) who looked at 19th-century American progressive conservationism, and the British historical geographer, Richard Grove (1990, pp17–20), who examined early colonial encounters with the unfamiliar tropics. Both historians perceived an antecedence to sustainability rooted in a combination of emerging science, colonialist guilt, a 'starburst' explosive economy, capitalist protectionism, and the exercise of raw political power in such a way that the vulnerable were made weaker in the cause of caring for the planet.

The 19th-century combined scientific discovery with capitalistic enterprise and technological optimism. This heady brew created a mixture of propulsion and reflection. This mix is one of the most paradoxical yet vital human qualities. Progress requires also that we assess change. The sustainability transition forever embeds us within this creative compromise. Grove (1990, p17) suggests that the rise of global merchantilism in the 15th-century re-evaluated the indigenous European notion of nature. Gone was the fear of the wild; enter the Garden of Eden with all its tropical luxuries. By the seventeenth century the evidence of Edenic despoilation, notably of tropical islands, coincided with the first serious scientific exploration of what we now call biodiversity. By the mid 17th-century:

> *...a coherent and relatively organised awareness of the ecological impact of the demands of emergent capitalism and colonial rule started to emerge and to grow into a fully fledged theory about the limitability of the natural resources of the earth and the need for conservation.* [Grove, 1990, pp17–18]

He concluded that the 19th-century became a symbolic precursor to the modern sustainability debate. The ravaging of tropical paradise and its indigenous peoples confused the practices of the early engineers and economic entrepreneurs. In order to protect the soils and waters, forest conservancies were created under police-like regimes where local people were forced out of their homelands, suffering abject livelihoods in the name of protecting resources partially despoiled by colonial predation. Yet contact with oriental and other non-Western spiritual traditions also inspired, amongst explorers and philosophers, a different ethos of caring and stewarding the land and its native peoples, many of whom were marginalised in the spirit of Christian conservation and proto-global capitalism. The practice of earthly salvation was therefore muddled and flawed; it was not surprising that the conservancy ideal received very bad press.

Hays (1959, pp264–266) was even more political in his critique of 19th century American conservation. He regarded it as the servant of an efficiency-maximising age; a decentralised, non-technical, loosely organised society in which waste, despoilation and the thoughtless destruction of animals, plants and native peoples were rampant. This was converted into a highly technical, ordered and entrepreneurial political economy that could confront a complex world 'with efficiency and purpose'.

> *These goals required public management – of the nation's streams because private enterprise could not afford to undertake it, of the western lands to adjust one resource use to another. They also required new administrative methods, utilising to the fullest extent the latest scientific knowledge, and expert, disinterested personnel...The conservation movement did not involve a reaction against large-scale corporate business but, in fact, shared its views in a mutual revulsion against unrestrained competition and undirected economic development.* [Hays, 1959, p266]

What Hays and Grove describe is pertinent to the age. Non-sustainability is an intrinsic and inescapable condition of a colonising species. Both Simmons (1989, pp6–8) and Mannion (1992, pp21–40) confirm that humanity is at its most aggressive when external stresses cause imperialism. These stresses may be environmental, technological or social. The outcome is a society that is out of kilter with itself, and hence institutionally proscribed from achieving self-regeneration. But, as Simmons (1989, pp26–28) emphasises, the net result is a cultural learning process: we do reflect on what we are doing to our ecosystems, and this is incorporated into our science and our ethics.

The American sociologist Bill Burch Jr (1971, p38) summarised this human condition (in language that preceded the current age of political correctness).

> *Cultures are a functional part of their ecology, and* homo sapiens *have a persisting tendency to make nature into his own image. After all, man is basically a weak creature, and nature has played some frightful jokes on him. For most of his history he has been compelled to make rather direct accommodation to non-human conditions, though his symbolic tendencies have strained along opposite lines...Such considerations may compel us to stop treating modern man as morally reprehensible and to begin recognising [that] he is but fulfilling a characteristic trait of survival – a capacity that may be directed in a fit or unfit manner, that is influenced by the nature of a given social order, its symbolic directives, and the limits of its habitat.*

The sustainability transition is thus painful yet pragmatic. Humans seek to find a compromise between supremacy and survival. Removed from the straightjacket of ecological and technological determinism, and freed of the needs to cooperate simply to keep alive, the trickle towards non-sustainability becomes a tidal flood. Institutions of thinking and acting, linked to an open social order, or a totalitarian dictatorship, are honed to accept a balance of intent that, either by optimistic self-delusion or enforced servitude to a political order, shifts the transition progressively towards non-sustainability.

The power of these historical analyses is that the very act of seeking a more sustainable salvation is embraced by a political order which incorporates sustainability in protecting efficiency, progress and vested interests. Wolfgang Sachs viewed this process as follows:

> *As governments, business and international agencies raise the banner of global ecology, environmentalism changes its face. In part, ecology – understood as a philosophy of a social movement – is about to transform itself from a knowledge of opposition to a knowledge of domination...The purpose of global environmental management is nothing less than the control of the second order; a higher level of observation and intervention has to be installed in order to control the consequences of the control over nature.* [Sachs, 1993, pxv]

If these analysts are to be believed, then it is by no means certain that the sustainability transition will be a force for liberation and survival. It might well be another version of human colonialism, but this time on a global scale. We attempt to answer this important point more clearly as the book evolves, and more particularly in the concluding chapter.

THE DISCOURSE OF SUSTAINABILITY

We shall see in the case studies of national responses to the sustainability transition that the very words used to describe sustainable development have different meanings. This rhetoric, designed for communicating ideologies as well as substantive messages, is referred to as 'discourse' (see Hajer, 1995). The British anthropologist Kay Milton (1996, p166) defines discourse as a process 'through which knowledge is constituted through communication'. In this sense, discourse has two roles. One is shorthand for a set of ideas that become universally acknowledged, even if ill-defined, and that are not necessarily coherent. The other is an active agent in interpreting events which, unconnected, have fragmented meaning. We argue in this book that sustainable development has both these elements. It is an organising discourse in its own right in the sense that it shapes beliefs, behaviours and organisational form and relationships. It is also a field of discussion in that sustainable development gains political currency because it is embraced by, and propels forward, other social and political dynamics that gain synergy through their relation to the sustainability transition. Social movements in areas such as civil liberties, gender liberation, animal welfare, rights to information, communicative participation and do-it-yourself civic activism are all part of a late 20th-century trend of democratic mobilisation. Similarly, fiscal reform, policy integration, ecoauditing, ethical investing and local food production and business development located around Local Agenda 21 (LA21), are also being energised by the sustainability debate. Without these two complementary faces of the sustainability discourse, the transition simply could not take place in anything approaching a purposeful manner.

Looking in a little more detail at the first arena of the sustainability discourse, Basaigo (1995, pp111–114) takes us through various definitions that are used by biologists, economists, planners and philosophers. To this list we add political scientists.

The Ecological Perspective

Biologists look at human interference on natural systems and their self-regenerating processes. There is a danger of converting humans and nature into respective bad guys and good guys. As a consequence, biodiversity is almost wholly reinterpreted as a benign process of maintaining genetic complexity through habitat renewal. Edward Wilson (1994), the Harvard guru in this domain, regards biodiversity as a key symbol of sustainability since a healthy and diverse ecosystem is presumed to be stable and efficient in its use of energy. But Andrew Watkinson (1997, p11) is by no means convinced that ecologists know enough to make such a statement. 'Basically we do not know how much biodiversity is essential to maintain ecosystem function', he concludes, 'and our ignorance of the processes that control the distribution of the millions of species worldwide is almost total.' The Wilson analysis appears to be more rhetoric than science.

BOX 1.1 SCIENTIFIC UNCERTAINTY AND SUSTAINABILITY

Science proceeds by formulating laws, developing models, verifying by observation, and falsifying by experimental analysis. This approach is fine when uncertainty can be managed by probabilistic statistics and error displays. But the problem arises when three types of uncertainty cannot be readily overcome:

1) *Insufficient data over space and time.* Many natural processes fluctuate over varying periods and spatial scales in an unpredictable manner. So any given set of measurements only provides a snapshot of relationships that may lurch from one phase state to another, and which may interact with other variables in a random synergistic manner.

2) *False positives can mean false negatives.* The false positive is a provisional acceptance that there is no evidence of a causal link between two measurable factors – for example, exposure and toxicity. So the preference is to assume no link until one is unequivocally proven. But in areas of public concern, such as the recent scare over bovine spongiform encephalopathy (BSE), the unwillingness to jump to a premature conclusion created a lot of public distrust and cost many billions of pounds.

3) *Indeterminacy of global cycles.* The big global cycles are all but impossible to model with any accuracy. Therefore, predicting what may happen if, say, all the tropical forests were to be removed is beyond calculable imagination. Best guesses may be erroneous. More to the point, any prognoses actually affect policy and subsequent human behaviour. So there is an interactive effect between the prognosis and the outcome. This is essentially a coupled science of natural processes and human endeavour and culturally framed expectations. This is more the science of the transition to sustainable development.

The dilemma facing the evolutionary biologist is the amoral aspect of creative change. The Darwinian and, indeed, Lovelockean legacies are that nature has no moral purpose. There are no ethics, equity or futurity in the natural world, or at least not in any way that is discernible to humans. The process of evolution has taken a terrible toll and continues to inflict pain and destruction on all manner of life. Yet, as humans, we appear to want some sort of manageable homeostasis in our natural world. We do not seem to want too much disorder, and we intervene if valued animals and plants are (naturally) becoming extinct. In short, we try to impose some sort of cultural straightjacket on evolution in the interests of 'comfortable' sustainability.

This is one difficulty. Another is the problem alluded to by Watkinson and taken further in Box 1.1. This is the harsh truth that scientists remain very vulnerable to immense uncertainty when trying to assess survival thresholds or capacities of tolerable resource depletion. What, for example, would be the true indicators of the ecological health of the North Sea? Since keystone and indicator species alter so frequently in their ecological roles, we are left with the uncomfortable conclusion that we may have to impose our own political discourse on ecosystem processes and critical loads.

The significance of scientific uncertainty, and its implications for genuine democratic policy-making, have been explored in Lemon (1996) and especially by the American commentator Kai Lee (1993). The conventional scientific approach is to establish laws, falsify hypotheses by observation and experiment, and presume that the tested laws hold if no conclusive evidence to the contrary is forthcoming. But as McGarvin (1994, pp88–92) pointed out, many ecological systems cannot be placed in such a conceptual straightjacket. It is often impossible to recognise the chaotic fluctuations of an ecosystem because there is neither the time series nor the observations to support the underpinning of a scientifically based ecological law. Thus, the very heart of the ecological discourse on sustainability, namely the 'natural' resilience of an ecosystem is essentially unknown and unpredictable. There may not be a natural resilience; on the other hand, if there is that resilience could be enhanced by the caring hand of human kind. We simply cannot be sure. Hence the argument advanced by Lee (1993, pp51–86) of adaptive and responsive management, of learning from experience, and of sharing with stakeholders the choices and possibilities of each successive stage.

The Economic Perspective

Economists use the phrase 'a sustainable economy' mostly in the conventional macro-economic sense of sound money, low inflation, manageable levels of borrowing, and stable exchange rates. These are regarded as the essential conditions of reliable and continuous wealth creation and job formation. On this basis, the 'environment' normally does not get a look in, and this is a primary reason why, even today, environmental economists are marginalised in the financial sector, the finance ministries, the lending institutions, and in business schools worldwide. The British business economist Richard Welford (1997, px) complains that 'industry has hijacked the more radical environmental debate by taking it out of its traditional discourses and placing it in a liberal productionist frame of reference'.

Ever since the days of Pigou (1926) economists have recognised that market transactions insufficiently cover all costs and benefits involved. Indeed, this almost self-evident observation can probably be traced to the beginning of independent judgement, and certainly features in the enlightenment economics that lead to the profession's mainstream. The difficulty, as is well documented, is not just that these so-called externalities cannot always be costed, and hence given commensurate value in an economic calculus. The major institutional failure for the sustainability transition is that these externalities are neither trivial nor peripheral to all economic activity. They are central, unavoidable, deeply distributional, often future orientated, and hence fundamentally politicised.

Economists have no practical discourse for this centrality, universality and cultural diversity. This is why the sustainability transition is so difficult to launch. The institutions of economic analysis simply cannot grasp the essence of self-regenerating ecological and sociological capabilities. There is no value that can be placed on such capabilities because they cannot be identified by ecologists or sociologists as measurable discrete phenomena (which, in any case, they are not). So the mainstream economist has no effective discourse to describe the fundamental essence of sustainability.

Instead, some economists prefer to think of ingenious devices for evaluating the life-support processes that ensure vitality and provide spiritual nurture. These devices are now widely summarised (for example, Turner et al, 1994; Bateman, 1995) and also widely critiqued (see Hildyard, 1992, and Sachs, 1993, for representative opinion). This is a well-trodden arena, so we do not propose to trample in it any further. Nevertheless, for the purpose of this book, it is important to say that the three major flaws with the environmental economists' approach to sustainability appear to be:

- there is still a presumption that externalities are peripheral and can be incorporated into a market or regulatory transaction by means of a surrogate value that does not become useless even in the face of huge variations of cultural interpretation;
- there is sufficient scientific knowledge amongst earth science analysts and ecologists to provide reasonable guesstimates of these external factors, both now and in the future; and
- where there is serious uncertainty, then the rules of 'playing it safe', or precaution, can be invoked. These may contain a more explicit ethical or political dimension, which in itself can be costed by virtue of the extra resources such prevarication entails.

Critics contest these conclusions on the grounds that any ethical or equity-based analysis would place more emphasis on the quality of experience and the perspective of gainers and losers, and not just monetary benefits. As the British philosopher John O'Neill put it:

Evaluation of objectives under different descriptions invokes not just different practices and perspectives, but also different criteria and standards for evaluation associated with these. It presupposes value pluralism. [O'Neill, 1993, p108]

The challenge lies not just in comparing valuation by a common measure. The serious charge is that to do so may distort preexisting cultural values. So the very act of evaluation may both cause and subsequently ignore cultural discrimination.

One interesting example of this ecological valuation effort is the clever, but incomplete, attempt by ecological economists led by Bob Costanza (1997) to come up with a means of valuing the life-support and waste assimilating functions of the planet. They selected 17 critical functions and applied these to

16 different blomes, or major ecosystem types, ranging from dense tropical forest to open ocean. They looked at a variety of calculations to estimate the ecological and cultural value of this matrix of 272 combinations. Here is where the dangers of asymmetrical discourse creep in. If information was patchy, they averaged where rich and poor people value differently. These valuations are assumed to differ not because of intrinsic cultural worth, but because of varying willingness to pay; therefore, Costanza and his colleagues weighted outcomes by population and income. Where no reliable evidence was on offer, they left a blank. Where some possible future outcome was potentially costly, they discounted. All of this reflects the mainstream economic paradigms. Income is regarded as a neutral mediator reflecting willingness to pay. Yet in a sustainability context, income is by no means neutral. It is a highly politicised variable that has gained its worth on the backs of the very damages the team is trying to cost. Equity considerations are also fundamentally politicised, with the powerless often left to suffer indignity and distress without compensation. Yet these very real 'costs' were not incorporated into the analysis. To be fair, the Costanza team stressed, in the early stages of their analysis, the huge uncertainties involved, and the scope for more focused regional research.

Nevertheless, the omission of any thoughtful analysis of both equity and justice considerations is an important criticism for anyone seriously interested in the politics of the sustainability transition. One has only to recall what Grove and Hays concluded. In the interests of sustainable futures, orientations and management regimes need to be ordered and made reliably efficient. Ecological economists have not fully crossed the threshold into true interdisciplinarity. This is not a fault of mendacity or mischief. It is a very real indicator of the difficulty facing contemporary integrated science to find a formula that links ecology with society and ethics with sustainability economics. Tinkering at the margins of conventional paradigms is simply not sufficient. However, one should have no illusions that the process of reconstructing science will be long and painful.

The Costanza team, nevertheless, still came up with some figures that suggested that the value of the planetary ecosystems may be worth at least the equivalent to the total world economic output (US$18 trillion per year), and possibly two or even three times this figure (US$54 trillion per year). At one level this is a fantastic advertisement for the fledgling field of ecological economics, where research grants remain low and prospective careers still indeterminate. So this ingenious piece of soft sell through the world's most prestigious scientific journal – *Nature* – warts and all, and on the web (<http://www.nature.com>) proclaims a particular variant of the economist's discourse, virtually without cost. And it is given further ventilation by encouraging dialogue amongst enthusiastic and disgruntled colleagues.

But at another level, this exercise may well be trivialised by politicians and financial interests in the manner described by Sachs and Welford. This is on the grounds that the evidence will be forever sketchy, the figures forever disputed on both technical and interpretative grounds, with the trump card, played by consumer (as opposed to citizen) opinion, namely that of differential property rights. A hectare of Malaysian tropical forest may be 'worth' US$3000 per hectare on the basis of its soil-protecting, gene-maintaining, and possible medicinal properties (Pearce, 1993, p86). But that cash is 'virtual' because these property rights are not owned by anyone in particular until some private entrepreneur 'captures' some of them, or the global community chooses to expropriate them by paying local people to act as stewards. The same Malaysian hectare is worth US$300–500 'cash in the bank' when the timber is felled, transported and sold to, say, the Japanese veneer market. The two sets of dollar values are simply not the same, even though, in sustainability terms, the higher figure has a very real symbolic role in the discourse.

Nicholas Hildyard (1992, p131) has argued persuasively that the true crisis of non-sustainability is the enclosure of the global commons – in effect, the very processes at all scales of human existence that Costanza and his colleagues reckon are worth more than we earn. 'The modern nation state', comments Hildyard, 'has been built only by stripping power and control from commons regimes and creating structures of governance from which the great mass of humanity (particularly women) are excluded'.

> *To achieve the condition of economic progress, millions have been thrown onto the human scrapheap as a calculated act of policy, their commons dismantled and degraded, their cultures denigrated and devalued and their own worth reduced to their value of labour. Seen from this perspective, the processes that now go under the metric of 'nation-building', 'economic growth' and 'progress' are first and foremost processes of appropriation, exclusion, denial and dispossession. In a word, of enclosure.* [Hildyard, 1992, p131]

The Costanza exercise will only take on meaning for the sustainability transition when his team's valuation is seen as representing genuine assets. We shall look at the progress and the disputes over green accounting in the chapter that follows. But even this well-intentioned effort has yet to affect investment decisions and macro-economic policy. Futures trading does not value a coral reef in its 'sustainability' account. It values it as a basis for attracting tourists and sees it as adding value to the nearby international hotel chain. When, eventually, that chain along with local people repossess the reef commons in a Gaian partnership so that coral watching becomes a greater economic asset than coral 'mining' for tourist takeaways, then the process will be approaching the sustainability transition. But is the international hotel industry ready for such a partnership, to the point of investing cash in coral stewardship? Welford (1997, p227) thinks not. 'We cannot begin to imagine', he muses, 'how we can stop the steamroller of large corporations in capitalism. This is now taking a heavy toll on humanity in terms of helplessness, lethargy and despondency. Are the investment analysts out there listening? Stewardship is not a money spinner for hot capital flows.'

One final point regarding the Costanza exercise. Is it wise to play the numbers game with ecological life-support functions in all their mystery and holism? Putting a cash value on phenomena that are part of the essence of earthly vitality is not only faintly ludicrous, it is also dangerously arrogant; how

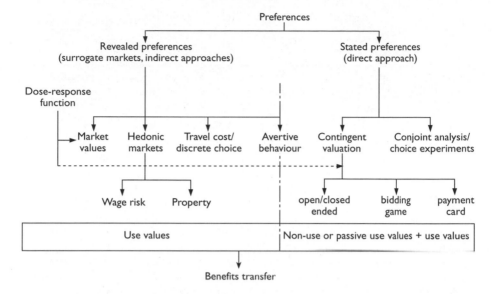

Economists have devised ingenious ways of valuing the sustainability transition via various simulated markets. These approaches are criticised by non-economists such as O'Neill (1993). The result is a healthy, but unresolved, debate.
Source: Pearce, 1996, p19

Figure 1.3 Economic valuation schema

can one assume that dollars call the shots? The real danger of the Costanza exercise is that it diverts attention away from the spiritual timelessness of creation to the equivalent of a bag of chips. The upshot is that economists argue over willingness-to-pay methodologies, and the significance of marginal valuation tradeoffs, while the essential fabric of the planet is torn open.

Despite these criticisms, the discipline of economics provides many ingenious ways of approaching sustainability, as is indicated in Figure 1.3. These are imaginative, relevant and beginning to be incorporated in indicators and green accounting techniques. The sustainability transition needs a focus and an internal energy. Economics of the innovative ecological sort are terribly important. Here, for example, is the basis of a language and a way of assessing the unquantifiable that does not frighten or attract ridicule. It operates at the margins but not beyond the status quo; in any meaningful early stages, the sustainability transition will only be possible if the status quo is, to some degree, protected. This, at least, is the lesson of history, and for dedicated sustainability pioneers, this is an extremely aggravating reality.

The Political Science Perspective

Political scientists are confronted by a situation that we shall term the *democratic paradox* when it comes to the sustainability transition. This paradox is based on

Table 1.1 The transition to sustainability

	Environmental Policy	Economic Policy	Public Awareness	Public Discourse
Stage 1: very weak sustainability	Lip service to policy integration	Minor tinkering with economic instruments on a case-by-case basis; some reinvestment of income toward the goal of sustainability	Dim awareness and little media coverage	Corporatist discussion groups and consultation exercises
Stage 2: weak sustainability	Formal policy integration and specific targets, backed by new institutional structures	Substantial restructuring of economic incentives; large-scale reinvestment of income toward the goal of sustainability	Wider public education involving 'perforated' classroom walls	Roundtables, stakeholder group participation, and legislative surveillance
Stage 3: strong sustainability	Binding policy integration and strong international agreements coupled to performance targets and indicators	Full valuations of the cost of living, green accounting, and creation of a 'civic income' for social use	Curriculum integration, with local educational initiatives geared to community growth	Community involvement, pairing of initiatives in the developed and developing worlds
Stage 4: very strong sustainability	Strong international conventions, national duties of care, and statutory and cultural support	Formal shift to sustainability accounting locally, nationally and internationally	Comprehensive cultural shift coupled with technological innovation and new community structures	Community-led initiatives become the norm

Note: This figure shows the four stages of sustainability. Each stage is characterised by particular environmental and economic policies, degree of public awareness, and type of public discourse. Generally speaking, moving from one stage to the next involves more serious environmental commitments, closer alignment of economic policy to environmental goals, greater public awareness of environmental problems and possible solutions, more democratic decision-making, and a greater role for local government.
Source: based on Jordan and O'Riordan, 1993, p186

the assumption that in any shift away from non-sustainability, those who benefit from the unsustainable state will become losers, unless appropriately compensated. Therefore, to initiate the transition, there will have to be some form of reconstructed democracy where the powerful willingly give up their influence for the greater global good. This point is more fully developed by O'Riordan (1996, pp144–149) and summarised in Table 1.1. To receive compensation from an economy that reallocates the composition as well as the size of the pie seems to be an impossible condition, unless the pattern of gain and loss is treated with great care and social dignity. Take, for example, the 90,000 lignite (brown coal) workers in Germany, or the 3000 fishermen in the UK. On sustainability grounds the lignite workers should have no future, and the fishing families should suffer the loss of their livelihood. In practice, even where there are subsidies which promise continued lignite production (as is currently the case), little is done politically to exercise a variant of 'sustainability dictatorship' over local electoral considerations, in the name of sustainability. To do so, workers would require the cash and the training in order to 'exist with dignity'. And here is where the valuations of the ecological economists do not help. There may be no money in the conventional economy for transition payments on the scale required. The result is a backing off from the confrontational politics of sustainability. This is, in symbolic form, the democratic paradox at work.

Paelke (1996, p27) looks at the proposition that the sustainability transition should create greater democratisation of political decisions simply because the sustainability ideal is more inclusive, more empowering and more transparent. Of this so-called 'reflexive modernisation' (as advanced by Beck, 1992; following Giddens, 1990, 1992), there will be more in the sections below. Our immediate purpose here is to emphasise the narrative of political bias in the discourse of sustainable development. Along with many others, Paelke recognises that for countries or communities at low levels of development, democracy and environmental protection simply do not figure highly, and that civil rights abuses are rampant in countries that are developing rapidly and care little about biodiversity.

For a central theme of Gaian sustainability, namely the stewardship of the intertropical genetic pools, the democratic paradox reveals itself in a discourse that is highly attuned to maintaining existing power structures. Posey (1997, p7), for example, points out that the richest biodiversity is found in areas of a coevolutionary relationship between humans and nature. The huge fuss that followed the passage of the UN Convention on Biodiversity centred on the degree to which natural systems and indigenous peoples have rights to existence, and to knowledge, which give them a stake in any prospecting for commercial advantage. At present, argues Posey (1997, p43), the indigenous property rights law is being mercilessly exploited 'for the unethical and unsustainable exploitation of local communities and their resources'. He even accuses some scientists of flouting these basic principles of democracy, let alone ecology. But, more akin to Paelke's argument, Posey concludes:

> *Ultimately, placing value on indigenous technologies threatens the ideological base that many countries have used in the past to justify the marginalisation and exploitation of local communities' resources. Given such a history, it is highly unlikely in many places that benefits will ever trickle down to local communities.* [Posey, 1997, p43]

This analysis can also apply to the other great post-Rio conventions, namely those on climate (O'Riordan and Jäger, 1996, pp346–360) and desertification (Toulmin, 1997, pp60–63). This is not the place for an extensive examination of capacity and compliance in international environmental treaties; these have been extensively treated elsewhere, for example by Jacobson and Brown-Weiss (1997, pp324–330), amongst many others. What is worth commenting upon is the significance of coalition-building when preparing a compliance regime. If that coalition does not meet with the approach of those who have the power to resist compliance, then the treaty is only relatively effective.

> *In the cases when activities that the treaty deals with are highly dispersed – as in CITES, the Tropical Timber Agreement, the World Heritage Convention – these levels of political authority must be coordinated, which is not always an easy task. Sometimes the authority of central government, which accepts international obligations, does not reach deeply into local areas. Moreover, these countries contain within their borders widely different ecological regions, which require variation in the way administration is conducted.* [Jacobsen and Brown-Weiss, 1997, p330]

Posey's critique is very relevant. The nature of power relations and compensatory deals becomes crucial in the delivery of sustainable development. This is why we cautioned earlier about the discriminatory and inequitable discourse of culturally insensitive approaches to ecological economics. It is also a reason why we place so much emphasis on locality and its post-Rio manifestation, LA21, in the latter part of this volume.

We now turn to the notion of reflexive modernity, or active civil society and its implications for the sustainability transition. This is a complicated notion since it has many contemporary meanings, not all of which are consistent. Dryzek (1996, pp117–119) defined civil society as public action in response to failure by the state or the economy. This may emerge in two ways. One is constructive coalition-building through citizens' initiatives, local partnerships or mediation-based visioning exercises, as is cautiously criticised by Penny Street (1997, pp143–153) and developed theoretically by O'Mahoney and Skillington (1996, pp43–45) and by Dobson (1996, p407). Here the initiative is taken, usually locally, and an institutional framework facilitates it. One such framework is LA21. But there are other consultative procedures, some of which we analyse below. Dobson (1996, pp406–420) attempts to widen this discourse to encompass political economy. By his own admission (p423) he has not fully satisfied his own thinking on this issue.

The second version of the active civil society is less constructive. Civil society, as a form of social mobilisation for informal protest through direct action – of the kind witnessed in the UK over the transportation of live animals and opposition to roads and airport extensions – can occur even when the decisions to proceed have passed through legitimate democratic processes. There is a fine line between the legitimate activism of civil protest and the less legitimate troublemaking of civil disruption.

Adopting the constructive tone, the political science discourse takes the social dimension of sustainable development one step further into the realm of *empowerment*. Empowerment does not so much mean granting or transferring power as it does increasing civic awareness of the efficacy of democratic involvement, through self-respect, mutual esteem, capacity-building, genuine responsiveness and open accountability (see Schwerin, 1995, pp55–57). The German sociologist Ortwin Renn and his colleagues (1995, pp21–25) take the notion of 'communicative discourse', or the symbols and biases through which thoughts are shaped and attitudes are framed, as a basis for examining empowerment. They conclude that the key conditions are the building of trust between the polity and governments in their various manifestations; authenticity (or feeling comfortable in the knowledge that others are sincerely understanding the message); transparency of response; and accountability when making a decision or establishing a programme. Paradoxically, empowerment should encourage the political conditions that render the protest element of civil society irrelevant. We examine this in our case studies of LA21, but develop the theory more specifically in the chapter that follows.

For successful political discourse within civil society, therefore, a more open and legitimate form of democracy is required. O'Mahoney and Skillington (1996, p43) refer to this as 'communicative governance', involving 'the substitution of a model containing a governing actor (the state) and an object to be governed (society), by a model that comprises a plurality of governing agents located in a civil society and amongst whom a more democratic relationship prevails'. Procedural fairness in such an 'open' democracy, therefore, relies on legitimacy, which is founded on the principles of empowerment, and on efficiency. The difficulty is in restraining consultative arrangements which may prolong an outcome because of the volume of evidence and the numbers of participants. This is probably best achieved by creating or encouraging informal networks of interested parties on a come and go basis.

We still have not come to terms with the darker side of civic society, namely the tendency to initiate active, illegitimate protest even though protest is adopted sincerely in the name of a more declaratory empowerment. Here the early stages of the sustainability transition are more problematic. A fractured society breeds trouble from within. Therefore, the key is to create networks of shared experiences, trust and outcome. This process we call *revelation* (see O'Riordan, 1997, pp180–181), or what Sabine O'Hara (1996, pp96–102) terms 'discursive ethics'. She describes this as 'a process of uncovered and undistorted communicative interaction between individuals in open discourse'. The task is to open up people's 'life world' to a host of ethical, ecological, economic and sociological experiences that will influence all societal-environmental inter-relationships. O'Hara justifies this approach on the basis that it:

- integrates ecosystem valuations by seeking to overcome the disciplinary blind spots, assumptions and value judgements exposed in any ecological economic approaches to valuation;
- copes with uncertainty by combining scientific rationalities with stakeholder biases and negotiated judgements; in this way it extends the basis of peer group authority; and
- reconstructs life worlds by breaking down existing patterns of power and privilege that otherwise shape the norms and outlooks of participants, in order to reestablish an authentic and trustworthy context for debate and resolution.

Reconciliation, therefore, is a valuation process, set in a context of empowerment and legitimacy through which people can come to terms with other positions and interests. However, unless the political system is prepared to deliver these shared and negotiated strategies, then the whole process becomes invalid. This is why political scientists continue to struggle with representative and participatory democracy. Penny Street (1997, pp156–157) concluded that an imaginative scenario-evaluating workshop covering sustainable urban futures for the medium-sized British town of Preston is in danger of falling into disarray because of the failure to carry through the process to political delivery at the LA21 level. We shall see in the case studies which follow that this particular variant of pluralist politics is the hardest to deliver in the early stages of the sustainability transition.

We cannot leave this topic without devoting a little more attention to the active protest side of civil society. In part, this is a feature of social mobilisation that is represented, most notably, by the environmental movement in the spread of animal rights; ecological feminism; the consumer movement; the anti-risk lobbies and the increasing distaste for the road vehicle – see Dalton (1994) for a general review and Jordan and Maloney (1997, pp40–46) for a more specific account. However, of equal significance is the emergence of civil disobedience in the name of community empowerment and environmental liberation. The rise of the anti-road and airport protestor in the mid 1990s is a feature of the active and anarchic groups that expose damage and disruption as objects in their own right – for example, Earth First! and Sea Shepherd. The act of civil disobedience requires a cause, an uncertain policing response, the media, and sympathetic, but wary, public opinion. In many respects it is like a drama. The general public are the audience, the media are the spotlights, with the protestors and the police as opposing choruses.

An example of such a group is Reclaim the Streets (RTS), a loose collection of young and not-so-young activists, originally based in London but now more widespread. RTS believe that ridding society of the car 'would allow us to recreate a safer, more attractive living environment, to return streets to the people that live on them, and perhaps to rediscover a sense of social solidarity' (in *Earth First!* 1997, pp3–5). RTS is typical of the modern direct action group – resentful of, yet dependent upon, advanced capitalism, alienated from government, yet protected by the civil state, and imbued with media attention and short-term, precision power. The key to their relatively high profile lies in their ability to empower, and often to overempower, individuals, to forge common ground over a wide range of grievances, and to inspire others to follow their example.

However, activists worry about their longer-term effectiveness. They cannot see a socially supported way forward in terms of their own ideals, and recognise that their popular support is paper thin and easily undermined by negative images. They are also troubled by the possible infiltration of those who are not sustainably 'high minded' but are only troublemakers. These recruits, or 'cuckoos', encourage the recently formed police public-order units to increase surveillance and to immobilise protestors with a record. David Rangecroft (1997, p22) assistant director of public affairs with the London Metropolitan Police, estimates the cost of disruption over the M11 link alone at £1.2 million, with over 60,000 hours of police time diverted from other duties. He also quotes (*ibid*) the head of the Metropolitan Police's Public Order Branch as recognising the difficult 'piggy in the middle' role in such circumstances:

> *Such protests take place in the communities we serve. They do not exist in a vacuum. This means that our planning has to take into account community needs and the long-term effects of our actions. When trust with a community is destroyed, the rebuilding process is likely to be long and hard.*

The serious-minded activists are genuinely concerned by the infiltration of troublemakers. Overempowerment, in the sense of exhilaration caused by disruption and huge media attention, breeds unnecessary damage and adverse publicity. Here again is a case where the discourse of the sustainability transition is confused. The allure of keeping close to the democratic status quo is overwhelming.

The Ethical Discourse

Much of what has been discussed above has an ethical dimension, at least in terms of democratic rights and the restructuring of power. But lying in wait is a more profound discourse, namely how far the sustainability concept will return humanity to its natural roots, or what Shiva (1992, p189) terms 'a recovery of the recognition that nature supports our lives' and 'is the primary source of sustenance'. Economists (such as Turner *et al*, 1994, pp13–15) define this as strong or very strong sustainability. Here 'criticality' is applied to vital life-support functions so that these are not impaired. And when in doubt, the economist applies 'safe minimum standards' (see O'Riordan, 1993, pp47–48), though it is doubtful that this notion has much of an ethical component; rather, it is a 'playing safe because error will result in avoidable costs' interpretation.

From an ethical perspective, then, we need to apply two additional principles. One is that of stewardship, or the application of management to ensure health, resilience and a capacity to regenerate in both social and ecological systems. The other is precaution, or systematic bias which ensures that the most damaging outcome is avoided by proactive mitigation measures and ethically loaded valuation procedures (see O'Riordan and Cameron, 1994). While stewardship is essentially a matter of taking due care for all relevant interests, precaution in the Shiva (1992) sense of 'natural humility' means shifting the balance of power towards the would-be victim. Returning to the Posey analysis raised earlier regarding indigenous property rights, precaution would extend those rights not only to the local people but also to ecosystems. This is a dramatic shift indeed; it would provide legal standing both to citizens' groups bent on protecting these rights, and also to the political efficacy of the very vulnerable whom most commentators such as Hildyard (1992) reckon lose out even in the sustainability transition. What we see, inevitably, is a standing back from the full force of stewardship and precaution, largely because these notions are too hot to handle.

Since sustainability has much to do with futurity, the equity issue takes on a longer and more troubling dimension. According to a useful review of climate change politics by Banuri *et al* (1996, pp85–88), equity applies to two separate categories. One is procedural fairness, which we have discussed here under the rubric of the emerging civil society. The other relates to outcomes – namely, the consequences of a decision where democracy, the law and judgemental rationality intertwine. At one level, nation states find it difficult to evolve procedures that guarantee the rights of all their citizens now and in the future. Despite being incorporated within various treaties and international declarations, the legal basis for ensuring sustainability rights is essentially non-existent. The American lawyer Edith Brown-Weiss (1989, p148) is particularly concerned about this ethical void. She argues for a Commission on the Future of the Planet, backed by a resolution from the United Nations (UN) Commission on Human and Environmental Rights, with power to promote the principle of trusteeship for the future of the planet. As we shall see, the fact that the UN has repeatedly ducked anything resembling a universal 'sustainability right' shows just how alienating this notion is for those who gain by non-sustainable rules.

On the consequentialist front, five rules of justice concerning distributional equity appear to prevail.

1) *Parity* is a formula for equal distribution of burdens and benefits, and is closely associated with the principles of egalitarianism. Because we live in an unequal world, the parity paradigm is of less significance for the sustainability transition.
2) *Proportionality* asserts that burdens or benefits should be distributed in relation to the responsibility of claimants. This, of course, begs the question of proof, which is why the science of modelling and scenario development is so contested; citizens' groups like to set their own risk agendas (see Irwin, 1995, pp135–167).
3) *Priority* argues that those with the greatest and most deserving need should be especially advantaged. This is the principle of removing vulnerability, or the enforced incapacity of a community to regenerate in the face of external stress. This forms part of the 'basic needs' theme that was applied to the 1970s notion of ecodevelopment – namely, the guarantee of access to

health, water, sanitation, food and shelter. Today, this notion has been extended to civil rights, financial credit and educational opportunity, and has been caught up in the sustainable consumption debate (Dowdeswell, 1997, pp210–211; Redclift, 1996, pp151–173).

4) *Classical utilitarianism* proposes that burdens should be distributed so that the greatest good is shared by the largest number. This is a rationalist approach to maximising utility, or satisfaction, but begs the question as to how far utility takes into account the 'ecological and social burdens' generated in the pursuit of fulfilling needs and wants, as discussed earlier in this chapter.

5) *Rawlsian distributive justice* adopts a variant of utility theory by ensuring that the most disadvantaged are singled out where they can be identified. Again, the cultural variations underlying utilities are not adequately explained. Precisely because of this, it is arguable that Rawlsian distributive justice would be difficult to put into effect, unless procedures of the revelatory sort were set in motion.

To incorporate an ethical dimension within the sustainability discourse is demanding enough. The task is made all the more daunting because of a failure to create measures or evaluative yardsticks for any of these different interpretations. But even if a common ethical discourse was agreed upon, and the priority ethos looks the best bet, how this would be incorporated within decision-making under conditions of the democratic paradox remains a mystery. We may have to rely on a future economy buoyed up by the 'information-efficiency' revolution to create sufficient wealth in order to redistribute capital. This may conceivably be a possibility for North America and northern Europe. It looks less plausible the further South one gets. Incorporating ethics into pragmatic decision procedures may require a special form of revelatory civic science; there will be more on this in the chapter that follows.

The Planning Perspective: Strategic Synthesis

Arguably, the planning profession, along with economists, engineers, accountants and lawyers, has still to come to terms with the sustainability transition (we look at accountancy in the next chapter). Planners present a paradox. They adopt spatial futurity in their structure and strategic plans, yet fail to use the planning system in a stewardship or precautionary manner. This is partly a feature of their training. Empowerment, equity, stewardship and futurity generally do not rank high in their professional training or qualifications. However, this is more an institutional failure. Planners lack the tools and the political punch to change those biases which we have already examined in this chapter. For example, the introduction of strategic shoreline, water, landscape and forestry perspectives in the UK in recent years has not resulted in proactive protectionism for planners, exercised through development procedures.

One way forward is strategic environmental assessment (SEA). This is the application of environmental appraisal to policies, plans and programmes

(Therival *et al*, 1992, p30). In practice, however, SEA is ineffective because neither the evaluative apparatus nor the organisational clout is in place.

> *In an ideal world, SEA should be based on sustainability, and in turn it would cascade this down into project planning. Sustainability should be based on carrying capacities, which then set environmental thresholds that are not to be exceeded. Within these constraints, other factors (social, economic) can be optimised. However, in our less than ideal world, changes take place incrementally. SEA is at present coming about as an application of a known technique to a slightly higher level of decisionmaking'.* [Therivel *et al*, 1992, p130]

We describe the efforts to upgrade the strategic evaluation of policies in the chapters that follow as part of our assessment of policy integration within the sustainability transition. At this point we note the struggle that characterises the domain of strategic planning. Here, concepts such as carrying capacity, thresholds of sustainable use, access limitation, planning restrictions on primary aggregates (to push up the price of secondary, or recycled aggregates) and the whole image of land use and transportation choices are evaluated by a profession that traditionally has facilitated development, not shaped sustainable development. Planners are still creating the appropriate discourses and are some way off from having the legal powers, or political empowerment strategies, to conduct a stewardship role over the nation's waters, soils, forests and shoreline; they are even less able to deal with greenhouse gas emissions and the protection of biodiversity.

It is highly likely that the sustainability transition will cause an interesting set of partnership alliances between the 'custodial' regulatory agencies in health and safety, environmental protection, countryside and urban amenity, and land-use planning. For this to take place, there will have to be a revolution in pricing and other regulatory techniques, and the bureaucratic isolationism that affects 'non-environmental custody' will have to be reformed. We return to these regulatory procedures in the chapter that follows.

PERSPECTIVE

We conclude that the sustainability transition is plagued by a clash of interpretations and reactions regarding the purpose of sustainable development in a globe that: exhibits the differential power and growing chasms in the rates of growth and wealth accumulation; is bedevilled with the democratic paradox; cannot establish a meaningful ethical position with regard to international agreements and the protection of the commons; and features custodial agencies that are still at cross purposes with each other. This transition is symbolised in intellectual discourse, in science, in coalitions of new governance, in various characteristics of an emerging civic society, and in the application of empowerment, stewardship and precaution.

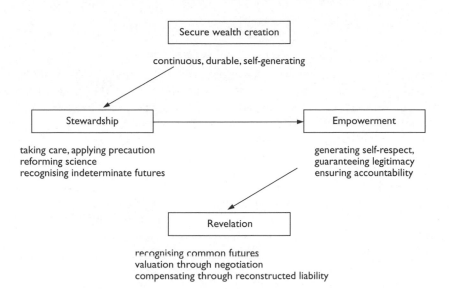

Source: O'Riordan and Voisey, 1997, p7

Figure 1.4 Four components of sustainable development

This is why we have produced Figures 1.1 and 1.4, (O'Riordan and Voisey, 1997, pp7–11) – namely a set of principles of the sustainability transition that provides a conceptual umbrella for the chapter which follows and is a guide for the detailed case studies that continue throughout the book.

The transition to sustainability must contain a language that is comforting to the finance ministries and their client groups. Therefore, our emphasis is on reliable and continuous growth. The transition must also contain the language and principles of stewardship and precaution so that the interests of the vulnerable are properly taken into account in valuation and decision procedures. Furthermore, the transition needs to embrace the wide-ranging notion of empowerment, with all its implications for equity. Finally, because the transition is a self-transcending process, with vitally important spiritual dimensions, the experience of 'revelation' must be introduced. Without revelation, losers would talk of sacrifice instead of promoting collective self-interest.

In the absence of revelation, procedural equity would be confronted with the constraints of the democratic paradox. And without revelation, society's personal identification with gaia, which lies deep within all our consciences, could not be articulated. Therefore, the sustainability transition is the merging of the inner and outer worlds of self and gaia, of community and humanity, of local and global perspectives, of responsibility and trusteeship, and of science and empowerment. What a heady brew: it is little wonder that the institutions of local, national and international governance still have to come to terms with the full force of the transition towards sustainability. This is evident in the sorry aftermath of Rio.

UNCED, UNGASS AND BEYOND

We assume that most if not all readers of this book are aware of the issues that led to the UN Conference on Environment and Development (UNCED), held at Rio de Janeiro in June 1992. If not, then we suggest that you read the Brundtland Report (1987), Adams (1990), Moffatt (1996) Clayton and Radcliffe (1996) and Dodds (1997). There are many other references, but these key books admirably set the scene, along with the critiques by O'Keefe et al (1993) and Sachs (1993).

The fact that UNCED was held at all is something of a miracle, a statement of faith by the participants that the trasition could be achieved. Indeed the heady debates which took place and produced agreements during the conference could, arguably, be seen as the beginning of the transition for many attending interests. The conference was characterised by an important combination of factors.

- *Intensive preparatory consultations* and agreements across a large variety of themes for the five years leading up to the conference: these took the form of intergovernmental negotiating committees, international workshops, and non-governmental organisation (NGO) forums operating intensively across the globe. These consultations were always awkward and often cantankerous. But they created networks of fellowship across nations, ideologies, interests and individuals that have lasted in the form of coalitions and networks. Cynics have labelled some of this the 'eco-circus', and certainly there are many groupies who have made a comfortable living out of the Rio process – arguably disinterested in the outcome so long as the circus is well financed. Nevertheless, the breadth and depth of the pre-Rio deliberations established a series of negotiating institutions that have lasted and helped to create the framework for the all important UNCED agreements.
- *Unreconciled disputes over North–South sharing:* sustainable development was not at the heart of UNCED; rather, it was the long-running issue of trade, human rights, and capacity-building. The South, or crudely the group of 77 developing countries (G77) (though this definition is imperfect – see Patterson, 1997), looked for more development with fewer ecolimiting strings attached, greater say in global security affairs, and a modicum of freedom to retain their own peculiar mix of political democracies and (un)civil rights. Above all they expected cash, technology, innovation and investment for their despoiled lands and impoverished peoples. UNCED simply did not deliver, and this has rankled in negotiations ever since. Barbara Bramble (1997, p200) has emphasised that the increasing unwillingness of the G77 countries to entertain the wider UN agenda of social policy, and women's rights in population futures and in trade relations can be traced to this deep sense of resentment. For many in the South, UNCED has essentially a Northern agenda. The negotiations in New York in June 1997 at the UN General Assembly Special Session on sustainable development (UNGASS) at the five-year review of A21 were bedevilled by

huge and, this time, irreconcilable rifts between North and South, and especially amongst the ideologically sprawling G77 delegations.

- *The rise of the NGOs* in official delegations and as a force for transmitting sustainable development in its own right, especially for countries with corrupt dictatorships or with administrative capabilities (see also Bichsel, 1996): prior to Rio the NGOs were, for the most part, marginalised. But in the run up to Rio, and especially in the various UN conferences that followed, NGOs increasingly became a formal part of the official delegations and are powerful brokers in the negotiating ranks. This meant that grassroots opinion and practical issues of capacity and delivery received an airing at the point of agreement rather than in the irrelevant aftermath of contract signing. It also destabilised many negotiations; the demands of the frustrated were so strident at times that they occasionally domineered the NGOs. All was by no means sweetness and light.

- *Treaties, non-treaties and variable compliance:* much is made of the failure of the Rio parties to agree to tough treaties with strong targets on climate change, biodiversity, forests, deserts and oceans. But one should stand back for a moment. All these issues affect economies across a wide swathe of activities and interests at all levels of social organisation and governance, and across every human culture. To obtain binding agreement on such meta-themes would be impossible in the short run, no matter how righteously the NGOs scream. This sounds apologist. However, one should recognise what has been achieved in the form of monitoring, audits, programmes for action (irrespective of how many initial targets are missed), and various legal and political institutions for measuring compliance, to say nothing of the huge outpourings of academic literature, scientific reports and research institute analyses. This is no mean achievement and a necessary precursor to harder agreements. Nevertheless, we have to conclude that the current rate of progress is too slow, highly unsatisfactory and deeply troublesome in that no novel institutions of governance, at any level, are in place to administer serious programmes of commitment on these areas of global concern.

In the chapter that follows we look more closely at those arenas where there is some movement, notably in the business world, in green accounting, in ecotaxation and, above all, in LA21. Meanwhile we return to the general scene and the progress towards A21, UNCED's framework for sustainable development (Lindner, 1997, pp12–14), as reviewed in UNGASS. Here the outcome is more sober. Let us look at the few bright spots first.

- *The social agenda was at least recognised* as an integral aspect of sustainable development. The Brundtland Commission (1987, pp42–50) never quite got to grips with the social justice and civil rights themes that have occupied our attention in this chapter. But in New York, there was a more explicit reference to this link. This will hearten those who see in development the liberation of human rights and the emancipation of the spirit. One would like to think that this admission will lead to a greater coordination of effort amongst the developmental, civil rights and environmental protection NGOs along lines that are already beginning to take shape. But NGO coordination, notably at international level, is not easy – there are budget pools and competing client groups to bear in mind. A lot of housekeeping politics is still required.

- *The Convention to Combat Desertification* entered into force before UNGASS but was promoted a little more by the meeting. The Conference on Highly Migratory Fish Stocks created a forum for looking at the crises of declining fish catches and depleting fish resources generally. This is very much a talkshop, however, with little in the way of urgency, given the dramatic levels of overfishing worldwide. An Intergovernmental Forum on Facts Relating to Forests has been formed with the purpose of working towards consensus on an eventual convention. This was a small concession, but at least some institutional innovation has taken place.

- *Freshwater resource depletion* was also given attention where insufficient interest had previously been shown. This is an arena widely recognised as a potential flash point for international and subnational conflict, especially since a report from the Stockholm Environment Institute concluded that by 2020 over a third of the world population will experience water shortages (Bigg, 1997, p15). However, no new money or any innovative institutional arrangements are in place, so the water issue will probably have to fall under the aegis of a future convention. This will be highlighted by an international conference to which Britain has put its name and political weight as president of the European Union in 1998.

All this is thin gruel indeed. The main problem is that UNGASS came too early for most countries, especially the developing countries. As a result, there was nothing like the preparation that characterised the Earth Summit in Rio, nor was there a conference of the Maurice Strong variety (the director-general of both the 1992 Rio and 1972 Stockholm conferences). Finally, UNGASS took place when expectations were high but when 'green fatigue' was in vogue. Germany is preoccupied with the huge economic and social costs of unification, France is struggling for its own political credibility, the UK sees a huge crisis over welfare spending in the offing, and the US remains effectively isolationist. There is no coordinated impetus on the OECD agenda to initiate the sustainability transition. In any case, a number of formerly poor countries are beginning to taste the success of economic growth, unhindered by too much talk of sustainable development. Therefore, UNGASS was all the more disappointing precisely because it was disappointing.

> *We let the South down! We can't even get started with the objective of sustainable development until rich countries put real resources behind what they know to be their responsibility. I expected statements to be made here on commitments to increase what they are spending. I am not saying that the 77 countries are all the good guys, but they feel that we have not fulfilled our part of the Rio bargain, and*

I can't say I blame them. [Former UK Environment Secretary John Gummer, cited in Bigg, 1997, p1]

Since 1960, the ratio of income of the top 20 per cent to the lowest 20 per cent has increased from 30:1 to 78:1 in 1994 (UN Development Programme, 1996, p5). Levels of official development assistance have fallen from an average of 0.34 per cent of GDP (gross domestic product) in 1992 to 0.25 per cent in 1997 (Bramble, 1997, pp192–193). France (–12 per cent), Britain (–6 per cent) and, above all, the US (–28 per cent) have led the doleful backtrack to reduced assistance. The total debt of the developing countries has risen to over US$2 trillion, up 8 per cent in 1995 alone (Bramble 1997, p194).

What is becoming all too apparent is that virtually all the developing countries are losing their ability to shift to sustainable development. They are not obtaining sufficient financial assistance for basic scientific analysis, for systematic monitoring, for technological innovation in waste and energy reduction, or for improved regulatory and enforcement regimes. It is not just the various international treaty regimes that suffer as a consequence. Local officials, NGOs, and citizens' groups become disheartened at the fundamental lack of capability to shift to sustainability in an orderly and sustained fashion. Even the basics such as the provision of adequate information and investment arrangements to assist public and private donor flows are not in place. This is a largely unrecognised area of the sustainability transition. What is worse is that in UNGASS, very little was done to recognise and improve the situation. No new money or any extension of the remit of the global environment facility (GEF) was on offer, apart from a vague reference to a 'satisfactory level of replenishment' at some time in the future. Similarly, the NGO Working Group on New Financial Mechanisms which proposed a special Intergovernmental Panel on Financing Arrangements was sidelined for consideration by the UN Economic and Social Committee.

The failure to upgrade multinational finance was bad enough. Equally serious was the failure to encourage world trade agreements to adopt sustainable development. Ekins (1997, p3) points out that under the rules of free trade, a country cannot use trade policy to protect its environment from foreign production, or to protect the global commons – nor may it impose charges or any import restrictions on any goods in relation to their processed production methods, even when it may be doing so for its own benefit. Furthermore, various environmental regulations can be classed as technical barriers to trade. In essence, countries have very limited room for manoeuvre when using sustainability principles as a means of directing trade to sustainability ends. Martin Khor of the Third World Network (quoted by Bigg, 1997, p9) states:

In the five years since Rio, globalisation is undermining the sustainable development agenda. Commerce, and the need to be competitive in the global market, have become the top priority in many countries. The environment, welfare of the poor and global partnership have been downgraded on the agenda. The World Trade Organisation (WTO) is now institutionalising globalisation. This globalisation process seems to reward the strong and is ruthless in marginalising the weak. Its paradigm emphasises the gaining of more market share, profits and greed above all else, values that are opposite to sustainable development and global partnership.

Ekins (1997, pp15–16) points out that the WTO Committee on Trade and the Environment is essentially moribund. There is no apparent interest in the WTO to look seriously at the sustainability transition in relation to any of its current rules. Yet, as Ekins (1997, p10) concludes:

Attempts by individual countries to implement the policies necessary for sustainable development while exposed to the full competitive rigour of globalised markets could cause industrial and economic pain, or perceptions of such pain, beyond social and political endurance.

The UNCED–UNGASS story is essentially one of failure. Every year of inaction increases the structural inability to come to terms with the sustainability transition. This is particularly serious for vulnerable people in parts of the world where environmental change is already imposing an intolerable burden. As we noted at the outset, the 'Gaian echo' is not being heard in international negotiations. All the signs are that the post-Rio institutional reforms are weakening rather than strengthening that echo, despite the international civic activism that is such a heartening feature of the post-Rio age.

However, the flame of sustainability simply will not be doused. There is a fundamental acceptance at a very visceral level that 'something has to change' if we are to get through the next millenium in a civilised way. There are many interpretations of this combination of fear and hope. Some rely on the prospect of increasing civil strife over depleting renewable resources such as fish, fertile soil and portable water. Some see the ever constraining legalities of international environmental protocols. Others view the prospect of an enlightened civil society which reorganises naked acquistition to encompass spirituality. Others believe in actively engaging in a process of technological innovation, managerial adaptation, local democratisation and civic identity, which is taking place the world over, miles away from the sustainability debate but close to it in practice. Whatever the impetus, humanity moves on through a combination of love (hope) and fear (realism). The sustainability transition will not avoid that embrace.

Chapter 2

THE POLITICS OF AGENDA 21

Tim O'Riordan and Heather Voisey[1]

The case studies that follow assess the nature and the significance of the institutional changes triggered by Agenda 21 (A21). To aid analysis, we will first summarise the history and objectives of the actual A21 document. We will conclude that A21 takes on institutional meaning when it reinforces or regenerates various other political and social initiatives that are essentially independent of, but increasingly incorporated into, the A21 process. A21, on its own, would not have been as effective and as influential as A21 in synergy with these various activities.

This conclusion begs the question as to whether A21 is an institutionally framing process in its own right. Does A21 create its own momentum in the political and social order of the member states of the European Union (EU), with which we are principally concerned? We shall see in the next chapter that the amended Maastricht Treaty, signed in Amsterdam in July 1997, contains a much more specific reference to sustainable development. In essence, the principle of sustainable development is enshrined as an organising principle, or *chapteau* in the Treaty; in legal terms, this means that sustainable development addresses all the purposes of the union. In addition, the treaty has used the sustainable development organising principle as a basis for promoting further integration of environmental protection into all other policies of the union, and the principle of subsidiarity, or directing action at the most suitable focal point of government. We shall see that this presents something of a dilemma between the principles of competitive markets and free trade, on the one hand, and subsidiarity and sustainable development on the other. Constructive ambiguity is the name of the game in European law making, largely for political reasons and partly because politicians like to leave choices open, and interpretations become a matter for legal debate. If policy is fundamentally muddled, then its reflection in law will also be muddled.

In the case studies that follow, the following questions will be examined in an attempt to assess the institutional significance of A21 in the political economy of the European Union.

- Is there a clear and consensual vision of sustainable development?
- What new institutional structures or mechanisms are being put in place for the implementation of sustainable development?
- What signs of change are emerging within the administrative cultures of government?
- Is there any coherence in the responses so far?

To answer these questions, we also address just what is an institution in the context of the A21 process, and on what basis it is possible to identify institutional responsiveness. The broad conclusion remains that the transition to sustainability has been assisted by a myriad of institutional changes that are not of themselves directly promoted by A21. However, there are also distinctive features of sustainable development that specifically create important and discernible institutional change. This chapter provides the broad context for both of these conclusions.

The case studies cover the United Kingdom (UK), Norway, Germany, Portugal, Greece and the European Commission itself. The selection was designed to be representative of the European scene. Norway and Germany have long standing responses to environmental protection generally, but are beginning to recognise the important differences of following through the sustainability transition as outlined in the previous chapter. The UK is the most advanced nation in the A21 stakes, at least in terms of documentation and policy rhetoric. Yet, in the UK there is much ambivalence over the relationship between environmental policy generally and sustainable development as a more comprehensive policy framework. This is even more so the case for the commission, which has now a more purposeful legal mandate – but insufficient institutional mechanisms in place to deliver the new arrangements. Portugal and Greece are selected as developing Southern economies assisted in their growth and competitiveness through EU funds, some of which are designed to promote environmental protection and sustainable development policies, but most essentially favour the unrestrained expansion of a single market and the physical infrastructure to enable this. From this cross section of studies, and bearing in mind the principal conclusions of the theoretical framing of the sustainability transition, we believe that we can stand back a little and assess the significance of A21, and increasingly its local government counterpart, LA21, on the political economy of the EU. This theme forms the basis of the final chapter of the book.

THE HISTORY AND SIGNIFICANCE OF A21

The Brundtland Commission (1987, p343) was determined that its report would not gather dust. 'The rate of change', it noted with some alarm, 'is outstripping the ability of scientific disciplines and our current capabilities to assess and advise. It is frustrating the attempts of political and economic institutions which evolved in a different, more fragmented, world to adapt and cope.' Accordingly, the commission recommended that:

...an active follow-up of this report is imperative. It is with this in mind that we call for the UN General Assembly, upon due consideration, to transform this report into a UN Programme of Action on Sustainable Development... Arrangements will be needed to set benchmarks to maintain human progress within the guidelines of human needs and natural laws. [ibid]

The commission therefore initiated a process of regional conferences to set the broad pattern for the UN Conference on Environment and Development (UNCED) at Rio. These in turn triggered four preparatory negotiating conferences (known as PrepComs). Chip Lindner (1997, pp4–6) summarises what subsequently happened. The Programme of Action called for by the commission became *Agenda 21* with 40 chapters. All the key themes addressed in our previous chapter were touched upon, though the sensitive themes of ecological justice, civil rights and fair trade were side-stepped, as was the general principle of empowerment. We shall see that Chapter 28, creating an LA21, encouraged the fullest and most effective citizen participation in any process. But even that chapter did not convey the emancipating and democratising qualities that are beginning to emerge as LA21 in the modern age.

A21 was most notable in that it singled out stakeholder groups for special inclusion, responsibility and respect in its implementation. These groups were in the sights of A21 across the whole swathe of subject matter, with a call for institutional changes in the law, economics, politics and civil society specifically to take their interests into account.

The nine stakeholder groups are:

- indigenous peoples;
- women;
- youth;
- agriculture;
- business;
- science;
- trades unions;
- local government; and
- environmental/development NGOs.

In principle, each of these target groups has an identity and a mission within A21. In practice there are notable and persistent failures in the areas of civil rights, laws of information, laws of democratic participation and the enablement of local self-reliance. All of these issues were implicit in the Brundtland analysis but never received a proper airing. This in turn means that these targeted groups are not as comprehensively treated as they ought to be. Part of the remit of the UN Commission on Sustainable Development (CSD), created post-Rio, is to put this to rights (see Bigg and Dodds, 1997, pp262–265). The commission is a subset of the UN ECOSOC, the principal economic and social development committee, and has 53 members, whose renewal requires election. Its task is to examine the sprawling components of A21 within a host of workshops, special sessions, policy papers and endless diplomacy. This is why we created Figure 1.4 in Chapter 1. Sustainable development is primarily a process of revealing personal and institutional approaches to stewardship and to empowerment if it is ever to work. It is noteworthy that the CSD, established in the wake of Rio as a reporting and reviewing body, has no powers to audit compliance or to investigate how progress towards stewardship or empowerment is being (or not being) achieved. Nevertheless, Bigg and Dodds (1997, p35) conclude that without the CSD slowly and painfully evolving into these areas, 'there would be a gulf between local and national implementation of Agenda 21 and the global follow up'.

At UNGASS, delegates applauded the work of the CSD, but gave it no new powers of audit or surveillance, despite prolonged lobbying by the NGOs. Though the NGOs spoke for the nine stakeholding groups, national governments were simply not prepared to submit themselves to independent scrutiny. It is ominous to note that the greatest opposition came from those countries emerging into the economic spotlight, and whose civil rights records are widely criticised. A21 may be symbolically important, but it carries no weight against a determined economic and political hegemony. The CSD is too harried by an overambitious agenda, too many networks, and insufficient support on the crucial areas of multilateral financing and capacity-building, the type of necessary institutional changes which were examined in the previous chapter. It is confronted by confused policy signals fuelled by too many competing aspirations to be resolved in a single case. A decision moving from the status quo is prevented by a fear of destabilising the whole system.

A21 is soft law in the sense that its text and message are regarded by national states as highly discretionary and interpretative.[2] Yet A21 is also formally a process of (partial) inclusion and recognition for the nine stakeholders mentioned earlier. This gives us a clue as to institutional reform. At least some attention should be given to policy coordination, to some form of published yardsticks, or indicators, and to means of financing change. In addition, science, business and LA21 are obvious zones for special attention. It is in these six areas that we propose to examine institutional change. However, before we do so, something on the nature of institutions is necessary to set the scene.

ON THE ROLE OF INSTITUTIONS FOR THE SUSTAINABILITY TRANSITION

Institutions hold society together, give it a sense of purpose, and enable it to adapt. A summary of the wide-ranging literature on institutions can be found in O'Riordan and Jordan (1996), and Jordan and O'Riordan (1997). For the purposes of this analysis, the concept of institutions applies both to structures of power and positional relationships – as found in organisations with leaders, membership, clients, information flows, resources for mobilisation, and the usual distortions of communication to suit their mandate. All organisations seek to generate knowledge and to shape it to promote their political ends. The notion of institutions also applies to socialised ways of looking at the world as influenced by culturally ascribed values, patterns of status and associations, and procedures through which any information or analysis is given weight and significance. In a nutshell, institutions serve to maintain social relationships, preserve social cohesion, organise political change, and enable shifts in outlook to take place, peaceably or in anguish (Jordan and O'Riordan, 1997, p4). Law is one institutional arrangement which arbitrates amongst other institutions in order to select those which are properly and generally authoritative. This is something the law needs to do to fulfill its function of providing authoritative resolutions to contested claims of political or social validity.

Jordan and O'Riordan (1997, p12) summarise the main features of institutions as they apply to global environmental change generally.

- Institutions embody rules that encapsulate values, norms and views of the world. Rules define roles and the social context. Institutions determine what is appropriate, legitimate and proper. They define obligations, self-restraints, rights and immunities, as well as the sanctions for unacceptable behaviour. Institutions also define the 'game' of politics, establishing for players both the objectives and the range of appropriate tactics or moves.
- Institutions evolve slowly, but over time they tend to become characterised by procedures and outlooks enshrined by habit. In doing so they help to stabilise perceptions, interpretations and justifications.
- Institutions therefore take on an element of permanence, a kind of enduring regularity for human action (Giddens, 1984, p24). They also confer identity on members, and separateness on non-members.
- Institutions are also changing in that they are constantly renegotiated in the interplay between human action and the organisational structures that influence outlooks and actions. Yet each institution forgets information that challenges its organisational principles or political mandate.

In order to carry out their role of ordering social evolution and personal action, institutions have to adopt various regulations and legitimating devices. These organising procedures require some sort of acceptable framework and it is this framework to which we now turn. Figure 1.4 in Chapter 1, and its A21 context, provides the basis for the text that follows.

Reliable Wealth and Sustainable Markets

We believe that there is a kind of evolutionary staging in the transition to sustainability, a pattern that requires institutional shape. We propose to examine this by introducing Table 2.1 to accord with the key themes introduced in Figure 1.4. The reliable growth paradigm remains the primary positional focus. No democratically elected government can hope to become so unless it espouses permanent and real economic wellbeing for its electorate. Where environmental threats loom, that promised growth comes about through technological innovation and regulatory belt tightening. This is the essence of Factor 4, the pathway to ecoefficiency so lovingly promoted by Ernst von Weizacker and Amory and Hunter Lovins (1997). These authors show how creating two times as much with half the input requirements, the so-called Factor 4, can be both more efficient and less expensive, and therefore much more profitable.

In fact still too little of this apparently miraculous win–win actually takes place and we need to ask why. The answer lies in a plethora of adverse factors running from adverse subsidies and taxes, weak information flows, and variable degrees of management vision, to the sheer inertia of existing market structures, even when a higher level of profit is in the offing. Bhargava and Welford (1996, p21) look critically and comprehensively at why some forms comply and others resist sustainable development. They emphasize the ROAST evolution (resist, observe, accommodate, seize, transcend). This is the sequence of responses by companies when being 'sold' Factor 4 or, much more threateningly, sustainable development.

- *Resist*, deny and avoid strategies that inevitably end in trouble. Look at Shell's behaviour over the Brent Spar issue. Even today, companies regularly hide ethically embarrassing information from their employees and shareholders.
- *Observe*, comply and pronounce in public what you are doing so that, once a threshold has been crossed, the evangelical mission is trumpeted about. Smart companies are wary of too many 'good news' stories. They know they still have a long way to go.
- *Accommodate*, adjust and discover that new management approaches result in new marketing niches and cost savings. The key here is the venture capital link to another company or a new operator. For example, Greenpeace and Friends of the Earth (FoE) are signing up with electricity utilities to promote photovoltaics.
- *Seize* and preempt the agenda by building in a comprehensive strategy for total product stewardship. This is the difficult task. Some companies such as Dow Chemicals and Monsanto are nearly there, as is ICI Polyurythenes. But total product stewardship means closing the loop in the production–waste chain and that is still very difficult to do.
- *Transcend* to produce a complete corporate culture, within the workforce and amongst the suppliers, distributors and the local communities, of awareness of, and action towards, the responsibilities of stewardship and 'managed' empowerment. This is the objective of so-called sustainable business. Note, however, that even the strongest sustainability action here is nowhere near self-generation and a zero ecological footprint. We must always be careful to put sustainability into commercial perspective.

Factor 4 is not as widespread as von Weizsacker and his friends would have us believe, and the transcendental aspects of modern business management are difficult to hear in the uproar of competitiveness, efficiency strategies and financial audits. For Factor 4 to succeed, many institutional relationships will have to be reorganised and reconnected.

The scope for ecoefficiency as one routeway to reliable growth leads us to place one key marker down in Table 2.1. This is the role of sustainability markets. In the sustainability transition, market institutions refer to arrangements in the competitive economy which aim to ensure that ecological and social tolerances to expansion and change are not exceeded. This in turn leads to a consideration of how wealth is construed in a more sustainable age, and how the tax regime might be adjusted to cope. So, along with markets we need to look at the system of national accounts: these are creating improved measures of ecological and social burdens attached to particular sectors of the macro-economy. We shall see that 'green budgets' become one of our key institutional devices for evaluating sustainable development as it evolves. Along with such market forces will come various indicators of sustainability's progress or regress. We shall also discover that the process of selecting and using indicators is highly institutionally framed, with its own set of political interpretations.

We therefore begin with a link between reliable or desirable growth which aims to be self-regenerating and which requires the signals of reformed markets, green budgets and politically sympathetic indicators to help monitor the transition. In institutional terms we will be looking at the evolution of new accounting techniques, of indicators for monitoring any progress to sustainable development, and at the scope for ecological tax reform. This last phrase means the use of charges and levies on polluting and depleting practices, identified through environmental burdens via indicators, so that the reserve can be earmarked for specific sustainability measures (see O'Riordan, 1997a, for a fuller treatment of ecotaxation).

Regulation in the Sustainability Transition

Markets on their own cannot complete the transition to sustainability. This is all part of the interactive evolution depicted in Figure 1.4 and Table 2.1. So there needs to be institutions for regulation. These can be in the form of formal patterns of control and guidance established by international or national order and operated through identifiable agencies. There is a slow but steady trend in regulatory agencies to incorporate the slippery term of sustainability into their remit. This is, for example, the case for Scottish National Heritage and the two environment agencies of Britain, namely the Environment Agency in England and Wales, and the Scottish Environmental Protection Agency in Scotland.

In effect, the sustainability remit poses an opportunity but also a headache for these organisations. The opportunity lies in the dynamism of constantly reinterpreting what sustainability means to allow these organisations to evolve into new partnerships and valuation techniques. The headache lies in the incomprehension on the part of most of their clients and members as to how they should behave and think just because a new word has appeared on the horizon. In practice, therefore, these agencies are thinking strategically but acting pragmatically. This is typical of the early stages of the transition to sustainability; as a result, the forthcoming experience of these two organisations should be worth watching. We note here that this concept has begun to unravel a host of innova-

tions in cost-benefit analysis, environmental appraisal and in consultative procedures, a number of which have manifested themselves in European directives.

Another feature of regulation for a more sustainable age is the rise of the
voluntary contact, or interactive compliance regime. This emerging arena for
institutional change is summarised by Dan Beardsley and his two colleagues
Terry Davies and Robert Hersh (1997) in a useful review of US and international experience. These authors look first at the shift towards comprehensive
integrated pollution control instead of single-media pollution reduction
programmes. This is reflected in business ecoaudits and in the more general
swing towards integrated management for product stewardship. Developments
in this arena are well summarised in Welford (1996, pp35–200). Beardsley *et al*
also emphasise the rise of economic incentives which are now being coupled to
voluntary programmes of regulatory compliance. This particular arena is given
prominence by Gary Davis and his colleagues (1977, pp12–13) who show how
more targeted patterns of incentives stimulate extended product responsibility.
The point here is the coupling of formal and informal regulation, flexible
targeting of incentives and responsive management regimes, both in business
and government. The hopeful signs are that real institutional reform is beginning to appear in this context. This is because of a growing synergy between a
reforming business culture and a responsive regulatory scene. But, be careful,
the signs are more in the intent than in the practice. The upper part of the
ROAST transition still prevails. Enforced or voluntary cooperation between
companies challenges the paradigm of perfect or workable competition inherent to the legal concept of the single market. Ostensibly, it is only legal for the
community to approve anti-competitive behaviour under certain, reasonably
well-defined, circumstances. Measures shown to have anti-competitive effects
on a European scale are void unless they get prior competition clearance.

Beardsley *et al* (1997, p8) also conclude that this reform needs to extend to
the zone of empowerment and trust, outlined in the previous chapter, but that
this is best done by formal codes of practice coupled to transparent accounting
procedures. Here is where environmental auditing and management systems
still break down. Business is happy with voluntaristic approaches where the
internal room for manoeuvre is hidden from a critical external gaze. But put
this into a formal reporting programme and industry generally gets nervous. As
Davis (1997, p37) summarises:

> *…while voluntary adoption of extended product responsibility is promising, it will*
> *never completely eliminate the need for rigorous governmental oversight… There*
> *has to be shared responsibility between governments and the private sector up and*
> *down the product chain.*

This suggests a form of regulation that recognises ecoefficiency and provides the
incentives to facilitate it, yet also enshrines the rights of access to all relevant
information for monitoring compliance against agreed and externally imposed
targets. For this mix of formal and informal regulatory regimes to work effectively, there has to be a link to indicators, to environmental impact burden studies,

and to the parallel accounts of green budgeting. This is why we suggest that the two diagrams reproduced in Figure 1.4 and Table 2.1 should be read as one.

Social Equity and the Sustainability Transition

The third institutional arena for this transition is that of social equity or empowerment. This means applying the principles of institutional fairness outlined in the previous chapter to non-human and human life. In turn this will require some form of ethical weighting or reverse discounting to take into account the rights of future generations that are encompassed in stewardship and precaution. Within that notion of equity will be a set of legal measures to guide institutional arrangements such as monitoring, protecting, evaluating and compensating. It follows that the extended consultative procedures outlined under the discussion of empowerment will increasingly play their part here.

One arena where equity considerations loom large is science for a sustainable age. The critical issue here is how far ethical and spiritual matters should be incorporated into the heart of scientific analysis. The British philosopher John O'Neill (1993, pp148–152) adopts an Aristotelian approach to this question by arguing that intrinsic values of self-awareness, reflectiveness and caring for others through caring for oneself are all elements of both the individual persona and the scientist. Like Shrader-Freschette (1996, p13), another philosopher but this time American, he recognised that science is presently institutionalised and does not easily cope with genuinely uncertain outcomes. Nor does the act of knowing always carry with it the pleasure of perceiving the value of the non-human world, and the significance of other values in forming one's own position. Shrader-Freschette (1996, pp30–32) is more circumspect over the science of valuation knowledge but, like O'Neill, argues for a more extended science of civic incorporation. She believes that under such conditions, ethical conditions of fairness become paramount. In the rules of maximin there would be embodied an avoidance of irreversible changes. The maximin rule, in particular, indicates that the worst outcome for each policy decision is systematically sought so that the option with the least worst consequences is explicitly selected. That, in turn, involves appropriate compensation, or evidence of irreversibility as a form of compensation, so that there is a real empathy with the intrinsic values of those not otherwise incorporated within the decisions. In this sense, the ethical outreach of the science for the sustainability transition is that of deliberately weighting, through empowering mechanisms, the interests of those whose feelings and hopes would not otherwise be articulated.

This extended, or potentially communicative, form of scientific enquiry is termed civic science by the American environmentalist Kai Lee (1993, p161).

Managing large ecosystems should not rely merely on science, but on civic science; it should be irredeemably public in the way responsibilities are exercised, intrinsically technical, and open to learning from errors and profiting from successes.

Civic science politicises the process in the sense that science evolves via adaptive human choices about means and ends. One version of this can be found in the community through its collection of scientific committees (comitology), made up of national government scientists. However, in practice, these bodies are remote and politicised in a manner which may not reflect the priorities suggested in the demands of civic science. Hence, the comitology committees are also under fire. Options for local choice are therefore built into the prognoses: the act of creating any future state becomes an agreed political choice that in turn shapes the political conditions for designing the 'future' state.

One could take, for illustrative purposes, the issue of transport futures for a medium-sized town. One approach would be to model how commuting and leisure patterns might alter on the basis of various price hikes in petrol (gasoline) or due to the imposition of progressively higher charges, or via an electronic 'gate' that monitored and priced vehicle movements in and out of town. Such models would have to assume how various commuters and pleasure-seeking drivers with different travel options and incomes might behave. This would be gathered into a geographical information system data base and indicators of response could be mapped in terms of alternative travel patterns. So far, so good. But such models tell us little of the equity issues involved, of how those with no travel options, but on low fixed incomes, might have to cope with alternative spending plans, or how various interest coalitions might form to oppose the proposals and force a political rethink. In short, deterministic and probabalistic models do little to create a community collective 'valuation' or 'knowingness' in O'Neill's (1996) terminology, and to address the issue of 'sustainable mobility' in a conscious discourse, leading to equitable and politically acceptable outcomes.

One way of tracking this would be through the route of empowerment and revelation. This would mean establishing participatory techniques and mechanisms involving sensitive contacts with all representative interests, and building up consensus while recognising areas of conflict and commonality. The aim would be to devise policy routeways in the course of the negotiations to ensure that viable alternative means of transport were provided, for example through 'green commuting plans'. These plans would themselves be the outcome of participatory consultative approaches at the level of the employer or neighbourhood. Therefore, the civic science of the sustainability transition could build in equity and compensatory arrangements into the process itself, so that trust and respect were introduced as an intrinsic part of the procedures. We are still some distance from that vision. But here is where civil society merges with LA21 in a cooperative venture. What it requires is real support from the top.

Revelation and the Sustainability Transition

Finally, to enable all this to happen, we refocus on the process of revelation. This is the capturing of the spirit of communal obligation and citizenship which, in part, will come about by the 'de-enclosure' of the commons.

Revelation is the institutional mechanism of creating consensus on common interests. We shall see in the chapters that follow how experiments under the umbrella of LA21 are facilitating this process.

As a result, we can now create Table 2.1, where the columns are the principle institutional discourses of markets, regulations, equity and revelation, and the rows encompass seven dimensions that emerge from the four principles outlined in Figure 1.4. These are:

- *myths of nature*, or views of natural tolerances central to the analysis of stewardship and precaution, and hence critical in the role of valuation, indicators and national accounts; we saw from the introduction to Chapter 1 that such myths are institutionally framed;
- *social values* or views of social tolerances which relate particularly to empowerment and to equity and mini–max considerations;
- *policy orientations*, or the performance of policy instruments such as the integration of policy measures, cross-ministry coordination of policy instruments, and measures of policy effectiveness – the changing face of regulation is highly appropriate here;
- *distributional arrangements* or the revelatory devices which help stakeholders to appreciate who is likely to gain or to lose in the sustainability transition and how compensation with dignity can be established;
- *generating consensus* via a combination of empowering and revelatory techniques, coupled to mini–max approaches to compensation;
- *ensuring intergenerational responsibilities* by applying formal and informal regulatory measures centred around stewardship and precaution, yet bringing into the frame the democratic paradox of 'sacrificing' for the future; and,
- *liability arrangements* which ensure that compensation is worked towards through a variety of measures such as performance bonds, safety nets and popular epidemiology programmes to permit a civic science of risk communication and reduction.

In diagrammatic form, the pattern of discourse around sustainable development might look as proposed in Table 2.1:

One can see that there are many ways of shifting towards sustainability by means that have similar goals but are different in approach. This suggests that there can be no commonly accepted definition of sustainable development, nor can there be any collective position as to which institutional means or forms are best able to facilitate the transition. By producing this table, we are not assuming that the differing strands of outlook and values conflict to the point of immobility. Indeed, we argue that all parts of the discourse need to be accommodated in any tolerated transition, for it is only by weaving these different strands together that a truly democratic transfer towards sustainability can be determined.

Table 2.1 Patterns of discourse applying to the transition to sustainability

	Market	Regulatory	Equity	Revelatory
myths of nature	expandable limits	precautionary limits	breached limits	negotiated limits
social values	enterprise	protection of the vulnerable	citizenship	community
policy orientations	price signals	rules of contracts	equality of opportunity	communication
distributional arrangements	markets	by agents of rule-makers	by democracy	by negotiation
generating consent	compensation	by agreed rules	negotiation and compensation	by reasoned discussion
inter-generationality	future looks after itself	future helped by present	future planned by present	future envisioned
liability	spread losses	fine redistribution	burden-sharing	by negotiation mechanisms

Source: O'Riordan and Voisey, 1997, p10

On the basis of the argument above, any institutional adaptation for the sustainability transition may be summarised as follows:

- it must reflect all the levels of discourse outlined in Table 2.1;
- it must be responsive to visions of a more ecologically protective and fair future state;
- it must be created by negotiated consent, and when that consent cannot be guaranteed, then by understanding and tolerance;
- it must be measurable, set in parameters that have ecological and social references, and linked to agreed norms and targets; and
- it must be carried out according to agreed rules and norms, both of a formal and informal kind, located in markets, in regulatory practices, in the law, and in social values.

If sustainable development is non-threatening, the four visions outlined above can emerge side by side. They are articulated by different interests, but can cross over in the discourse of, say, sustainability indicators, green accounting, and formal or informal regulation. The tension is most obvious when the discourses are institutionalised, as for example in the UK Round Table on Sustainable Development (see Chapter 8). In the early stages of the Round Table the transformation was too raw and the level of understanding too recent to permit effective dialogue. Respect for legitimate positions is beginning to occur, largely because of 'retreats' involving all or part of the membership. This innovation is helping to hold the Round Table together and to bestow on it a sense of collective solidarity.

INSTITUTIONAL SIGNS OF THE TRANSITION TO SUSTAINABILITY

The original objectives of the research project that forms the basis of this text were to extend the earlier work on institutional adjustment to climate change in selected European countries, and in the community itself, to the national and EU response to A21 (see O'Riordan and Jäger, 1996). Specifically for this project, the aim was to develop a fuller understanding of the political dynamics associated with the organising focus that is sustainable development. To do this, the project team examined a number of indicators of both policy shift, including policy integration, and structural or positional adjustment in the pattern of forces guiding and coordinating policy. These organizational and procedural modulations are associated with a host of actors and agencies, including government departments, non-departmental public bodies, regulatory agencies, business, local government, the voluntary sector, communities, and citizens.

Throughout our assessment we were influenced by the conclusions of the climate politics study (O'Riordan and Jäger, 1996, pp351–360). These observations suggested that the following themes should be addressed in any future analysis of institutional dynamics in response to global environmental change initiatives.

- Institutional adjustment takes place in a number of policy arenas, working cooperatively but not necessarily with the same set of political triggers. Thus, response to the transition towards sustainability can and should come in a number of guises.
- Robust institutional adjustment has to be backed by economic ministries and economic policy strategies. Tackling the roots of macro-economic philosophy with an environmental agenda will fail unless the two approaches can be made to reinforce one another.
- Because policy networks are constantly coalescing and fissuring, the most successful institutional adjustments require linkages of policy coalitions and fresh groupings of interests whose unequivocal, cooperative support buttresses a number of policy innovators and executors at a variety of levels. For the transition to sustainability, such coalitions have to shape a common political space and to combine economic, social and environmental interests.

Therefore, the project team approached this task by searching for policy indicators that might herald a shift towards more sustainable patterns of economic development and social welfare.

As a means of identifying how far any country has moved in its institutional redesign towards sustainability, we propose eight indicators for testing response and adaptation:

1) *the language and meaning* of sustainable development as expressed in official documentation and popular discussion during the early years of the debate over sustainable development;

2) *the scope for policy integration* where earlier policies were neither united not mutually reinforcing;

3) *the nature of interdepartmental coordination* promoting and reflecting these new policy alliances, backed by widened risks and evaluative procedures;

4) *the role of legislative (parliamentary) surveillance* of both policy integration and administrative cohesion, including improved means of identifying targets and performance indicators, according to open procedures and agreed ethical principles;

5) *the compilation of environmental and social indicators* of quality of life and ecological tolerance as a basis for legitimising action, changing course and evaluating the sustainability transition;

6) *the creation of 'green' accounts* covering indicators or resource depletion, environmental disruption, price incompatibilities, inappropriate subsidies, and measures of human welfare and social justice, coupled to tentative moves towards ecological tax reform;

7) *the involvement of the business community* in addressing sustainability through full-cost accounting, internal housekeeping, full regulatory compliance, product stewardship, supply chain audits, and awareness-raising for shareholders and customers; and,

8) *the emergence of local action*, along the lines of LA21, to bring about a locally responsive version of all of the above points, set in a drive for fresh democratic mandates.

These eight themes emerge from the discussion earlier in this chapter, from the theoretical analysis of the introductory chapter, and from the amalgamation of approaches embodied in Figure 1.4 and Table 2.1. We fully realise that there could be other organising foci for the transition that forms the centrepiece of this book. We could have looked, for example, at education, community mobilisation, or in formal structures of consultation. We propose to extend our analysis in the future to cover these themes, but that is for another book.

To assist the reader in following both the story so far and the subsequent material, here is a basic summary of the findings, along with various observations on their significance for the transition towards sustainable development.

FINDINGS OF THE STUDY

The overall conclusion of this study is that sustainable development is indeed a very important organising force for political, social and economic response, covering far more than environmental problems and destined to evolve into a broader social agenda as Europe continues both to federate and decentralise. Its influence will be shaped by political and economic processes that will evolve, mostly independently, from the sustainability transition. But its significance as an organising force depends ultimately on its own identifying focus. To date, that crucial aspect of institutional response is only barely discernible, and even then only in a fragmentary way.

There are two fundamental challenges to the progress of sustainable development in Europe. The first is the lack of an intrinsic policy focus that channels patterns of political, social and economic change towards the specific direction of economic durability, precautionary stewardship and citizen empowerment as a unifying transitional engine. The second is the potential incompatibility between the economic and technological forces of economic globalisation, as seen in the drive towards international competitiveness, freedom of trade and movement generally, and the privatisation of former state-supported responsibilities in both business and social services. All of this is predicated on the principles of growth through innovation and comparative advantage, set in the context of ever-increasing economic and cultural integration. Against this is a call for self-reliance, for community identity, for cultural tolerance and for 'people-centred' means of debating and reconciling future choices of sustainable development. This line of analysis supports an awareness that the locality is the principle avenue of change for most people, as well as the site of cultural variety, collective identity and a sense of community control over the nature of change.

At all levels of government, European, nation state, regional, and local, this tension between competitive globalisation and empowering localism is beginning to emerge in the politics of the sustainability transition. At present these tensions are manifest in the dismay over the closing of factories and local services in the name of efficiency; in the debate over the funding of services such as schools, post-school training, social care, prison and probation services, health care and pensions provision; and in the emergence of a host of new socially concerned self-help groups around such neglected issues as AIDS, domestic violence, rights of asylum, and drug addiction. The evidence is beginning to emerge that active groups have little faith in the ability of government at any level to handle such issues in a comprehensive and caring manner. Hence the shift towards civic activism, political disobedience, and collective efforts to achieve greater measures of security in local economies. We regard these 'empowering' moves as a vital aspect of any sustainability transition. We also believe that many social and political mechanisms and movements are in place to promote this objective. But there is no conscious connection between the two in any sustainable development agenda. This is a lost piece of institutional innovation, whose non-appearance is all the more alarming because of its significance.

Language

In terms of translation, the phrase sustainable development has caused some difficulty. In some cases (Greek, Irish) the wording had to be invented. In all cases the translation adopted in formal treaties reflected national biases. The British liked the notion of continuity and reliability, the Germans, stewardship, the Greeks, life support, the Portuguese, something akin to self-perpetuation, and the Norwegians, 'being upheld' by self-generating investment. There may be no agreement as to language, but in the Portuguese and Norwegian texts there is an innovative sense of the Brundtland Commission's notion of self-limiting and self-perpetuating closed-loop economies. This is mostly rhetoric.

The core concept of sustainability is linked to the language of continuation and stewardship.

As for the European Community, the language of article 2 of the Maastricht Treaty is a classic example of politically ambiguous draftsmanship. As noted earlier in this chapter, the revised text of the Maastricht Treaty describes sustainable development as an organising principle for incorporating environmental policy across the board in European Union activities. And one of the principle objectives of the union is 'to achieve', not to 'promote' as in the original wording, 'balanced and sustainable development'. To assist this process, the codecision procedure (involving qualified majority voting in the Council of Ministers and a joint liaison with the European Parliament) extends to all environmental matters. Unanimous voting, however, still applies to landuse, water resources, energy matters, and taxation generally. This is a blow to the integrationists, since all these sectors are intrinsic to sustainability. This is one important case where the organising focus is weakened.

Assessing the implications of the sustainability transition for the European Union is fraught with difficulty. On one level, treaty amendments concerning sustainable development and integration at the top of the treaty leave room for some weak readjustment of ever more complex and centralised rules concerning justifying sustainability-motivated action at a national level. This is the case, despite the reinforcement of the subsidiarity principle based in major part on the competition-driven demands of the single European market. Any more radical interpretation of sustainability is unlikely, given its deliberate ambiguity and the entrenched neo-liberal economic position that the treaty adopts. Europeanisation of politics based on the power of the market to transcend national boundaries, and on the concurrent demand of politicians for European- and global-level policies to steward these forces, lies at the core of the European project. Globalisation only weakly mirrors Europeanisation in terms of institutional acceptance of the market ideology. Abandoning liberal and neoliberal ideology which drives political integration is unlikely unless an equally powerful but alternative integrating discourse becomes available. In the absence of such a discourse, European integration, the dominant political force since the war, may fail. Whether this is desirable or not in terms of the sustainability transition is itself questionable. In institutional terms one may doubt whether competing global science or ethical discourses can keep pace with the globalising tendencies of the economic discourse. These points are given further discussion in Chapters 4 and 6.

Policy Integration

Policy integration requires a common evaluative yardstick, coalitions of supportive interests, and a machinery of execution that coordinates a host of governmental and non-governmental actors. Such conditions are rare, let alone a conjunction of them, despite the current trend towards policy coalitions and interest groups realignments. One cannot expect much movement here, except where there is genuine policy ambiguity and an overwhelming political demand to get things done. Transport policy which touches the interrelated areas of public health, economic decline in urban centres, pedestrian and cyclist safety, and road-related damage to wildlife sites, is one such arena.

The evidence emerging from this study is that effective policy integration is not taking place. There are various institutional innovations, including coordinating cabinet-level committees, interdepartmental working groups on environmental valuation and green accounting, so-called 'green-ministers', and important new combinations of interests across business, environmental, consumer and justice groupings. But none of this has any serious political or administrative force at present.

We conclude that the discourse for sustainability is itself too ambiguous and used by too many different actors, for widely differing purposes, for policy to be fully integrated or to achieve consensus. However, we shall see below that mechanisms for improving procedures for scientific analysis and policy evaluation at an interdepartmental level offer hope for a better transition to policy integration over time. We should recall that bureaucracies do not readily cede auditing of budgets to other bureaucracies: a necessary discourse called sustainable development is only likely to go so far in terms of genuine policy integration.

In the European Commission, the legal requirement under Section 130(r), now in the Maastricht Treaty, namely to integrate environmental considerations into other policy arenas, has, to date, had little administrative or even political effect. Again, movement is taking place for reasons other than those of policy integration, notably in agriculture and energy. As David Wilkinson shows in Chapter 6, there are institutional innovations in the form of an integration unit in Directorate-General (DG) XI (which is responsible for environmental matters generally). It coordinates: 'integration correspondents' within each DG, environmental appraisals of various policy moves, and an internal management accounting system.

In practice, however, little of this has any effect. DGs are not attuned to thinking laterally or environmentally. Sharing of responsibility may be a European ideal, but it has yet to become part of the highly sectorised and self-protecting administrative culture of Brussels. However, the European Parliament has used the integration clause to require much greater environmental accountability for the area of cohesion and structural adjustment funds, and this certainly is a policy innovation. Adjustments at this level can have significant national impacts on progress towards sustainability. Yet our Portuguese and Greek case studies both contain examples where cohesion funds were used to promote economic development in a palpably non-sustainable manner. The institutional reasons for this lie in the contradictory interpretations of the use of funds and in warring ministers, short ministerial tenure, and the huge payouts linked to large construction projects in these countries.

The ultimate barrier to sustainability lies in the lack of encouragement from the top, namely the prime minister or president, the unwillingness of the main economic departments (finance, industry, employment, energy, transport) to address sustainable development within the mainstream economics focus, and the relative political weakness of the environment ministries. From this perspective, it is hardly surprising, but not helpful, that responsibility for sustainable development rests with the environment ministries. They may seek to coordinate but they have no effective power. No prime minister, not even Mrs Brundtland herself when she was in power, places sustainable development high on their political priorities. They may like to talk a language of stewardship and empowerment, but they do not carry it out. This is political rhetoric at work.

Interdepartmental Consultation

Any departmental policy requires clearance and the support of related departments. So interdepartmental working groups are the coinage of administrative discourse. In the name of sustainable development there is movement on green accounting in the form of shadow accounts by statisticians, sustainability indicators of varying degrees of sophistication, and economic valuation of environmental change. At present most of this is in the form of data gathering and seminars on valuation techniques. There is little in the way of discernible policy shift, in any of the countries studied, with regard to the improved use of sustainability accounting methodologies. However, this is not to say that all this effort is wasted. Far from it. It is actually a vital part of institutional adaptation during the transition. We perceive the early stages of this all-important interdepartmental relationship in the European Environment Agency, in the Department of the Environment, Transport and the Regions (DETR)[3] in Britain, and in the OECD's and the European Commission's work on ecotaxation, or ecological tax reform as it is more formally known. But without high-level political encouragement, this is still embryonic.

The research team concludes that there is a small, but discernible, cultural shift taking place in the bureaucracy of official ministries. Officials are beginning to think in a precautionary manner, in the long term, in a language of ecological economics and risk management, and are working through more integrated structures of accounting and assessment. The younger members of the administrative 'tribes' are especially interested and sensitive to these developments. There are huge structural and attitudinal blocks to this process – make no mistake about it. But the pace of movement is both exacting and progressive. We regard this as a very important form of institutional innovation.

Legislative Surveillance

This, by contrast, is the least active arena of institutional innovation. The various national parliaments and the European Parliament have not been able to organise or to undertake any meaningful audit function of national or departmental responses to A21. Beyond the UK there is frankly no political push for this, nor any established mechanism to make it work well. Parliamentary surveillance is very much a matter for the legislators and their committee structures, as is the perceived responsiveness of the administrative departments and the states of law. Without formal 'duties of care', and in the absence of any coordinating committee structure, parliamentary surveillance is always likely to be wanting.

In speeches to UNGASS, Prime Minister Tony Blair and John Prescott, Secretary of State for the Environment, Transport and the Regions, proposed a 'powerful new environmental committee of Parliament to scrutinise policies and actions across government (Prescott, 1997, p3). In the same speech, Mr Prescott stated that he would chair a new cabinet committee on the environment 'on which colleagues from all key departments would sit'. We will see if this extends to the Treasury (O'Riordan, 1997b, p13). Legislatures have to be prepared to return to a topic many times if they want it to be effective. There is, as yet, no stomach for this with regard to sustainable development, at least in national governments. The European Parliament, however, appears to be more aggressive, with a much more focused interest in the 'integration' remit of article 130 (r), and it is intensifying its demands for more specific performance targets through which to evaluate the effectiveness of the various environmental action programmes. The recent Maastricht Treaty amendments should assist, if only by providing more facilitative pathways.

Sustainability Indicators

The OECD is pioneering an approach to sustainability indicators, and this is having an influence on the European Environment Agency, the Norwegian Environment Ministry and the UK DETR. Greece has no formal indicators, nor does Portugal. The commission is considering this, but nothing official has emerged. It may do so in the run up to the Sixth Environment Action Plan now that the European Environmental Agency has commissioned a study on sustainability performance with regard to targets. Despite this apparent sluggishness, many official statistic organisations are analysing the scope for more comprehensive performance indicators towards set environmental goals. In this early stage, most of the indicators are either economic or ecological in character.

The pioneering British study of national sustainability indicators (Department of the Environment, 1996) is nevertheless an important starting point to institutional evolution in this connection. This study combined the speculations of statisticians and policy analysts across the sweep of Whitehall. It created bodies of data, and interpretations of trends, that no single department would have recognised if working entirely on its own. It also created a shift in policy, notably towards more social cost pricing of private road vehicles. The fact that the study is published, with a request for its collaborative improvement in future editions, is a good example of institutional dynamics that probably will be copied elsewhere in Europe, and certainly in the European Environment Agency.

However, if we look at empowerment, equity and revelation for our guide, then sustainability indicators need to enter the realm of social auditing, economic emancipation, and political liberalisation. In a study commissioned for Charter 88, the leading constitutional reform lobbying organisation in the

UK, Mary Lenton (1997) combined the evidence of a wide range of informed opinion to produce a fine summary of these conditions. In addition, Andrew Mullaney (1997, pp162–163) shows how auditing social equity can be handled using a combination of consensus and community empowerment measures. The empowerment theme means that the process of reaching understanding and consensus about the content and purpose of indicators is as important as the indicators themselves. The evolving participatory techniques in the LA21 experience provide a basis for exploring such procedures. Ideally the following conditions should apply:

- there is real commitment to a more representative democracy;
- there is a willingness to experiment with a more pluralistic power structure;
- participatory mechanisms must try honestly to be inclusive of all relevant and legitimate interests, even those disempowered interests who do not readily reveal themselves;
- the tests for participatory success are trust, accountability, authenticity, and transparency; and
- to meet this level of effective involvement, all participants must be prepared to accommodate each others' interpretations of the sustainability transition, and accept the resulting manifestation of consensually shared indicators.

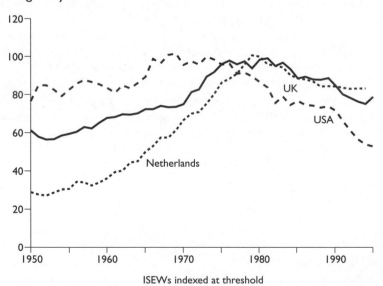

Can't get any better?

ISEWs indexed at threshold

Source: Friends of the Earth and NEF, 1997, pp6–7.

Figure 2.1 Indices of sustainable economic welfare (ISEWs)

The main points to emerge from any innovative approach to indicators are:

- indicators are deeply politicised since they are set in the context of power, variable social rights and biased interpretations of experience; and
- the indicators that are not presented may be the most important since these would otherwise have come from disempowered groups and interests who are not in a position to alleviate them; identification of these indicators is crucial for any process .

We shall see that the theme of indicators spills over into green accounting and LA21. For example, there is now a huge industry of creating custom-made indicators at the local level, work based on that summarised by the Local Government Management Board (LGMB) (1995), and promoted more controversially by the New Economics Foundation (NEF) (1997). In the LGMB's case, the main conclusion is the ubiquitousness and inventiveness of indicators for community involvement. In the NEF instance, the aim was to produce an index of sustainable economic welfare (ISEW) (see Figure 2.1). This depleted the typical gross domestic product (GDP) by incorporating estimates of resource degradation, spending to offset social and environmental costs, deterioration in the distribution of income estimates of long-term environmental damage, and estimates of the value added by household labour. This pioneering and somewhat opinionated work has been criticised by economists who tend to approach matters from the vantage point of neoclassical theory. More to the point, one index or indicator of such a hugely meta-variable as sustainable economic welfare is bound to cause trouble. The whole point of the previous discussion is that it is highly distorting to try to combine discourse into a single variable. For one thing, the analysis takes little account of efforts to reconstruct natural asset gains and losses in satellite accounts. For another, the ISEW combines data when there are no meaningful estimates. So the analysis becomes more a basis for political leverage and increased exposure for the NEF than a basis for reasoned debate. The NEF naturally disputes this. But this is why we pointed out how institutions frame mandates and determine insiders and outsiders.

Green Accounting

There is a lot of interest in green accounting methodologies in the World Bank, the UN and the OECD (try the web site at the CSD: <http//:www.un.org/dpcsd/dsd>). Today, GDP is formally recognised as having no bearing on social or ecological wellbeing (Vaze and Balchin, 1996, p43). The Office of National Statistics (ONS) in the UK has begun a series of pilot environmental accounts that include physical measures of emissions and monetary measures of resource depletion, environmental pollution, environmental degradation and emission abatement costs (*ibid*, p45). This scheme is an important step forward in the institutional redesign of national accounts and will be placed on the internet by early 1998. The ONS specifically requests assistance and commentary in a creative dialogue. This is also an important institutional innovation, especially as it is widely regarded that the accounts will mix qualitative and quantitative variables, and will introduce a measure of equity considerations. For that to happen, however, the statistician will have to go beyond multidimensional modelling.

In Norway, NGOs have allied themselves with the local authorities and the environment ministry to establish a network of commentators who promote more sustainable consumption. Still, it is not clear precisely what that means, but at least it involves a relatively high-profile Norwegian institutional innovation. The Norwegians have also a 'green book' of green accounts, mostly environmental protection expeditions, and a green tax commission to examine the scope for ecotaxation. Neither the Portuguese nor the Greeks have developed green accounts. In both countries the environment ministries have responsibility for public works and infrastructure investment. As a result, these are neither politically nor administratively conducive conditions for developing green accounting. The European Commission remains silent on the issue, but who knows what is going on in the bowels of DG III.

Ecotaxation

Ecotaxation is a generic term to cover both the Pigouvian (or correctional) adjustments to market prices necessary to take externalities to the producer, and the policy measure of directing the tax system to change human behaviour and to release revenue for more sustainability-driven investments. This latter element is sometimes referred to as ecological tax reform and O'Riordan (1997a) provides a full analysis of this process.

We shall see in the chapters that follow that though the idea of ecological tax reform originated in a European Commission (1993) white paper, so far the commission has not taken it much further, at least not as a policy measure. However, the OECD (1997) has recently reviewed the state of both environmental charges and taxes and has concluded that more of this should be tried, so that environmental protection measures and fiscal policy are mutually reinforcing (*ibid*, 1997, p7).

This is a fine example of an arena in which the sustainability transition and various other approaches to policy and institutional change provide synergy. The OECD report looks to fiscal instruments as a substitute for costly regulation and distorted price signals. Treasuries look for new sources of revenue that are politically acceptable in a tax conscious age. Social ministries believe equity considerations can be overcome and that, with directional spending, equity can be improved as a result. Furthermore, the Norwegian Tax Commission (1997, p93) believes that the introduction of green taxes will influence the pattern of overconsumption in Northern countries, a theme in the sustainability transition to which the Norwegians are particularly attached.

This combined momentum is important. But we are also aware of the huge institutional barriers to ecotaxation. The US President's Council on Sustainable Development (1996, pp47–52) proposed a national tax commission, but none has materialised. The UK's new Labour Government (Labour Party, 1997, p12) argued in opposition for a change in the balance of taxation towards rewarding labour and punishing environmental degradation, but no fundamental policies are yet in place, though promises to investigate are widespread. The real politics of ecotaxation test the transition to this most important institutional change to its limits. We shall see in the case studies that the huge institutional biases in the form of policy coalitions around current tax arrangements make it all but impossible for a tax-reforming government in a highly competitive global market. More to the point, the organisational practicalities of ecotaxation are seriously problematic – defining what to tax, how to predict future revenue, how to collect it and what to spend it on – if the sustainability transition is to be pursued.

Business and Sustainable Development

Europe-wide, business is beginning to adopt the mode of ecoefficiency. For a broad review, see Easterbrook (1996); for a more industry-focused perspective of this management issue, see Fussler and James (1996), Welford (1996), and von Weizsacker *et al* (1997). We have already covered the theme where business should concentrate on housekeeping measures that help to make a company more profitable yet less environmentally harmful. Therefore, not much more will be added here. This drive is especially noticeable amongst the larger corporations whose chief executives are influenced by public image, cost saving measures, the need for a competitive edge, and the growth of regulations on environmental auditing and product stewardship. This is an area that is more voluntaristic than regulated, but only to a point. The growth of more open government, the surveillance of company accounts, the increasing move towards voluntary regulatory compacts under the ecoauditing schemes, and the acquisition of more environmentally and socially concerned younger recruits have helped to promote this trend. But beware, there is no such thing as a truly sustainable corporation, only those who make money and profits by being less unsustainable. Here is where the discourse is especially muddled.

In Norway, Germany and the UK, the business community has mobilised sufficiently to be a new institutional force in the progress to sustainable development. It is cautiously supportive of moves towards greater environmental accountability and encouraging of shifts towards a greater duty of care. But, paradoxically, it also forms significant political impediments to innovations such as green taxation and green accounting. So, like everything else in this report, institutional innovation is very much at an early stage, with a contradictory influence between structure and procedure. One can hardly expect anything different in a highly ambiguous policy arena.

The Local Focus

LA21 is the local government-located version of A21, featured in Chapter 28 (Brugman, 1997, p101). By the end of 1997, over 2000 local authorities in the world were able to provide an account of how they had moved, or were preparing to move, towards sustainable development in the form of their own LA21. The success of this initiative lies in its ability to capture the imagination, to promote action amongst community groups that would not otherwise have been stimulated or involved, and to give local action and ingenuity a place on the international stage. LA21 should be about involving and empowering to establish the structures which will perpetuate locally responsive action and which will create a shared vision of the future. The research team found that by far the most vibrant institutional innovations were taking place at this level, most noticeably in the UK, and to a lesser extent in Germany and Norway. In Greece and Portugal the constitutional arrangements for local autonomy in local government are not suitably developed for LA21 initiatives. It thus may be some time yet before LA21 takes off everywhere.

Although there is evidence of vision and community participation, and there is great potential for linking environmental, social and economic agendas, most local government environment-orientated policies still follow more traditional environmental protection lines. Such activities include: waste reduction, energy efficiency, preventing unnecessary private car usage and promoting composting and nature reserves. LA21 moves beyond these activities to new ways of planning, discussing, delivering, and evaluating progress on environmental, social, economic and political objectives.

The highlights of this initiative so far are:

- the emergence of full ecoaudits in about a third of local authorities in the UK, less in Germany and Norway;
- a serious attempt to enable partnerships to form between local government and the business and voluntary sectors;
- the employment of coordinators or strategists to act as facilitators within local authorities, and between them and the wider community, towards establishing action programmes;
- a revaluation of the relationship between central and local government, with a strong political move towards greater local autonomy, and for cross-sectoral policy initiatives; this is connected to demands from some sectors of society, including some important segments of local government, for a greater push for political decentralisation; and
- the beginning of a serious effort at local governance in the form of environmental forums, involving people and interests in a common vision of local areas, and the mobilisation of local groups and people to work towards achieving these visions. This aspect contains the potential for real change in behaviour, attitudes and goals.

LA21 could be the grassroots catalyst for serious institutional innovation in the areas of discourse and action suggested in Table 2.1 It is by far the most appropriate forum for informal community initiatives in job trading, credit unions, civic protest, and educational reform. It is also the basis for both empowerment and revelation through such devices as visioning and coordinated round tables. The key is the internal mobilisation of collective self-respect amongst local authorities and their stakeholder alliances in the context of more political autonomy, a greater sense of democratic proximity, and a voice in the noisy clamour of the globalisation–locolisation accommodation process. This is bound to be a highly active area for institutional innovation in the next stages of the sustainability transition.

The European Union and Sustainable Development

This research has already shown the fundamental ambiguity and legal muddle between integration and sustainable localisation. At present, legal norms promote the interests of a competitive single market at the expense of any right to the self-determination of sustainable local futures. This means that unless there is a wider civic awareness, there will always be a legal fudge, and the local cultural aspects of sustainability may forever be secondary in European Community law. Yet, paradoxically, community law is also adopting a *de minimus* approach to local and national diversity via its subsidiarity principles.

This dilemma is surmountable. To begin with, both legal and political rules applying to unanimous and majority voting suggest that protectionist positions on national and local autonomy will have political and legal support. Furthermore, moral principles underlying the activities of the European Court of Justice allow individuals to claim the benefits of community rules before national courts. This would include the promotion of more local autonomy if it could be shown to be in the interest of balanced and sustainable economic activities, and to lie in accordance with clearly defined national priorities. Any action here will depend on the evolving liberalisation of community legal principles in favour of greater individual and environmental rights, coupled with the freedom and ability to use a variety of courts for arbitration.

The record of spending in both community cohesion and structural funds, and in investments in the new federal states of former East Germany, shows that the economic development paradigm is still dominant (see Chapter 7). In these cases there is no formal procedure for guaranteeing stewardship, let alone public participation in project planning. Cohesion funds have been almost exclusively directed towards transport and water supply or water treatment works: large capital investments with huge environmental side effects. There may be an institutional basis in the form of integration, but there appears to be no political will.

PERSPECTIVE

Sustainable development is a deliberately ambiguous concept that can mean conservatism and liberalism in proportion to the general drift of social and political change. This is its staying power. Its organising focus coalesces around more ecological and human sensitive accounting, the application of a precautionary duty of care, and the scope for civic activism at local level. This provides it with a distinctive role in the evolution of human and natural wellbeing.

Institutional innovation is a permanent feature of the human condition. What is relevant here is the relationship between general trends of institutional change, promoted by a host of factors: laws, treaties, communication, value change, and civic activism. Such change is, by definition, continuous and unpredictable. The most important propulsive effect is the drive towards political liberalisation, openness of information, more effective accountability, and the constructive pluralistic activism of civil society. We regard these as institutional panacea for any transition to sustainability. We also regard these trends as an indicator of an advanced modern state, sufficiently self-confident in its governance as to tolerate and accommodate criticism. Admittedly, this is still rare, but the trends are persistent and without them there would be no transition towards sustainability. The more specific change promoted by A21 is rather more variable, with some very distinct moves in the form of policy integration, indicators and targets, green accounting, business initiatives and local empowerment. The contradictions between open markets and the social democratic principles which favour the protection of individual and natural rights have become more sharply defined. This is the area in which the next phase of sustainable development will evolve. For that to be effective, the mood of the body politic will have to shift to favour greater local autonomy and greater collective responsibilities to protect the rights of the vulnerable and of future generations. The law will follow attitude shift, but it need not be far behind. The key lies in juxtaposing the basic principles of growth with the application of stewardship, and the cry for greater local control over uncertain but manageable futures. It is possible that this somewhat more ideal juxtaposition will take off in the next decade. If so, it will be due to the institutional innovation spurred on by sustainable development, which we record in the chapters that follow.

Part II

The European Union and Sustainable Development

EDITORIAL INTRODUCTION

The European Community was created for the purpose of economic expansion and to encourage peace in the region through greater political cooperation and the liberty of its people as a reaction to the horrors and hardships preceding the First and Second World Wars. Specifically, it developed after the failure of an attempt at political union by federalists. Therefore, the European Coal and Steel Community and the European Economic Community, now the EU, were adopted as a more modest and technocratic alternative to political union. The underlying idea was that this sort of cooperation would inevitably draw in other connected areas of policy such as environmental and social measures. The original Treaty of Rome was signed in 1957, at the beginning of the postwar boom, when entrepreneurial innovation was taking off. The operational and constitutional ethos of the community was growth, and the member states did not mind pumping money into agriculture, roads, ports and airports, and latterly into telecommunications to make the point. Sustainable development simply was not a concept that had any meaning in 1957. Indeed, there was no formal legal basis for environmental protection until 1973, and even then it had to come in through the back door.

What we are witnessing is an example of institutional concentration and evolution. Over the past 30 years, the EU has increasingly become a legal entity with a powerful collective political force and separate constitutional identity, as the founding fathers Monnet and Schuman intended. It is the product of 30 years of political co-operation and judicial activism characterised by sporadic periods of political realignment (treaty amendments) and redefinition (by the case law of the Court of Justice, and application of the single market provisions). For example, Haigh and Lanigan (1996, p19) quote Derek Osborn, the former director-general of the UK's then Department of the Environment:

> *In a relatively brief period of time the nature of the community has evolved and expanded, so that its many strands are now worn into most areas of public policy. This is certainly true of environmental policy, where in the last 20 years the European Community has rapidly become a major factor, or even the dominant one.*

However, it is the implementation of these policies which has provided a key insight into the political reality of the EU. Haigh and Lanigan note that political attention to implementation really only began seriously in 1983, following an incident where a container of hazardous dioxin-rich waste was found in northern France, having been shipped from the site of the notorious chemical plant accident in Seveso, northern Italy. This shipment highlighted the possible dangers of a common economic market without giving adequate attention to the safety of cross-border trade. Couple this with the resulting interest in regulation in connection with an expanded market (as we discussed in the previous chapter) and one sees the emergence of an institutional conflict in the sustainability transition.

That conflict is the freedom of trade in goods, capital and workers' service provision, set against the guarantee of environmental protection standards desired by electorates, which can be very stringent and hence a possible threat to free trade. Free movement requires common standards since different standards prejudice free movement. Therefore the basis for a trade-motivated environmental policy is common. However, a purely environmentally motivated policy may require different standards which conflict with the free trade motivation. This tension, which is inherent in trade and environment relations, is noticeable enough when it comes to environmental protection, but is much more problematic when sustainable development comes into the frame. The various treaties remain deliberately vague about the status and definition of sustainable development, and how it is to be integrated into the existing legal and political framework. So the notion of sustainability as an organising force for institutional reform in the EU remains very clouded.

In Chapter 3, Nigel Haigh points out that the language of the Treaty affords a lot of room for cultural and national redefinition of the phrase sustainable development. One has to accept, at least for the time being, that the politicians and legal drafters did not want anything too specific but recognised the need to absorb A21 into European action in some way or another. Law is an essential influence in its own terms, providing the ultimate justification for action and inaction at community level. Its political interpretation is of key importance, but the final interpretation lies with the European Court of Justice (ECJ). In Chapter 4 Martin Hession refers to principles governing the court's interpretation of its core text: the Treaty. He refers to the historical legal dynamism of the ECJ in its promotion of the European Project, and links this to judicial interpretation, essential to allow the political contribution to adapt to changing circumstances. The conditions for judicial activism are also examined and the likelihood of a judicial role in defining sustainable development is assessed. While the mood of the times is very much the currency of legal judgement, the ECJ is always mindful of precedent, political realities, and the wish to be circumspect when innovative challenges are placed before it.

Nowhere is this more evident than in the ECJ's response to subsidiarity and sustainable development. Both the court and the commission are aware that the past decade has seen a shift towards including, within the primary objectives of economic growth and competitiveness, a more diffuse set of parameters, including regional development, local cultural diversity, and more geographically explicit indicators of economic and social change. Nevertheless, the economic globalisers have effected strides in trade liberalisation, while the adoption of European Monetary Union by bankers has absorbed a huge amount of political time and attention; even the big geopolitical issue of reforming the EU's institutions for expansion to the east has begun in the recent intergovernmental conferences preceeding the Treaty of Amsterdam.

The social dimension has been expressed most vigorously vis à vis the employment chapter and surrounding debates over a citizens' Europe, and articles 2 and 3 have quietly been redefined. Nigel Haigh describes the evolution of these amendments, while Hession places them in the context of the treaties' philosophy as defined by the courts. Subsequently, Hession and Macrory look at the legal consequences of the integration duty in a purely legal context, while David Wilkinson and Claire Coffey examine the political impact of this agenda within the commission and European policy respectively.

For our purposes, therefore, the incorporation of the sustainability discourse into the European Union sidesteps the *acquis communitaire* of legal norms and constitutional niceties. It is expressly excluded from areas of competence; it has lead to no repeal of legislation; it has been used indifferently as an excuse for some restyling of existing and future legislation; and it has no legal force at all – as far as can be told. Turning to Table 2.1, the sustainability transition has to pass into the equity and revelatory realms if it is to succeed. The EU has made progress in the market and regulatory discourses – but only a step, not a stride. For this additional transition to occur, the EU will need to evolve further a set of ecological and human rights principles enshrined at the local level more than at the national level. The tools for this exist – embodied, for instance, in establishing the direct effect of environmental requirements or more radically the integration requirement – but this approach is fraught with conceptual and practical difficulties: who exercises these rights, against whom, in respect of what? It is important to understand that establishing local rights at an EU level means the content and exercise of these rights is made dependant on a very centralised institution, namely the ECJ since, ultimately, rights are enforced by their guarantor. This is the inherent contradiction of all rights-based approaches. In guaranteeing rights you have to delimit them and structure legal relations according to a fixed pattern, in a sense denying the right to be different from this centralised pattern. This global–local relationship still has to be played out. This is why Hession talks of an ecological civic order for the community: a distant dream right now, but a vision worth contemplating.

One of the crucial indicators of the sustainability transition is policy integration. In Chapter 6 David Wilkinson spots various organisational changes that still have to reveal themselves in the bureaucracy of the commission. As we noted in Chapter 1, sustainable development has to activate a personal gaian echo if it is to work. Arguably, that echo still has to be heard in Brussels. Hession's 'new ecological order' will only come about when the hearts and minds of European citizens and officials move it along. One role for the courts is consciously to assist this process. The early cases following the so-called 'environmental obligation', tucked into Article 130r and analysed by Richard Macrory and Martin Hession in Chapter 5, may give us a clue. The legal apparatus is broadly in place via the various action plans on the environment and the wording around sustainability. What is missing is the institutional apparatus to make this transformation possible. What is present is the glimmer of a legal order that could reshape the political order. The sustainability *chapteau* will not go away.

Right now there is little to go on. David Wilkinson is sombre in his assessment of the institutions that promote integration. Certainly empowerment and revelation are not on everyone's lips. But the community is slowly evolving into a more civil state. The social and regional distresses of economic integration are showing up in the various forms of civil protest and redoubled efforts to retain local self-determination. The push towards greater economic competitiveness clashes with cultural values, a concern that should grow in electoral significance the larger, geographically and culturally, the community becomes. Yet the liberalisation of trade is propelled by an urge to free up individual choice and unleash the creative capabilities of a modernising Europe. Hession and Macrory (1996) worry about the tendency for legal separateness in trade and environmental policy. This merely reflects and reinforces the political reality. Here the law demonstrates a political problem that trade and environmental agendas are separate and perhaps even inconsistent. The courts are, as usual, left with the dilemma of resolving the inconsistent aspirations that politicians place in the law at the behest of their citizens. Maybe that sought-for fusion will only come about when social rights and environmental rights are incorporated within the stewardship mode and beyond that into greater social justice and democracy. We believe that this could be the future of the community, and that A21 can be used as an organising medium to nudge the process along. But civil society will have to be unusually active and interventionist across a swathe of political and economic cultures. In the short run, that is a tall order indeed.

One other way forward is a greater interdependence of the European Commission and the European Parliament vis à vis the Council of Ministers. Again, there is a constitutional evolution in the making with the parliament enjoying greater scrutinising powers over policy and financing than ever before. In Chapter 7, Clare Coffey explores this relationship by suggesting that the parliament is anxious to intervene in cohesion and structural fund project financing; this palpably strikes against the protection of critical natural resources such as coastlines, wetlands and urban environmental health. As we noted in Chapter 1, the push towards strategic environmental assessment (SEA), compared to the more laborious, inflexible and manipulative environmental impact assessment technique, could be another example of how the sustainability transition is nudged forward by sympathetic and resonant institutional innovations. To date, SEA is neither a well-grounded evaluative tool, nor appropriately embedded in the political firmament in order to be as influential as it might become in the reallocation of structural funds.

The following chapters in this section show that the European Community is poised to embrace the sustainability transition, but not quite yet and not as its fundamental rationale. The legal evolution of constitutional reform, allied to a strengthening social justice agenda and an emerging civil society, will assist this process. Maybe, too, the steady acceptance of politicians and officials with a sustainability conscience will help push the commission towards creative policy integration, more stewardship-orientated indicators of development, and ecological tax reform. The institutions of the European Union are poised for this transition and the chapters that follow should help the reader to assess the factors that will promote or impede that trend.

Chapter 3

Introducing the Concept of Sustainable Development into the Treaties of the European Union

Nigel Haigh

The Treaty of Rome that established the European Economic Community, as it was called in 1958, made no mention of the environment nor did it suggest that there were any limits to the 'continuous and balanced expansion' that was to result from establishing a common market and approximating national economic policies. This was to be the task of the community as set out in Article 2 of the treaty.

While the treaty was truly original in creating an entirely new kind of 'community' in which sovereign states ceded legislative powers in certain fields in order to achieve objectives that were beyond the reach of them individually, it remained a creature of its time in its call for 'continuous expansion' without any recognition that in a finite world environmental considerations must impose some limits. Not until some 30 years later was the treaty amended to provide a legal base for environmental policy. Even then, the amendment made by the Single European Act in 1987 left untouched the language of the 1950s in which the task of the community was defined. By coincidence, the amendment to the treaty was made in the same year that the Brundtland Commission gave currency to the concept of sustainable development, which recognised that the needs of future generations must not be compromised by the type of development pursued today. The Brundtland concept was quickly endorsed by many governments. When, therefore, some three years later, an intergovernmental conference began negotiations on what eventually became the Maastricht Treaty, the conference was receptive to the idea of amending the call for continuous growth in article 2. Unfortunately, for a reason that we explain below, the wording adopted in the amended article 2 was not ideal: as a result, the intergovernmental conference that began reconsidering the Treaty in 1996 decided to look at the subject again. The resulting draft Treaty of Amsterdam – which had yet to be ratified at the time of writing – finally introduced the word 'sustainable development' but alongside 'sustainable growth'.

This chapter traces the introduction of the concept of sustainability in the

European Community and its treaties, a process that can conveniently be divided into the following four periods:

- 1957–1972: the dark ages;
- 1972–1987: environmental policy is established;
- 1987–1991: after the Single European Act; and
- 1991–1997: from Maastricht to Amsterdam.

THE DARK AGES (1957–1972)

During the first 15 years of the community's existence there was nothing that could be called an environmental policy. The task of the community, set out in article 2, was as follows:

> *The community shall have as its task, by establishing a common market and progressively approximating the economic policies of member states, to promote throughout the community a harmonious development of economic activities, a continuous and balanced expansion, an increase in stability, an accelerated raising of the standard of living and closer relations between the states belonging to it.*

While a few items of legislation which we would now call environmental were adopted during those 15 years, they were always secondary to some other purpose. In 1967 a directive was adopted on classifying dangerous substances and their appropriate packaging and labeling, but the driving force was the desire not to allow barriers to trade by differing national rules set to protect workers and the environment. The same applies to the first directives adopted in 1970, setting standards for emissions and noise from vehicles. While individual member states may have seen the need for some environmental protection measures, the role of the community was then only to prevent the undermining of the common market.

One subject which the community did recognise from the beginning as requiring environmental standards was ionising radiation. The Euratom Treaty, signed in Rome in 1957 at the same time as the better known Treaty of Rome, was intended:

> *to contribute to the raising of the standard of living in the member states ... by creating the conditions necessary for the speedy establishment and growth of nuclear industries.* [Article 1]

The next article then went on to say that in order to do this the community should 'establish uniform safety standards to protect the health of workers and of the general public and ensure that they are applied'. The first Euratom standards relating to ionising radiation were accordingly laid down as early as 1959, but here again they were ancillary to the main purpose of advancing the nuclear industry, then optimistically seen, in the aftermath of Hiroshima, as turning swords into ploughshares.

Towards the end of this period (1957–1972), the community was placed in a dilemma by the worldwide recognition that environmental protection was not just a minor or local matter – the very future of human life on the planet was at stake. It was seen not just as an adjunct to other policies but as a subject that deserved attention in its own right and one requiring that other policies be reshaped. Several member states at that time established ministries for the environment (both France and Britain did so in 1970) and the subject was firmly placed on the agenda by the great UN Conference on the Human Environment held in Stockholm in 1972. The community had either to decide that it should not involve itself in this newly found subject, since it was not provided for in the treaties, or that it would have to respond in some way.

ENVIRONMENTAL POLICY IS ESTABLISHED (1972–1987)

The community had originally been founded with six member states (France, Germany, Italy, Belgium, the Netherlands and Luxembourg). The first enlargement took place in 1973 with the accession of the UK, Ireland and Denmark (Norway had applied but rejected membership in a referendum). During the discussions leading to enlargement, the community replied to the criticism that it was too concentrated on a common market – that it was a 'businessman's club' – by deciding to expand its activities in three fields: consumer protection, regional policy and environmental policy. This was described at the time as giving the community a 'more human face'.

At a summit meeting in Paris in 1972, the heads of state and government, including those from the applicant countries, declared that the community would embark on an environmental policy:

> ... *economic expansion is not an end in itself: its first aim should be to enable disparities in living conditions to be reduced...It should result in an improvement in the quality of life as well as in standards of living. As befits the genius of Europe, particular attention will be given to intangible values and to protecting the environment so that progress may really be put at the service of mankind.*

This declaration neatly side-stepped the issue of whether it was necessary to amend article 2 before the community could embark on a new policy. The declaration effectively accepted that the existing treaty was flexible enough to allow for environmental policy without having to be modified. The declaration can, according to taste, be regarded as either a denial of the impossibility of continuous expansion in a finite world or a redefinition of the quality of that expansion. There was an implication that if 'progress' in the past had been pursued for its own sake and not for the service of mankind, this could now be changed.

The declaration called on the commission to draft an Action Programme on the Environment, and the programme was published in 1973. When approving the Action Programme, the commission also indulged in sleight of hand. It declared that the task of the community set out in article 2 'cannot now be imagined in the absence of an effective campaign to combat pollution and nuisances or of an improvement in the quality of life and the protection of the environment' (OJC, 1973). The use of the word 'now' is revealing: although the treaty had not changed, society's views apparently had. The action programme resulted in an explosion in the number of items of European Community environmental legislation over the next 15 years, and while many were rather narrow and technical, some are of major importance by any standard and have come to influence all of the member states.

From time to time during this period attempts were made to suppress environmental policy as distracting the community's main purpose. The hostility that environmental policy encountered may be difficult to understand today; there was great resistance at that time to treaty amendment. But environmental policy survived and managed gradually to consolidate itself. Nevertheless, doubts continued to be raised about its legality (see House of Lords, 1977–78). All items were then based either on article 100 or article 235. Article 100 provides for an approximation of laws among member states so that trade is not distorted, and article 235 empowers the community to take measures to deal with any unforeseen circumstances which would otherwise impede the objectives of the community – but as we have noted, environmental protection is not mentioned in the treaty. Various pronouncements of the European Court of Justice gave some reassurance, such as the statement in 1983 that 'protection of the environment is one of the essential objectives of the community which may justify certain limitations on the principle of the free movement of goods' – despite the lack of any authority in the treaty for such an assertion.[1] Whatever the reassurances, pressure for a clear legal base for environmental legislation continued to come from lawyers; from policy institutes and parliaments (von Moltke, 1977; House of Lords, 1979–80); and also from the German Länder who were concerned with the uncertainty over the loss of their powers whenever community legislation was negotiated by their federal government.

Simultaneously, pressure for amendment of article 2 to redirect the priorities of the community came from environmental pressure groups. For example, the European Environmental Bureau (EEB) (1977) in its manifesto for the first direct elections to the European Parliament in 1979 advanced the concept of sustainability and called for Europe to invent 'a new industrialism, a mature pattern of growth, that will enable its own great population to live more fully, yet press more lightly on the planet'. The manifesto ended with a call for amendment of article 2.

It is probable that the first calls to remove 'continuous expansion' from article 2 were made in Britain, possibly because accession to the community had led many to read the treaty closely. The Civic Trust (1974) in a pamphlet entitled *Growth Limits and the Treaty of Rome* proposed amendment of article 2, and the Conservation Society proposed a form of words for a new article 2 in 1975 (quoted below).[2] These bodies were both members of the European Environmental Bureau, which at its first meeting in December 1974 decided that its primary aim was 'to work for a sustainable life style in the European Community'. This was then written into its constitution, providing an early example of the use of the Brundtland concept in a developed world context. Previously the phrase sustainable development had only been applied to developing countries.

Three key ideas about inserting the environment into the treaty had developed by the end of the 1970s: the need for a clear legal base for environmental legislation; the need to replace 'continuous expansion' in article 2 with wording that showed respect for environmental quality and the needs of future generations (sustainability); and an obligation that all European Community policies should take account of the environment (integration). These three ideas were rehearsed in 1979 in evidence before a House of Lords Committee (1979–80), and had already been elaborated upon, in 1977, in an article by Konrad von Moltke, founding director of the Institute for European Environmental Policy. Indeed, the competence of the community in the field of the environment was one of the first themes the institute tackled when it was formed in 1976.

Calls for a structuring of the community in different ways also came from other quarters. In 1984 the European Parliament adopted its draft Act of European Union (CEC, 1984), inspired by the Spinelli report (European Parliament, 1983) which foresaw the community developing along the lines of a federal state, with the European Commission being elevated to the status of parliamentary government, and the council and parliament being coequal partners in a bicameral legislature. Encouraged by proposals from environmental bodies, the parliament's draft act included a title on environmental policy.

Meanwhile, certain governments were pressing for faster progress in one of the community's original tasks, a process that came to be known as 'completion of the internal market'. This resulted in the commission publishing a White Paper on the subject in early 1985. In the ensuing discussion it became evident that in order to take several difficult decisions necessary to complete the internal market, the power of individual member states to veto decisions would have to be reduced. Amendment of the treaty was therefore necessary and this provided the opportunity for the parliament's draft act to be taken forward at an intergovernmental conference. This eventually produced the treaty known as the Single European Act which inter alia amended the Treaty of Rome. The agitation of environmental bodies and others was transmitted via the European Parliament and resulted in a new treaty title on the environment; we turn to this now.

AFTER THE SINGLE EUROPEAN ACT (1987–1991)

The Single European Act marked the coming of age of European Community environmental policy by more than just confirming its legitimacy. The stated objectives of environmental policy were broad and allowed for subjects that could well have been excluded even under the elastic interpretation of the treaty that had previously prevailed. One example is the directive on freedom of access to information on the environment (for an analysis of all community environmental directives, see Haigh, 1992).

The new title also set out certain principles of community environmental policy which, although already in the action programmes, gave them greater authority. It then added the important new principle that 'environmental protection requirements shall be a component of the community's other policies'. This requirement for integration is arguably the most important feature of the new title; for the first time it gave authority to those concerned with environmental matters to question other bodies, such as departments of agriculture and transport, who were developing the community's other policies. No longer was community environmental policy just a matter of legislation covering water and air pollution and nature protection, which might well cause pain in the member states but did not much touch other directorate-generals of the commission: now it had the capacity to influence the policies of other directorates-general. Increasingly, this became a matter of dispute and so raised environmental protection to a higher political level. The new integration requirement is essential in shifting the community in the direction of sustainable development, as is described in Chapter 6.

The Single European Act made another important innovation relating to environmental policy. It introduced 'qualified majority voting' for the adoption of legislation relating to the internal market, together with the associated 'cooperation procedure' with the European Parliament. Although most environmental legislation required unanimity in the council, items relating to traded products, for example, could now be agreed upon by qualified majority voting. The best known example is the emission standard for cars that effectively made catalytic converters compulsory. Several member states were opposed to the standard which would never have been agreed upon unanimously. Despite these significant changes, which embodied two of the three ideas developed in the 1970s, article 2 was left intact with its original 1950s wording so that pressure for amendment to that article continued.

One of the difficulties was that during the late 1970s and early 1980s no phraseology with some chance of winning broad political support had been put forward as an alternative to 'continuous expansion'. The EEB suggested none in its manifesto for the 1979 elections which called for amendment of article 2, one of its members, the Conservation Society, had proposed the following words: 'the highest quality of living conditions for all the people within the community that are consonant with the paramount need, having regard to the interests of succeeding generations, to conserve the natural resources and the environment'. This formulation, which approximates quite closely to the Brundtland definition of sustainable development (quoted below), had the disadvantage that it was rather long winded.

By coincidence it was in the same year that the Single European Act came into force (1987) that the Brundtland Commission published its report giving currency to the phrase 'sustainable development' and providing the well-known definition: 'development that meets the needs of the present without compromising the ability of future generations to meet their own needs.' Rather surprisingly, the Brundtland report was quickly endorsed by a number of governments so that, when in 1990 another intergovernmental conference

began to negotiate what was to become the Treaty of Maastricht, the conference was receptive to the idea of replacing 'continuous expansion' with
'sustainable development'. Unfortunately, there were two parallel intergovernmental conferences, one on monetary union and one on political union. While
the conference on political union apparently found no difficulty with 'sustainable development', the conference on monetary union wanted: 'sustained
non-inflationary growth'. The draftsman who had to reconcile the work of the
two conferences produced the following English language formulation that
appears in the ratified version of the Maastricht Treaty. While the intention to
introduce the Brundtland concept certainly underlies the wording, it is arguable
that the combination with another, quite different, intention has resulted in
wording that is either meaningless or at best ambiguous:

> *The community shall have as its task, by establishing a common market and an*
> *economic and monetary union and by implementing the common policies or activi-*
> *ties referred to in articles 3 and 3a, to promote throughout the community a*
> *harmonious and balanced development of economic activities, sustainable and non-*
> *inflationary growth respecting the environment, a high degree of convergence of*
> *economic performance, a high level of employment and of social protection, the*
> *raising of the standard of living and quality of life, and economic and social*
> *cohesion and solidarity among member states.*

The Maastricht Treaty also made three other changes that are significant to
environmental policy and sustainability (Wilkson, 1992). It stated that community policy should be based on the precautionary principle, it strengthened the
integration requirement, and it made qualified majority voting the standard
procedure for environmental legislation subject to only a few exceptions.

By the time the commission proposed the Fifth Action Programme on the
Environment in 1992 it felt able to call it *Towards Sustainability* (OJC, 1993). To a
large extent it aimed to ensure that environmental considerations, including
those of the long term, were integrated within a number of other community
policies.

FROM MAASTRICHT TO AMSTERDAM (1991–1997)

The intergovernmental conferences that drafted the Maastricht Treaty recognised that some matters had been left unresolved and called for a new
intergovernmental conference (IGC) to meet in 1996 to deal with unfinished
business. Since one of the tasks of the new IGC was to fit the community for
the challenges of the 21st century, it is no surprise to find that environmental
bodies again argued that the wording of article 2 should be improved.[3]

The task of finding an appropriate phraseology that is agreed upon by 15
countries would be difficult enough if the community conducted its business in
only one official language, but there are 12 official languages. And there is not
a widely accepted equivalent of the English words 'sustainable development' in

all of these languages. This is shown by Table 3.1, which sets out the use of the word 'sustainable' in all official languages of the community in the following three separate treaties:

- the treaty establishing the European Community – the Treaty of Rome – (as amended by the Treaty of Maastricht but before the Amsterdam amendments);
- the treaty on European Union (the Treaty of Maastricht); and
- The Agreement on the European Economic Area which came into force in 1994 and governs relations between the European Community and certain European countries that are not part of the European Community.

In some languages the same word is used in all four columns of the table, while in others different words are used. An extreme case is provided by the German text in which a different word is used for the English 'sustainable' in all four columns. In particular, in the important article 2 the word *beständig* is used. This can be translated as continual, continuous, permanent, lasting, and stable. The word has not elsewhere been used as a translation of 'sustainable' in the sense defined by the Brundtland Commission, and as used in article 2 the context suggests the traditional economic sense of continuous growth. Thus in German the Maastricht version of article 2 is little different in this respect from the 1950s original.

Table 3.1 was published during the IGC to stimulate debate in different countries about the need for appropriate language (Haigh, 1996; Haigh and Kraemer, 1996).

The ideas put forward in early 1995 by environmental bodies for improving the treaty included clarifying the wording on sustainable development and revising appropriate articles on specific policies, such as transport and agriculture, to take environmental considerations fully into account.[3] These ideas caught the attention of ministers, or reinforced ideas that were already there because, one year later, just before the beginning of the IGC, a number of member states announced that they were seeking environmental changes. The European Commission and the European Parliament said the same. The countries concerned were mostly the smaller ones: Sweden, Denmark, Finland, Austria, The Netherlands, Belgium and Luxembourg. Some said they wanted the concept of sustainable development stated as an objective of the treaty and also wished to reinforce the requirement to integrate the environment within other policies. Sweden in particular stated that its government 'intends to propose that an environmental goal for the Common Agricultural Policy is introduced into article 39 of the Treaty of Rome'.

When in March 1996 the European Council agreed the agenda for the IGC, the environment was one of the items listed, and the Italian presidency's conclusions expressed it in these terms:

A healthy and sustainable environment is also of great concern to our citizens. Ensuring a better environment is a fundamental challenge for the Union. The

Table 3.1 The language of sustainable development in the treaties and agreements of the European Community

	Rome Treaty article 2	Rome Treaty article 130u (Objective of Development Cooperation)	Maastricht Treaty article B	Agreement on the European Economic Area Preamble (1993)
English	'sustainable and non-inflationary growth respecting the environment'	'the sustainable economic and social development of the developing countries'	'economic and social progress which is balanced and sustainable'	'the principle of sustainable development'
French	'une croissance durable et non inflationniste respectant l'environnement'	'le développement économique et social durable des pays en développement'	'un progrès économique et social équilibré et durable'	'principe du développement durable'
German	'beständiges, nicht-inflationäres und umwelt-verträgliches Wachstum'	'nachhaltige, wirtschaftliche und soziale Entwicklung der Entwicklungsländer'	'ausgewogenen und dauerhaften wirtschaftlichen und sozialen Fortschritt'	'der Grundsatz der umweltverträglichen Entwicklung'
Dutch	'een duurzame en niet-inflatoire groei met inachtneming van het milieu'	'de duurzame economische en sociale ontwikkeling van de ontwikkelingslanden'	'een evenwichtige en duurzame economische en sociale vooruitgang'	'het beginsel van duurzame ontwikkeling'
Italian	'una crescita sostenibile non inflazionistica e che rispetti l'ambiente'	'lo sviluppo economico sociale sostenibile dei paesi in via di sviluppo'	'un progresso economico e sociale equilibrato e sostenibile'	'principio che lo sviluppo dev'essere sostenibile'
Portuguese	'um crescimento sustentável e não inflacionista que respeite o ambiente'	'o desenvolvimento económico e social sustentável dos países em vias de desenvolvimento'	'um progresso económico e social equilibrado e sustentável'	'princípio de um desenvolvimento sustentável'
Danish	'en bæredygtig og ikke-inflationær vækst, som respekterer miljøet'	'en bæredygtig økonomisk og social udvikling i udviklingslandene og særlig i de mest ugunstig stillede blandt disse'	'at fremme afbalancerede og varige økonomiske og sociale fremskridt'	'princippe om bæredygtig udvikling'

Spanish	'un crecimiento sostenible y no inflacionista que respete el medio ambiente'	'el desarrollo economico y social duradero de los paises en desarrollo y particularmente, de los mas desfavorecidos'	'un progreso economico y social equilibrado y sostenible'	'del principio del desarrollo sostenible'
Greek*	'synexi ke isorropi epektasi tis economias'	'ti statheri ke diarki economiki ke kinoniki anaptyks. ton anaptysomenon horon'	'isorropi ke statheri economiki ke kinoniki proodo'	'tin arxi tis viosimis anaptyksis'
Swedish	'hällbar och ickeinflatorisk tillväxt som tar hänsyn till miljön'	'varaktig ekonomisk och social utveckling i utvecklingsländerra'	'främja välavvägda och varaktig ekonomiska och sociala framsteg'	'principen om en varaktig utveckling'
Finnish	'ympäristöä arvossa pitävää kestävää kasvua, joka ei edistä rahan arvon alenemista'	'kehitysmaiden kestävää taloudellista ja sos.aalista kehirys.ä'	'edistää tasapainoista ja kestävää taloudellista ja sosiaalista edistystä luomalla alueen'	'erityisasti noudattaen kestävän kehityksen sekä ennalta varautuvien'
Irish	'les fás inbhuanaithe neamhbhoilscitheach a urramaíonn an comhshaol'	'le forbairt inbhuanaithe eacnarraich agus sóisialta na dtíortha I mbéal forbatha'	'is iad seo a leanas cuspóiri an Aontas: dul chun chinn eacnamaíoch agus sóisialta atá cothromuil inbhuanaithe a chur ar aghaidh'	'ar bhonn phrionsabal na forbartha inbhuanaithe'

Non-Member State (applied for membership – but membership rejected in a referendum)

Norwegian	'en bærekraftig ikke-inflasjonsdrivende vekst som tar hensyn til miljøet'	'en bærekraftig økonomisk og sosial utvikling i utviklingslandene'	'a fremme likevektig og varig økonomisk og sosial framing'	'Principe om en bærekraftig utvikling'

* The text provided in the table is a transliteration of the Greek script

IGC will have to consider how to make environmental protection more effective and coherent at the level of the Union, with a view to a sustainable development.

Nine months later in December 1996 the Irish presidency issued a general outline for a draft version of the treaties based on the work already undertaken by the IGC. This amended article 2 to introduce 'sustainable development' and a new article 3d (now 3c), which strengthened the integration requirement 'with a view to promoting sustainable development'. The Irish text of article 2 was virtually unchanged in Amsterdam in June 1997 so that the third idea developed in the 1970s finally entered the treaty – subject to successful ratification.

The new article 2 reads:

The community shall have as its task, by establishing a common market and an economic and monetary union and by implementing the common policies or activities referred to in articles 3 and 3a, to promote throughout the community a harmonious, balanced and sustainable development of economic activities, sustainable and non-inflationary growth, a high degree of convergence of economic performance, a high level of employment and of social protection, a high level of protection and improvement of the quality of the environment, and the raising of the standard of living and quality of life, and economic and social cohesion and solidarity among member states.

This wording, unlike in the Maastricht version, separates 'balanced and sustainable development of economic activities' from 'sustainable and non-inflationary growth' and also adds 'a high level of protection and improvement of the quality of the environment'. It is not immediately clear that 'sustainable development' is to take precedence over 'sustainable growth', nor what is meant by sustainable growth. However, if the Brundtland definition of 'sustainable development' is followed, then sustainable growth cannot mean an ever increasing consumption of limited resources since it would not then meet 'the needs of the present without compromising the ability of future generations to meet their own needs'. The definition would have been clearer if the needs of future generations had been introduced explicitly. Nor is 'sustainable development' linked to environmental protection, though the link is made by the new article 3c which reads:

Environmental protection requirements must be integrated into the definition and implementation of community policies and activities referred to in article 3, in particular with a view to promoting sustainable development.

This brief new article 3c does four other things. It makes clear that 'integration' is intended to result in sustainable development. It applies to all policies and activities in article 3, which is more precise than the existing wording which just says 'other community policies'. Sustainable development, having been connected to environmental protection, is made to run through all policies. It strengthens the integration requirement politically, and probably legally, by lifting it out of article 130r and placing it more prominently. The result is that were it ever to be tested, the Court of Justice would be likely to say that the changed position was intended to have an effect, and would accord the environment greater importance. It is not impossible to imagine a member state who is dissatisfied with an item of legislation for being insufficiently environmental, and challenging it for not fulfilling the requirements of article 2 or 3c. The Treaty of Amsterdam did not amend articles dealing with specific subjects such as agriculture and transport, but if and when they come to be amended at another IGC, they too can be brought up to date by introducing appropriate environmental objectives.

Has the struggle over many years to introduce appropriate environmental language been worth the effort? There are those who argue that changing words is just playing with words and that action is what matters. They overlook the fact that the wrong words make the right action more difficult and the right words make it easier. The treaty is important as a symbol but it is also a legal text. Certainly the new treaty provides a better frame for the EU as it moves into the 21st century. Without a strongly expressed environmental objective which recognises the needs of future generations, the EU is unlikely to hold the support of the European public. Ultimately, however, continuing support depends on the right action.

Chapter 4

THE LEGAL DYNAMICS OF EUROPEAN INTEGRATION AND SUSTAINABLE DEVELOPMENT

Martin Hession

Any examination of institutional change in Europe demands examination of law and legal processes of the European Community.[1] The Treaty of Rome and its interpretation by the Court of Justice has effected considerable institutional change in the member states of the European Community, albeit in limited policy fields. This may appear counter-intuitive to some. Legal systems are ordinarily thought of as conservative or stabilising institutions, a structural impediment to social change rather than a facilitator of transformation. Nevertheless, even a preliminary acquaintance with the history of the US Constitution, for example, suggests that the role of law cannot be confined to that of stabilising social or political expectations. While these remain fundamental objectives of law, the impact of a codifying or constitutional law, where it is superimposed on diverse subsidiary legal systems, is often radical change (Ely, 1980).

Though the Treaty of Rome is not a fully formed federal constitution, the increasing constitutionalisation of community law under the stewardship of the Court of Justice has been the subject of some comment (Temple Lang, 1991).[2] Viewed in these terms, compared with other constitutional documents that reflect the aspirations of often revolutionary political and social reformers, the European Treaty can appear a less ambitious document, even mundane. Despite the ambitious political intentions of its sponsors (Monnet, 1962), simple textual analysis of the treaty system reveals provisions of a purely technocratic nature, obscuring the fundamental processes the European treaties have set in train. Legal analysis and understanding is important; its impact can only be fully understood in a broader context.

This chapter seeks to understand better what is meant by the term 'integration'. Describing law as a process of integration enables direct comparison to be made with other political and economic processes. Similarly, sustainable development, when viewed as a process, can be expressed as the integration of new environmental perspectives into political, economic and social processes. In the same way European integration can be described as a process of legal, economic and political transformation affected in the member states. It is the outcome of interaction between political, legal and economic processes at a range of scales (Liberatore, 1997). Broader notions of sustainable development imply a reorientation of these processes at all scales. Though there is an extensive literature on the political, economic and legal processes that drive European integration, this has not been linked to the literature on sustainable development. O'Riordan and Voisey's description of patterns of discourse around sustainable development in Chapter 1 is the starting point here. Using their typography it is possible to relate the European integration process, at least in part, to these patterns.

WHAT IS INTEGRATION?

Integration is defined here as the resolution of inconsistent objectives, positions or patterns of activity (described as systems). Integration can occur in a variety of ways, described in terms of fields, modes and models. It should be noted that descriptions of integration are coloured by the agency/structure debate, potentially occurring as part of a deliberate plan or as a result of inevitable processes. The following is suggested as a useful typography of integration.

Horizontal and Vertical Fields of Integration

- **Horizontal integration** occurs between systems organised on functional lines (eg between directorates within the European Commission).
- **Vertical integration** occurs between systems organised in terms of scale (eg between national and European environmental policies).

Hierarchical, Competitive and Discursive Modes of Integration

- **Hierarchical integration** suggests integration is determined by rules that order the process (eg top–down integration). Current regulatory (political and legal) models of sustainability have some expression here.
- **Competitive integration** suggests integration occurs through the competitive behaviour of individual agents. If individual behaviour is predictable in accordance with economic rules, it is also in this sense hierarchical. The market interpretation of sustainability can be seen here.
- **Discursive integration** suggests integration as the product of consensus derived from discussion.

Legal, Political and Economic Models of Integration

- **Legal integration** is the legal process whereby the legal rules and concepts of several systems are merged to form one legal system. Legal integration occurs through a process of interpretation and the formation of a single hierarchy of rules and principles. It may be horizontal (between trade and environment law) or vertical (between federal and local legal systems). Law relates to politics in that it polices the exercise of political power.

- **Political integration** is the process whereby a whole range of political institutions integrate their decision-making processes. The process may be hierarchical or consensus orientated and can occur between functional and geographical units. The term 'political integration' may be used expansively to encompass other models. In a democracy the political sphere seeks to represent and implement public opinion through law and other instruments.

- **Economic integration** may be described as the integration of economic activity and is particularly important in the European context, as this process creates and supports the conditions for integration across other policy fields. This process occurs in vertical and horizontal fields and is competitive, but is also arguably hierarchical in the sense that individuals are both presumed and encouraged to act according to economic rules. Economic integration can also be the product of usually hierarchically politically-motivated and legally-mandated market intervention which prevents or modifies the operation of free competition.

The interplay of these models of integration is of particular importance. All share a particular emphasis on the individual as actor, demonstrable in terms of the rights granted to individuals in the model; key elements of a liberal, capitalist democracy.

- **Legal rights** determine both individual interests protected from state control, and the extent of individual participation (political rights) in the formulation of state policy (common interests). Legal and political rights are generally individual in nature. They are granted to groups only insofar as they fulfill recognised and limited political functions.

- **Political rights** determine the mode of individual participation in collective action and are also held by individuals. In the model of liberal democracies common to all member states and adopted at the European level, political rights are necessarily limited. Democracy is representative rather than participative and therefore excludes more radical republican, communitarian or discursive democratic models.

- **Economic rights** determine an individual's economic opportunity and may act as a guarantee on individual autonomy and as the chief means whereby the individual's freedom of choice is maintained. The concentration on individuals as actors competing in a system within uniform rules means the economic model of integration is at least partially supportive of a particular legal and political model based on the individual. In the European context the economic model of integration is reflected and reinforced in the other fields of integration, not least the legal.

Environmental integration, approximating if not synonymous with sustainable development, must be considered. Again it may occur both vertically and horizontally, and this may be expressed hierarchically competitively or discur-

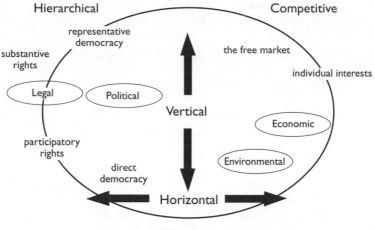

Figure 4.1 Modes, Fields and Integration

sively, corresponding to legal, market and revelatory interpretations of sustainable development. In practice it occurs according to well-established political, legal and economic models which determine the extent to which the environment is represented and the mode in which it is integrated. Other social and political aspirations (elements of equity) may also be subject to these disciplines. Insofar as varieties of environmentalism require representation of certain interests there is some question as to which model is most effective at doing so. Representation of non-human and intergenerational interests implied by equitable interpretations of sustainable development are most difficult to incorporate in all the models.

The economic and legal nature of the integration process is one that emphasises the autonomy of the individual in direct relation to a uniform set of economic and legal rules determining her rights. A strong combination of economic competition and legalism suggests that the process is market or regulatory in style and that European integration is primarily hierarchical and competitive in character. As a result, equitable and revelatory interpretations of sustainable development are limited or effectively excluded.

Having connected interpretations of sustainable development to descriptions of integration, it is necessary to connect these to the extensive literature on the European integration process. The object is to assess the possible effect of the adoption of sustainable development as a treaty objective in a broad context, and to relate existing legal analysis to the other modes of analysis available.

Winacott (1995) has identified three different perspectives to the process of European integration adopted by legal and political analysts:

1) **Legal analysts** who 'typically concentrate on the internal dynamics of the jurisprudence of the Court'.

2) **Neo-functionalist political scientists** 'who direct their attention towards the development of a pattern of interest groups around a supranational Commission'.

3) **Realist and intergovernmentalist political scientists** who 'downgrade Community distinctiveness completely, comprehending it as almost unmodified international relations models'.

Alternatively, Weiler et al (1995) have identified three characters of integration, each individually favoured by different analysts, but which he suggests operate simultaneously to explain elements of the overall process.

1) **The intergovernmental** corresponds to the traditional model of inter-state relations. This view is basically external to legal analysis, concentrating on the council as an international forum, and conforming most to the realist and intergovernmentalist frameworks described above.

2) **The supranational** applies the metaphor of the nation state, or the federal state, to European political and legal processes. This view is that of legal practitioners and policy analysts who concentrate on the formal legal and political institutions of the community. This explanation conforms most to the neo-functionalist framework adopted here.

3) **The infra-national** is concerned with the formal and informal linkages between national bureaucracies and local and sectoral institutions, put in train by the day-to-day management of community policies. This viewpoint is characterised by a lack of transparency and limited legal consideration. It is the realm of technocratic politics and includes structures through which the commission is attempting to transform community–state relations via cooperative and stakeholder politics.

Combining these viewpoints and the triple character of the integration process, it is clear that legal and political analysis concentrates on supranational and, to a lesser extent, on intergovernmental models of integration. To date the infra-national sphere has had limited attention. The following section deals chiefly with supranational and neo-functional accounts of the integration process to explain the framework for market, regulatory, and equitable and discursive inter-pretations of sustainable development.

LEGITIMACY AND THE ECONOMIC MODEL OF EUROPEAN INTEGRATION

An historical perspective reveals that the Treaty of Rome and its associated treaties are creatures of their time. They reflect the (then) pragmatic basis for cooperation between the governments of six European states, which was intended ultimately to secure a profound, if at that time idealistic, aspiration towards greater unity amongst the peoples of Europe. Intergovernmental consensus was possible only through practical cooperation in economic matters.

Table 4.1 Interpretations of sustainability and the European Union

interpretations of sustainability	definition of sustainability	model of integration	mode of integration	environmental developmental representation	European integration	typical instruments of representation (state of play)	sphere of integration
markets	needs defined by individual and limited by resource scarcity	economic	competitive	externalities	single market rules	taxes, charges (weak, requires unanimous vote)	economic actors and supranational
regulatory	needs defined and limited by individual legal rights and collective justifiable state interests	legal	hierarchical	legal rights duties	new legal order	rights and duties (limited categories of liberal rights)	legal persons and supranational
		political	hierarchical	political rights (representative)	the democratic deficit	direct elections/legislative powers (limited by instance maintenance of national representation)	supranational v inter-governmental
equitable	needs defined by equitable redistribution	political	hierarchical	regional and social redistribution	regional and structural funds	backward regions and social groups (priorities defined in terms of economic integration)	supranational v infra-national
revelatory	needs defined by participation of citizens	political	discursive	direct politics	partnership and voluntarism	citizens groups/social partners (weak experimentation)	infra-national

Functionalist and neo-functionalist approaches to the process this set in train describe how cooperation on economic policy led inevitably to greater political integration, through a 'spill-over' effect. Three processes are interlinked.

1) **Political integration** occurs through the intermeshing of economic and other policies, and is reflected in subsequent legislation and treaty amendments by political agreement amongst the member states' governments.
2) **Legal integration** is derived from legislation but also the reaction of the judiciary to the slow pace of political change. Active interpretation and enforcement of economic rules combined with a liberal approach to community political power has supported political and legal integration. Adoption of the rights thesis has enabled legal integration to play a substantial role in driving economic integration through the application of treaty rules in a range of sectors.
3) **Economic integration** is derived from the operation of economic actors trading across community boundaries and creating economic conditions for political responses at national and community levels. Legal and political rights have allowed at least some undertakings to remove national legal barriers to this trade, either by action to invalidate national rules, or encouragement of European legislation.

A general starting point is that the economic model of integration, through its promise of economic prosperity, was and remains the model most capable of commanding political consensus at international level. This is most apparent amongst governing elites but extends also to interpretation of opinion poll evidence (Slater, 1982; Eurobarometer, 1998). The power of an economic model to command political consensus is a prominent feature of nearly all intergovernmentalist and supranational explanations of European integration. Indeed, in political terms economic integration is the ultimate, or at least preeminent, basis for legitimacy in European politics. The marked failure to establish transparent and representative politics is rendered tolerable either through intergovernmental explanations of the community's role, or pending the political success of the integration process.

In legal terms exclusive reliance on this basis for legitimacy is problematic, particularly as the court has authorised broad intervention by the community in national policy and rendered invalid cherished national policies in pursuit of market goals at the suit of individuals (Barents, 1990). Intergovernmental accounts of the community have become less and less attractive as the legal systems of the member states and the community have become integrated in a new legal order. National conceptions of individual rights have been recognised as applicable to community action where this has led to dispute with national constitutional courts, and the rights thesis has provided general cover for the court's extension of economic and other rules by direct effect[3] (De Witte, 1991; de Búrca, 1995).

The legal and policy spheres share a common approach in that the treaty defines community activity in functional sectors. Collusion of principle and

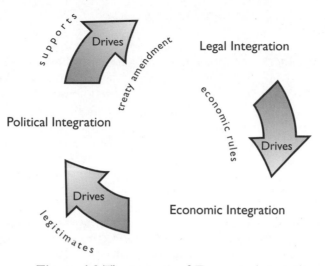

Figure 4.2 The process of European integration

integration of these sectors is inevitable no matter how carefully they are defined. The inescapable interconnection of economic, social and environmental policies can be demonstrated in both legal and political experience. In general, the economic model has proved stronger than either environmental or social policies in dictating the integration agenda. In political terms, the European community has been granted legislative responsibility in respect of elements of economic policy, namely the single market which has been extended to those areas which increasingly indirectly affect its operation. The logic of both horizontal and vertical integration demands the integration of ever more national policy sectors with developing European policy. Arguably, a lack of greater political integration between policy sectors at a community level renders different national policy spheres ever less integrated because vertical integration has taken a priority.

In legal terms, the Treaty of Rome and its guardian, the Court of Justice, guarantees economic policy through the application of economic rules. The legal application of these rules can no more be confined by sectoral definition than can political activity. As a result, vertical integration occurs where European rules render invalid a range of state practices which demand either a political response at European level or judicial supervision of the national activity involved.

There are of course a variety of attitudes as to whether continuing application of the market as the model for political integration can be successful. As the market touches ever more areas of national policy it tests the ability of states to find political consensus at a European level to replace those policies it has overridden, and makes ever more transparent the political nature of the exercise. Full political integration has not yet been achieved according to any model.

Ironically the centrality of the market model may itself operate as much as an impediment as a spur to true political integration. This is particularly the case where the political integration it demands is less than successful. Expressed in political terms the practical basis of the European model is clear: '(i)f Europe lacked a flag capable of touching men and women of different national and ethnic groups, it took economic progress to be its substitute faith' (Hoffman, 1994). The results of the spillover effect may be disputed in political terms, at least in terms of a desire to create a true European identity. Hoffman (1964 and 1994) in particular has suggested that his statement that 'Europe today has no clear identity other than that which the process of industrialization and economic integration has given it', is as true in the nineties as it was in the sixties. This is a matter of concern as despite the relative success of this integrating identity there are signs that 'within Europe itself, even in the more prosperous segments, there is new preoccupation with whether what was once thought to be inevitable progress is in fact likely to continue' (Graubard, 1994).

In radical terms sustainable development is one reflection of dissatisfaction with current models of progress (WCED, 1987; Schnaiberg, 1997). Arguably, doubts about the current models has led the community to expand its objectives into other spheres. Whether these in themselves present as powerful an alternative to the economic model may be doubted. In the search for alternative legitimation, environmental policy, given its popularity, has been often suggested as a candidate for the revitalisation of community politics. But the fundamental difficulty here, as elsewhere, is that whereas the market presents a simple and universal model for political integration, the environment does not. Arguably, it is not a coherent model upon which to order a supranational entity.

The market is a rational and universalising system, subject to a variety of interpretations, but the basics of which are generally accepted and understood. Both in legal and social terms it has been the most effective driving process of internationalisation within Europe and beyond (Barents, 1990; Giddens, 1990). The programme of environmentalism is comparatively less coherent, more contested even where its fundamental tenets have been generally excepted. At least according to some versions of environmentalism, environmental demands are positively inimicable to the process of integration, particularly those that contradict the economic model upon which Europe has been built to date, and those that demand an explicitly local perspective. On the other hand alternative internationalist but environmentally driven demands for global perspectives appear more promising. Nevertheless, global problems will at least sometimes demand global solutions and these themselves may not be satisfied by Europe alone. This dichotomy may be reflected in the different attitudes of environmental non-governmental organisations to Europe (Dahl, 1995). Nevertheless, the preference for locally-based diversity and revelatory styles of government need to be reconciled with the need for more integrated approaches to policy development regardless of the future of Europe per se.

A Narrow Legal Interpretation of Sustainable Development

Turning to the text of the Amsterdam Treaty itself, it finally makes explicit that the promotion of sustainable development forms part of the European Community's task.[4] While the framework has been altered and some adjustment might be expected, the legal and political impact of the amendment might be doubted for a range of reasons.

Firstly, the course taken at Amsterdam was a deliberate choice to pursue a general amendment at the beginning of the treaty rather than line item amendments of some of the more criticised policies later on in the text (Climate Network Europe et al, 1995). In theory a general amendment particularly tied to a specific integration requirement has as much impact as specific amendments later on, allowing for greater judicial discretion in determining its precise effects on subsequent policies at the expense of making these amendments explicit. Nevertheless the political and legal implementation of article 2 is dependent on the development of more precise principles in respect of defined community activities. These principles will only be influenced by the court if it adopts a deliberately activist policy in its interpretation of the treaty and its implementation.

Secondly, the form adopted is important. Sustainable development is one among many objectives promoted by the community and is not a meta-narrative designed to mould either the shape of Europe or of European integration. Similarly, article 2 makes it explicit that sustainable development shall be achieved by specific means, establishing a common market, an economic and monetary union and the implementation of various other policies which include an environmental policy. Taken together this suggests sustainable development becomes a legitimate but additional objective of the European project; one which existing processes and concepts survive, though to which they may be expected to adapt. This view is confirmed by article 6 which states that integration of environmental protection requirements into *existing policies* is an identified mechanism for promoting sustainable development. European sustainable development is part of the community's existing model rather than fully transformative of it.

Thus, the European Community's institutional response to sustainable development as represented in the treaty can be categorised as cautious. The fundamental structure of the treaty system, contained in the rules established and powers defined in later articles, remains intact. Sustainable development has been incorporated in statements of general principle rather than wholesale recasting of the treaty or by piecemeal amendment of some of the more criticised policies. On another level, a formal, if cautious, rededication of the community to sustainable development suggests a fundamental change to the shape of the treaty. Though this change can be understood only in terms of a process of legal interpretation of pre-existing provisions rather than as the explicit result of expressed amendment, it nevertheless deserves some specific examination.

LEGAL INTEGRATION

A Structural Account of the Legal System

Some general observations can be made, concerning the internal logic of the law, which may be termed the dynamics of legal integration. The law in particular demands integration. The first demand placed on judicial authority is insuring overall systemic integrity. This leads to a holistic interpretation of the law and reconciliation of the competing objectives it sanctions or demands. The process often involves courts in seeking to divine a single overall framework where in reality there is none or at least none has been formally laid down (Ely, 1980). The meaning and effect of all community provisions is determined with reference to the objectives they have been designed to achieve: *teleological interpretation*. Specifically, all community activities are defined in article 3 to be 'for the purposes set out in Article 2'. Insofar as sustainable development is a core objective there is at least the theoretical possibility that all existing rules and policies have been redefined with reference to it. More specific still is article 5 which defines the limits of community powers with relation to objectives and requires that the community does not go beyond what is necessary to attain the objectives of the treaty.

There are three approaches to ensuring this integrity. First, the overall political philosophy of the system may preclude recognition and implementation of some objectives as legal principles or rules. In a liberal democracy certain limits must be observed out of deference to political authority. Only those principles that can be expressed as individual rights or other categories of legal limitation on state power can be readily implemented. Provisions may be declared aspirational or political in character to be resolved in the political sphere by reason of their political character. As a result of the courts' role in the political process, collective, social and political principles are left to be resolved in the political sphere. The court confines itself to the enforcement of clear limits to defined state interests, through the exercise of community powers and the application of provisions capable of enforcement as an individual right. Most difficult in this regard is the scant regard given to the other rather broad objectives contained in article 2 in the course of policy definition or legal interpretation; objectives amongst which sustainable development is not the least ambiguous or contentious. Sustainable development may achieve similar status as the rest. It is not clearly intended to give rise to individual legal rights and its effect on the limits of community power is at best ambiguous. Nevertheless, the general character of the community has been referred to and acted on in some seminal cases, and amendment provides a resource for new directions in legal interpretation of the treaty text.[5]

Second, a hierarchy of principles may be established (Hession and Macrory, 1996) where two principles conflict, allowing for certain interests to prevail over others or to enable a balancing of interests according to well-established principles such as proportionality. Whether or where sustainable development fits into the established hierarchy is in doubt, as is the place of the integration requirement, even if some interpretations suggest at least some environmental principles are capable of modifying the operation of even such entrenched principles as non-discrimination or proportionality.[6] Again, the principle supports modification of the existing hierarchical and competitive system but does not remove existing barriers to equitable and revelatory accounts of sustainable development.

Third, and related to the first, access to the court may be controlled to limit application of principles in favour of individuals or groups to those directly affected by the failure to apply those principles. Whether sustainable development is capable of giving rise to pre-emptive rights and whether the court will be willing to entertain such cases must be in doubt. Standing has traditionally been granted to the community institutions and the member states and only in very limited circumstances to individuals or groups (Krämer, 1996). Only if the court adopts a policy of opening up procedural review, imposing transparency and accountability demands on hitherto-protected community policies, can more equitable or revelatory interpretations of existing policy be envisaged.

An Agency Account of the Role of the Court

Within these observations, it is clear that the European Court of Justice has confounded political expectations on several occasions leading to analysis of its 'activism'. The court's role and activism can be explained in terms of: its role to see that the law is observed; its dedication to meet the overall objectives of the Treaty; and, more particularly, its adoption of a particular philosophy as to the meaning of the text it has been called on to interpret. The supremacy of law over imperfect representative politics, a particular interpretation of economic integration and the rights thesis have combined to enable the court to force the pace of integration.

Cappelletti (1987, p5) proposes that there are three fundamental explanations for activism, reflecting the attachment to internal consistency of the law: legislative inertia, statutory or regulatory 'pollution', and 'the existence in particular of a hierarchy of norms with all the conflicts of law that ensue from such a hierarchy'. Though these incentives to activism are common to all constitutional systems and affect all constitutional courts (see Cappelletti, 1987; Ely, 1980; Rasmussen, 1986), all are demonstrable in terms of the interpretation of economic rules to establish the single market, as illustrated by the list below.

- **The council's inability to agree measures**, where unanimity was the order of the day (prior to the SEA in 1987), provides one (institutional) explanation of the court's shifting interpretation of the requirements of a single market (Armstrong, 1995). Here the legal mandate for economic and political integration is adopted as a motivation of legal integration. A failure by the community's institutions to implement sustainable development insofar as it can be reduced to clear principles would satisfy this incentive.

- **The indeterminacy of the market ideal**, constructed out of a mix of rules and principles, demands some definition and provides space for development by interpretation, and provides an alternative (legal) explanation of judicial action.[7] Here, and in the two following points, the need for legal certainty and systemic integrity motivates legal integration. Sustainable development provides ample space for judicial interpretation of its requirements.
- **The confusion of legal provisions** engendered by the collision of 15 legal systems with a uniquely powerful treaty regime, and the complexity of the regime itself, provide a (legal) explanation of the court's willingness to resort to general principles to resolve conflicts and gaps in the community's 'new legal order'.[8] The adoption of local and national policies under the sustainability rubric presents further fuel for European interpretation.
- **The introduction by treaty amendment of new policies** (including the environment) which are allegedly philosophically inconsistent with the previous legal order again provides a (legal/institutional) explanation of the court's current problems reconciling trade and environment. These conflicts provide rich material for the modification of community law.[9] Whether sustainable development introduces yet further normative confusion remains to be seen.
- **The Court's autonomous role as guarantor** 'that in the interpretation and application of this Treaty the law is observed' has justified its manipulation of the legal system to guarantee individual access to and enforcement of community law vis a vis member states at national level. Here the autonomy of law from legal and political processes is the motivation for legal integration. Drawing on the language of rights it has shifted the institutional context within which the legal system is developed. This concentration on individual rights is perhaps the greatest structural impediment to judicial activism in respect of sustainable development.[10]

In summary, these explanations show that the court's interpretation of its responsibility to see that the law is observed has demanded action in the absence of political will, interpretation of general principles and extended access to the law by individuals to achieve this. Whether the promotion of sustainable development will result in similar activism depends on the extent to which the entrenched market ideal can realistically be subverted, supplemented or modified with reference to the principle. Given the overarching dedication of the community's institutions to a hierarchical and competitive mode of European integration per se, promotion of sustainability is most likely in market interpretations. Synergistic promotion of market rules designed to ensure resource efficiency through the removal of subsidies to promote eco-efficiency is an obvious starting point.

The Economic Framework

> *We thought that both these objectives [political and economic] could in time be reached if conditions were created enabling these countries to increase their resources in a large and dynamic common market and if these countries could be made to consider that their problems were no longer solely of national concern, but were mutual European responsibilities* [Monnet, 1962].

Turning to the economic framework of integration, it is clear that economic theory drives political and legal processes. The concentration here is on legal processes, which, by invalidating national policies, have both driven political agreement at a community level, and deregulated member state economies according to broad market principles.

The idea of a single market has, by very deliberate political choice of the treaty architects, become the foundation of cooperation and the motor for the development of shared policies in respect of those areas which economic activities touch (Monnet, 1962). The basic structure of the current treaty is an economic order based on the market. In essence the treaty demands free competition between undertakings in a single European market in which national public policy interventions are limited, either to favour well-established European policy interventions, or in the hope that these restrictions will lead to agreement on an ever greater range of European policies. Full examination of all the treaty provisions cannot be attempted here; it is, however, possible to make some general observations.[11]

Firstly, there is a tendency towards a broad interpretation of the requirements of the market. A liberal interpretation of the rules prohibiting state or private intervention in the operation of the free market has led to political or judicial control of national policy responses. Insofar as the establishment of a market provides a starting point for political integration and legitimates interference in national policy, it at once embodies a political ideology and a concept whose 'outer limits' require constant redefinition (Chalmers, 1995). The 'market' therefore provides the condition for vertical and horizontal integration and judicial activism. But arguably, the nature of the market is as much the result of the court's approach to questions with regard to the implementation of the single market, and in particular that relating to goods, as to any pre-existing underlying philosophy. In as much as the influence of any particular philosophy surrounding the nature of the market can be detected it is derived from the answers to these questions.

Secondly, there is some confusion concerning the underlying philosophy of the market system. Chalmers (1995) cites the ordo-liberal tradition of the Freiburg school as the defining influence on the community's market philosophy and the touchstone of the initial model for economic constitution building. Accordingly, the community market philosophy is directed at political as much as economic ideals. The internal or single market embodies not merely free market philosophy but is based on the premise that an economic order is deliberately created and therefore reflects ethical and political views of society. Economic theory not only drives and legitimates integration in the political and legal spheres but also determines the mode of integration. According to this view, the political choice involved necessarily limits social choice by virtue of ideological and structural constraints implied by an economic constitution, namely the market economy. To this extent the market limits the operation of social choice (including presumably environmental choice) in the interest of individual (economic) freedom. The ultimate justification for economic freedom, the rationale for a market system, lies not in the proposition that a market economy leads to the optimal allocation of resources, but on the basis that economic freedoms form the basis of protection of human dignity and are as indicative of a free society as political freedoms (Petersmann, 1995).

Thirdly, there are two broad approaches to market structure: one which stresses the beneficial character of market freedom in itself, another which recognises the market only in terms of the benefits that market freedom delivers. In political terms these approaches reflect the ideological divide between those endorsing political and economic freedom as a good in itself, incorporating maximum individual choice, and those endorsing political and economic freedom for the social and political ends delivered. These philosophical distinctions also reflect the liberalist and dirigist traditions (Belassa, 1994), which underlie the more famous ideological conflict as to the purpose and direction of European integration (Margaret Thatcher and Jacques Delors' Bruges speeches, in Nelson and Stubb, 1994, pp 45–50 and 61–64).

In conclusion, social and environmental policies are evaluated broadly in terms of the legitimate incorporation of market externalities, though the market is a social construction adapted and adaptable to human ends rather than a naturally occurring and immutable fact of life; intervention in the market is possible only for defined purposes. Equitable redistribution and environmental intervention is theoretically confined to that which is justifiable in terms of market externalities.

LEGAL IMPLEMENTATION OF THE MARKET MODEL

Two examples are chosen to explain the court's implementation of the market model, an approach which displays a bias towards European integration. This bias subjects national environmental measures to market discipline whilst allowing member states and the community to subsidise environmentally damaging activities.

Cases that Illustrate Legal Difficulty Concerning Authorisation of National Market Intervention Based on the Precautionary Principle

While the framework reflects the ordo-liberal idea that intervention in the market order is subject to overriding protection of market freedom, the treaty allows intervention nevertheless (Climate Network Europe *et al*, 1995). But the legitimacy of any intervention is dependent on its extent, and the treaty, while recognising these justifications, requires that measures are proportionate to the interest involved (de Búrca, 1993). The effect of the proportionality principle in particular is of importance as it determines the relationship between autho-rised intervention in market rules and market freedom and the exercise of recognised member state power in particular.

Proportionality is particularly problematic as it demands justification of trade-restrictive or anti-competitive measures in terms that they are capable of attaining their legitimate objective, go no further than is necessary to do so, and ultimately that the benefit achieved by the intervention is proportionate to the restriction on trade (de Búrca, 1993). This tends to suggest that all intervention and the interests that justify intervention can be evaluated in terms of a common standard of trade restrictiveness or some equivalent weighting with regards to market freedom. The adoption of precautionary measures is partic-ularly vulnerable to such weighting in the absence of internationally agreed scientific evidence (Sedemund, 1988). In some cases intervention is justified only with respect to an 'objective' standard of protection,[12] in other cases proportionality is applied to the means adopted to achieve levels of protection which are freely determined by the member states.[13]

Proportionality applies much more loosely to community measures. Member states are subject to burden of justification which may vary (de Búrca, 1993), but the community is required only not to lapse into manifest error. As a result, there is a preference for uniform community incorporation of environ-mental externalities over differential incorporation at a national level. Judicial intervention to ensure transparency and participation in the elaboration of policy in powerful technical, scientific and economic committees might be one way to ensure a more discursive approach to precaution.

Cases Illustrating a More General Reluctance to Intervene in Community Policies where Treaty Objectives Authorise Action which may Exacerbate Environmental Damage

Here in particular the court expresses a general reluctance or inability to balance broad environmental, social and regional policy objectives. If community action is less stringently controlled and therefore enables broader discretion in the plugging of market externalities, certain community policies operate in a manner which actively promotes environmental degradation – so-called 'non-market failure'. Nowhere is this more evident than in the allocation of the community budget, for example, to the common agricultural policy (CAP) (Conrad, 1993); the common fisheries policy (Coffey, 1996); or the structural funds (Scott, 1997a). The possible inconsistency of social, economic and environmental policies is clearly demonstrated here.

Experience suggests that there is a serious question as to whether the community can be policed in respect of the environmental degradation its own intervention causes. A relatively liberal attitude to subsidies by the member states, adopted where serious social and political problems might be expected to result from their removal, provides member states with the freedom to promote unsustainable development (see, for example, the subsidisation of the German coal industry by its government). Challenges to national state aid as well as to community funding allocations remains difficult if not impossible. Rigid application of market discipline would support environmental objectives, in terms of promoting resource efficiency ('the prudent and rational exploitation of natural resources') but would be inimicable to the social protection of the social and economic priorities CAP and regional policy represent.

In practice, whatever the economic theory adopted, the law demonstrates some inconsistency in the application of the ordo-liberal model application. The departure from strict application of the principle of limited intervention on the basis of market externalities has several causes. Certainly a general preference for community intervention over member state intervention is one. Similarly political and legal sensitivity to certain national policy priorities means that justification for national intervention in the market is assessed on varying criteria. The introduction of non-market policies (including the environment) through treaty amendment has allowed for alternative justifications for the community's and member states' action. These new justifications have an uneasy relationship with the strict ordo-liberal interpretation of justified market intervention, and have too often escaped adequate political and legal control in the area of deleterious subsidies, while simultaneously restricting national environmental initiatives in the interests of competition.

INCORPORATING SUSTAINABLE DEVELOPMENT INTO THE LIBERAL LEGAL AND POLITICAL MODEL

The pre-eminent difficulty posed by sustainable development for law, politics and economics derives from problems the liberal, human-centred model has with the representation of concerns extraneous to the human system (Sagoff, 1995; Ladeur, 1996). In broad political, even ethical, terms the inability to incorporate these concerns into decision making derives from several elements inherent to the liberal, contractual political model.

Who and What is Represented or Legally Protected?

The 'who' is a particular conception of the participant – the rational and current actor – which prevents the legal, economic and political direct representation of non-human actors, and those who do not currently exist (Midgely, 1995). The 'what' rests on a need for certainty in deliberation or legal rules. Defining environmental protection requirements questions the need for knowledge before action (or lack of it). In particular, determining the economic, political or legal justification of environmentally motivated action is dependent on clarity. This attitude is partially expressed in terms of difficulties in the simultaneous application of the proportionality and the precautionary principle in European law (Sedemund, 1988).

Environmental integration in this context presents fundamental difficulties. Market interpretations demand the expression of environment in terms of the internalisation of external environmental costs, calculated and justified in market terms. Regulatory interpretations require sustainable development to be expressed as enforceable legal or political rights and duties. Equitable interpretations imply some modification of the market model, which remains subject to overarching environmental as well as developmental goals, including the protection of interests of future generations and the intrinsic value of the non-human environment. Revelatory interpretations demand discursive integration which depends on individuals' appreciation and ability to express the interests of non-participants, assuming that these interests are amenable to individual choice or representation – in other words, that these sustainability rights may be defined, delimited, and exercised and operated in a manner which satisfies or defines the overall collective interest, including those of 'naturally extrane ous' interests. The vision of individuals challenging others, both claiming to exercise or represent the rights of portions of environmental concern, demonstrates the difficulty (Sagoff, 1995). Still, only participatory or representative rights seem capable of combining individual concern and responsibility with collective concern and responsibility for nature.

Liberal Market Designations of Sustainability

In a liberal market system sustainability may be expressed as a public or private interest effected as legal or economic rights, but there are problems in doing so. At least in a representative democracy, attribution of sustainability interests to the public sphere (namely the state) leads to problems of accountability in the absence of clear guidelines. Whether establishing true environmental costs or appropriate regulatory standards to meet these interests, one requires a clear and agreed basis upon which to determine the relative value of the environment with respect to a whole range of already internalised or legally protected values and needs. Judicial reluctance to enforce substantive environmental rights derives from the legal interpretation that such a basis does not exist in law (du Bois, 1996).

Instead, deference to economic or scientific expertise in the public sphere tends to disguise the complex ethical or political nature of decisions demanded of supposedly representative institutions. Where complex precautionary and value-laden choices are exercised by the state on behalf of the individual in the absence of social consensus on the values that these choices are designed to protect, trust in representative institutions or expertise declines. This is the same whether a market or regulatory method is adopted.

The alternative is the attribution of sustainability interests to the private sphere of the individual through market or regulatory approaches. Substantive rights, whether the creation of new forms of property or the definition of legal rights to a particular standard of protection, suffer from the same complaint as that made in respect of regulatory and market definition and implementation of the public interest. This approach merely transfers current problems with hierarchical integration of the scientific and ethical complexity and uncertainty involved in the public sphere to an alternative mode of integration in the private sphere. Such integration is competitive, where some form of property is created, as it occurs as the result of individual behaviour and understanding affected through the market.

In this context, recent moves towards negotiated or voluntary agreements with industry in the environmental sector might be viewed as attempts to subvert the rigid distinction between public and private approaches and between regulatory and market instruments. Though indicative of a more discursive approach to regulation, the adoption of a voluntary model has marked hierarchical features, and raises concerns as to the accountability and transparency of the participation it encourages. Within the existing model of economic competition, even truly voluntary measures may also be criticised as reducing competition and being in breach of legal rules designed to maintain it (see articles 85 and 86).

LIBERAL RIGHTS, LEGITIMACY AND EUROPE

Legal Rights and Accountability

Turning to the process of European legal integration in particular, incorporation of sustainable development within the legal process is doubly problematic. Within the legal process the discourse of economic integration is both supported and, at times, placed in conflict with the discourse of human rights. The former occurs where individual economic rights are established and enforced through the conception of the market citizen, the latter particularly where the effects of economic integration have impinged on those human rights which member states have traditionally treated as inviolable. The direct effect of economic rules and the applicability of human rights principles to community action are well established. As a result it is fair to say that while the court has been keen to extend market rights to individual citizens in order to promote economic integration, other civil rights have been recognised only indirectly.

In terms of its legitimating function, according to de Búrca (1995), the development of a language of rights in the European Court may be explained as a direct result of the spillover effect of the neo-functional approach to integration. The court's activism in pursuit of the single market requires legitimation affected in the language of universal human rights and thence access to a moral content and context for community action in areas of expansion surrounding its functional competencies, depriving the member states of traditional competencies.

On the other hand, member states are reluctant to sanction a general standard of protection to liberal democratic rights as this may subvert their status as sovereign states to an extent not already experienced. So, community protection of human rights per se remains limited; another example of the fundamentally economic nature of the Union. Human rights apply to community action and action undertaken by the member states under community law by reason of the need to guarantee protection of rights the supremacy of EC law would otherwise cause to be overridden.[14] Any general protection of human rights would enable the invalidation of national law for non-compatibility on similar conditions to those currently enabling individual enforcement of economic rights granted by the treaty. This would imply a massive transfer of power to the community and is something the member states are unwilling to countenance at present. Even were this to be the case, there is considerable difficulty with placing environmental rights in the liberal agenda. This reluctance emanates not only from the political problems associated with direct challenge to national measures before the court, nor just from a possible overloading of the court's limited time, but also from the politico-legal conception of environmental rights. These problems do not apply exclusively to the community (Ladeur, 1996)

Judicial Review in the Community

Continuing denial of direct access to the court by anyone other than direct participants in the legislative process or individuals with 'direct and individual concern' protects community decisions from the scrutiny of outsiders. Cappelletti (1987, p7) rather optimistically emphasises the democratic credentials of legal activism in that the judicial process is itself participatory in nature 'its commencement and contents being determined by those individuals, agencies or groups which are most directly involved [and] hence best informed on the interests at stake'. Even if this is the case for those treaty rules judged to have direct effect, it occurs mainly in respect of national legislation and in respect of economic and certain social rules. How such an interpretation applies to the representation of environmental interests must be doubted given the exclusion of environmental interest groups from direct access to the court (Dahl, 1995).

The recognition of an individual right to enforce European environmental law before national courts against member states is also subject to these difficulties. The direct effect of environmental provisions (dependent on clear, precise, unconditional provisions capable of giving rise to individual rights) is still in doubt. As yet no environmental legislation has been found to have such effects though there is a backlog of cases on the point awaiting a court decision (Krämer, 1991). As Krämer (1996) points out there are many arguments against such an *actio popularis* despite the apparent disparity in the enforcement of economic and environmental law in community law. Even were direct effect clearly extended to environmental directives, national standing rules liberalised, and judicial review of community decisions liberalised, it is questionable whether such exercises in judicial democracy are truly participatory, still less that they conform to discursive or revelatory models of sustainable development.

Political Rights and Legitimacy

In the political sphere, reform of the community's institutions to allow for greater representative democracy has not yet been achieved for similar reasons. Intergovernmentalism and supra-nationalism remain alternative explanations of Europe in the absence of a fully defined political settlement. According to the former, the member states are willing to pool sovereignty provided it is protected to some degree by the legislative role of the council and the voting mechanisms adopted there. Supra-nationalism remains suspect in the absence of general political control of community legislation effected by an elected community institution, the European Parliament. The introduction of new legislative procedures is one context within which intergovernmentalism and supra-nationalism are defined and played out. It has to be asked whether any attempt to adopt a more discursive democracy founders in the face of the community's apparent inability to establish even traditional representative models of democracy.

REVELATORY INTERPRETATION AND PARTICIPATORY CITIZENSHIP: INFRA-NATIONAL DEVELOPMENTS

Truly revelatory politics demand some reconsideration of traditional representational democracy. Supra-national and neo-functional accounts of the European Community have delivered neither option at present. Supra-nationalism is an attempt to forge a European state on liberal democratic lines; neo-functionalism has provided little more than a limited market citizenship at present, despite the adoption of European citizenship at Maastricht (Closa, 1992). Before turning to infra-national accounts of integration, two general approaches to citizenship may be sketched out, one more consistent with revelatory accounts of sustainable development, the other describing a citizenship the European community has yet to attain (Wiener and Della Sala, 1997).

The 'modern' creation of the citizen–state relationship places the collective interest firmly in the hands of the state as a defined state interest. In general terms, citizenship has defined the individual's relationship with the state in two ways. One posits an expansive role for individual participation in political decision making of the state as a natural expression of collective good; the other preserves an area of self sufficiency and autonomy against the state constructed as a necessary evil. These two definitions co-exist in many legal systems in the form of individual rights of participation and substantive fundamental rights. In political terms they reflect two fundamental notions of citizenship: liberal, and civic republican/communitarian (Cohen and Rogers, 1995; Etzioni, 1996; Streeck, 1995). The first defines the individual against the state and gives law the role of mediating between these positions; the latter promotes the active participation of the citizen in the state and places law in the position of facilitating this process. Ironically, reaction to attempts to bring institutions closer to citizens and re-establish political communication between groups and players in the process can be viewed both as progressive or regressive. According to these views, it is either empowerment through the transformation of social relations (between industry and government or locality and central government) or alternatively the return to corporatism or feudalism, subverting individual freedom in the liberal transparent pluralist state to secretive exclusivist or myopic stakeholders.

The broadly liberal model has been pre-eminent in modern mass democracies of the last two centuries. Ironically, this rational and universalist model has been dependent on constructed nationalisms to maintain relative stability (Smith, 1997). The continuing transformation of traditional socio-economic and cultural structures based on the enlightenment model of individual autonomy acts to undermine the national model through economic and other processes of 'globalization', and drives attempts to transform individual collective relations according to another model.

If such a process is to occur within the European Community, signs of its development, and of more revelatory interpretations of sustainable development, rest in the infra-national sphere. Whether a progressive or regressive model is adopted, experience suggests ideas that these institutions may foster a more discursive democracy must be viewed with some suspicion. Efforts to maintain a relationship with infra-national bodies by the commission are diverse and derive from consciousness of the democratic deficit as well as the general absence of an implementing bureaucracy in the usual sense of the word. They are also limited in scope. Arguably, existing consultation processes are better described as transnational and involve national policy elites in contact through commission-established committees (Bulmer, 1983). They have also been dominated by economic rather than other actors (Schmitter and Streeck, 1994).

Deeply contested, subsidiarity represents a more general initiative to deal with the democratic deficit. While some interpret the principle as reducing the drive to supra-nationalism, the commission views it as mandating a new, more discursive implementation of agreed objectives (Axelrod, 1994). The following list of the community's relationships does not purport to be exhaustive but is illustrative of the sphere within which direct infra-national contact is maintained.

- As is envisaged by the Fifth Environmental Action Programme (CEC, 1993), direct contact with stakeholder groups in the implementation of voluntary and other measures implements both sustainability and subsidiarity. But there are problems; in particular, the agreement of 'voluntary measures' is not clearly within the commission's competence. Even if this were the case, the process cannot be assumed to be consensus-oriented and some hierarchical features might be expected.
- The member states have imposed various committees on the commission to assist in the legislative implementation process. These committees are principally creatures of national government though occasional independent experts will sit on bodies. There is little transparency in the process and minimal legal scrutiny of their operation (see for example the BSE debacle (Faulke and Winter, 1996)).
- The commission has the function of enforcing community law and has initiated a complaints procedure which enables individuals to assist and become involved in legal enforcement to a very limited degree (Krämer, 1996).
- There are partnership arrangements involving the disbursement of Community funds at a sub-national level. Insofar as these arrangements are transparent, they seem to be essentially hierarchical in nature (Scott, 1997b and 1997c).

Even accepting extensive contacts between the European commission and infra-national bodies through these networks, some doubt must be expressed as to the ability of the community to establish a truly discursive politics within the current framework. Direct contacts with citizen and stakeholder groups may develop in the future but whether these will develop towards a more integrated politics, and encourage environmental integration specifically, remains to be seen. The ability of groups to organise and represent diverse interests at European level is plainly an important factor, as is the assurance that, once formed, they themselves do not revert to a representative and therefore hierarchical mode of politics, or even undermine the limited representation which exists at a European level.

CONCLUSION

In an increasingly globalised world the European Union remains a rare model for re-establishing control over economic and other processes which have fashionably escaped national and sub-national control. Ironically, Europe has adopted the market as its primary legitimation and organising principle. It is the only model demonstrably capable of structuring and institutionalising a political system comparable to a state across national boundaries. More ironically still, should faith in the current model of progress fail there is some question as to whether an alternative discourse can supply both the legitimacy and similar certainty to act as an organising reference point for interstate politics necessary to sustainable development at a regional or global scale (Wieler, 1994).

Within Europe, alternative legal and political processes have developed to supplement and extend the market discourse, but have not as yet managed to replace the state as the ultimate focus of political and legal legitimacy. In terms of sustainable development these discourses are not promising. In terms of equity interpretations, they are based on a model of liberal democracy that appears to preclude or at least limit the possibilities for the representation of interests other than those of current human generations. Insofar as sustainable development incorporates integration at the global or regional scale, there is a very real question as to whether any social organisation can transcend market and regulatory models to enable truly revelatory involvement in global processes (Habermas, 1996). This said, Europe might present the best opportunity for the development of a more revelatory and discursive politics through alternative instruments of regulation pursued at an infra-national level, directly with local and functional groups. An activist policy on the part of the court, designed to promote re-interpretation of existing rules in favour of sustainability, and to increase accountability and transparency in the infra-national sphere, would facilitate interpretation of the concept, and the start of such a revelatory process.

Chapter 5

The Legal Duty of Environmental Integration: Commitment and Obligation or Enforceable Right?

Martin Hession and Richard Macrory

Environmental protection requirements must be integrated into the definition and implementation of other community policies.

article 130r(2), European Community Treaty

Why a Legal Analysis?

In its 1992 report to UNCED, the European Commission described environmental integration as 'the lynch-pin in the process of establishing sustainable social and economic development patterns'. All member states may now politically subscribe to the goals of sustainable development, but no national constitution or legal system contains an explicit legal requirement concerning the integration of an environmental dimension into other policy sectors. Only within the European Community Treaty, under article 130r, has the idea been given such an overt and broadly drawn expression in law. The presidency conclusions from the 1997 Amsterdam Treaty reaffirm the integration duty and expressly relate it to the promotion of sustainable development:[1]

Environmental protection requirements must be integrated into the definition and implementation of community policies and activities referred to in Article 3, in particular with a view to promoting sustainable development.

Other chapters in this section consider the policy and political implications of environmental integration, together with the tensions and difficulties apparent at European Community and national level as efforts are made to respect the requirement. The approach here is somewhat different. Given the distinctive legal dimension to the integration duty in the treaty, we feel it is important to consider the nature of a duty from a legal perspective, bringing to bear principles and conceptual approaches developed in the context of the discipline of law. In particular, we need to ask: to what extent does the provision, as a matter of law, require, provide, and constrain the operational criteria for its implementation?

It is tempting to dismiss a duty which is expressed, in such broad and apparently political terms, as merely 'symbolic reassurance' (Edelman, 1963) or one that implies no more than a reflection of existing policy developments. It is true that the community commitment to a policy of environment integration predates its express inclusion in the treaty in 1987 by some five years.[2] As Haigh describes in Chapter 3, the duty first entered the legal language of the treaty under the Single European Act 1987 and the wording was strengthened under the Maastricht Treaty in 1992.[3]

These developments, however, do not answer the question of the legal significance attached to the duty. Despite the Single European Act requirement, the European Commission made little progress in strengthening its own policy-making procedures to reflect the obligation. It did publish integrative policy documents in a number of sectoral areas (see Wilkinson, 1992). But it is only fairly recently, as considered by Wilkinson in the next chapter, that more substantial internal administrative changes have been made by the commission in order to pursue the goal of integration. A number of these reflect similar administrative initiatives already introduced by member state governments at national level. It is fairly fruitless to speculate whether these developments were brought about by the existence of the duty in the treaty, or whether these provisions simply reflected pressures for policy changes that were occurring in any event. Certainly, the developments that have taken place at community level cannot be said to have been the result of any dramatic, interventionist decision by the Court of Justice. This has happened in some other policy areas, such as the common transport policy.[4] The fact that the legal duty existed for almost ten years without any significant internal administrative change at community level indicates that the motor for change was not sparked by a legal dynamic.

It does not follow, however, that the duty is devoid of legal significance. It has already been referred to by the Court of Justice in a number of cases concerning the appropriate legal basis for community environmental legislation.[5] The thrust of the case law to date has been to interpret the duty in the light of measures based on the treaty's non-environmental provisions even where their substantive content has an environmental dimension.[6] In that sense, the integration duty can be said to have an enabling or legitimising effect on community action already being proposed. But from a legal perspective, perhaps the more critical question for the future is whether the requirement goes further: does it imply a duty which *constrains* community activities, and which fails to reflect the integration concept or *requires* positive steps to be taken? In other words, the duty to integrate must fall somewhere in the continuum of an expression of general interest in environmental protection and a general duty to protect the environment.

The bald conclusion of the European Court in the Chernobyl I case, namely that the integration provision under article 130r in its pre-Maastricht version implies that 'all community measures must satisfy the requirements of environmental protection', hints at something more than a mere enabling provision.[7] But closer analysis is required to test the validity and practicality of that assertion. Ordinarily, the expression of a legal duty implies a concomitant right, as a consequence of the general need that duties should be enforceable. Therefore, in seeking to define its place on the continuum, it is important to consider how and by whom the duty/right is enforceable. In the absence of any enforcing power a duty risks becoming 'a statement of public policy that is contradicted by practice' and 'is nothing but an empty shell...It may even be pernicious to the reputation of the constitution as a whole and detract from the credibility of the constitutional system derived from it.'[8]

In pursuing the analysis further we can identify five interrelated but essentially distinct lines of inquiry. These are purposely framed in terms of a legal perspective on the issue.

1) Is the integration duty legally binding or merely exhortatory in character?
2) What does the duty apply to?
3) By whom is the duty owed?
4) What is the substance of the duty: what must be integrated, and when is the duty satisfied? Is it a substantive or procedural requirement?
5) To whom is it owed, and if it is legally binding, by whom is it enforceable?

THE INTEGRATION DUTY IN CONTEXT

Before considering these questions in more detail, it is important to place the duty in the context of the environmental provisions of the treaty. Although these represent something of a mishmash from a legal perspective, one can provide an analytical overview of the structure.

- Ostensibly the treaty does not guarantee environmental quality or sustainable development nor does it place a duty on the community to achieve these goals. To paraphrase article 2, the community has as one of its fundamental tasks to promote sustainable growth while respecting the environment, which it will achieve by various measures (establishing a common market and an economic and monetary union and by implementing common policies or activities, including the environmental policy). The Amsterdam amendments would expressly add as one of the tasks 'a high level of protection and improvement of the quality of the environment'.
- The community does, however, have a recognised *interest* in environmental protection, and has legal authority to adopt measures with reference to a range of policies including those contained in article 130r of the treaty relating to community policy on the environment.
- The three key objectives are: preserving, protecting and improving the quality of the environment; protecting human health; and the prudent and rational utilisation of natural resources.[9] These indicate that environmental

protection is defined according to a variety of philosophical approaches – ecocentric, anthropocentric and what might be described as economic rationality (the rational use of resources).

- The community authority for action is confined to the range of community policies listed in article 3 and their relevant legal base. For those policies which are not exclusively the preserve of the community but exist concurrently with those of member states (of which the dedicated environmental policy is one), community authority is further constrained by the principle of subsidiarity.
- Nevertheless, where the community does take action, there is an identified standard of protection to be achieved, albeit expressed in qualitative terms. In its proposals concerning the internal market and environmental protection, it *must take as a base* a 'high level' of protection (article 100a), or alternatively in proposals under the environment policy it must aim at a 'high level' of protection, taking into account the diversity of situations in various regions of the community.
- According to article 130r, there are express principles upon which environmental policies must be based, notably: the precautionary principle; the principle that preventative action should be taken; the need to rectify damage at source; and the principle that the polluter should pay. Again under article 130r, additional factors must be taken into account when preparing environmental policy. These are: available scientific data; environmental conditions in the various regions of the community; the potential costs and benefits of action or lack of action; and the socio-economic development of the community and its regions.
- Finally, there is the integration duty, currently contained in article 130r and analysed in more detail in the chapter that follows. The positioning of the duty is potentially significant, as are the Amsterdam amendments which place it higher up in the treaty, in a new article 3. Currently, it falls within the definition of the community's competence on environmental matters, and after the stated objectives for environmental policy and the principles of environmental action. Its position suggests a requirement that is exercisable only in the context of community policy formulation and implementation rather than any absolute duty in respect of existing and presumably superior legal principles. Repositioning the provision is intended to give the principle far greater policy significance. As Hallo (1997) has noted, there may be an analogy with the repositioning and reformulation of the subsidiarity duty as a general principle following Maastricht, which brought in its wake considerable political attention designed to flesh out the implications of the requirement.[10]

IS THE INTEGRATION DUTY LEGALLY
BINDING OR EXHORTARY?

From a practical point of view, only a self-executing [judicially enforceable without the enactment of implementing legislation] constitutional provision seems to be worthy of adoption, since it alone has true constitutional value. Any other type of clause could be easily ignored: it would lack the weight and timeless authority of a constitutional provision. [Brandl and Bungarth, 1992]

Most systems of public law, and especially those that require the interpretation of written constitutional provisions, recognise two categories of legal statement:

* *directory duties* which are essentially exhortatory or policy statements not intended in themselves to be legally enforced, though they may colour the interpretation of other duties; and
* *mandatory requirements* which are self-executory in the sense that they impose duties which are enforceable in themselves, without requiring the implementation of further legislation.

The fact that a directory duty may not be legally enforceable does not necessarily render it mere rhetoric. It may influence the legal interpretation of other provisions, as has already happened with the integration duty.[11] Moreover, the existence of such a duty may elevate the status and influence of those parts of government already convinced of the need for such goals, and in turn affect the approach of others. As Cotterrell (1984) put it, 'the behaviour of officials and individuals may change even though the legislation does not create enforceable rights and duties ... non-justifiable legislation performs important functions'.

There are a number of arguments for considering the duty to be directory in character only. The duty is expressed in positive terms ('environmental protection requirements must be...'), and therefore, from a legal perspective is generally less susceptible to enforcement than is a negative requirement ('the community may not promote policies damaging the environment...'). It relates to the exercise of judgement in policy development and implementation in which a court would ordinarily allow a greater margin of discretion to the decision-maker. The provision can be said to be ambiguous in that it fails to identify specific environmental protection requirements, an issue considered further below. This is a common response to environmental duties, but not necessarily fatal. Given the unconditional character of the duty, a proactive Court of Justice might insist that it has the authority to seek out the environmental protection requirements of the duty. But some commentators have detected a palpably less activist and more consolidatory phase in the court's current approach – and in any event the court has generally been less inclined to hold the community's actions as contrary to community law when compared to its tougher approach to the enforcement of community law against member states. Finally, as a general comment where duties exist with respect to the environment in national constitutions, experience has revealed considerable reluctance on the part of the courts to implement such environmental duties, in whatever language they are expressed (see Brandt and Bungert, 1997).

These are powerful arguments. But despite the ambiguity of the language, the literal meaning and legislative history of the integration provision tend to suggest that it is more in the nature of mandatory requirement. As Haigh notes in Chapter 3, at Maastricht the member states consciously took the opportunity to reinforce the mandatory tone of the provision by strengthening the language of the obligation. Furthermore, in the context of community law, it would be unusual for the court not to ascribe some effect to such a statement pursuant to the principle of *effet utile* – the idea that treaty provisions must have some useful purpose.

To What Does the Duty Apply?

The duty applies integration to 'other community policies' without defining the meaning of that term. Article 2 of the treaty sets out a range of European Community activities, but only a limited number of these are referred to explicitly as policies:

- a common commercial policy (external trade to developing countries);
- a common policy in the sphere of agriculture and fisheries;
- a policy in the social sphere comprising a European social fund – a common policy in the sphere of transport;
- a policy in the field of the environment; and
- a policy in the sphere of development cooperation.

A restrictive legal interpretation would suggest that the integration duty is confined to these areas only and does not cover other areas of community activity, such as competition law or free movement of goods, which are not explicitly on that list. The drafters of the integration duty could have used, if they wished, broader language. Our own view is that this is too limiting an approach. If the issue were to come before the European Court of Justice it would adopt a more generous interpretation, and not feel confined by the explicit list of policies in article 3. For a start, the treaty itself is not consistent in the use of the term 'policies'.[12] The court would be justified in considering the duty's underlying rationale and subject those policy-making activities of the community, whether or not they are formally described as policies, to the integration duty.[13] In any event, the Amsterdam amendments will remove the doubt. The new version of the integration duty applies to 'policies and activities' (our emphasis) referred to in article 3. This extends the scope well beyond narrowly defined policies to encompass, amongst others, free movement of goods, competition, consumer protection, and measures of energy.

So much for the substantive areas encompassed by the duty. But we also need to ask what exactly is meant by policies (and 'activities' if the Dublin proposals are agreed). Does it encompass only binding legal acts such as directives, regulations and decisions? Or would it include formal, but non-binding, acts such as decisions, or go further to include informal documents and statements which do not necessarily have a legal status under community law? Again, our view is that the court would be tempted to adopt a generous view, looking not so much at the legal form or status of the measure in question, but considering its significance in practice – is it, for example, a formulation of principles intended to guide or influence action within a field of community activity? Again the Amsterdam amendments would strengthen that view.

By Whom Is the Duty Owed?

No particular institution or body is identified by article 130r(2), but it is clear that it applies to those bodies with primary responsibility for defining and implementating the community's other policies. These include all relevant community institutions and member states in so far as they are charged with implementing community policies. The Declaration to the Maastricht Treaty refers to the commission's undertakings in respect of environmental integration, and most attention to date has been focused on the commission's internal administrative initiatives. But the above interpretation suggests a broader range of subjects than envisaged in current proposals, and would encompass at the very least all those community bodies involved in defining or implementing community policy, including the Council of Ministers, the European Investment Bank and the European Parliament.[14]

As to member states, they are clearly bound by the duty when acting within the Council of Ministers.[15] The duty, however, refers to 'implementation' as well as to 'design', and since implementation is often the responsibility of member states, it is arguable that the integration duty must apply here as well. This interpretation has considerable implications for member states. Much would depend on the level of discretion granted at national level, and the extent to which a failure at national level to integrate an environmental dimension could frustrate the effect of article 130r. To take one example, a national body such as a transport department might be given the responsibility to define routes for Trans-European networks under article 129b of the treaty and would, we suggest, be legally vulnerable if no regard were paid to the duty at the time it exercised its responsibilities. Or a national body might be given responsibilities concerned with implementing community policy, such as the distribution of community funds. Again, we would argue that it would be bound by the integration duty. This would be especially relevant where the body has a margin of discretion and choice – in other words, where regard to the duty could have a real influence on the outcome of its decision.

THE SUBSTANCE OF THE DUTY: REGARDING ENVIRONMENTAL PROTECTION REQUIREMENTS

The core of the duty refers to the integration of 'environmental protection requirements' and both phrases require interpretation in order to understand the substance of the requirement. But in the legal analysis of similar duties on governmental bodies, it has usually been difficult to disentangle the nature of the duty from the question: to whom the duty is owed. Each inquiry influences the other. The issue of enforceability is considered in more detail in the next section, but at this stage we can usefully identity three broad possible classifications of the duty.

1) *Internal integration:* this implies that the duty is one owed by community policy-makers only to other community policy-makers. The duty could take the form of one that is owed and legally enforceable by each institution, or one that is owed by community institutions to the others but is implemented only by internal administrative methods. The current administrative initiatives considered by Wilkinson in the following chapter can be considered as an example of the latter.
2) *Weak constitutional integration:* here the duty is treated as one that is owed by community institutions to member states as well as to other community bodies. This would permit member states to challenge, in law, policies and decisions on the grounds that they were in breach of the integration duty.
3) *Strong constitutional integration:* this classification of the duty treats it as one that is owed by the community to individual citizens, in effect creating an external individual right. Recent case law of the European Court has already treated the code of conduct on public access to information, developed by the European Council and European Commission and the decisions of those bodies to adopt it, as creating such external rights.[16] Nevertheless, as we discuss below, we see considerable difficulty in treating the integration duty as creating similar rights.

When considering the meaning of 'environmental protection requirements', there are several possible interpretations. The first, which we call conservative, is the simplest and most narrow. The word requirement implies a legal obligation and thus encompasses only those obligations concerning the environment contained in community environmental legislation. This has the advantage of providing a clear benchmark and avoids the difficulties elaborated below when determining other, more elusive reference points. This is the approach that appears to have been adopted by the commission in relation to structural funds, as indicated in the analysis by Clare Coffey in Chapter 7.[17]

Whatever its superficial attraction, this narrow approach hardly makes long-term sense. All it contributes to the existing legislative framework is an added mechanism for ensuring compliance with existing community environmental law – that is, a requirement to prevent other community policies from undermining compliance by member states with their obligations under community law. General principles of community law already exist to prevent this from happening. The general duty under article 5 of the treaty requiring member states to take all appropriate measures to fulfil community obligations imposes a reciprocal duty on the commission to assist member states, and by implication to refrain from action which inhibits implementation. Furthermore, the conservative approach fails to reflect the aspirations of the integration requirement.

The second approach to interpreting environmental protection requirements looks to objective standards of protection. According to this argument, in order to judge whether or not the integration duty has been followed, it is both legitimate and necessary to determine some standard of environmental protection which is neither contained in the treaty nor, necessarily, in community secondary legislation. To an extent, the idea that there are objective environmental protection requirements derives from the environmental rights ethos – wherever those rights are placed, it is possible to objectively determine what is necessary to protect the environment.

There are considerable difficulties in endorsing this interpretation. By cutting adrift the definition of environmental protection requirements, a court would potentially be involved in substantive moral and ethical choices with respect to the factors that ought to be integrated and the standard of protection to be adopted. The reference to a 'high level' of environmental protection in article 130r of the treaty might act as a useful pointer for a court, but remains an aim rather than an obligatory requirement. In general terms, the essential difficulty with enforcing an objective standard of environmental protection is that the standard is not one amenable to judicial application or confidence.[18] The essence of judicial reluctance to become involved in such issues lies in the difficulty of describing an effective dividing line between the application of a rule based on solid criteria and the substitution of judicial judgement for what should be a matter of political discretion. In contrast, reviewing a decision for its procedural regularity is more easily performed. Here, what is examined is the reasoning process of the decision-maker; the substantive result of the decision is not directly tested for its compatibility with some putative environmental protection requirement. Even this approach does not always let a court completely off the hook. Assessing procedural regularities requires some consideration of the facts leading to the decision, their relevance or irrelevance, and some minimum basis to justify the decision.

The limitations of the conservative interpretation and the conceptual challenges of the objective standards suggest that a third approach is required. The treaty itself contains certain obligatory policy requirements concerning the environment, which can be summarised as follows:

- a contribution towards the objectives of preserving, protecting and improving the quality of the environment, protecting human health, and the prudent and rational utilisation of natural resources;
- a high level of protection;
- adherence to the four principles of precaution, prevention, rectification at source, and polluter pays; and

- the need to take into account certain additional factors including the diversity of situations within various regions of the community, available scientific and technical data, and the potential costs and benefits of action or inaction.

These principles indicate the basis and direction of policy rather than specify a substantive result. The language used and the gradation of terminology (a 'basis in' to 'taking into account') suggest that they are guidelines – directional rather than prescriptive – and indicate a real difficulty in challenging measures claimed to be in breach of such principles, other than in the most clear-cut case of consciously avoiding their consideration. Nevertheless, if the integration duty is to be given any legal significance, we suggest that it represents a basis for interpretation which is consistent with the treaty rather than relying on the contents of existing secondary legislation.

THE SUBSTANCE OF THE DUTY: INTEGRATION

Article 173 of the treaty, which provides the means to review the legality of community acts, makes a classic distinction between infringement of a rule of law and infringement of an essential procedural requirement. Generally speaking, the former guarantees a particular substantive result, while a procedural right guarantees some form of participation in the process of determining a result. The distinction is important, though in practice it can become blurred.[19] As we have indicated, courts are more inclined to recognise a procedural right with respect to the environment rather than a substantive right.[20]

The duty to integrate environmental requirements is suggestive of procedural rather than substantive protection. The dictionary definition supports the idea of a duty with respect to formulating policy rather than identifying a *ne plus ultra* of policy results. At the very least, the duty requires that regard must be given to environmental requirements when developing other community policies. As Kramer (1990, para 4.45) points out, in the context of the 1987 version of the duty, all community measures 'must have one eye on the existing community legislation and the other on the environment, which is now a factor in all action [taken] by the community'.

A familiar requirement often imposed on administrative bodies is to 'take into consideration' certain factors, implying that once taken on board they may be rejected if they conflict with other goals. But the terminology of the integration duty implies more than this; conflict with other areas does not entitle environmental requirements to be dismissed. Courts frequently have to make sense of competing goals which appear on the face of law. The European Court is no stranger to this challenge and could adopt a number of tried and tested approaches. The first would be to apply principles of proportionality already seen in the context of conflicts between free movement of goods and environmental protection. According to this model, transport or competition policy, for example, would have to be the most environmentally compatible with the goals of these policies. This approach is not entirely satisfactory since it gives a predominance to those other policy objectives, whereas the integration duty is designed to redefine and redirect those policies.

Another approach that the court could adopt would be to accept that determining the balance of competing objectives should remain at the discretion of community institutions rather than within the court's domain. This essentially is the stance adopted by the court in the agricultural field where the treaty objectives are themselves potentially in conflict, and where the court has been reluctant to interfere with the commission or council's determination of the purpose or scope of particular measures – even accepting that at any particular time one objective may legitimately take precedence over another.[21] The third approach is to develop a restrictive attitude towards parties entitled to bring legal challenges before the courts, thus relieving the court of the difficult choices involved. This demonstrates the clear connection between the nature of the substantive duty and the question of locus standi, considered in the next section.

TO WHOM IS THE INTEGRATION DUTY OWED?

This is perhaps the most difficult of all the questions raised and the most important. It determines the true nature of the duty, and whether it gives rise to a responsibility in the sense that somebody has the right to enforce it. As we indicated in the section on environmental protection requirements, three categories of potential beneficiaries can be identified: community institutions; member states; and, individual citizens.

With respect to the community institutions, under article 173 of the treaty, they have general rights to challenge the legality of community acts and could conceivably enforce the integration duty against each other in this way. It must be observed that as the institutions share the responsibility of adopting community acts in most cases, breach of the duty to integrate during this process might arise in the context of disputes over the legal basis of measures. Here, both the European Parliament and the European Investment Bank may act only in respect of their own prerogatives (to protect their own particular rights), and it seems unlikely that either could hold rights with respect to the integration duty per se.

Similarly, member states are able to challenge the validity of community acts. Against a background of increased majority voting at council level, it is possible to predict that a minority country, concerned with the lack of environmental sensitivity in a proposed community measure, might take advantage of the remedy. But in areas such as structural funds, there has been a marked reluctance by member states to initiate any legal challenges – perhaps for the simple but cynical reason that all member states expect to gain from structural funds at some point and have been unwilling to rock the plentiful boat (Kramer, 1996, p9).

To the extent that the integration duty also applies to member states when defining or implementing community policy, the European Commission would have a primary duty to initiate enforcement procedures under Article 169 of the treaty. The decision whether or not to initiate such action is essentially a matter of discretion for the commission and is not reviewable by the court.[22]

Individuals bringing action before the national courts may also claim the benefit of treaty provisions, which are considered sufficiently precise and certain to have 'direct effect'.[23] In one sense, the integration duty is relatively precise and unconditional, but it is most unlikely that it would have such direct effects. There are sufficient ambiguities in the terminology (both of court overload and the substantive judgements demanded of the courts) to allow direct challenges of all community policies by almost anyone; these weigh heavily against such an interpretation.

The treaty also permits individuals to challenge the legality of community action directly before the European Court of Justice, although there are two critical limitations to the remedy. Firstly, the treaty rules, under article 173, only permit challenge to regulations or legal decisions. They do not allow individuals to challenge directives, resolutions and other non-binding actions of the community. Secondly, the applicant must show 'direct and individual concern' and the Court of Justice has consistently given a restrictive interpretation of this phrase. Essentially, individuals making the challenge must demonstrate that they are affected in some way which differentiates them from all others affected,[24] and recent decisions of the Court of Justice which deny standing to environmental groups and individuals demonstrate that the test is almost impossible to satisfy where an issue of general environmental concern is raised.[25] During the build-up to the Intergovernmental Conference, environmental interests made proposals to liberalise the standing rule, and in effect to introduce an actio popularis (Climate Action Network *et al*, 1995), but the current overload in the European Court and concerns about opening the floodgates makes any radical change unlikely. Nevertheless, for a system that is so fundamentally based on the rule of law, the present procedures represent a worrying lacuna (Kramer, 1996; Macrory, 1996).

Procedure and Substance Revisited

It is clear that to the extent that the integration duty amounts to a procedural requirement for adopting and implementating community legislation, the community institutions are at least bound by the obligation, and there is liberal standing for them and member states to challenge the legality of decisions made in breach of them. Article 190 requires that community regulations, directives and decisions must state the reasons upon which they are based – an important requirement to promote transparency in decision-making. It is a broad principle which is deeper in scope than are most equivalent rules under national legal systems.[26] The substantive content of the duty to give reasons has varied according to the nature of the act in question, and although a margin of discretion is afforded to the institutions with respect to the detail of reasoning required, the obligation can act as a significant lever to reinforce the application of the integration duty.[27] Interpreting the duty as a procedural requirement would imply a guarantee of certain procedural minima before a policy is agreed upon and implemented.

We have already identified the difficulty of viewing the duty as substantive and relating to specific results. The problem of determining by legal process (as opposed to political means) an objective environmental standard is one that bedevils the whole field of substantive environmental rights. We suggested, however, that the principles of environmental action contained in the treaty might serve as a basis for more substantive review. And, indeed, in case law concerning the conflicts between free movement of goods and environmental protection, recent legal developments have hinted that the integration principles have given a higher status to those principles of environmental action than previously.[28]

If, as we have suggested, the integration duty forms an essential procedural requirement, one can argue that a precondition of the legality of community measures should be a demonstratable compliance with an environmental appraisal based on the principles of environmental action contained in the treaty.[29] Difficult though this sounds, it merely supports the simple notion that policy development leading to European Community acts must display a minimum standard of reasoning. The environmental integration requirement is now an essential element of that reasoning process. Failure to reflect the broad criteria of the treaty's environmental principles should open the institution in question to at least a minimum review of the stated reasons. Where no reference is made to the basic environmental criteria, or the reasoning is unsupported by substantial evidence, the decision in question must be open to challenge. Applying legal analysis to the integration duty suggests that, despite the conceptual difficulties involved, it can be considered as something more than a political aspiration. But it will require a degree of bold foresight on the part of lawyers and judges to bring about that change.

Chapter 6

STEPS TOWARDS INTEGRATING THE ENVIRONMENT INTO OTHER EU POLICY SECTORS

David Wilkinson

INTRODUCTION

The principal vehicle employed by the European Union to implement Agenda 21 is the Fifth Environmental Action Programme *Towards Sustainability*, which was published by the European Commission in March 1992. A key theme running through the action programme is the need to integrate the needs of the environment within the development and implementation of other policies, particularly in five key sectors – agriculture, energy, industry, transport and tourism. Integration is seen as a fundamental prerequisite for sustainable development. The Fifth Environmental Action Programme, however, is not binding on the European Union's member states, nor in practice on individual directorates-general within the European Commission itself. A number of progress reports on the Fifth Environmental Action Programme produced by the Commission's Environment Directorate-General (DG XI) and the European Environment Agency have noted the limited impact so far of the programme and the need for greater political commitment to its objectives.

This paper does not seek to describe substantive examples of integration that have occurred in the various European Union policy sectors since the publication of the Fifth Environmental Action Programme. Rather, the paper is focused specifically on the procedural steps that have been taken by DG XI within the commission to influence the development of European Union legislative and policy proposals in sectors outside its own immediate responsibilities. In its dealings with other directorate-generals, DG XI has been obliged to rely on persuasion rather than on power, a 'bottom-up' as opposed to a 'top-down' approach to integration. So far this has had limited effect and DG XI has begun to enhance its power in relation to the rest of the commission in order to accelerate the process of integration.

SUSTAINABLE DEVELOPMENT, INTEGRATION AND THE FIFTH ENVIRONMENTAL ACTION PROGRAMME (5EAP)

Sustainable Development in the Treaties

It is not surprising that the original Treaty of Rome, signed in 1957, should have made no reference either to sustainable development or even to environmental protection. In article 2, the treaty set as the task for the community the promotion of: 'a harmonious development of economic activities, a continuous and balanced expansion, an increase in stability, an accelerated raising of the standard of living, and closer relations between the states belonging to it'. This was to be achieved by establishing a common market and progressively approximating the economic policies of the member states. Given that this wording was drafted in the mid 1950s, the call for 'continuous expansion' is not surprising, nor is the lack of any recognition that there might be environmental limits to growth.

When, 30 years later in 1987, the Single European Act came into force, it did not use the phrase 'sustainable development' – but it did for the first time provide a formal, legal underpinning for the community's already developing environmental policy. It also laid down the important principle of 'integration' (of the environment into other policies), which is generally regarded as a principal means for moving towards sustainable development. Article 130r(2) established the principle that: 'environmental protection requirements shall be a component of the community's other policies'.

In 1993 the Maastricht Treaty on European Union (EU) introduced into EU's statement of objectives the word 'sustainable' (not 'sustainable development', nor even the more limited concept of 'sustainability'). Article B of the treaty sets as one of the objectives of the EU:

> *...to promote economic and social progress which is balanced and sustainable, in particular through the creation of an area without internal frontiers, through the strengthening of economic and social cohesion and through the establishment of economic and monetary union, ultimately including a single currency in accordance with the provisions of the treaty.*

At the time there was legitimate scepticism that 'economic and social progress which is balanced and sustainable' could be achieved through the creation of an internal market, monetary union, and eventually a single currency. What occurred during the 1990 Intergovernmental Conference (IGC) was that the word sustainable was added almost as an afterthought to the pre-existing political objective of political and monetary union (which was the main purpose of the Treaty of Maastricht), without otherwise much disturbing those objectives (Wilkinson, 1992).

In addition, the Maastricht Treaty also amended article 2 of the Treaty of Rome by replacing the objective of 'continuous expansion' with that of 'sustainable and non-inflationary growth respecting the environment'. Although many environmentalists have pointed out the intellectual incoherence of the notion of 'sustainable growth', it nevertheless represented an advance that subsequently could be built upon. Maastricht also strengthened the 'integration' principle in article 130r(2) by now making it imperative: '[e]nvironmental protection requirements must be integrated into the definition and implementation of other community policies'. The practical effect of such legal formulations may, on the face of it, appear to be limited, but they have been used by the Environment Directorate-General (DG XI) and the European Parliament separately as a justification for introducing new, formal mechanisms and procedures aimed at ensuring that the environment is taken into account across all EU policy sectors.

Integration

Approaches to Integration:[1]
Strategies for integrating environmental concerns into sectoral policies with major environmental implications may take a variety of forms along what may be termed an integration continuum. Along this continuum the activities of sectoral departments are subject to increasing degrees of constraint in order to secure environmental objectives. The continuum extends from 'strong', or 'top-down' integration at one end, to 'soft' or 'bottom-up' approaches at the other. Top-down integration depends upon the possession and exercise, normally by an environment ministry, of formal power in relation to other departments. By contrast, a bottom-up approach is more incremental and piecemeal and, crucially, leaves sectoral departments greater freedom to determine the extent to which they modify their policy or programme objectives for environmental reasons.

• *Top-down integration* typically involves the establishment of binding frameworks which constrain the actions of sectoral departments. Mechanisms for enacting this approach include the development by the government as a whole, perhaps led by an environment ministry, of sectoral action plans with quantified targets and timetables. This is the approach adopted in The Netherlands in successive environment plans. Top-down integration requires effective review and reporting mechanisms to monitor progress in achieving targets. Therefore, in addition to playing a leading part in setting these priorities, the environment ministry or authority plays a crucial, 'horizontal' role, reviewing and regulating the environmental performance of other departments – somewhat similar to that of a finance ministry in setting the overall level of public expenditure and its allocation between different departments. Top-down approaches to integration might involve the following key steps as depicted in Figure 6.1.

• A *bottom-up approach* to integration reflects the application of influence rather than formal power. Environment ministries or agencies are not able to impose constraints on the actions of other departments, which remain free to develop policies and programmes in the light of their own sectoral priorities. The integration of environmental considerations into sectoral policies comes instead from a process, often very gradual, of cultural

The development of 'rolling' national sustainability and biodiversity plans

The development of sectoral action plans

Annual reporting by departments on their performance in relation to sectoral action plans

Regular review of annual environmental reports by parliament and the public

Figure 6.1 Top-down approaches to integration

change in which sectoral departments themselves take greater account of environmental considerations. The role of environment ministries or agencies in this process is to *influence* and *guide* rather than to direct. In this task they may be helped by parliamentary and public opinion. The key features of the bottom-up approach are not binding action plans but procedures designed to make sectoral departments more aware of the environmental consequences of their actions. The approach requires a process of continuous negotiation between environment and sectoral ministries, through, for example, the extensive use of interdepartmental committees or working groups, or the appointment of 'green' officials within sectoral departments.

• *Intermediate steps:* between the two extremes of the continuum, sectoral departments may face increasing degrees of constraint as they are required to apply one or more formal 'integrative' mechanisms. These may include some forms of strategic environmental assessment and appraisal (SEA), or the application of environmental auditing and reporting mechanisms.[2] The degree of constraint that these mechanisms represent will depend crucially on such factors as who undertakes the assessment or audit, and who takes the final decision on whether a policy should proceed and in what form.

The choice of Integration Strategy
The approach to integration adopted at EU or member state level will depend on the degree of formal power or authority at the disposal of the environment ministry, directorate or agency. Among EU member states, most environment ministries have only recently been established. The oldest of them have been in existence as separate ministries for less than 25 years and some, as in Italy and Spain, for less than ten. Generally they have not been sufficiently powerful in relation to other ministries to impose a top-down approach to integration, even if they wished to. Similarly, within the European Commission, the political weight of DG XI is limited in comparison with, for example, DG VI (agriculture) or DG III (industry), both longer established and with far greater financial

and staff resources. It is inevitable that powerful sectoral ministries will continue to insist on developing policies and programmes in the light of their own non-environmental priorities. In practice, therefore, environment ministries, agencies and non-governmental organisations (NGOs) seeking to advance integration need to focus simultaneously on several points along the integration continuum. Binding action plans may represent the most direct and potentially effective route to integration, but political realities need to be acknowledged and the development of softer, bottom-up approaches need to be encouraged as well.

Integration and EU Environment Policy
The subject of environmental integration was first given prominence in the European Community's (EC) Fourth Environmental Action Programme of 1987.[3] Section 2.3 states:

> *It will accordingly be a central part of the Commission's efforts during the period of the Fourth Environmental Action Programme to make major progress towards the practical realisation of this objective – initially at the level of the Community's own policies and actions; secondly at the level of the policies implemented by member states; but as soon as possible in a more generalised way so that all economic and social developments throughout the Community, whether undertaken by public or private bodies or of a mixed character, would have environmental requirements built fully into their planning and execution.*

Initially, emphasis was to be placed on the community's own policies and, to this end, the commission was to 'develop internal procedures and practices to ensure that this integration of environmental factors takes place routinely in relation to all other policy areas'. Action to give effect to this promise was not forthcoming until after the publication in 1992 of the 5EAP, and the strengthening of the integration requirement in the Maastricht Treaty.[4]

The 5EAP

The European Commission adopted the 5EAP on 18 March 1992, three months before the United Nations Conference on Environment and Development (UNCED) and the adoption of Agenda 21 (A21). Nevertheless, the 5EAP was prepared in tandem with the principal Rio agreements so that it shares many of the strategic objectives and principles of A21. The 5EAP marked an important change of direction for the community's environmental policy. Previous environmental action programmes had taken the form of lists of proposed legislation often selected in response to events, whereas the 5EAP attempted to address the fundamental causes of environmental degradation as a means of creating a more sustainable economy and society. In contrast to A21, its focus was exclusively environmental and it did not address the social dimensions of sustainable development such as poverty, gender or demographics.[5] In a Council Resolution of 1 February 1993 approving the 'general approach of the Programme', EU environment ministers noted that the 5EAP 'constitutes an appropriate *point of departure* for the implementation of Agenda 21 by the European Community and its member states' (our italics).[6] Subsequent A21 implementation reports from the community to the United Nations Commission on Sustainable Development have similarly emphasised that the 5EAP 'has been chosen as the Community's main vehicle for implementing Agenda 21 and the other agreements made at UNCED'.[7]

The 5EAP set the strategy for the EU's environmental policy until the year 2000. It focused on ten major environmental problems or themes, and five economic sectors which make a significant contribution both to their creation and, by the same token, their solution. These were industry, agriculture, energy, transport and tourism. For each of the themes and target sectors, the programme presented tables setting out policy objectives, the instruments and timetables for achieving them, and the key actors from whom action is required, including the EU, member states, local authorities and industry.

Fundamental to the programme was the principle that the environment must be integrated from the beginning into all the policies and actions of industry, government and consumers, especially in the target sectors. Other important features included a recognition that changes in society's patterns of behaviour must be achieved in a spirit of shared responsibility among all key actors, including central and local government, public and private enterprise, and the general public (as both individual citizens and consumers). It also emphasised that the range of policy instruments that are applied to solve environmental problems should be broadened beyond traditional command-and-control legislation to include economic instruments, voluntary agreements, and better information and education to enable the public to make more informed choices.

As a council resolution, the Council of Ministers' response to the 5EAP was non-binding. Moreover, EU environment ministers were careful to establish that the proposed actions, targets and timetables in the 5EAP did not immediately impose legal obligations upon the member states. It was only the general approach and the strategy of the programme that were approved. They also emphasised that, in accordance with the principle of subsidiarity, 'some of the actions in the programme fail to be implemented at levels other than that of the community'. Where appropriate, the commission was invited to come forward with proposals to give effect to the programme, which would be considered by the community's institutions in the normal way (and by implication could be rejected in the council). Less clear, however, was whether the commission itself was obliged to develop proposals in those areas identified in the programme as requiring a lead from the community. The view of the commission's DG XI was that since the commission as a whole had adopted the draft 5EAP, all DGs were bound to come forward with appropriate proposals. Other commission officials were less convinced, however. A review in mid 1995 of how far the commission had 'delivered' on its obligations to act by that date revealed that, in respect of over one quarter of its commitments, the commission had failed to act.[8] In contrast to A21, the 5EAP contained no suggestion that member states should present regular reports to the commission on their implementation of the programme. Only the UK produced such a report;[9] an annex to the commission's progress report on the 5EAP seeks to present in tabular form how far the member states had taken steps to implement the programme, but observes that 'information on some countries is limited because of too late input (*sic*) or no input by these countries'.[10]

THE EUROPEAN COMMISSION'S INTEGRATION PROCEDURES

The Commission's Approach to Integration

The commission's approach to integration has necessarily been an example of the bottom-up approach. DG XI has no formal power over other DGs, and the 5EAP is not binding on the member states, nor on the commission itself (but see next section). Environment Commissioner Ritt Bjerregaard has observed:

> *I am a bit like someone in charge of a car park where none of the issues which are parked there under the name of the environment are really ones I could call my own. In reality they are in fact issues which really need to be resolved elsewhere by some of my other Commission colleagues...*[11]

The commission's integration arrangements were set out in an internal (and unpublished) communication: *Integration by the Commission of the Environment into other Policies*.[12] This was drawn up by DG XI and DG IX (personnel and administration) in discussion with the commission's secretariat general and endorsed by commissioners at the end of May 1993. The proposed arrangements were the subject of very little discussion, however, and most commissioners seem not to have properly absorbed their full implications. In summary, the new machinery comprised five principal elements:

1) a new integration unit was to be established in DG XI, reporting directly to the director-general;
2) each of the commission's directorates-general were to designate an integration correspondent – a 'green' official whose task would be to ensure that policies took proper account of the environment;
3) all policy proposals with significant environmental effects were to be subject to an environmental appraisal (a form of SEA). Those selected for this procedure would be indicated by a 'green star' in the commission's legislative programme published at the beginning of each year;
4) each DG was to undertake an annual evaluation of its environmental performance. Such evaluations were to be published in the Commission's annual *General Report on the Activities of the European Union*; and
5) a code of conduct was to be drawn up for the commission itself, covering such green housekeeping issues as purchasing policy, waste minimisation, and energy conservation.

In September 1994, these requirements were elaborated upon and incorporated into the seventh revision of the commission's internal *Manual of Operational Procedures*.[13]

Implementation of the Commission's Integration Machinery

DG XI Integration Unit

A Unit for Political Coordination and Integration was established in DG XI in 1993 with five officials charged with monitoring the implementation of the 5EAP, both within DG XI itself and throughout the commission. More specifically, it was to be the point of contact with integration correspondents in other DGs. The unit has made information available to correspondents on developments in environmental policy and, to the extent that it can, has advised on such matters as the techniques of environmental appraisal. It has commissioned more structured training sessions on such techniques, including other skills related to environmental integration. In consultation with the commission's secretariat-general, it was responsible for proposing those items in the commission's work programmes for 1994 and 1995 that might be subject to an environmental appraisal (although it is the responsible DGs who ultimately decide if such appraisals should be undertaken).

Environment Integration Correspondents[14]

The commission's internal communication stressed that:

> *In each directorate-general a senior official closely linked to the central policy making operation of the DG will be made responsible for ensuring that policy proposals and legislative proposals developed in that directorate-general take account of the environment and of the requirement to contribute towards sustainable patterns of development.*

By mid 1994, integration correspondents were designated by all DGs. Most correspondents were senior officials (head of unit or above), but in practice many of the duties of the post have been delegated to subordinates. The appointment of integration correspondents was undertaken by each DG acting independently of DG XI. In several DGs the designation was given, as a matter of course, to officials with preexisting environmental responsibilities. DGs III, VI, and XVII (energy) each had one or more units dealing with environmental affairs, and have continued to develop their own environment-related policies. For example, Unit A/2 in DG XVII (analyses and forecasts) played a leading role in an interservice group on the community's carbon dioxide reduction strategy, which comprises representatives of nine DGs. In DG VI, there were no less than five separate sections dealing with environmental concerns. Inevitably, such units have each had their own agendas and ways of working.

For its part, DG XI has issued no formal guidance setting out in precise terms what the role of an integration correspondent should be. There is a range of possible models, including the following:

- spy – informing DG XI of developments in other commission services;
- postman – passing on information from DG XI on environmental developments and legislation;
- policeman – vetoing 'ungreen' policy proposals;
- technician – advising on whether and how to do, for instance, strategic environmental assessments;
- facilitator – negotiating between DG XI and the correspondent's own DG; and
- ambassador – modifying DG XI's policies to accord with those of the correspondent's own DG.

In practice, each integration correspondent has been able to interpret the role in his or her own way. Few, if any, can be regarded as DG XI 'spies' or 'policemen'; indeed, at one of the very few meetings of all the correspondents summoned by DG XI, a significant proportion failed to attend. In those DGs with an established environmental role or unit, integration is regarded as a two-way process in which the sectoral department has as much right to influence DG XI as vice versa. The case of DG III may be cited as an example. An environment unit B4 ('industrial problems related to environmental legislation') was established in April 1993, some months before the commission's internal communication. As early as November 1992, DG III had already produced its own communication: *Industrial Competitiveness and Protection of the Environment* (SEC (92) 1986). DG III's environment unit set itself three principal objectives:

1) to inform officials with sectoral responsibilities within DG III of relevant environmental developments within the Council of Ministers, the OECD, and other fora; this is done through meetings of an internal environmental network of some 30 DG III officials who meet monthly, the production of a newsletter, and the use of electronic mail;
2) to act as an élément modérateur by making DG XI aware of industrial realities in the development of the EU's environmental policy; and
3) to advance the 'greening' of industry by the direct encouragement of voluntary agreements, life-cycle analysis, and the diffusion of clean technologies.

Officials in DG III's environment unit have privately expressed the view that responsibility for developing aspects of environmental policy and legislation could be transferred from DG XI to DG III. DG III traditionally has had far greater contact with industry than DG XI, which is regarded as underresourced and suffering from excessive staff turnover.[15]

Environmental Appraisals of Commission Proposals
The commission's internal communication required environmental appraisals of any commission proposal with significant effects on the environment. These have been identified with an asterisk (a 'green star') in the commission's annual legislative programme, following consultation between DG XI and the

responsible DG. The ultimate responsibility for undertaking the work, however, rests with the responsible DG. Annex 6 of the *Manual of Operational Procedures* now lists a step-by-step procedure for undertaking environmental appraisals. A review of the environmental impact of relevant proposals was also to be included in communications to the council (COM) documents. However, there is no evidence that any such environmental appraisals have been undertaken. No references to such appraisals have been included in any commission communications issued since the new procedures came into effect. The attempt by DG XI to apply environmental appraisal on such a scale was overambitious. The appropriate methodology is underdeveloped and is still being investigated in research commissioned by DG XI. In respect of its proposals for Trans-European Road Networks, DG VII (transport) has also commissioned research on practice elsewhere. Against this background, it was certainly optimistic of DG XI to attach 'green stars' to so many of the legislative proposals in the commission's 1994 and 1995 legislative programmes.

Annual Evaluations of Environmental Performance
Each DG was to draw up annually an evaluation of its environmental perfor-mance, which would be published in the commission's annual *General Report of the Activities of the European Union*. Unpublished evaluations were submitted to DG XI covering the period 1993–94, which formed the basis of an internal DG XI information note to the rest of the commission.[16] Not all DGs, however, submitted complete information. DG XI notes that: 'numerous DGs have taken initiatives and developed measures in the environment sector, but to what extent and how the environment has been taken into account, on a systematic basis, as other types of measures and policies are devised, is rarely indicated'.[17] Some information on environmental performance was included in the *Interim Report on the Implementation of the Fifth Environmental Action Programme*. However, despite the requirement in the June 1993 internal communication, very little information is contained in the commission's *General Report on the Activities of the European Union* for 1994 and 1995.[18]

Internal Environmental Management System for the Commission
An internal consultation paper was drawn up by DG IX on the environmental impact of the commission's own activities, but has not been published. Only in early 1996 were consultants invited by DG XI to draw up an internal environ-mental management system for the commission.

Impact of the Commission's Integration Measures

The impact of the commission's June 1993 internal communication on practice in other DGs has been modest. Not all elements of the new integration proce-dures have been implemented, and where they have, their impact has been limited. Where substantive progress towards integration has occurred in the five key policy sectors identified in the 5EAP, this has been as much the consequence of exogenous factors as of the June 1993 measures. For example, what progress there has been on the 'greening' of the common agricultural policy (CAP) is a reflection of a coincidence of interests between the farming community and environmentalists, while in the energy sector attempts to reduce energy demand simultaneously serve a number of different policy objectives – the classic win–win situation – and are therefore more readily acceptable to DG XVII.

DG XI's disappointment with the new internal integration procedures was reflected in the *1995 Progress Report* on the 5EAP:

> *The measures so far have had limited impact…progress has varied according to sectors, but the message of the Fifth Programme has not been sufficiently integrated in operational terms within the commission. The process depends on persuasion and influence and will take time. In the longer term, change is likely to take place through increased education, training and changes of attitude. It will require continued adequate resources and sustained commitment.*[19]

This last sentence highlights the profound importance of integration for the future direction and culture of DG XI itself. Even a bottom-up approach to integration requires the application of considerable staff resources, new forms of expertise, and political commitment in the department responsible for driving an integration initiative. Substantial investment is required by an environment ministry or department to: develop expertise in policy sectors outside the traditionally 'environmental'; train staff outside the environment department in such environmental techniques as SEA and environmental auditing; and develop new management skills associated with team-building, influencing and negotiation. The willingness of officials to make this investment may be weakened by what is perceived as the uncertain outcome of successful integration. This may mean that responsibility for environmental protection shifts away from the environment department and towards sectoral ministries, so that measures, for example, to prevent or minimise agricultural or industrial pollution become the exclusive responsibility of the agriculture and industry departments, with the role of environment departments limited to advice and training. Successful integration entails a fundamental redefinition of the role of environment departments, and some loss of control over environmental policy. The dilemma this poses is that the focus for advancing integration across the activities of government may consequently become less distinct. It was for this reason that one of the earliest initiatives of the DG XI integration unit was to address these issues in 'reflection' meetings with all DG XI staff. Subsequently, the process of developing a new corporate mission for DG XI, which acknowledges its new integration responsibilities, has been given priority by its former director-general, Marius Endhoven. Work on this continues.

TURNING THE SCREW: MOVES TOWARDS A TOP-DOWN APPROACH

As discussed above, DG XI has had no formal authority of its own to direct other DGs to 'green' their policies, hence its reliance on a bottom-up approach to integration. This is necessarily a long-term and uncertain process which fits uneasily with the targets and timetables set out in the 5EAP. In these circumstances, it is not surprising that DG XI has tried to shift the integration continuum towards a more top-down approach. It has attempted to increase its power in relation to other DGs by: forming an alliance with the European Parliament; applying, for the first time, provisions in the Maastricht Treaty which enhance the legal status of general action programmes on the environment; and, at the 1996 IGC, seeking to reinforce the treaty commitment in article 130r(2) to advance environmental integration.

The European Parliament and the Power of the Purse

The powers of the European Parliament in relation to the EU's annual budget are considerable, and in the past it has not been afraid to use, or threaten to use, them to extract concessions from the commission or the council in other policy sectors. Prior to the parliament's examination of the draft 1996 budget, informal discussions were held between DG XI and the parliament's Environment Committee on the possibility of using parliament's budgetary powers to further the process of integration. An opportunity to take this forward arose after the 1994 elections to the European Parliament, when Laurens Jan Brinkhorst, former director-general of DG XI, was elected a Member of the European Parliament (MEP) and appointed to the Committee on Budgets. He helped to influence the views of Mr James Ellis MEP, the Budget Committee's rapporteur on the draft 1996 budget, on the need for 'greening' EU spending, and was himself appointed the Budget Committee's rapporteur for the 1997 budget. Together with the Environment Committee's rapporteur on the draft budget – Karl-Heinz Florenz MEP (a Christian Democrat) – a close triangular relationship was established between the parliament's separate committees on budgets and the environment, and a few key officials from DG XI. A long-term process was begun of inserting environmental conditions within key budget lines. According to Florenz, '[a]s far as your rapporteur is concerned, 1996 will be the year of the greening of the budget'. His proposed amendments to the draft budget were explicitly designed 'to make up for the inadequacy which still exists in the commission's internal procedures concerning the environment'.[20] Parliament's resolution of 5 April 1995 on the guidelines for the 1996 budget included the following statement:

> [The European Parliament] requests that the Commission, through the application of the principle of sustainable development, include environmental protection in Community policies, so that the impact on the environment of Community actions be taken into account before any appropriations are granted.[21]

For the 1996 budget, the Environment Committee's proposed amendments focused principally on the appropriations of the structural and cohesion funds – at 29 billion ECU, over one third of the 1996 community budget, and a category of 'non-compulsory' expenditure over which parliament has the final say. As a result of an effective campaign in the late 1980s by environmental NGOs who highlighted the environmental damage caused by large infrastructure projects supported by community finance, the revision of the Structural Fund Regulations in 1993 incorporated a number of new requirements relating to environmental appraisals and the participation of 'environmental authorities' in decisions on applying the funds (Wilkinson, 1994). The failure to properly implement these safeguards on the ground in the member states, and the sometimes casual attitude to their enforcement shown by DG XVI, continued to feed the NGO campaign and the concern of sympathetic MEPs.

Accordingly, the Environment Committee's key amendment to the EU's 1996 draft budget threatened to freeze 50 per cent of the funds for the structural and cohesion funds in reserve unless the commission (for example, DG XVI) produced, by a deadline of 15 November 1995, an environmental code of conduct governing the future use of the funds. According to the committee, the code of conduct was to: require an environmental appraisal to be undertaken and published of every programme and project to be financed by the structural and cohesion funds; require the continuous monitoring and evaluation of the environmental impacts of structural and cohesion expenditure; and require regular reports on the above to the parliament and the council. The committee's opinion concluded: '[t]he committee on the environment must therefore do everything in its power to ensure that the first stage of this "greening" of the budget is a complete success: only then will genuine integration with other community policies be possible in the future'.[22] These proposals were accepted by the Committee on Budgets (although the deadline for the code of conduct was put back to 8 December), and subsequently endorsed by the parliament as a whole on 26 October 1995.

The effect on DG XVI was dramatic. At the end of November the commission issued a communication, jointly authored by the Regional Policy and Environment Commissioners, entitled *Cohesion Policy and the Environment*.[23] It included a declaration from Regional Affairs Commissioner Monika Wulf-Mathies that: 'The environment itself is a major factor for regional development, and I personally regard cohesion policy as a significant opportunity to operationalise sustainable development.' The communication set out a ten-point plan for tightening environmental requirements in the current use of the structural funds, within the current structural fund regulations. The communication promised: more money for environmental pilot projects, and preferential differentiation of the community's rate of assistance for environmentally friendly programmes; better project selection criteria, monitoring and evaluation of the environmental impact of structural fund activities; a clearer role for 'environmental authorities' on structural fund monitoring committees; tougher action by the commission on member states who fail to apply environmental regulations; and safeguards set out in the structural fund regulations. The communication promised to incorporate these strengthened procedures into the new structural and cohesion fund regulations, due to be revised in 1999.

In addition, on the precise deadline set by the parliament (8 December 1995), a letter of intent was dispatched from the commission to both Florenz and Detlev Samland (chair of the European Parliament's Committee on Budgets). The letter was signed by the regional affairs commissioner and the budget commissioner (Erkki Liikenen) and was written with the express agreement of President Santer. The letter made the following key commitments:

- the environmental role of structural fund monitoring committees would be strengthened;
- all proposed structural and cohesion fund projects larger than 50 million ECU would undergo an environmental appraisal to establish that there are no detrimental environmental effects, or that any such effects will be 'adequately compensated';
- resources within the commission would be made available to review such environmental assessments;
- an annual list of large projects funded by the structural and cohesion funds for which an environmental assessment had been undertaken would be published in the *Official Journal*; and
- the European Parliament would be sent details of these environmental assessments on request.[24]

Despite some ambiguous and tortuous wording, the Committee on Budgets was satisfied with this response, calling it 'a serious effort to strengthen the environmental dimension of budget implementation'.[25] As a result, the threat to place structural fund spending in reserve was lifted. However, in the 1996 budget as finally agreed with the council, alongside budget lines dealing with each of the structural and cohesion funds, there is a reference to the 'integration' requirement in article 130r(2), including the statement that:

> ...*appropriations for the structural funds cannot be implemented unless the measures financed by these funds comply with the provisions of the treaties and acts pursuant thereto, in particular those concerning environmental protection, as stipulated in Article 7 of Regulation (EEC) No 2052/88. They should be accompanied by an environmental impact commentary according to the principles of the Commission's letter of understanding of 8 December.*[26]

The exact legal status of this statement remains untested, but at the very least it represents a political commitment by the European Parliament to use its powers to block structural fund spending if the commission's commitments are unfulfilled. However, during the parliament's consideration of the following year's budget, Florenz expressed some satisfaction with the response of DG XVI. In his report for the Environment Committee on the draft 1997 budget, he also noted that the next set of targets jointly agreed by both the Environment and Budget Committee for 'greening' were the EU's agriculture, energy and development cooperation policies. In the case of agriculture, Florenz called upon DG VI to establish a code of good practice for the sustainable use of fertilisers and plant protection products. For his part, Brinkhorst called upon DG XI to establish a unit for assessing the environmental impact of expenditure in the targeted sectors, and for advancing the use of green technology.[27]

The Codecision Procedure and the Review of the 5EAP

In addition to associating itself with the European Parliament's use of its budgetary powers, DG XI has also attempted to increase its influence in relation to other DGs by using powers in the Maastricht Treaty which give a new legal status to environmental action programmes. As discussed above, when the 5EAP was debated by the Council of Ministers in February 1993, it was considered to be binding neither on the commission nor on the member states, since the council approved only the 'general approach and strategy of the programme' and not its detailed targets and timetables. Moreover, this approval was given in the form of a non-binding resolution. However, nine months following the council's resolution, on 1 November 1993, the Maastricht Treaty came into effect. For the first time, it gave in article 130s(3) a new legal status to general action programmes on the environment. These were henceforward to be established under the codecision procedure with the European Parliament, the outcome of which must be a legal instrument. Moreover, under this procedure, MEPs are given considerable powers of amendment (Wilkinson, 1993).

The 5EAP contained a provision for an interim review of the programme to be undertaken by the end of 1995. The European Environment Agency and the commission both issued reports reviewing progress, and both concluded that there should be accelerated progress towards meeting the targets set in the 5EAP.[28,29] Although the review applied to an action programme that was adopted before the Maastricht Treaty came into effect, DG XI nevertheless sought to use the provisions of article 130r(3) by proposing a draft decision incorporating what it described as an 'action plan to ensure the more efficient implementation of the approach set out in the programme'. In an accompanying communication, Environment Commissioner Mrs Bjerregaard observed that the commission's internal measures, adopted in June 1993 to integrate the environment across the work of the commission:

> ...*have still to be fully internalised by the services of the Commission in operational terms. In order to ensure the success of the priorities contained in the enclosed proposal, it will be necessary to pay increased attention to the implementation of integration measures. The college should commit itself to integration and ensure that this message is passed on to its services for action.*[30]

Most of the priorities set out in the draft decision were already identified in the 5EAP, or in subsequent commission communications. In a number of cases, however, the proposed measures were either new or more sharply defined. This was the case in a number of measures in the agriculture, transport, and tourism sectors, and in relation to noise, the structural funds, the range of policy instruments, and implementation and enforcement. The draft decision was discussed extensively by DG XI with the relevant DGs. Their agreement to the draft was presumably facilitated by the fact that the language is imprecise (for example, 'will further develop', 'investigate possibilities', 'special attention will be given to', 'consider means how to improve'), and that, unlike the 5EAP itself, there are no quantitative targets or timetables.

Predictably, the European Parliament's Environment Committee was dismissive of the commission's proposed decision, describing it as 'a step backwards in relation to the original Fifth Environmental Action Programme'.[31] In its report to the parliament, the committee put forward over 100 amendments and observed that only fear of further delays prevented the rejection of the commission's proposals in their entirety. The committee's report pointed out that the continuing deterioration in the state of the environment, described in the European Environment Agency's 1995 *Environment in the European Union*, required 'binding community actions, underpinned by fixed time frames' to ensure that priorities are actually put into practice. Among the measures proposed by the committee were:

- reform of the common agriculture policy's set-aside arrangements to recreate permanent natural zones;
- setting targets and timetables for reducing the use of pesticides in agriculture; these should be tabled by the commission before the end of 1997;
- a sustainable forest policy, also to be developed before the end of 1997;
- measures to attain a 20 per cent reduction of EU carbon dioxide emissions by 2005, 30 per cent by 2010, and 50 per cent by 2030 compared with 1990 levels;
- tougher measures, to be proposed by the commission before the end of 1997, to ensure the proper implementation and enforcement of community environmental legislation; and
- 50 per cent of EU funds currently spent in central and eastern Europe to be redirected from the promotion of fossil fuels and nuclear energy towards energy efficiency and support for renewables.

By the end of October 1996, the committee's report had not been debated by the parliament as a whole, nor had the Council of Ministers adequately discussed the 5EAP review. Negotiations between the European Community institutions were expected to be protracted, not least because the exact legal status of an action plan (or programme) established by the European Parliament and European Council is unclear. EU decisions are binding on those to whom they are addressed, and the proposed decision throughout refers to actions taken by the community. Some member states, including the UK, have argued that this has no immediate implications for member states, and that the proposed measures in the action plan may only be implemented by separate detailed proposals, which will be subject to separate negotiation and agreement.[32] However, the decision (once adopted) will certainly be binding on all commission DGs, so that they will be bound to propose specific legislation relating to the measures listed in the decision. DG XI's leverage within the commission has therefore been enhanced.

'Greening' the Treaty

References in the Maastricht Treaty to 'sustainable growth respecting the environment', and to the 'integration' imperative, provided DG XI with a legal underpinning for the 5EAP, and opened the way for references to sustainable development to be included in some subsequent items of legislation.[33] The IGC, launched in Turin in March 1996, has provided a further opportunity for DG XI to reinforce the community's commitment to sustainable development. The commission's opinion on the IGC proposes to reinforce 'the provisions of the treaty directed at sustainable development and a healthy environment'.[34] These proposals were included in the commission's opinion only at the last moment, at the insistence of Mrs Bjerregaard. The support of Austria, Sweden, Finland and some other member states has insured that the EU's environment policy forms part of the IGC agenda.

The commission's opinion proposes that 'the environment should be specifically incorporated into the other policies of the union', implying a further reinforcement of the integration imperative in article 130r(2). The opinion does not say which policies, or whether references to integration should be peppered throughout the treaty in articles dealing with agriculture, transport, economic and social cohesion. One possibility is that a single, new article 3(c) establishing the integration principle might be included in the treaty, with a horizontal function similar to the 'subsidiarity' requirement in article 3(b). According to Irish Minister for the Environment Brendan Howlin, there is support for this option among a majority of member states, as there is for revising the tortuous wording of article 2 and replacing it with an explicit reference to sustainable development as a fundamental objective of the European Union.[35] Both of these amendments can be expected to reinforce the hand of DG XI in its dealings with the rest of the European Commission.

Chapter 7

EUROPEAN COMMUNITY FUNDING AND THE SUSTAINABILITY TRANSITION

Clare Coffey

INTRODUCTION

Using European Commission estimates, approximately 17 billion ECU of the European Community's (EC) budget will directly fund environmental measures between 1994 and 1999 (see Appendix 7.1). The majority of these resources originate from the EC's structural and cohesion policy instruments. Although the difficulties in making such estimates are notorious, this represents 11 per cent of the total EC budget over that period, a significant proportion. The approach adopted to community funding, including funding for environmental projects, should therefore be a major factor in the successful transition of the EC towards sustainable development.

The integration of environmental considerations into other EC policies is an obligation laid by amendments to the Treaty of Rome, most recently the Treaty of Amsterdam which placed integration among the basic principles of the EC, as described by Nigel Haigh and David Wilkinson in this book. In agreement with the integration concept and priorities contained in the Community's Fifth Environmental Action Programme *Towards Sustainability* (CEC, 1992), it is necessary to ensure that all community financial support mechanisms take full account of environmental considerations.

This chapter provides a brief outline of the principle funding opportunities for environmental projects provided under the three financial instruments: LIFE (L'Instrument Financier pour l'Environnement), the structural funds and the cohesion fund. It then focuses on the newest of these three instruments, the cohesion fund, and assesses the fund's contribution to sustainable development.

EUROPEAN COMMUNITY FUNDING FOR THE ENVIRONMENT

EC funding for the environment is available under three principal community financial instruments. Each of these instruments, structural funds, LIFE and the cohesion fund, have developed out of differing circumstances and present

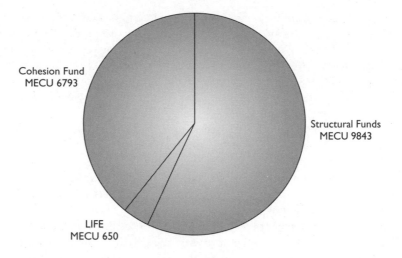

Cohesion Fund
MECU 6793

Structural Funds
MECU 9843

LIFE
MECU 650

Source: see Appendix 7.1.

Figure 7.1 Approximate EC financial contribution to direct
environmental measures, 1994 to 1999

specific opportunities for environmental programmes and projects. All three
are potentially significant tools for the institutional adjustment towards sustainable development in the EC, together amounting to over 157 billion ECU.
Figure 7.1 provides an estimate of the overall share of these funds which have
directly supported or are expected to support environmental measures under
each of the three financial instruments during the period of 1994 to 1999,
based on commission calculations.

Structural Funds

The structural funds are made up of four separate funds: the European Regional
Development Fund (ERDF), the European Social Fund (ESF), the Guidance
Section of European Agriculture Guidance and Guarantee Fund (EAGGF) and
the Financial Instrument for Fisheries Guidance (FIFG). The principal purpose
of the structural funds is to promote the economic and social development of
disadvantaged regions, groups and sectors of the community. Over the current
programme period, the total structural funds budget amounts to 141 billion
ECU (1994 prices). Expenditure under the funds is expected to represent
approximately one third of the community's total annual budget by 1999. All the
funds can potentially benefit environmental projects where these contribute to
regional development in any member state. Consequently, the structural funds
present by far the greatest opportunity for environmental projects.

The structural funds underwent considerable change in 1988, and their
combined resources rose in comparison to expenditure in previous years. While
still focused on the weakest economic regions in the community, their range of
objectives was also narrowed. For the first time, the structural funds' regula-

tions brought environment-related programmes and projects within the funds' remit, as long as such investment was linked to regional development. The effect was a substantial increase in expenditures on 'environmental protection' in the period of 1989–1993, estimated by the commission to be some 20 per cent of the total structural funds budget (CEC, 1991). However, as suggested below, such estimates give little indication of the actual environmental impact of expenditure on the ground.

The requirement that all projects contribute to regional development meant, in practice, that funds were administered and allocated by ministries with responsibilities in this area, to the exclusion of environmental authorities. Where 'environmental funding' occurred, it often came in the form of end-of-pipe technology: the environmental element of projects was generally added on to what were principally regional development projects. Many potentially innovative environmental projects failed to find a place in the programmes (Wilkinson, 1994). These problems and demands for improvements from key players such as the court of auditors, the European Parliament and heads of state and government led to pressure for a review of the funds and their relationship with EC environmental policy as embodied in successive EC environmental action programmes.

Following the 1989 elections, the European Parliament's environment and budget committees supported the introduction of an Environment 95 fund which was to represent 1 per cent of the EC budget by 1995. The 1990 budget, however, contained merely a token entry for an environment fund, prompting the parliament to threaten to block the 1991 budget. In addition to these parliamentary pressures, the Court of Auditors started to investigate community spending on the environment. At the European Council meeting in Dublin in 1990 a declaration by EC heads of state and government, *The Environmental Imperative*, called for a review of the overall level of budgetary resources devoted to the environment, in view of the unequal burden on member states to implement the community's environmental policy. As one response, the commission finally presented its proposal for a new fund, LIFE (see below), in 1991, though the fund's scope and budget fell considerably short of what the parliament demanded. A second and more significant effect was the eventual review of the structural funds in 1993 resulting in a proposal to extend the environmental provisions of the structural funds. In addition to the opportunities for funding environmental projects, the significant revision of the structural funds' regulations in 1993 introduced a package of 'environmental safeguards' to ensure that all (including non-environmental) projects supported by the funds should not inflict positive damage on the environment.

The revision of the structural funds introduced a requirement for 'environmental profiles' to accompany the submission of regional development plans by member states as the basis for future financial support. The profiles were to contain state of the environment reports, a strategic evaluation of the environmental impact of the Regional Development Plan, a description of the arrangements for involving environmental authorities in the various stages of preparation, implementation and monitoring of plans, and a description of arrangements to ensure compliance with community environmental legislation. In addition, the type of project to receive funds was broadened, allowing greater opportunity for more innovative 'environment' projects to be funded, including those falling under the guidance section of the EAGGF.

LIFE

As outlined above, in 1991 the European Commission presented a proposal for establishing a dedicated EC environment fund in reaction to pressures for increased and improved community spending on the environment. The new fund, now called LIFE, is the only financial instrument created purely for environmental purposes. In adopting the LIFE regulation (Council Regulation 1973/92), a number of smaller preexisting funds (ACE, ACNAT, NORSPA and MEDSPA) were replaced.

The initial drive to create a specific environment fund came from the fact that money was being spent on the environment in an uncoordinated fashion. A budget line entitled *Community Operations Concerning the Environment* was entered into the 1982 budget with an allocation of 6.5 million ECU. In 1984, following a commission proposal, an environment 'fund' was given legislative form by Regulation 1872/84 on Action by the Community relating to the Environment (ACE I), later replaced by Regulation 2242/87 (ACE II). ACE focused on demonstration projects for clean technologies and the protection of sensitive areas. At the end of 1991, new instruments were introduced to focus limited community environmental spending on three priority areas for the period 1992/1993: nature conservation (ACNAT); coastal waters and areas in northern European waters (NORSPA); and coastal waters and areas in the Mediterranean (MEDSPA). In total, funding allocations under these three instruments amounted to some 90 million ECU.

Demands in the early 1990s for a more substantial and unified fund for the environment finally led to the adoption of the LIFE financial instrument in 1992, with a budget of some 400 million ECU for the period of 1992–1995. LIFE was established to assist the development and implementation of community environmental policy, to provide assistance for non-EC member states bordering the Mediterranean and the Baltic Seas, and for relevant regional international agreements. In 1996 this was replaced by a new LIFE II instrument (Council Regulation 1404/96) with a budget of 450 million ECU and which is to run until the end of 1999. In comparison to the structural funds, however, the potential level of environmental investment offered by the LIFE instrument is comparatively small.

The Cohesion Fund

An additional source of finance for environmental projects, on top of the structural funds and LIFE, is the cohesion fund (Council Regulation 1164/94). In comparison to the structural funds, the cohesion fund is smaller but, with an allocation of some seven billion ECU for 'environmental projects' in only four member states in the period of 1993–1999, is nonetheless significant. The name cohesion fund reflects its ultimate aim of strengthening economic and social cohesion of the EC member states. To this end the application of the fund is restricted to the poorer member states, these being Spain, Portugal, Ireland and Greece at the start of the first phase of the fund in 1992. The broad nature of the fund, and its concentration on particular geographical regions which traditionally give a low priority to environmental protection, provides for a significant environmental improvement.

However, the cohesion fund was created quite simply as a financial transfer mechanism for moving funds from the richer to the poorer EC countries. In effect, the fund was created to enable Greece, Ireland, Spain and Portugal to comply with new conditions introduced to the Treaty of Rome by the Maastricht Treaty in 1992. These conditions called for reductions in the public borrowing levels of member states to meet the convergence criteria for the third stage of economic and monetary union. The Maastricht Treaty amendments (article 130d) thus included a requirement for the setting up of a cohesion fund by 1994 to facilitate this process. Eligibility for the fund is limited to countries with a GNP per capita of less than 90 per cent of the EC's average. In 1992 this criteria was met by Spain, Greece, Portugal and Ireland. If the fund is successful all four will eventually fall outside the fund's criteria, perhaps to be replaced by new 'cohesion' countries after 1999.

At the time of agreeing article 130d, public expenditure demands in the four countries were seen to stem especially from transport infrastructure projects and projects to implement EC environmental legislation relating to water and waste treatment. To limit the effect of such expenditure on public borrowing levels, article 130d specifically states the following: 'The cohesion fund shall provide a financial contribution to projects in the fields of environment and Trans-European networks in the area of transport infrastructure.' The overall size of the fund for transport and environment projects, and an indicative allocation among the eligible states, was agreed upon by EC heads of state and government meeting at the Edinburgh Summit in 1992. The fund was to amount to 15.15 billion ECU for the period of 1993 to 1999, to be allocated as follows:

* Spain   52–58 per cent;
* Greece   12–16 per cent;
* Portugal   12–16 per cent;
* Ireland   7–10 per cent.

The Edinburgh Summit clarified what constituted 'environmental projects': these were projects contributing to the achievement of the objectives of article 130r of the Treaty of Rome, including, though not limited to, projects resulting from measures adopted pursuant to article 130s of the treaty. Delays in ratifying the Maastricht Treaty meant that it was impossible to establish a cohesion fund by 1994. As an interim measure, the cohesion financial instrument was introduced in 1993 (Council Regulation 792/93) to run until the cohesion fund proper was eventually adopted in 1994.

The primarily financial nature of the fund was reinforced by arrangements adopted following Maastricht. At the time the fund was created, responsibility for administration was given to DG XIX – budgets of the European Commission, rather than to DG XVI – regional policy which administered other elements of structural policy, or to the directorates-general for transport (VII) or environment (XI). The criteria for project funding requires that the cost of individual projects, and in some cases groups of projects, not fall below ten million ECU, in effect allocating funds in favour of large infrastructure projects as opposed to labour-intensive, small-scale environmental projects. The cohesion fund contribution to individual projects is also unusually high compared to the structural funds and can represent as much as 85 per cent of the total project cost.

The apparent opportunities which the cohesion fund presents for environmental programmes and projects are considerably diminished by the emphasis on using the instrument as a financial transfer mechanism. Unlike the structural funds which had new environmental safeguards, similar safeguards were not applied to, or included in, the cohesion fund regulation. The latter includes only a reference to the fact that projects should be 'in keeping with' various community policies. Thus cohesion fund money can be applied to building a sewage works, since that is an 'environmental project' (to improve water quality), but there are no specific rules forming part of the cohesion fund regulation which say that the sewage works should not be built so as to damage sensitive habitats.

ANALYSIS OF COHESION FUND SPENDING IN THE FOUR COUNTRIES

The focus of the cohesion fund on investing in transport infrastructure projects and environmental projects presents opportunities for the environment in the following ways:

- the provision of significant investment in environmental projects which deliver genuine environmental improvements; and
- the greening of investment in transport projects in member states through the incorporation of environmental safeguards in order to adopt more sustainable transport systems.

This section provides an overview of community spending under the cohesion fund in order to assess the extent to which these opportunities have, in fact, been realised. As described earlier, the cohesion fund consists of 15.15 billion ECU, to be distributed over the period of 1993–1999 to the poorest member states in order to soften demands on their public borrowing levels. Projects, and in some cases groups of projects, are to be 'of a sufficient scale to have a significant impact in the field of environmental protection or in the improvement of Trans-European transport infrastructure networks' (article 10).

Projects are to cost at least ten million ECU in total, although exceptions may be allowed in justified cases. This criteria immediately indicates a preference for large-scale, infrastructure projects. Even groups of small, labour-intensive projects would be unlikely to amount to ten million ECU.

According to the cohesion fund regulation, when allocating finances, 'a suitable balance shall be struck between projects in the field of the environment and projects relating to transport infrastructure' (article 10). The fund may also provide 100 per cent finance for preliminary studies and technical support measures which contribute to the successful implementation of projects, including environmental impact assessments (EIAs). All projects financed by the cohesion fund are to be in keeping with the provisions of the treaties, including European Community policies concerning environmental protection, transport and Trans-European networks.

Allocating Funds to Transport and Environment Projects

The cohesion fund regulation stipulates that a balance must be struck between transport infrastructure projects and projects in the field of the environment. This should ensure that environmental projects are not ignored. Again the criteria that projects are of a 'significant scale' and should cost at least ten million ECU immediately indicates a preference for large infrastructure projects. The criteria would also appear to favour transport over environmental projects. Even groups of small, labour-intensive projects would be unlikely to amount to ten million ECU and would be costly to administer.

The evidence to date does indeed show a preference towards transport infrastructure expenditure, but not an overwhelming one. Of the total budget allocated within the fund between 1993 and 1996, some 52.7 per cent has gone to support transport projects. Table 7.1 provides a more detailed breakdown of cohesion fund allocation between environment and transport projects over the period of 1993–1996 in each of the four 'cohesion' countries. As the data illustrates, although only 52.7 per cent of the overall fund has gone to transport projects, yearly national allocations for transport infrastructure projects have regularly represented 60 per cent or more of the total. However, 1996 figures show an improvement in this regard.

The information indicates that the allocation under the cohesion fund has been biased towards transport projects, though this bias has been decreasing over the years. In terms of national expenditure, some countries show a clear imbalance, most notably Portugal where transport projects to the end of 1996 represent 57 per cent of total expenditure under the fund. Ensuring that the expenditure balance is reached in compliance with the cohesion fund regulation is one important aspect of using the fund for environmental ends. The commission's failure to ensure that a balance is achieved was highlighted by both the Court of Auditors (1995) and the European Parliament (1995).

Table 7.1 Allocation of the cohesion fund on environmental projects among eligible member states (million ECU – per cent)

	Greece	Spain	Ireland	Portugal	Total
1993	280	858	142	284	1565
Environment	175 (62)	252 (29)	56 (39)	123 (43)	606 (38.7)
Transport	105 (38)	606 (71)	86 (61)	161 (57)	958 (61.3)
1994	332	1018	168	334	1853
Environment	198 (60)	519 (51)	72 (43)	134 (40)	923 (49.8)
Transport	134 (40)	499 (49)	96 (57)	200 (60)	929 (50.2)
1995	388	1184	190	387	2149
Environment	228 (59)	574 (48)	93 (49)	147 (38)	1037 (48.2)
Transport	160 (41)	610 (52)	97 (51)	240 (62)	1113 (51.8)
1996	438	1342	222	439	2441
Environment	236 (53.8)	664 (49.4)	100 (46)	218 (49.6)	1217 (49.9)
Transport	202 (46.2)	678 (50.6)	122 (54)	222 (50.4)	1224 (50.1)
Total	1438 (100)	4402 (100)	722 (100)	1444 (100)	8008 (100)
Environment	837 (58.2)	2009 (45.6)	321 (44.5)	622 (43.1)	3785 (47.3)
Transport	601 (41.8)	2393 (54.4)	401 (55.5)	823 (57)	4223 (52.7)

Source: figures for 1993 and 1994, CEC, 1995a; figures for 1995 and 1996, CEC, 1997a.
Note: discrepancies in total figures are due to figures being rounded to the nearest per cent.

Projects Supported by the Cohesion Fund

Even if a balance of expenditure between 'environment' and 'transport' projects were reached, this would not in itself indicate that 50 per cent of the cohesion fund was being used for genuine environmental protection purposes. Both 'transport' and 'environment' projects have potentially adverse consequences for the environment. The potential impact of the fund can been placed in the following three categories (Karas, 1995):

- *direct effects* or impacts resulting from projects, such as the effect of road-building projects on sensitive habitats;
- *indirect effects*, such as the reduction of air pollution resulting from increased investment to reduce road traffic and congestion or greater environmental damage resulting from increased levels of road traffic; and
- *longer-term benefits from more sustainable forms of development*, such as decisions improving the efficiency in resource use.

Just as with the structural funds before it, the cohesion fund's failure to stem negative direct effects on the environment has subjected it to severe criticism. The possibility of further environmental damage continues due, in part, to the lack of environmental safeguards comparable to those introduced in the structural funds. The cohesion fund regulation requires only that projects are in keeping with the provisions of the treaty and community policies – that is, there are no specific requirements for environmental protection built into the regulation.

The following sections set out to assess specific projects, funded under both the environment and transport headings of the fund, in order to create a clearer picture of cohesion fund expenditure and its environmental impact, both positive and negative.

Environment Projects Under the Cohesion Fund

The cohesion fund regulation introduces a requirement that assistance for environmental projects will contribute to:

* 'the achievement of objectives of Article 130r of the treaty' – in other words, preserving and improving the quality of the environment, protecting human health, and the prudent and rational utilisation of natural resources, 'including projects resulting from measures adopted pursuant to Article 130s of the treaty'; and
* 'projects in line with the priorities conferred on community environmental policy by the Fifth Programme of Policy and Action in relation to the environment and sustainable development' [article 3(1)].

The commission's priorities in selecting eligible projects were those likely to have the greatest economic and social impact in relation to the cost of the investment (CEC, 1995a). In practice this has meant that large infrastructure projects required to implement just three directives relating to urban waste water treatment, drinking water and waste (directive 91/271) have been dominant among projects receiving funding. In some cases, nature conservation and natural heritage projects have also received financial support. Table 7.2 provides an overview of the main categories of projects funded by the cohesion financial instrument under the environment heading.

Table 7.2 Breakdown of environment projects approved under the cohesion fund in 1993–1994

Environment projects	Assistance allocated (million ECU)	Percentage of total
Water	582.79	76.3
Waste	18.78	2.5
Erosion	98.14	12.8
Heritage preservation	7.42	1.0
Industrial pollution	18.08	2.4
Nature conservation	29.87	3.9
Other	8.94	1.2

Source: CEC, 1995a

Table 7.2 shows clearly the weight given to water-related projects. Although some element of funding has gone to support small-scale, labour-intensive projects, such as financing measures in the Spanish National Parks, most projects consist of large engineering proposals. The main focus of the fund has been on the supply and quality of water, drainage and the treatment of waste water and sewage. Specific priorities of individual member states among different types of water projects have been variable. Ireland, for example, has been targeting waste water treatment in line with targets set in its environmental action programme.

The large water supply projects funded by the cohesion fund have been even more controversial. Such projects could be seen as falling within article 130r of the treaty by 'protecting human health'; however, strictly speaking they are not projects which improve the environment, and as such illustrate contradictions in the treaty. In the area of water management, the EC's Fifth Environmental Action Programme has, as its objective, to balance the supply and demand of water – which is to be achieved through the rational use and management of resources. In Portugal, Greece and Spain large portions of the cohesion fund have gone to water-supply projects in cities, to alleviate water shortages in the short term, while little or no money has been applied to demand management or improvements in the efficiency of water use. These projects were criticised by the Court of Auditors in 1995 as rarely forming 'part of a general action plan for water management, specifying the strategy to be followed for each basin and also including measures to prevent excessive withdrawals'. In some cases, water-supply projects offered no direct or indirect environmental benefit but caused a direct impact on the environment. Box 7.1 provides a brief case study on a Greek water-supply project funded under the cohesion fund's environment heading, and which is seen as compounding environmental damage already caused to a wetland complex by another project.

Transport Projects under the Cohesion Fund

The cohesion fund regulation states that eligible transport measures for assistance under the fund are:

> ...*transport infrastructure projects of common interest...which are identified within the framework of the Trans-European Transport Network (TEN) guidelines; and other transport infrastructure projects contributing to the achievement of the TEN objectives of article 129b (article 3(1)).*

The preamble to the cohesion fund regulation refers to the European Commission's *Green Paper on the Impact of Transport on the Environment* and its call for the development of more environmentally friendly transport systems which take account of the sustainable development needs of the member states. In general, projects are to be 'in keeping with community policies', including those concerning environmental protection, transport and TENs.

Community policies set out clear demands for the incorporation of

---

**BOX 7.1 WATER SUPPLY PROJECTS FUNDED BY THE
COHESION FUND: GREECE**

Environment projects in Greece include those relating to water, waste
management, soil and forest protection, and a separate category of projects
known as special projects. According to the Greek Ministry of National
Economy, special projects represented in excess of 65 per cent of total
funding under the environment heading of the cohesion fund. In 1993,
more than 85 per cent of the special project budget (99 million ECU) went
to the so-called Evinos water-supply project for diverting water from the
River Evinos to meet water shortages in Athens (Fousekis and Lekakis,
1995). A 1994 report by BirdLife International points to the need for priority to be given to water conservation measures before additional water
supply measures are initiated. The Athens water distribution system is
known as highly inefficient and presents enormous potential for reducing
water losses. According to the report, the Evinos project would remove
water from a wetland complex, compounding the environmental damage
caused by another water diversion project on the River Acheloos (see also
Chapter 12).

---

environmental dimension within transport policy. The Fifth Environmental
Action Programme refers specifically to:

- reducing mobility and the development of alternatives to road transport;
- improving the competitive position of environmentally friendly modes of
  transport; and
- maintaining biodiversity through sustainable land management in and
  around key habitats.

Nevertheless, the majority of transport projects supported by the cohesion
fund are for the construction of major road infrastructures. In the case of
Ireland, a 1993 draft Greenpeace report highlighted the fact that all Irish transport projects approved for funding in 1993 were road projects (Hey and
Tiltcher, 1993), although other types of transport projects have since been
funded. In a resolution on the cohesion financial instrument in 1995, the
European Parliament expressed its 'disquiet at the undue priority accorded to
road transport infrastructure, which accounted for 72.2 per cent of the total,
thus serving to marginalise other environmentally more acceptable modes of
transport'. A detailed breakdown of the type of 'transport' projects funded is
provided in Table 7.3.

With reference to the environmental effect of projects, it is road projects in
particular which have been attacked by environmental organisations. Such projects
have resulted in direct impacts on the environment, including damage to particularly sensitive areas such as those designated under the EC's Birds Directive

Table 7.3 Principal types of transport projects approved for assistance between April 1993–May 1994

Type of project	Cohesion instrument contribution (million ECU)	Total (per cent)
Roads	808	72
Rail	170	15
Airports	92	8
Maritime	33	3
Vessel traffic management system	16	1
Total	1118	100

Source: CEC, 1995a

(Council Directive 79/409). Box 7.2 provides a case study of a transport project heavily criticised by environmental NGOs for its environmental impact.

Apart from the direct impacts on surrounding areas, there is the obvious danger that provision of extra road space will lead to an increase in road traffic, contrary to the objective noted above in the Fifth Environmental Action Programme. Even where it has been alerted to possible infringements of EC environmental legislation by NGOs, the European Commission has not always initiated proceedings. However, DG XVI (regional and cohesion policy) has recently indicated a possible change in the approach to projects seen to be in violation of environmental policy (IER, 1996).

TENs Guidelines

In allocating funds, the commission has given priority to those projects falling within the approved or proposed guidelines on trans-European networks ('TENs). Guidelines for high-speed trains, roads, internal waterways and combined transport were adopted in October 1993. However, a number of projects have received support before the adoption of corresponding community plans for such networks. In the case of multimodal projects, according to the Court of Auditors' 1995 report, proposed TENs guidelines were in fact drawn up around the funded projects, rather than vice versa. This is arguably a general weakness of the TENs guidelines, in that they tend primarily to reflect the investment priorities of individual member states and as yet lack any overarching strategy, far less a strategic environmental assessment. Steps are currently under way to carry out a strategic environmental assessment of the TENs plans, but it is difficult to see how, if at all, this will influence the project selection procedures of individual member states.

When approaching the cohesion fund, the commission selects projects rather than programmes. In the absence of a broader framework for evaluating plans or programmes, individual projects are assessed on a case-by-case basis, irrespective of the cumulative effect a number of such projects might have. The absence of a framework also precludes presentation or assessment of a

---

BOX 7.2 COHESION FUND TRANSPORT PROJECT RESULTING IN A NEGATIVE IMPACT ON THE ENVIRONMENT: PORTUGAL

In 1991 a government office was created to select the preferred roadway crossing of the Tejo River outside Lisbon. Three alternative routes were analysed in terms of their potential traffic diversion, with the results indicating the west corridor route to be preferable. From economic and social perspectives, the central corridor option represented the best option. Yet, in 1992, the eastern route, between Sacavém–Montijo, was chosen by the government. Construction of the bridge along this route was to impinge upon a designated Special Protection Area under the EC Birds Directive but, contrary to national and community requirements, was agreed without an environmental assessment or public consultation.

The estimated total direct cost for constructing the Sacavém–Montijo bridge was 1000 million ECU. The project was presented to the cohesion fund in 1994 with a request for some 300 million ECU. An EIA was performed as required under EC legislation and public consultation took place in the three months following. The works were to involve five kilometres of construction within an area in the Tejo Estuary designated as a Special Protection Area and a wetland site of international importance under the Ramsar Convention. Despite the importance of the area and the existence of alternative routes, the commission did not lodge a complaint against the Portuguese government. Instead, it accepted compensatory measures in respect of the site, namely a 400-hectare enlargement of the zone. In March 1995 the contract to build the bridge was signed.

The construction of the bridge directly led to an encroachment of the sensitive natural area. In addition, and more importantly, the existence of the bridge will have the effect of raising considerably the value of land and creating a new urban area in the rural municipalities of the Tejo Estuary. This in turn is likely to engender additional road traffic. This was one aspect not considered by the EIA, which also failed to look at alternatives in terms of the environmental impact or technical advantages.

Source: CEEETA, 1995a/b; see also Chapter 11.

---

package of projects which might, for example, contribute to a modal shift in favour of rail. Within the structural funds, by contrast, a more strategic analysis is employed which enables the impact of overall plans on the environment to be assessed using strategic environmental assessment.

Preliminary Studies and Technical Support Measures

The commission and member states are to ensure the effective monitoring and evaluation of projects funded by the cohesion fund. Where they are considered appropriate, systematic appraisals and evaluations of expenditure also take place. However, in the majority of the 'cohesion' countries, and within the commission itself, there is often insufficient technical support available for *ex-ante* and *ex-post* monitoring and evaluation of projects. As a support measure for carrying out these activities, the cohesion fund regulation allows 100 per cent financial assistance to be granted in two specific areas (article 3(2)):

- 'preliminary studies related to eligible projects'; and
- 'technical support measures', including studies contributing to the 'appraisal, monitoring and evaluation of projects and ensuring the coordination and consistency of projects, particularly their consistency with other community policies'. Other eligible measures include 'comparative studies to assess the overall impact of community assistance'.

Studies in this area may represent up to 0.5 per cent of the total financial allocation under the fund, in other words 75.8 million ECU. This provision therefore presents an important opportunity to ensure that existing environmental safeguards are applied to the full in these countries.

In practice, only a small proportion of the support allocation has been used to ensure that environmental safeguards are applied. In some cases money has been used to bolster the commission's own technical capacity for handling project applications. Several studies have been carried out to improve project selection in the member states and a further set of studies has been funded at the request of the member states.

Monitoring and Evaluating of Projects in the Four Eligible Member States

The size and distribution of the cohesion fund provides for substantial financial support for a wide range of environmental projects. Yet the fund's actual operation to date has failed to meet the expectations of many environmental organisations and actually inflicted environmental damage in many cases. A major contributing factor has been the absence of adequate mechanisms for *ex-post* and *ex-ante* monitoring and evaluation of projects.

One of the strengths of the cohesion fund, in contrast to the structural funds, is that projects are directly funded by the commission, thereby enabling the commission to apply monitoring and evaluation procedures more rigorously in order to ensure that each project fully respects community policies. At a basic level, the following monitoring and evaluation mechanisms are important for integrating environmental concerns in cohesion fund spending:

- *ex-ante* evaluation, particularly prior environmental impact assessment using indicators;
- project selection arrangements;
- monitoring and evaluation of project impacts; and
- institutional arrangements and the role of environmental authorities.

The sections below aim to outline the current role of these individual mechanisms, and suggest a number of opportunities for improvement.

Prior Environmental Impact Assessment

While the arrangements for funding applications under the cohesion fund allow for direct intervention by the commission, no strategic framework is provided to set priorities over the lifetime of the fund. This is in contrast to the strategic 'programmes' applied under the structural funds system.

In the absence of strategic environmental assessments, a crucial environmental safeguard that can be introduced at the project selection stage is the prior environmental appraisal of individual projects. In practice, however, the application of environmental assessments has fallen short of requirements, as illustrated by the case of the Spanish Adra bypass project (see Box 7.3). In this instance, an assessment of the project's environmental impact was undertaken after completion of the project itself.

In the case of large infrastructure projects, there may be a legal requirement for an EIA to be undertaken by the member state in compliance with the EC directive (council directive 85/337). Even where assessment is required by law, however, fundamental problems in relation to such assessments have been identified, particularly in countries where the implementation and enforcement of the directive is considered to be weak. In many cases, inadequate EIA procedures have led to numerous problems, including the following:

- failure to identify key impacts, particularly those relating to indirect and long-term effects of projects;
- the fragmentation of an EIA, where impacts of individual sections of projects are assessed, rather than the overall effects of the project as a whole;
- failure to examine meaningfully all alternative project options;
- an insufficient level of expertise in relevant authorities to conduct an EIA; and
- failure to require and monitor environmental mitigation as part of the EIA (BirdLife, 1995).

The approach to an EIA may simply be as an after thought or 'add-on' to a project proposal rather than allowing the EIA to influence the contents of the proposal (Karas, 1995). Some or all of these problems have arisen in several cohesion fund projects, including those described in this paper, and call for tighter procedures to avoid their repetition in the future.

Clearly, there are also projects which are not subject to the EIA directive at all, but which may nevertheless have a serious impact on the environment. In the case of all projects, the member states are to submit information to the commission enabling the possible impact on the environment to be assessed. From the many decisions to grant financial assistance, it would appear that such information is not, in fact, provided. In numerous cases information given on the 'assessment of environmental impact' points to the positive environmental

---

BOX 7.3: ENVIRONMENTAL IMPACT ASSESSMENT OF THE ADRA PROJECT: SPAIN

The Adra bypass project involved the upgrading of a road into a motorway. Payment of EC money was made in instalments. The second instalment was conditional on the agreement of the Spanish authorities to apply corrective measures to minimize negative environmental impacts. The undertaking and the EIA for the project were completed, however, after the work itself. Clearly, few environmental considerations could be built into the project at this stage, nor could alternative solutions to traffic flow problems be considered.

The 1995 Court of Auditors report on the implementation of the cohesion financial instrument was critical of the commission for effectively failing to assess the project, both in terms of cost-benefit analysis and EIA, and for not considering possible alternative means of accommodating the relevant traffic flows.

---

effects of projects, and in some cases states that an EIA has been carried out. It is rare that unforeseen impacts are discussed in detail. Furthermore, it is not uncommon for there to be no mention of environmental impacts at all.

Project Selection, Monitoring and Evaluation

Once a project has been selected by a member state an application is forwarded to the commission. The cohesion fund regulation stipulates that a cost-benefit analysis of the proposed project is to be included. It is still the case that in terms of cost-benefit analysis, the emphasis is on conventional 'value for money' considerations and excludes external 'environmental' costs from calculations. In relation to environmental projects, the commission accepts that traditional cost-benefit analysis may be inconclusive, and that other forms of quantified analysis may be acceptable. The same qualification is not, however, applied to transport projects.

Before projects are approved, the commission determines the expected impact of the project, so that the potential and actual impact of the project can be assessed as part of an ongoing monitoring and evaluation process. More detailed rules for monitoring and evaluation are set out in individual decisions which approve projects (article 13).

The importance of using appropriate physical and financial indicators in the monitoring and evaluation process is identified in the 1993 structural funds regulations, as well as in the cohesion fund regulation. The proper quantification and assessment of a project's impact on the environment might be improved through the use of agreed indicators. Indeed, the use of suitable indicators could improve the integration of environmental concerns at all stages, including the ability of monitoring committees to monitor and evaluate projects effectively. Traditional indicators are of limited value for environmental assessment – for example, in the case of transport projects where the focus is on the length of roads or the general physical size of the road network. Although some examples of more positive environmental indicators exist, a much broader range of appropriate indicators is required to assess and evaluate projects and groups of projects on an ongoing basis.

In order to incorporate the wider effects of projects, in terms of the environment and sustainable development, it is important that the definition of costs and benefits is sufficiently broadened, or that a sufficiently robust environmental assessment is placed alongside the cost-benefit analysis in the assessment process. Improvements in the environmental component of the project selection criteria could also be used as a powerful force for promoting sustainable development by filtering out less environmentally desirable projects.

Institutional Mechanisms and the Role of Environmental Authorities

National studies on the application of community support in Greece (Fousekis and Lekakis, 1995) and Portugal (CEEETA, 1995a/b) illustrate shortcomings in incorporating environmental safeguards within cohesion fund projects (see Box 7.4). Although partly resulting from inadequate selection, monitoring and evaluation mechanisms, the overarching political and institutional framework is an important factor. Greece and Portugal in particular have a limited capability, technically and practically, to ensure that adequate measures are taken to evaluate projects before, as well as during and after, the work is carried out. The result is that responsible ministries may not give proper attention to the administration of the fund and instead select projects primarily in order to secure large sums of community funding, irrespective of the project's environmental impact.

In terms of transport projects under the cohesion fund, responsibility for initial project selection at member state level is often vested solely in those ministries with transport responsibilities. Environmental authorities or NGOs are often found to have little or no input during the project identification process. The integration of environmental considerations, particularly in the case of transport projects, would be improved considerably by the meaningful participation of environmental authorities at these initial stages of project selection.

After agreeing to fund a project, the respective member states must establish a monitoring committee. In three of the four cohesion countries, monitoring committees consist of representatives from various government ministries. However, unlike monitoring committees set up under the structural funds, their membership is smaller and not representative of 'local partnerships'. The make-up of the committees was criticised by the European Parliament, which called for elected regional and local authorities to be present on the monitoring committees and for these to be given additional powers in areas of project selection and management (council regulation 1164/94).

Despite these significant shortcomings, environmental NGOs are more effective in raising awareness of the issues. Already, cooperation between

---

BOX 7.4: INSTITUTIONAL ARRANGEMENTS FOR EVALUATING PROJECTS: PORTUGAL

Approximately 2700 million ECU will be allocated to Portugal under the cohesion fund. Approximately 58 per cent is to be invested in the transport sector according to the transport operational programme which focuses on road transport. Transport projects are selected by the Ministry of Public Works, Transport and Communications whose policy is directed towards the implementation of the National Roads Plan. In the past, the ministry has been in conflict with the Ministry of Environment, particularly in relation to environmental impact studies.

Environment projects are selected by the Ministry of Environment, which focuses expenditure on projects involving water, waste water and solid waste facilities, and water resources, including construction and increasing the capacity of dams. Some remediation measures in fragile coastal areas and wetlands are also covered. A major area of concern is the lack of resources for ensuring that funds are allocated to appropriate projects. In the early days of the cohesion fund, Portuguese authorities were keen to select big projects which were 'available' to soak up the financial allocation. In some cases this involved reviving otherwise dead project proposals. In effect, the funding had little impact on reducing the national public borrowing requirement the principal aim of the cohesion fund.

Source: CEEETA, 1995a/b; see also Chapter 11.

---

national and European NGOs has become more commonplace, as the highly controversial Acheloos project in Greece demonstrated (Fousekis and Lekakis, 1996). Organisations such as BirdLife International and the Worldwide Fund for Nature (WWF) have contributed by providing technical expertise, financial support and access to an environmental network of similar organisations. The result is the building of networks with the collective capacity and information to increase pressure for improvements.

GREENING THE COHESION FUND

Significance of Greening the Fund

Considerable attention has been focused on greening areas of European Community funding, particularly under the structural funds. Visible improvements, such as the introduction of new environmental safeguards, have resulted. Much of the pressure for change has come from the European Parliament and a number of key international NGOs operating in the field. Less attention has been paid to greening the cohesion fund for a number of reasons, including the fact that the size of the fund is smaller and that environmental pressure for change has been weaker in those countries where the fund is applied.

However, the size of the overall fund means that it represents a significant aspect of community policy and therefore has a significant impact on the shift towards sustainable development in the 'cohesion' countries, where environmental priorities are often secondary to economic priorities. The potential of the fund to support direct and genuine environmental measures is important, as is the need to reduce the positive damage inflicted upon the environment – as a direct or indirect result of projects being funded. Even if changes cannot be achieved within the lifetime of the first round of expenditure under the cohesion fund, the greening of any future cohesion fund regulations should nonetheless remain a priority. The commission's 1997 communication *Agenda 2000* (CEC, 1997b) sets out a proposed future financial framework for the period of 2000 to 2006. In this document, the commission proposes that the cohesion fund is 'maintained in its present form' for the period of 2000 to 2006, and that the fund should have available a total of some 20 billion ECU for the current member states, thus increasing the size of the fund by 30 per cent. Furthermore, it is proposed that aid of one billion ECU per year is made available to central and eastern European countries applying to become members of the EU. Funds would be primarily intended to bring the applicant countries' infrastructures up to community standards, particularly in the transport and environment fields, along the lines of existing cohesion fund transfers. Large sums could thus be allocated in the future, using the present cohesion fund as a blueprint.

Advances in Greening the Fund

A somewhat limited mid term review of the cohesion fund arrangements took place in 1996, and a full evaluation is to be undertaken by 1999. The principal purpose of the 1996 review was to evaluate the ongoing eligibility of the four 'cohesion' countries. The opportunity was not taken to improve the institutional mechanisms and assessment procedures in order to maximise the potential offered by the existence of the current fund.

The full review of the cohesion fund regulation in 1999 could be used to alter the approach of the fund from a project-based to a more strategic plan or programme approach, with attendant clarification of the aims and objectives and environmental statements comparable to the structural fund requirements. DG XVI is launching its evaluation process on the environmental dimension of projects financed by the cohesion fund in preparation for the 1999 review. In the meantime, several important changes have already occurred. A significant institutional development has transferred responsibility for the cohesion fund, originally with DG XIX, to DG XVI at the time the new commission was installed in January 1995. In institutional terms, this brings the cohesion funds closer to the structural funds, and provides a greater impetus for the introduction of the environmental component of the structural funds to the cohesion fund. The contrasting environmental arrangements between cohesion and structural funds are therefore an increasingly obvious focus for both DG XI and DG XVI.

As a result of DG XVI gaining responsibility for administering the cohesion fund, continuing attempts by the European Parliament to use its budgetary powers to influence structural fund spending are now also being used to influence cohesion fund spending. In the EC's 1996 budget, the European Parliament inserted calls on member states to comply with community legislation on the environment in order to have access to the cohesion fund. All financed projects are to be covered by a prior environmental impact assessment and must indicate the authorities and environmental organisations involved in that operation. However, the parliament's demands have only partially been met.

In November 1995 the commission adopted a communication from the environment and regional affairs commissioners on options for achieving greater synergy between the community's 'cohesion' and environmental policies. The paper (CEC, 1995b) was in response to European Parliament threats to block spending under the EC's structural and cohesion funds for failure to provide adequate information on their environmental impact. Contained within the paper are proposals to take measures within the framework of the current regulations, including improved monitoring of member state projects, improved assessment of measures having an indirect effect on the environment, and a review of selection criteria applied by member states, to reflect a project's contribution towards sustainability. The commission proposes to play a more active role in monitoring infringements of environmental legislation within the operation of the cohesion funds. In addition, non-governmental organisations and the general public are to be allowed greater involvement, in order to increase transparency and the environmental quality of structural fund and cohesion fund activities. Despite the various options set out in the 1995 communication, however, there has been rather limited evidence of real progress towards 'greening' expenditure under the cohesion fund.

CONCLUSIONS

The cohesion fund was established as a financial transfer mechanism to increase economic and social cohesion among the EC member states. Despite its principal purpose, the fund offered a significant opportunity for supporting genuine environmental measures in countries where the environment is often low on the political agenda. In allocating 'environmental' funding, however, the fund has been primarily targeted at large infrastructure projects, which in many cases have had detrimental direct and indirect effects on the environment. Among the projects selected as 'environmental', many have involved excessively large, concrete projects aimed at protecting human health while causing damage to the environment as a result. Similarly, transport projects supported by the cohesion fund display few if any of the characteristics needed in the transition towards sustainable development.

Historically, the European Parliament has been instrumental in greening the EC's expenditure and, in keeping with this tradition, is now taking measures to improve environmental integration within the cohesion fund. The parliament's current activities could have far-reaching implications for the future implementation of the cohesion fund, including instruments adopted in its place thereafter. In the first instance, it could result in the adoption of a code of conduct for applying safeguards to cohesion fund expenditures similar to those which were introduced within the structural funds in 1993.

Increased pressure to improve the environmental aspects of the cohesion fund also stems from stronger participation of national and international environmental NGOs. Together with the parliament's actions, these pressures may be sufficient to force the commission's hand in terms of correcting many of the current shortcomings of spending under the fund. Such improvements could be of enormous significance for the future funding of sustainable development, particularly in light of the commission's Agenda 2000 proposals and the EC's enlargement to the east.

APPENDIX 7.1 EC FINANCE FOR DIRECT ENVIRONMENTAL MEASURES IN THE PERIOD 1994–1999

Many of the calculations contained in the table below are based on estimates of one form or another. Nevertheless, the table is produced to provide a rough indication of EC financial expenditure on direct environmental measures during the period 1994–1999.

Total allocation to fund (MECU)	Allocation for period 1994–99 (MECU)	Contribution to direct environmental measures (MECU)
Structural Funds 1994–99		
141,000	141,000	9843[1]
LIFE Instrument 1992–99		
850	650[2]	650
Cohesion Fund 1993–99		
15,150	13,585[3]	6793[4]
Total	155,235	17,286

Notes
1   The figure includes expenditure on direct environmental measures under Objectives 1, 2 and 5b, using commission calculations set out in the commission communication *Cohesion Policy and the Environment* (COM(95)509). The total figure for Objective 2 is derived by doubling the figure given for the period 1994–96.
2   Calculated by adding 50 per cent of LIFE I budget (200 million) and LIFE II budget (450 million).
3   Calculated by subtracting expenditure for 1993 (1565 million).
4   Calculation based on 50 per cent of fund going to 'environmental' measures.

Part III

THE EVOLUTION OF NATIONAL SUSTAINABLE DEVELOPMENT STRATEGIES

EDITORIAL INTRODUCTION

The national reports in the succeeding chapters indicate a variety of experiences of implementing Agenda 21. No single country has made exemplary progress, and no one country has failed to act at all. Instead, there is evidence that A21 has not been ignored and that there has been some form of response across the board; it is the extent, nature and quality of this response that we have tried to capture. Each national report is a snapshot of the initial implementation of A21. However, by the time this book is published, events will have happened to make some of this material out of date. Hopefully the analysis of the underlying processes, trends and structural forces will continue to ring true and provide insight into the evolving politics of the transition towards sustainability.

In Chapter 1, we pointed out that there are three key concepts of sustainable development, namely reliable growth, stewardship and empowerment. To achieve a synthesis of all three, we have proposed a process through a variety of formal and informal devices. The national reports that follow indicate that there have been no moves towards processes of this kind. Institutions of democracy are key to this element of the sustainability transition. We note that democracy, locality, and sustainability are inherently part of the political culture of European nations. This means that the triggers of change will vary enormously. For instance, in the social democratic countries of Scandinavia, Austria and the Low Countries, the levers are primarily governmental and regulatory. But in more anarchic France, local political opinion counts for much, while in Greece, Italy and Spain governments at all levels are largely discredited. There, the people look to the media for their assurance, and to the robust activism of watchdog pressure groups. In the UK there is a fascinating tussle between the growing power of local government set against a modernising but still centralised nation state.

In general, we observe that the state of democracy in Europe, notably in Greece and Portugal where party allegiance is passed through families, is not in a position to cope with the new demands being placed upon it. Environmental impact assessments are rarely taken seriously, and are certainly not used to generate public discussion on the need to reach the chosen objective. As for the more strategic level of integrated environmental assessments, these are not evident in any of the countries studied. In short, efforts are made to produce more codified information, notably in the UK, Norway and Germany, but there are few effective mechanisms at a national level for integrating that information into strategic sustainability objectives. Without adequate information-gathering, dissemination and assessment procedures to inform policy, vital evaluation mechanisms which feed back into policy objectives are unable to operate properly. Therefore the democratic process required to support sustainable development is weak and undernourished. Citizens are barely informed, let alone empowered, except by political change that lies well beyond the domains of the sustainability transition.

The national studies also reveal the problematic dependence of environment ministers and their ministries on the more politically and economically powerful ministries in order to achieve any meaningful response to A21. Notably in Norway, the UK and in Portugal, political astuteness has been required to combat the relative apathy or even hostility of the powerful economic ministries. Indeed, it is unlikely that any realistic moves towards sustainable development could rely on the sole initiative of an environment minister or ministry. The key economic ministries have to be in a pole position, and there has to be some element of support from other powerful ministries, such as health, agriculture, transport and education. The transition cannot rely solely on the relative power and political tactics of environmental politicians, although they can provide impetus at crucial times in the policy-making and implementation process.

The national reports show that the indifference to the sustainability idea by finance, trade and industry, transport, and employment ministries means that any hope for integration in key sectors of policy (green accounting, ecological tax reform) are all but non-existent, at least for the time being. In Norway the environment ministry led a green tax commission that included finance ministry economists. So the conclusions had political weight, particularly because the finance ministry was, in any case, anxious to streamline distorting tax burdens. The trick, as in the case of climate protection policies (see O'Riordan and Jäger, 1996), is to seek allies early on whose interests coincide for non-sustainability reasons. The more difficult trick is to translate this support into permanent acceptance of the wider and more fundamental principles of sustainability; action can then be taken. So far that has largely defeated even the most shrewd and active of environmental politicians and ministries.

This set of essays reveals that only tentative steps are being taken in the direction of sustainable development, and that these are primarily of a developmental kind, with stewardship in the distance and empowerment out of sight. We shall note in the subsequent section that LA21 is beginning to bite in these areas, notably in the UK and more recently in Norway and Germany. However, this is prevented in all countries, most noticeably in Portugal and Greece, through electoral-democratic reforms because of the changing and uncertain role of local government. At the national level the important signs of hope lie in the slow shift to wider evaluation mechanisms, policy integration, and the recognition of a need to drive sustainability indicators forward. Even if these are not working very effectively there is at least a recognition that such elements need to be in place. Therefore, embryonic efforts to develop them are very much underway. The development of green accounts in the UK, Norway and Germany, for example, is progressive, as is the publication of targets and indicators in the UK and in Norway, even though these are still primitive in character. The use of interdepartmental guidance on valuation techniques that embrace green accounts, ecological economics and risk management is a sincere attempt to change evaluation procedures. But until the policy signals encourage longer pay-back periods and the rigorous application of the precautionary principle, only a small step in the transition will be achieved. The 'continuation' rather than the 'stewardship' ethos still holds sway.

Technocratic bureaucracy also hampers this progress. The almost universal drive to adopt efficiency-management measures, competitive tendering, annual budget allocations that disrupt long-term strategies, and short-term, part-time contracts for facilitators and coordinators all serve to penalise the transition. Nevertheless, there is a response to A21 in all the countries studied. That it emerges within the discourse of markets and regulation should come as no surprise. Indeed, the response of the business sector is highlighted in some of the national reports as evidence of this. Firms are undertaking full environmental audits, and they are beginning to look at sourcing of products and to embark on the tortuous road to ecoefficiency. However, social and critical audits are a rarity and are normally hidden from probing NGO eyes. Product stewardship is enshrined in regulatory codes of practice, primarily in northern Europe, but again this potentially innovative approach to sustainable consumption is sporadic and ephemeral.

In short, all these reports suggest a mixed response. Part of the problem is the longevity of the environmental idea. This breeds fatigue at the 'continuation-stewardship' interface, and encourages many to see success in the old endeavours of pollution control, recycling and nature conservation. The main reason is that the sustainability message is not institutionalised in moves towards empowerment and revelation. Until that happens, there will be no reservoir of public pressure and community-led initiatives to amalgamate with a powerful social movement towards sustainability. Tinkering at the top is certainly not enough, but it is a start.

Chapter 8

SUSTAINABLE DEVELOPMENT: THE UK NATIONAL APPROACH[1]

Heather Voisey and Tim O'Riordan

INTRODUCTION

The UK takes its international reporting obligations relatively seriously. Its A21 response has been incorporated into a longer running environmental policy reporting exercise. This exercise is an attempt to integrate departmental performance and planning into a series of targets and reporting measures which themselves are innovative. Upon this structure has been placed further innovative mechanisms of awareness raising, policy integration and review that are external to central government. These form the essence of the A21 response and the beginnings of the sustainability transition.

This chapter will look first at how the concept of sustainable development is defined, arguing that there are three separate but interlinked approaches within policy-making in the UK. It subsequently looks at the two processes framing the UK's response to A21: the white paper (HM Government, 1990) process, which was the first comprehensive statement of environmental policy in the UK; and the sustainable development strategy (HM Government, 1994a), which guides the UK's response to sustainable development until 2012. A final section will look at recent progress towards implementing sustainable development in the key areas of: economic instruments, indicators, green accounting, and business.

Although some progress in implementing Agenda 21 (A21) is apparent in terms of policy innovation and institutional change, it is slow and uncertain because it is not propelled by sufficient political momentum. Greater signs of progress are evident at the local level, as discussed in Chapter 13. A new Labour Government has been in place since April 1997, instituting many changes outlined here, but it is still too soon to indicate how effective these are likely to be.

LANGUAGE AND DISCOURSE

To paraphrase Sachs (1993, p9): definitions tacitly shape the perception of problems, highlight certain solutions and consign others to oblivion; they feature certain types of social actors, marginalising others, and certain types of social transformation, degrading others. Sustainable development tends to be defined and conceptualised in three ways in the UK, all of which have taken the Brundtland Commission's definition as their starting point (WCED, 1987, p8).

The first definition is framed in economic terms and is an extension of academic debate among economists, emphasising market and regulatory discourses.[2] It uses interventions in market prices and in regulatory mechanisms to correct the imperfections of undervaluing environmental losses, such as the depletion of non-renewable resources. It is not a comprehensive statement of sustainable development, more an attempt at fine-tuning to create a more ecologically sensitive market economy. The second definition uses the language of development, calling attention to the North–South divide, intra-generational equity, poverty, and population growth. Sustainability strategies involve helping developing economies to progress in accordance with environmental protection objectives so that economic growth is not hindered by environmental degradation. The third definition emerges in the literature of local government and NGOs through their efforts to implement Local Agenda 21 (LA21); (see Chapter 13).[3] This emphasises the local social structures that should be implementing the sustainability transition, such as the processes of public participation and local involvement. Here it is as much a social transition as an environmental one. However, at national level, it is not currently an influential interpretation. Let us consider the first two in more detail.

As part of the government's belated response to the Brundtland Commission, in 1989 the Department of the Environment (DoE) produced *Sustaining Our Common Future*. This prioritised economic development and highlighted the problems of developed countries with regard to environmental degradation resulting from growing populations and poverty. Despite claiming that: 'the government is making sustainable development an integral part of its domestic and international policies' (HM Government, 1990, p47), and declaring its support for the principle of sustainable development, the subsequent white paper on the environment – *This Common Inheritance* – confined discussion to a few sentences tucked away in the 'world environment' section, or referred vaguely to 'sustainable growth'. The white paper's continued emphasis on economic growth and development in its discussion of sustainable development indicates a very 'weak' definition of the concept.

At the time of the white paper, Chris Patten, then Secretary of State for the Environment, in a bid to reassert the department's influence in this area, stated that the basis for environmental policy was 'stewardship', to preserve and enhance, moving away from purely environmental protection towards sustainable development (HM Government, 1990, p10). Despite this, environmental degradation is perceived as a problem to be solved either by international diplomacy or by existing national institutions. In the first, second and third DoE reviews of progress towards the targets of the white paper, the concept of sustainable development was referred to only in the context of aid programmes to developing countries, or in response to the Fifth Environmental Action Programme of the European Commission (HM Government, 1991; 1992; 1994b).

Sustainable Development: the UK Strategy, published in 1994 as part of the government's response to UNCED, says that:

> *The challenge of sustainable development is to find ways of enhancing total wealth while using common natural resources prudently, so that renewable resources can be conserved and non-renewables used at a rate which considers the needs of future generations.* [HM Government, 1994a, p33]

Notably, however, it contained no discussion of sustainable development as a concept and therefore no new thinking, stating only that it was 'difficult to define', hence the tendency to rely on the Brundtland Commission's definition and environmental concerns. The lack of debate at national level is a barrier to institutional change and therefore to the implementation of A21 and ultimately the principles of sustainability. The following sections, although not referring again to this lack of debate, illustrate that without broader debate and discussion on sustainability there is not the required understanding of the concept, impetus or opportunity for action.

AN ENVIRONMENTAL STRATEGY

The 1990 white paper *This Common Inheritance* set out the UK's environmental strategy until the year 2000 in response to the rapid greening of UK politics in the late 1980s (HM Government, 1990). Prior to this, the UK had no coherent policy strategy on the environment. However, even before its publication there were indications that the potentially innovative and ambitious paper would be compromised. This was largely because of the lack of high-level political support and opposition from other departments keen to protect their policy areas from DoE encroachment.

The white paper's four key innovations, discussed below, were largely institutional, focused on central government, and aimed at policy coordination. In fact, Patten's successor claimed that the government had put in place 'some of the most sophisticated machinery to be found anywhere in the world for integrating environment and other policies' (quoted in Green Alliance, 1995, p539). On the negative side, the white paper suffered from short-termism and lack of vision, with very little in the way of targets, deadlines, firm commitments, and new initiatives. Much of it was simply a restatement of established policy and actions that the government was already committed to under various EU directives and international agreements. Key issues, such as enforcement inconsistencies or the administrative weakness of the DoE, were ignored. In many areas, such as agriculture, energy or transport, little or nothing was envisaged in terms of policy change. However, despite the criticisms, the ray of hope for environmentalists was that it had been produced at all, and that its existence appeared to create a documentary process against which government policy and action could be measured and assessed annually.

Ministerial Committees

The white paper gave the two committees which were formed to produce it responsibility for coordinating action on the environment within central government. Secrecy and a lack of accountability have characterised their activities, and they have rarely met, supposedly because there are few serious disputes for them to deal with: 'although it is fair to argue that if the [DoE] was pushing a radical agenda there would be rather more disputes to deal with' (Green Alliance, 1995, p540). In 1992 the most important of these committees, the cabinet committee, was disbanded and a new ministerial committee, the EDE, was created. Its chairman was the leader of the House of Lords, not the prime minister as previously, denoting a significant loss of prestige and a lessening of political influence. In practice the EDE was an ineffective institutional device, mainly due to the continued territorial preoccupation of the departments and hostility within the central government machinery towards the relatively new DoE, particularly from the 'economic' departments. Nevertheless, the existence of a cabinet committee on the environment at this level, which the policy arenas of health and education did not have, suggested that it was considered politically important, and thereby increased the relative status of the DoE and its ability to encourage greater policy integration. The new government has dissolved the EDE and created the Cabinet Committee on the Environment. This cabinet status indicates a resurgence in the fortunes of environmental issues on the political agenda. It is to be chaired by the Deputy Prime Minster John Prescott, MP, who also presides over the newly created superdepartment, the Department of Environment, Transport and the Regions (DETR).

Green Ministers

Green ministers in each department are nominally responsible for 'greenhouse-keeping' matters, departmental annual reports, and coordinating environmental initiatives between departments. However, to date they have had little impact on departmental policy in these areas. Their status has either been low, or it is one responsibility among a multitude for the respective secretary of state. They meet as a committee to facilitate policy integration, constituting the second ministerial committee announced in the white paper, under the chairmanship of the Secretary of State for the Environment. But they do so infrequently, meeting just seven times in five years (ENDS, 1997a). They have no power to make major policy decisions and have remained focused on internal issues (Hill and Jordan, 1993). One of the main reasons for their creation was to deflect the focus of public attention, criticisms and queries over environmental matters away from the DoE when other departmental policies were involved. However, this has not happened.

Green ministers have rarely been the focus of lobbying and questions in parliament, so there has been little pressure to take a more visible or productive position. Their low public profile in relation to sustainable development policies has been recently noted by the House of Lords Select Committee on Sustainable Development (HOLSCSD) (1995), who felt that their reported role, compared to actual achievements and responsibilities, was misrepresented to such an extent that it could undermine confidence in the government's institutional mechanisms. However, they do seem to be reevaluating their role in response to this criticism and increased questioning in parliament. In January 1996 the green ministers announced that they would be publishing a number of case studies to illustrate good environmental practice within departments (HC Debates, 1996a). The new Labour Government has reviewed this mechanism and revamped it into a 'network' of green ministers, who will support the new Cabinet Committee on the Environment, and ensure that the policy appraisal process described below is improved. This means a higher status and greater responsibility for the ministers, which they hopefully will live up to, closing the credibility gap which they have faced so far. It also heralds a higher profile for green ministers in the future, but whether this facilitates further policy integration and illustrates good practice remains to be seen.

Annual Departmental Reporting

Analyses of annual reporting by central government, announced in the 1990 White Paper, have shown a noticeably poor level of environmental content (Green Alliance, 1991 and 1992). Reports in the main fail even to reflect departmental action on the White Paper's commitments. Virtually no targets against which future performance could be assessed have been produced and almost no hard data have been presented – when it has, the picture has not been good. After five years, the overall improvement in energy efficiency was 14.8 per cent, just short of the 15 per cent target (now risen to 20 per cent) by the year 2000, with some departments showing a drastic deterioration: such as education (85 per cent) and health (54 per cent) (ENDS, 1997b).

Some positives notes are sounded in the recent reports. For example, the 1995 Department of Transport report (1995, pi) includes minimisation of environmental impact in its guiding principles, and refers to the environment throughout rather than consigning it to just one chapter as in many reports. Although this is not a statement of support for sustainable development, but an adaptation of the language to departmental objectives, it is at least an acknowledgement that the issues need to be addressed. The benefit of this mechanism is that it helps to formalise the involvement of the DoE in other departmental policy-making, and allows a greater amount of transparency in environmental performance. It also appears that interdepartmental meetings set up to discuss the environmental content of reports have led to improved communications and debate, and so have proved to be a positive integration mechanism (Hill, 1996).

Guideline Documents

Published as a guide for civil servants, *Policy Appraisal and the Environment* (DoE, 1991) set out how departments could assess the environmental impacts of their policies in a systematic way. The intention was to encourage all government departments to undertake such an exercise at the early stages of decision-making. It was backed up by procedural guidance that papers produced for cabinet and ministerial committees should, where possible, cover significant environmental costs and benefits. However, the appraisal process was in danger of being emasculated before it began, since some departments claimed that their policies had no environmental impacts and so implementation was not necessary. It also came under criticism for its focus on monetary valuation techniques, and for starting with the policy as a given rather than assessing whether it was the appropriate solution to the problem. By the summer of 1993 it seemed to have disappeared without trace within the opaqueness of central government decision-making – until, that is, pressure was exerted to produce some evidence of implementation when 12 environmental groups wrote to the Environment Secretary complaining that there were no published environmental policy appraisals for several major policy decisions, including the roads programme.

The DoE subsequently published *Environmental Appraisal in Government Departments* (1994), consisting of a number of brief case studies illustrating how the appraisal process has been applied in a number of government departments. It indicated, as has the recent consultant report on the process (DETR, 1997; ENDs, 1997c), that departments are taking such techniques more seriously than before, but that there is little actual policy change or integration. Few, if any, appraisals have been carried out, and full copies of the case studies contained in the second report were not available for examination. Putting the guidance into practice has been problematic, with a lack of expertise and resources to undertake the appraisal adequately; there is also a perception amongst civil servants that the techniques are not easy to understand, operationalise, or that 'the results were not sufficiently reliable to merit the expense of the work' (ENDS, 1997c). The deficiencies of the second document, particularly in terms of comprehensiveness and projects covered, are evidence of a number of underlying issues: departmental expertise is still evolving; the Treasury is suspicious of some of the economic tools available; and there is a need to widen the scope of these tools and reports to embrace social policy, industrial strategy, international relations, education and health, or even to move beyond project appraisal to policy appraisal.[4]

The mechanism of policy appraisal is potentially the most important in terms of policy integration. The potential is for a less ad hoc, more explicit, structured and transparent tool to be established for policy analysis and to be used in decision-making, which will enable clearer comparisons between the decisions of different departments and policy arenas. With this the move of departmental cultures towards greater environmental awareness should follow. In response to the recent consultant report, green ministers have agreed that where there is a significant environmental impact they will consider publishing the appraisal. The new Sustainable Development Unit within the DETR will produce an aide-memoire for policy advisors, reminding them of the necessity and technique of policy appraisal, and will act as an information point for departments on policy appraisal. Further technical guidance will be drafted by an interdepartmental group of economists and will replace, with the aide-memoire, the 1991 guidance.

Reviewing the 1990 White Paper

Since 1990 six reviews of the white paper have been produced and continue to disappoint observers. The reviews published since 1995 are combined updates of activities resulting from the white paper but mainly from *Sustainable Development: the UK Strategy* (HM Government, 1994a) and will be discussed later. The white paper process appears to have missed the opportunity to address issues such as green taxation, the link between the environment, economy and social policies, and real institutional reform. It represents no strategic assessment of future needs in terms of environmental policy and lacks a commitment to those measures it has considered. The opportunity for more accountability and openness was ignored. Significantly, there has been a lack of impetus to take environmental considerations into account in more than a mechanical way and so there has been no change of departmental cultures. Evidence given to the HOLSCSD (1995) highlights the importance of greater transparency in the process creating greater external surveillance opportunities. An important part of this process, is a strong critical voice from NGOs and individuals, but at present this is floundering (Green Alliance, 1995).

So far, it appears that the four main institutional innovations have had little real effect in terms of integrating environmental considerations within other policy areas, and even less with regard to sustainable development. However, it is important to note that these form a significant institutional structure for implementing sustainable development in the future and that although they have not fulfilled their potential, mainly as a result of poor cooperation from ministries, their continued existence does represent progress in terms of policy integration. What is interesting is how the new Labour Government has retained them, attempted to review their weaknesses, and put in place measures to strengthen them. Hopefully it will give these mechanisms what they most need – support from the centre of government: political will.

THE SUSTAINABLE DEVELOPMENT STRATEGY

The national response to A21, *Sustainable Development: the UK Strategy* (HM Government, 1994a), was submitted to the CSD in 1994. It was criticised for having no targets or clear vision of the future, no sense of urgency, and no inspirational capacity. Although it exhorted action from many other groups and stakeholders, action by the government itself was lacking. Criticism centred on the lack of any real position and action on the international front, the ad hoc consultation process and the ineffective institutional arrangements. The high point was the acceptance of the principle of demand management by central government, particularly by the Department of Transport where a change in policy substance occurred, breaking the deadlock between it and the DoE. When John Gummer was appointed as Environment Secretary in 1993, such interdepartmental battles, required to produce a strong strategy, were seen as a test of his skills and influence – perceived to be waning (Green Alliance, 1993). The appearance of the strategy and the subsequent publication of sustainability indicators (DoE and Government Statistical Service, 1996) represent a significant victory for the DoE. It is debatable whether any other environment minister could have achieved as much in the same time.

Policy integration in Whitehall does not, however, appear to have moved any further. There was no role mentioned or explored for the Treasury in the strategy, and nothing of substance, beyond the landfill tax, is suggested in terms of the economic mechanisms. Although the aim was to present a broader approach than the white paper, its only innovation was to create new institutional machinery, this time 'external' to departments.

The Government's Panel on Sustainable Development

The panel has a roaming brief to advise the government on topic areas of its own choosing, and it has access to all ministers and the machinery of government. Its terms of reference are:

* to keep in view general sustainability issues at home and abroad;
* to identify major problems or opportunities likely to arise;
* to monitor progress; and
* to consider questions of priority.

It has now published three reports, (Government's Panel on Sustainable Development, 1995; 1996; 1997), hilighting subjects chosen for their topicality and general interest. The government's formal response (HM Government, 1995a) has been both cautious and non-committal, reiterating its major achievements, mostly already laid out in the white paper process. It has promised nothing new as a result of the panel's reports, but welcomes the panel's role in stimulating debate and defining priorities for the government. The panel is gaining respect for its consistently critical but constructive approach to the government's policies on sustainable development; it appears now to be carving its own niche and adding its voice to the chorus of other actors in this policy arena, evaluating government policy. The real influence of this panel is, however, difficult to judge. Its success in winning political support and action depends on the personal influence of its members, something which is practically impossible to gauge.

The UK Round Table on Sustainable Development

The UK Round Table meets around four times a year and had its inaugural meeting on 23 January 1995. Its role is described as 'driving forward environmentally sustainable development' (DoE, 1995b), and its objectives are to:

- develop new areas of consensus on difficult issues of sustainable development and, where this is not possible, to clarify and reduce differences;
- inform and involve others, building wider support for emerging consensus;
- help identify the agenda and priorities for sustainable development;
- provide advice and recommendations on actions to achieve sustainable development; and
- help evaluate progress towards objectives.

Along with environmental NGOs, members were specifically invited by the DoE from academia, the church, trade unions, business, local government associations, the medical and farming professions, and consumers' associations. The environment secretary is the government's representative and president, with Sir Richard Southwood as the sole chair.[5]

So far the round table has focused on transport, energy efficiency, and mechanisms to secure environmental improvements, concentrating on the obstacles to sustainability. It published two annual reports (UK Round Table on Sustainable Development, 1996 and 1997). The second reviews progress to date, and summarises the most recent topics its working groups have considered: transport, housing and urban capacity, freshwater, energy and planning. The new Labour Government has made an interim response, flagging those areas where it agrees with the Round Table or is already planning on action (ENDS, 1997d).

The significance of the round table as a mechanism for change in government policy, and its facility as a forum for debate and consultation, remains to be seen. It is, however, more transparent than the panel, with more concrete objectives and therefore easier to monitor. So far it is making its presence felt on a wide range of issues and has made a start on networking with other initiatives, interest groups and government departments. However, at the launch of its first annual report when it came under substantial pressure to show evidence of its influence, it was unable to point to anything specific. A lack of interdepartmental communication and cooperation is still the major obstacle facing it (ENDS, 1996a). After conflicting with the Department of Trade and Industry and the gas industry regulator (OFGAS) over the role of economic regulators in achieving sustainable development (ENDS, 1995a), the round table's members appeared to lose their enthusiasm for the process. In Canada and in Australia, similar round tables have failed. The UK initiative appears to be enduring, despite the aforementioned problem, and will officially continue until 1999, but experience suggests that the attitude of ministers in the new government will be crucial to members' continued commitment.

The Citizen's Initiative

The Citizen's Initiative has now been renamed Going for Green (GFG), and was formally launched in February 1995 with all party support. It is intended to be a citizen-driven, civic-minded campaign (DoE, 1995c) that is local and small scale: 'Going for Green aims to identify and explain what sustainable development is and what we as individuals can do about it' (DoE, 1995c, p1). At present it appears that there is little governmental support, outside of the DoE, or cohesion of effort with other initiatives; there is also little funding and uncertain long-term prospects. In 1996 it became a limited company and attained charitable status in order to secure private sector funds, improving its chances of survival. The DoE provides £1.5 million a year, but between April and November 1996 it had already secured private sector sponsorship of £360,000, with an additional £950,000 of similar support (HC Debates, 1996b and 1996c).[6] So far it has worked on several fronts: developing a public relations campaign; a 14-point code for individuals to encourage sustainable behaviour patterns; an eco-schools project; and recently it has launched Eco-Cal, a computer programme describing how 'green' people live in their everyday lives. However, until recently it has only undertaken small-scale initiatives that represent no real advances in terms of local or individual sustainability compared to its larger objectives, or the work of some NGOs and local authorities. In the past it has suffered from the low level of government support for sustainability initiatives. Its status under New Labour remains circumspect but it has received the support of the new environment minister, Michael Meacher.

A Successful Strategy?

So far there appears to be little connection between these initiatives, although the panel and the round table have supported the recommendations of other government appointed bodies, such as the Royal Commission on Environmental Pollution, keeping them on the political agenda. The lack of support at the prime ministerial level and continuing departmental wariness means that there is little evidence so far that these innovations will facilitate institutional change in the machinery of government or in wider society. More generally, the strategy represents another missed opportunity since it has not attempted to tackle the 'bigger' issues, such as integrating environmental considerations within economic and social policies. The trajectory of departmental policies remains largely intact; and there is no attempt to define a strategy since there are no specific long-term goals in any area of policy.

In March 1995 the government quietly produced its first combined review of the white paper and the sustainable development strategy (HM Government, 1995b). Uniquely, this set out a number of agreed and quantifiable targets for global atmosphere, air and water quality, landfill and biodiversity. March 1996 and 1997 saw the even quieter release of the second and third reviews (HM Government, 1996 and 1997). All were short on new ideas, restating commitments made elsewhere, fudging targets set in previous

165

reviews and policy statements, and failing to plug the holes left by the sustainable development strategy. This is really just a continuation of the white paper exercise in that: 'it does not drive policy, it reiterates and probably consolidates, so that all those who are supposed to deliver are aware of what they need to do' (Hill, 1996). As such it requires greater commitment outside the DoE to build upon the institutional and policy innovations, and for the mechanisms to go beyond consolidation and towards progression in implementing sustainable development.

In June 1995 the HOLSCSD called for environmental considerations to be given a higher priority in government thinking in all policy areas, and requested a 'clear and prompt restatement of the functions and purpose of the government's own internal integration mechanisms' (HOLSCSD, 1995, p75). Its main criticism was a lack of targets, and varying performances between departments, with the DoE making encouraging attempts in this direction, while the Ministry of Agriculture, Fisheries and Food (MAFF), and the Department of Transport have not. Beyond these concerns, the committee felt that there is a leadership role for the government in the dissemination of sustainable development. The government's response to the report was disappointingly defensive, glossing over or dismissing many of the HOLSCSD's key recommendations. Apart from rejecting all the criticisms of its climate change strategy, the government: denied the need for a further greening of the tax system; claimed that the Treasury was already involved at the early stage of all policy development; and only acknowledged the need for further environmental targets in a limited way (ENDS, 1995b).

INDICATIONS OF INSTITUTIONAL INNOVATION

Economic Instruments

In 1992, the second review of the 1990 White Paper stated a 'new presumption in favour of economic instruments rather than regulation' and unveiled a number of initiatives that 'marked a significant advance towards more market-based solutions' (HM Government, 1992, p5). This was the first positive move since the 1990 White Paper announced that there were definite environmental benefits in shifting from regulation to economic instruments in terms of flexibility and cost-effectiveness. New instruments were now proposed in the areas of:

- *water:* consultation on charging for effluent discharges, water abstraction, and a paper on charging for water to discourage water wastage;
- *waste:* a waste management White Paper to promote the use of economic instruments to encourage recycling, and levies to increase the relative costs of landfill;
- *air:* consultation following a report on the viability of tradable emission permits for SO_x; and
- *transport:* an exploration of the case for urban congestion and road pricing.

A number of areas previously identified in the 1990 white paper were ignored – for example, the introduction of incentives for the recycling of chlorofluoro-carbons (CFCs), waste oil, batteries and tyres. The 1994 strategy also announced a series of new initiatives on demand management regarding energy, water, minerals and transport. Despite all these statements of intent only a few instruments have been, or are being, developed:

- water conservation;
- incentives to farmers to protect the countryside;
- recycling credits;
- VAT on domestic fuel and power, rising from zero rating to 8 per cent (and under the new government back to 5 per cent);[7]
- road fuel duty set at a minimum of 5 per cent increase per year in real terms;[8]
- a differential for unleaded petrol of 67 per cent over leaded petrol;
- the duty advantage for diesel of one pence per litre; and
- cost recovery charges for administrating pollution control, which are now standard practice.

In the case of at least two of these measures there has been little effect on behaviour because of downward pressures on energy prices. The imposition of VAT on domestic fuel has been largely swallowed up. Over the period of 1984 to 1994, real prices have fallen by 20 per cent (DoE and Government Statistical Service, 1996) and look set to continue as energy markets are liberalised and regulators push for lower bills (*The Guardian*, 1996a). Road fuel duty has raised petrol prices by 2.5 pence per litre, but has been offset by a 2 pence per litre fall in pump prices, resulting from low crude oil prices and fierce competition between petrol retailers. This has meant that there is little incentive to invest in measures to improve domestic and industrial energy efficiency.[9] There have also been practical problems with tradable permits for sulphur emissions and congestion pricing (ENDS, 1996b and 1995c).

Evidence given by the Treasury to HOLSCSD not surprisingly indicates that there has been no shift in the burden of taxation thus far from labour, income and profit towards consumption (ENDS, 1995d). The Treasury asserts that it is proving difficult to devise economic instruments which are 'robust and actually do what we want them to do rather than something else' (ENDS, 1995d). Therefore, the bulk of measures to support sustainable development continue to be regulatory in nature. This is also partially because, as the Treasury has indicated, it sees its role as responding to DoE proposals for instruments rather than taking an active part in their development (ENDS, 1995d). The Treasury also remains ideologically opposed to the hypothecation of tax revenues, although there is evidence that it is being forced to accept some element of this in energy initiatives, the landfill tax, and new charges on transport and water pollution.

To be supported by the Treasury, a tax needs first and foremost to be financially robust and to have an environmental rationale. The landfill tax has both

---

BOX 8.1 THE LANDFILL TAX

In the 1994 budget the former chancellor announced a new tax on waste disposal to landfill, introduced in October 1996. This is the first move away from taxation on labour towards pollution and environmental disbenefits, and it is geared to a defined social purpose. The revenue produced is used to offset labour costs via reductions in national insurance contributions (proposed at 0.2 per cent), so that it is a zero effect tax. It is expected that £450 million of revenue will be raised in its first full year of 1997–1998. The environmental rationale is fulfilled through the creation of environmental bodies, funded by voluntary payments from landfill site operators (LOs) who receive a 90 per cent tax rebate. This allows the revenue to be directed, in part, to a specific environmental purpose without the Treasury having to agree to hypothecation (HM Treasury, 1995). These bodies are in the private sector, but are non-profit making and are able to invest in activities approved by the government, such as land restoration and good practice in sustainable waste management, regulated by Entrust. Entrust is a private sector, not-for-profit company, funded by an enrolment fee from environmental bodies and an administration charge. It is estimated that LOs will generate up to £100 million of private sector expenditure for environmental improvement (Sills, 1997). Despite a slow start in its first year of operation, by 1 December 1997, LOs had contributed £49 million (more than double forecast figures), and about 350 environmental bodies had registered and submitted almost 1500 projects (Sills, 1997). The landfill tax has no specific environmental target; for example, there is no direct mechanism for reducing domestic waste, indicating that the environmental rationale is not strong. However it is hoped that through the projects of environmental bodies its environmental effects will be significant. [Powell and Craighill, 1996]

---

but is a rare success story. The politics also need to be right: without a political window even the most technically and environmentally proficient tax is unlikely to become policy. The recent political failure of the proposed increase in VAT on domestic fuel burned the DoE's fingers and reduced confidence in the likelihood of similar fiscal measures being approved in the near future (Hill, 1996). But there are also concerns over the future scope of such instruments. Industry has responded well in the main to regulation and the idea of voluntary agreements. The costs of implementing such instruments are high since there are many practical and political obstacles to overcome, not least of which are the distributional implications. A further problem is presented because many EC directives do not give the UK a choice of instruments. Finally, and most importantly, there needs to be support across central government. However, this is still the government's preferred approach and there are a number of areas where future developments are possible:

- pricing water to limit abstraction in water shortage areas (HM Government, 1996b);
- pricing aggregates to raise the cost of new aggregates and to encourage the recycling and reuse of existing aggregates;
- commitments to international conventions, which mean that tax or permit approaches to limiting SO_x, NO_x, and VOCs may still be on the agenda; and
- measures to limit total emissions on the use of specific polluting substances.

Green Accounting and Sustainability Indicators

Green accounting is still external to political decision-making and has a long way to go before it will inform these processes. There are a number of constraints on the development of robust indicators, primarily: a lack of agreement on methodology; a lack of transparency in government and expert decision-making processes; and a large number of conflicting interests.

In *Sustainable Development: the UK Strategy* the former government indicated that it would be produce a preliminary set of sustainable development indicators. It did this on 12 March 1996. John Gummer, the environment secretary, claimed the indicators were a significant element in making sustainable development 'the touchstone of the UK's policies' (*The Independent*, 1996). Altogether, 120 indicators in 21 areas are set out in the report, about a third show progress away from sustainable development, while for many no interpretation of good or bad is attempted (DoE and Government Statistical Service, 1996).[10] Significantly, only 12 have targets attached, something that is surely required if there is to be a move beyond information to action.

The production of these indicators was welcomed by environmental NGOs. In particular, the statistics on transport have already provoked considerable public debate (*The Guardian*, 1996b; *The Financial Times*, 1996).[11] The former government came under criticism for its choice of standard economic indicators and its failure to relate these to social and environmental objectives in the long term: '[t]he assumption is still that growth in GDP increases standards of living, and a healthy economy is more able to afford environmental goods' (Green Alliance, 1996a). However, the government was able to announce during the same week that costs associated with damage to the environment by pollution would be incorporated, for the first time, into official economic data in August 1996 – pilot environmental accounts. The production of indicators appears to have been a useful coordination exercise for Whitehall, if nothing else, but the interest generated highlights the potential for an annual exercise to stimulate debate and possibly policy change; assessment of the indicators is expected in 1998.

Business and the Environment

Business can never be fully self-sufficient in environmental and social terms and still remain competitive and profitable. True sustainability means leaving no footprint on the planet. That is simply not possible for any business. But methods of reducing the spread of the ecological footprint are being sought by UK business. For the most part this action is spurned by increasingly tough, European regulation-driven, articulate and inquisitive consumer and environmental groups. However, there is evidence of: a new breed of environmentally literate managers; huge technical and accounting opportunities to reduce wastage; and a strong ethical envelope in which concern for possible impacts on indigenous peoples and high-profile ecosystems means that attention is now being paid to the origin of goods and what happens to products in use and disposal.

A study by a consulting organisation, EFTEC, in association with Green Alliance, an environmental lobby (Green Alliance, 1996b), found that:

- 70 per cent of leading UK firms take environmental issues more seriously than a year ago;
- 58 per cent of companies are proactive in the sense that they take initiatives beyond compliance; and
- there is a willingness to accept tougher regulations and tax regimes to make all competitors face similar performance requirements.

Nevertheless, the vast majority of business leaders hold back from environmental investment because of costs, lack of awareness of long-term benefits and a general absence of knowledge and information. There is movement in environmental performance through environmental management schemes and certified standards such as BS 7750 and international standard ISO 14001. But this is primarily confined to major companies with good housekeeping procedures who are conscious of their public image. Unless the perceived penalties of losing competitiveness are overcome by more commonly applied regulations, and unless there is a much higher-profile policy promoting good business practice, this element of the sustainability transition will always lag.

Implementing A21 under the New Labour Government

While still in opposition the Labour Party produced *In Trust for Tomorrow*, an environmental policy blueprint, drafted at a senior level in the party and endorsed by the full party in 1994. This contained several elements which, if implemented, would have been an improvement over the mechanisms put in place by the then Conservative Government. However, although it is early days, it appears that it is largely to be ignored, and only the very watered down parts that made it to the Labour Party election manifesto are to be implemented (ENDS, 1997e).

The new government has created under the deputy prime minster a 'super-ministry': DETR. Crucially, the environmental part of this department no longer has a cabinet minister (whereas transport still does). Commentators have so far viewed this arrangement in two ways. Firstly, the deputy prime minister can give the department a strong voice in the cabinet, which previous secretary of state John Gummer, MP, never could, despite being seen as one of the greenest incumbents of the post. In particular, the deputy prime minister is less likely to be outgunned and disregarded by other, notably economic, ministers. Secondly, the new environment minister Michael Meacher is seen as competent, with an understanding of the environment brief, but he is not part of the prime minister's favoured circle. Environment and sustainability issues could be demoted out of the cabinet, if the deputy prime minister should decide to concentrate on his other portfolios. In addition, the merger may provide opportunities for policy integration but make less transparent the differences which have been semi-public between the former departments (Green Alliance, 1997).

The promised sustainable development plan will revise the 1994 sustainable development strategy but will not be ready until autumn 1998. This plan was to have been drawn up by the Cabinet Committee on the Environment, supported by a Sustainable Development Unit. The unit, in theory, consisted of high-flying civil servants and was situated in the cabinet office to ensure that it was central to all policy-making. However, in reality it was established in the DETR, with a remit to review the sustainable development strategy and to act as a contact and information point for other departments.[12] Therefore, its influence is to some extent dependent on ministers pushing for a wider environmental agenda in their departments (ENDS, 1997a).

In terms of parliamentary surveillance, a regular mechanism which has been lacking, the new government established an Environmental Audit Committee in November 1997. Its 14 (relatively inexperienced) members have already decided to investigate the environmental aspects of the pre-budget statement. One aid to greater transparency that has not appeared is the Green Book, which assesses environmental implications, to accompany the Red Book, which elaborates on the chancellor's budget statement each year. None was published for the July pre-budget statement, and although one is promised for the first full budget, the scope and timing remain unclear (ENDS, 1997f). The Environmental Audit Committee will focus on the process of greening government, in order to complement the scrutiny of environmental policy already undertaken by the Environment, Transport, and the Regions Select Committee. This could provide an invaluable surveillance mechanism within the machinery of government that allows for greater transparency and accountability in achieving sustainable development.

The Scottish Dimension

The devolution of Scotland by 1999, with a separate parliament elected by proportional representation, offers a new opportunity for sustainability to flourish north of the border. It is far too soon to speculate with any confidence, but there is already evidence of genuine institutional innovation. The scope for tax variance beyond 2001, even with only a 3 per cent range off the central norm, offers a real opportunity for ecotaxation. The Scots see the option of using this money for sustainable ends, notably in the social sphere, with growing excitement. The commitment to a peculiarly Scottish national park regime offers a fresh look at protecting and enhancing biodiversity and encouraging more accessible green spaces in and near urban areas.

Right now the Scots have their own Advisory Panel on Sustainable Development, a Scottish office minister with special responsibilities for sustainable development, a series of non-departmental public bodies with sustainability as part of their statutory remit (notably Scottish Natural Heritage and the Scottish Environmental Protection Agency), and a high-level Lord Provost's Commission on Sustainable Development for the City of Edinburgh. All of these initiatives have overlapping membership, all are held in open session, and all are reasonably well reported in the Scottish media. What emerges in this region is an articulated sense of a special Scottish identity for sustainable development, a great willingness to cross policy arenas with joint budgets, and a surge of real excitement about linking social uplift and community empowerment to the sustainability theme. Scotland's progress towards sustainability will be interesting to observe.

CONCLUSION

The UK takes its obligations to international conventions and European Union directives very seriously. The Labour commitment of a 20 per cent reduction in greenhouse gas emissions by 2010 is bound to be modified in the light of the Kyoto agreements on the Climate Change Convention, but will still be hard to deliver. Obligations under the Montreal Protocol are largely met, as are the targets on sulphur and nitrogen oxides, and volatile organic compounds, under European legislation. These trends are well spelt out in official documentation and should not be underestimated. They are an important component of the UK's sustainability strategy. Yet, despite the fact that the UK is prompt in discharging its documentary commitments with regard to A21, being one of only 13 countries that submitted a national report for 1996 to the CSD by the end of January 1996, the real signs of progress can only be seen with regard to institutional change. There are institutional mechanisms and tools that are developing in many areas, but these are only the beginnings of institutional adjustment towards sustainable development. At present this adjustment appears to be falling into the pattern of material change but producing little in the way of progressive policies and administrative cultures which are required to initiate real results in the long term. In this paper we have suggested that this is because:

- there is *no clear consensus on the definition of sustainable development.* Evolution from the concept of reliable and durable economic growth, through stewardship, towards civic empowerment is only barely discernible, and there is certainly little political debate driving it, and no intellectual leadership or vision of sustainable development from any of the three major political parties;
- the *administrative and regulatory cultures are operating conservatively and incrementally;* departmental territorial attitudes and inertia continue to place the administrative focus for sustainable development in the environment ministry;

- *altering the tax regime, no matter how alluring, is difficult and politically contentious;*
- *the pattern of responses is currently very haphazard.* Taken collectively, these still could produce a considerable effect. Greater high-level political support and leadership could produce this coherent effect, but the environment continues to remain low on the political agenda in comparison to employment, taxation and welfare; and
- *the role of the citizen is seen as a rhetorical focus but a practical nightmare.* To involve citizens requires changes in the patterns of power and representation that the political parties are unwilling to condone at present.

At this point one can only look for signs of policy and process links that could herald a more robust shift towards sustainable development. In the UK context, the following developments are worthy of note:

- *cross party interest* in the topic, at least at the level of a manifesto chapter;
- *general interest in sustainability indicators, green audits, and budgetary and policy assessments;*
- *landfill tax and environmental bodies,* which could be possible precursors to charitable public–private partnerships across a range of policy areas;
- *increasing interest in environmental citizenship* through entitlement and education at all levels;
- *the emergence of a civic activism* across a range of environmental and social issues that remains to be tapped and coordinated; and
- *the relative success of LA21* in the UK, more so than elsewhere in Europe, as a possible primary focus for a more socially just and empowering political culture (see Chapter 13).

Sustainable development presents a bigger challenge as we move away from an economist's definition to the wide, social and political aspects of the concept. Its survival as a challenging organising force relies on support from all levels of society; this support can be engendered by evidence that there are threats to society and that progress can be made in countering them which will benefit society in the long term. There is just about sufficient evidence of innovation in the UK to be confident that there is a shift towards addressing sustainable development beyond the rhetoric.

Chapter 9

THE GERMAN RESPONSE TO THE SUSTAINABILITY TRANSITION

Christiane Beuermann and Bernhard Burdick

INTRODUCTION

Compared to other countries, the concept of sustainable development in Germany was established late on in public discourse; it was also relatively late in arriving both on the political agenda and in scientific discussion. Today it seems that although ozone depletion was the major concern of the late-1980s, and global climate change subsequently, the issue of sustainable development will acquire an overriding importance in the early part of the next decade. Owing to growing problems of unemployment and economic recession, 'the future' has recently started to dominate public debate. Discussions concerning Germany's industrial base and economic future are torn between the high hopes placed on sustainable development by the more ecologically and socially oriented parts of society, and the lack of imagination, or even the fear, about following a sustainable development path in conservative and economically oriented parts of the society.

This paper provides an overview of the steps that have been taken so far to introduce and implement sustainable development in Germany. In doing so, a short description of how the issue of sustainability is perceived in Germany is given. Subsequently, the emergence of sustainability on the political and NGO agenda is reviewed. Given the fact that, in 1992, Germany signed A21, compliance with the resulting reporting obligations is taken as a first indicator of how committed the federal government is to sustainable development. In the following section, the effectiveness of the German approach towards sustainability is evaluated on the basis of three groups of sustainability indicators derived from A21:

- the increasing involvement of different actors in society in preparing and implementing sustainability, as well as their approaches;
- the development of public-awareness building and the implementation of 'green' instruments, namely green accounting and ecotaxation; and

- the implementation of A21 at the local level, including an evaluation of whether this has inspired a redefinition of local–central government relations.

GERMAN PERCEPTIONS OF SUSTAINABILITY

Sustainability is not a new issue in Germany. Historically, the ideas underlying the concept of sustainability have origins in forestry management practices going back to the early Middle Ages. At the turn of the 19th century, these practices resulted in the concept of 'lasting forestry' (*nachhaltige Forstwirtschaft*). The basic idea was that in a certain period of time the amount of wood harvested and consumed must not exceed the regrowing capacity of that period. In the early 1980s, in response to general environment discussions, the focus of public awareness on transboundary air pollution, and the related issue of *Waldsterben* (forest dieback), the concept of 'lasting forestry' was rediscovered. Because of this deep-rooted connection to forestry, from the mid 1980s up to 1990 the term sustainability was connected with the issue of tropical deforestation and, hence, climate change. Sustainable forestry management was controversially discussed as an option to protect tropical forests and, generally, to protect and improve sinks of greenhouse gas emissions. Moreover, at that early stage, discussions on sustainability were still related to both questions of development and environmental policy.

Due to the high political priority of the issue of climate change in that period, several political and scientific institutions, such as the German Parliament's Enquete Commission 'Protecting the Earth's Atmosphere' and the Scientific Advisory Council on Global Change, were established (Beuermann and Jäger, 1996).[1] The intense discussions between experts and politicians in the Climate Enquete Commission ensured that in every political party – regardless of their general interest in environmental issues – knowledge and expertise on the complexities of climate change were made more generally available. Furthermore, the analysis of the scientific and socio-economic causes of the greenhouse effect made the connection with development problems (such as increasing population) obvious (Deutscher Bundestag, 1989a). Referring to these difficulties, the social democratic opposition party demanded that the concept of sustainable development, as formulated by the Brundtland Commission, should be the basis of the relationship between the environment and the economy. In addition, sustainable development, however defined, should be taken as the main criterion to evaluate the effectiveness of federal development policy (Deutscher Bundestag, 1989b).

Translations and their Use in Public Debate

An interesting feature of the German sustainability discussion is that there is no common understanding of how the terms should be translated. Confusion about which translation should be employed is not restricted to the use of the term sustainability by different actors. Inconsistencies can also be found in different translations made by the same group of actors. For example, as Nigel Haigh demonstrates in Chapter 3, different words are used in German translations of EU legal texts, demonstrating different perceptions of what is meant by sustainability. Somehow, this situation reflects the openness of discussion on sustainable development and the lack of consensus in interpreting sustainability, with different elements of sustainability highlighted by the terms chosen. The following list of German translations is not exclusive. Some of the translations, such as *tragfähig* (tolerable; acceptable) and *durchhaltbar* (something that can hold out), have been used occasionally but are of minor importance in the discussion process and are not explained further, whereas the translations that follow are significant.

- *Umweltverträglich* (eg Preamble of the Treaty on European Economic Area): environmentally compatible. This is a very broad term describing the generaal goal or principle of taking into account the compatibility of measures and decisions with the environment. It is very similar to the term *umweltgerecht,* which means environmentally sound.
- *Nachhaltig* (eg Treaty of Rome, article 130u): lasting; to have a strong, deep effect or to deeply impress someone. The Federal Environment Ministry (BMU) uses this translation in official documents, for example in the German translation of A21. Although it has a positive connotation it is disputed by the German Council of Environmental Experts (SRU) as not having a strong public environmental interpretation and a perception of being 'insistent' and 'intensive' (Thones, 1994, p46).
- *Dauerhaft* (Maastricht Treaty, article B): durable; (long)lasting. This word was consistently used in the German translation of the Brundtland Report (Bruntland and Hauff, 1988). However, it is disputed for its focus on continuing the status quo, which disregards the required reorientation of long-term policy strategies. In combination with economic terms (especially growth), it is likely to be interpreted as continuous growth. In addition, it has a nationalistic connotation: 'sustainable Germany' translated as '*dauerhaftes Deutschland*' sounds like 'Germany forever' (Loske, 1995).
- *Beständig* (Treaty of Rome, article 2): continual, continuous; permanent; lasting, stable. Beständig is only used in one document. Both the translation and the context make it obvious that sustainable was interpreted in the traditional economic sense as continuous economic growth – as such it is in keeping with the German tradition of the 'magic square'.[2]
- *Zukunftsfähig:* sustaining future opportunities or actions; developing future capacity. This has a very general meaning; it did not have an environmental or economic connotation prior to the sustainable development debate but expresses a positive and progressive feeling. It was invented in 1991 (Simonis, 1991) and was used mostly in scientific discussions (WBGU 1993; BUND and MISEREOR, 1995). With the publication of the study *Zukunftsfähiges Deutschland* it became a slogan in the public debate on sustainable development and has subsequently been applied to discussions about future issues.

- *Dauerhaft-umweltgerecht:* durable and environmentally sound. The SRU used this translation in its 1994 environmental report *For a Sustainable Development*. The SRU argued that, in contrast to others, its translation makes the concept of sustainable development evident: starting from the widening of the time perspective (*dauerhaft*), the ecological conditions are of priority significance (*umweltgerecht*) under a dynamic concept (*Entwicklung*) (SRU, 1994, p46).

The three most commonly used German translations for sustainability (*dauerhaft, nachhaltig, zukunftsfähig*) are increasingly found in almost every context, and it appears that in many cases the term sustainable development is used for green or social labelling or as a non-committal slogan (SRU, 1996).

SEARCHING FOR EVIDENCE: THE SUSTAINABILITY TRANSITION IN GERMANY

Establishing Sustainable Development on the Political and NGO Agenda

During the preparation of the UNCED, sustainable development was discussed constantly but very vaguely by the federal government and in parliament. Just before the conference discussions were intensified with the efforts made by the social democratic opposition to focus attention on the content of the concept rather than on the rhetoric. It was only in early 1992 in response to a parliamentary question that the federal government presented its interpretation of sustainable development as:

> ...*a policy which harmonises the economic and social development of a nation with the preservation of the environment and of the natural resources, also with respect to the interests of future generations. This implies the consequent development or rather the further development of a precautionary environment policy and the integration of environment protection in all areas of political action in industrialised and developing countries.* [*Deutscher Bundestag*, 1992a]

However, this was again a vague interpretation, and the measures taken into account did not go beyond those that were discussed in other environmental policy contexts. As an important first step in the discussions on sustainable development, in February 1992 the Enquete Commission 'Protection of Man and the Environment' was established.[3] The commission based its recommendations in its first interim report primarily on the results of earlier international studies, such as the Club of Rome's reports of 1972 and 1992, the report of the Brundtland Commission, and the generally accepted connection between global environmental problems, production processes and consumption patterns. In 1995 it was given a mandate to work out goals and approaches to the operationalisation of sustainable development.

For a long time national and European environment and development policies, and also public awareness, were characterised by selective and regional environmental problems in the North or analogous, mainly regional, social problems in the South. The first NGO-initiative on the theme of sustainable development was the One World for All Project, initiated in 1989 by more than 30 NGOs (consisting almost exclusively of development NGOs). Its aim was to raise public awareness about sustainable development by preparing information campaigns and working through the media (Geschäftstelle Eine Welt für Alle, 1991). The German environmental NGOs were relatively late in responding to this issue because they were more focused on local issues. The larger NGOs (BUND, DNR and WWF) claim that they began to work internally on the issue of sustainable development in 1986–87, in preparation for, and in response to, the work of the Brundtland Commission.[4] But until 1991 there were no public campaigns on the theme of sustainable development; indeed, the main obstacles to an earlier response were (Unmüßig, 1995):

- insufficient teamwork and networking between environment and development NGOs within Germany, and on the international and global level;
- weak positions of the NGOs on 'the new themes'; and
- the lack of experience in actual political and media work, especially by environmental NGOs.

As a result of these problems the NGOs missed their chance to work within the National Committee, which was founded in June 1991 by the German government to prepare the national position in UNCED.

In June 1991, however, more than 20 NGOs (among them: DGB, BUKO, DNR, BUND, WEED, and different church organisations) founded Clearinghouse 1992.[5] The main objective was to stimulate discussion on the environment and development between different social groups. Their work was aimed not only at UNCED but at the world economic summit in July 1992 in Munich. Primarily on the initiative of BUND and DNR, a national NGO secretariat called UNCED '92 was founded in August 1991 to help prepare an NGO position for UNCED. The BMU, together with BUND and DNR, partly funded the NGO secretariat which ended its operations in September 1992. During the whole process there was disagreement between the NGOs, weakening their influence and partly damaging their potential for participation, which they had demanded.

The Federal Government's Reporting to the CSD

This report is almost exclusively a description of the past and present (successes of) German environmental policy; it is not a strategy for implementing sustainability in the future. In its progress report on implementing the EU's Fifth Environment Action Plan, the EU Commission stated that Germany has no national sustainable development strategy at all (European Commission, 1995). The CSD reports were prepared both by the BMU and the Federal Ministry of

Economic Cooperation and Development (BMZ). Both reports emerged through close coordination with the federal chancellor and all federal ministries. The BMU and BMZ are jointly in charge of coordinating the Earth Summit follow-up, particularly the implementation of A21. This procedure is not a new development resulting from the sustainability discussion, since interministerial coordination is usual on cross-sectoral issues.

The federal government explicitly declared its commitment to the concept of sustainable development in its official documents for UNCED and the CSD (BMU, 1994a). Moreover, there is a consensus among the political parties, the confederation of German trade unions and numerous industrial federations in acknowledging the importance of the concept. In the government's opinion, the German environment and development policy is based on the principle of precaution, implemented in the first environment program in 1971; therefore, it is already to a large extent identical with the aims and demands of A21 (BMU/BMZ, 1994; BMU, 1994b). Furthermore, there is a belief that Germany's good example leads international efforts and has done so since the early 1970s.

The basis for the federal government's judgement that it has made a good start towards sustainability are the successes achieved by past environmental policies, for example in water conservation and air quality control (Wessel, 1995). The BMU's low level of interest appears to be partly linked to the departure of the former environment minister, Professor Klaus Töpfer, at the end of 1994; this led to a weakening of environmental policy, particularly in the areas of internationally oriented climate-protection and sustainability policies.[6] In the reorganisation of ministries, Töpfer switched to the Federal Ministry for Regional Planning, Building and Urban Development (BMBau), where he is again taking up the progressive environmental policy which he developed in his previous ministry and as former CSD chairman. It seems that in his new area of responsibility, he was able to put his ideas into practice (such as thermal insulation, solar energy use), and this has resulted in a growing interest in sustainable development in BMBau. In point of fact, Herr Töpfer was only able to achieve modest reforms in this area due to the reduced availability of public spending in the run-up to European monetary union. In 1998 he took up the role of director general of the UN Environment Programme. Other ministries widely ignore and neglect the concept of sustainable development and A21. This is also evidence that progress on sustainable development strategies initially depends on the personal engagement of innovative politicians and other actors.

EFFECTIVENESS: DEVELOPMENTS POINTING THE WAY FOR THE SUSTAINABILITY TRANSITION?

Germany's sustainability transition is only in its initial phase, if at all. In order to investigate the opportunities for implementing A21 in Germany, the response of different groups of actors towards A21 and their involvement in the process is described below and in Table 9.1. The adaptation of economic and social institutions to sustainability is then reviewed briefly.

Table 9.1 Prototype projects for a German contribution to the Earth Summit process in Rio

Field of action / level of action	Energy	Transport	Foreign trade	Foreign investments	Social sustainability	Development cooperation
Global	Protocol on reductions in CO_2 emissions certificates	Protocol on reductions in CO_2 emissions certificates	Reform of GATT/WTO through inclusion of ecological and social standards	Environmental guidelines for OECD investment agreement	Optional protocol for social pact	Tobin tax
European Union	Energy/CO_2 tax	Tax on kerosene	Removal of export subsidies for agricultural products	Social standards in promotion of commercial enterprises	Job opportunities for women	20/20 Initiative
Federal government	Ecological reform of energy sector	Rail network	No arms-exports to non-NATO countries	Environmental and social clauses for capital protection agreements	Wealth report	Basic education for all
Region	Regenerative energy sources/-energy saving measures	Local public transport	Environmentally and developmentally sustainable promotion of foreign trade	Transfer of environmental technologies	Sustainable regional development	One-World awareness work
Local government	Energy-saving programmes for local-authority buildings	Mobility/goods-distribution centres	Fair trade	Research and development for environmental technologies	Non-skilled jobs/expansion of not-for-profit sector	Local versions of Agenda 21

Source: Feus, 1997, p9.

The Role of the NGOs

Partially funded by the federal government prior to UNCED, the NGOs almost failed to assure the continuation of that funding afterwards through administrative error. Due to power conflicts between the different NGOs, an application for further funding was not filed. As a result, the NGO secretariat was dissolved. In December 1992, however, DNR applied for and received funding, becoming the sole coordinator of a new NGO Forum for Environment and Development (Bleischwitz, 1995). This forum brings together some 60 individual environment and development associations and NGO networks with more than 100 member associations. A steering committee has been established consisting of representatives from each environment and development NGO and from women's and youth organisations. It defines the tasks of the forum and voices the positions and demands of the forum to the government and the public. It has been suggested that the ministerial pressure to ensure effective working procedures, which initiated the steering committee, is an indication of the interest of the BMU and BMZ in a qualified and coordinated input from the NGOs to back up their own position in inter-ministerial games (Unmüßig, 1995).

The BMU and BMZ have also funded an NGO secretariat which: distributes position papers drafted by the forum members or its working groups; maintains contacts with organisations in developing countries; works with international organisations and networks on joint activities; and monitors the international Earth Summit follow-up.[7] One of its main tasks is public and press relations, in order to inform the German public on the link between the environment and development. After initial mistrust and minor quarrels, the secretariat has worked quite well for almost four years and has established a network of contacts in relevant parts of the governmental machinery.

Beyond simple funding, cooperation between the federal government and NGOs on the issue of sustainability takes place in two bodies, the forum and the National Committee for Sustainable Development (formerly National Preparatory Committee for UNCED).[8] The forum is the main point of contact with NGOs for the federal government, who funds NGO participation in the CSD through this body. Moreover, a number of the forum's working group representatives are widely recognised for their competence and now advise BMU officials in preparing for, and during, CSD sessions. For the first time, in 1996, the environment minister invited five representatives from major stakeholder groups to the CSD session (BMU, 1996). However, contacts between the federal government and NGO representatives during preparation for CSD sessions are judged by some to be no more than lip service as the government appears to have accepted few of their demands or recommendations.

Business and Industry

Business and industry 'discovered' environmental protection quite some time ago. Ecology is used as a marketing strategy for advertising and public relations. Sustainability grows in importance, and meanwhile also appears as a motive for enterprise policy or even as an advertising slogan. The development of new instruments (product liability, ecoaudit) is closely watched and questions of norms and standardisation have gained strategic importance (Leitschuh-Fecht and Burmeister, 1994). The aim is to make the environmental compatibility of production and products clear to customers; in this way, there are criteria on which to base the decision to buy, as experiences with the 'blue environment angel' label, introduced in the 1970s, show.

More interesting developments with regard to the reorientation of business and industry towards sustainability include the forming of new coalitions between the environment and the economy, for example: the 'strategic alliance' between the BUND and 16 firms (Wuppertal Bulletin, 1995; BUND, 1995). This coalition was formed in order to promote the introduction of ecological tax reform (Leitschuh-Fecht and Burmeister, 1994; Beuermann and Jäger, 1996). Another example of a new NGO–business coalition is the European Business Council for Sustainable Energy Futures. It was founded in February 1996 in Brussels, mainly on the initiative of the German developmental NGO, Germanwatch. Meanwhile more than 30 German and European enterprises and numerous associations have joined this business council. However, the number of businesses and industries participating in these coalitions is still very small, with some of the more progressive companies waiting for action by the federal government, for example, ecological tax reform (Leitschuh-Fecht and Burmeister, 1994).

The Scientific Community

Numerous research activities exist on the subject of sustainability. All too often they deal only with minor, though detailed, problems, but there is some discussion about comprehensive strategies for the operation and implementation of the concept of sustainability in Germany.

When it started its work, the Enquete Commission *Protection of Mankind and the Environment* did not explicitly concentrate on the issue of sustainable development. Concerning itself first with the ecological effects of material flows, the commission then extended its perspective to social and economic dimensions. At this point the topic of sustainable development entered the discussion and became the theme. Rather than working out binding measures and aims, the commission contributed important work on a common interpretation of sustainable development across party lines, based on the equal representation of different parties in the commission (Thones, 1996). Other governmental advisory groups, such as the Global Change Advisory Council and the SRU, have dealt with sustainable development since 1993 and have published different studies on the issue. The Global Change Advisory Council is primarily working on sustainability indicators, while the SRU is working on environmental quality targets and the institutional implications of sustainable development.

In April 1992 Milieudefensie (Friends of the Earth, The Netherlands) published the study *Sustainable Netherlands* (*Nederlands Duursam*). This study was the starting point of an intense public discussion on how to implement sustainability. As a reaction to this the European Commission commissioned Friends of the Earth (FoE) Europe, together with Milieudefensie (The Netherlands), to carry out a series of studies in all European countries. At the moment studies are being, or have been carried out in more than 30 European countries (Spangenberg, 1995). The German case study was carried out by the Wuppertal Institute on behalf of BUND and the Catholic Church organisation MISEREOR. The study, entitled *Zukunftsfähiges Deutschland*, was published in October 1995 and gained much political and public interest. Other studies by governmental advisory bodies and research institutes have been carried out but failed to gain as much popular attention. The English version of this text has recently been edited by Sachs *et al* (1997).

Education and Public-Awareness Raising

The Federal Ministry for Education, Science, Research and Technology (BMBFT) supports research projects, modelling experiments and conferences, often in cooperation with NGOs. In Germany the responsibility for education lies mainly at the state level in the hands of the Länder ministries for education. The curricula for the different school levels (including universities) are still being revised to include the cross-cutting issues of sustainable development. Teaching materials and new school books are being developed. The environment, in general, is perceived by the government to have become an integral part of school education. Furthermore, there is some governmental funding of education programmes – BMZ and BMBFT support NGO school and non-school projects, as well as adult education programmes. Most activities deal with climate change, but there are also some on sustainable development.

With regard to public awareness of sustainability, this and the topic of future needs have increasingly gained importance during the last two years – for example, the enormous public interest generated by the study *Zukunftsfähiges Deutschland*. At the launch of the study, there was a panel discussion with different high-ranking representatives from political, economic and trade union sectors. Furthermore, the media gave the study and the issue of sustainability a very high profile. Since publication, the authors of the study have been asked to give lectures or to participate in panel discussions, particularly in several German Länder ministries. The Enquete Commission arranged a hearing, and in parliament the ecological party Bündnis 90/Die Grünen made a minor interjection on the influence of the study for the work of the federal government. Furthermore, there were numerous talks, discussions and scientific congresses with interested industry federations, with the DGB (German Trade Union Federation), the Carl-Duisberg-Society, and NGOs. More than 13,000 copies of the study have been sold since January 1996. Several follow-up research projects are planned on the themes of 'globality and locality'. Moreover, industry has taken part in and observes this public discussion intensively as well as critically (Loske, 1995).

Ecotaxes

In its several reports, the BMU states that the German sustainability transition is happening because of an early commitment to a precautionary environment policy. These statements are marked and influenced by the recent intensive public debate on shrinking locational disadvantages and the necessity of deregulation. Therefore, instead of introducing new rules, taxes and decrees, policy seems to be confined to voluntary self-regulation and actions by industry and households. In the opinion of BMU officials, the first steps towards ecological tax reform are well underway but this refers only to the noticeable increase in public fees for waste disposal and waste water management (Wessel, 1995). In its 1996 CSD report the German Government stated:

> *Since 1992 no environmental taxes/levies/charges have been introduced in Germany. In Germany taxes and charges with an environmental component are already levied (eg waste water charges; petroleum excise duty differentiated by unleaded and leaded gasoline; emission-oriented motor vehicles tax). These are taxes in which the environmental aspect is one of several important aspects.... It is not possible to supply any isolated information about the proportion of revenue from these taxes and levies that is due to the environmental component.* [BMU and BMZ, 1995]

In scientific and environmental circles, and small parts of the business community, taxes on the consumption of resources have been intensively discussed for years with varying momentum. Starting from discussions on the introduction of ecotaxes (most prominent were taxes on energy consumption and CO_2 emissions) not linked to a reduction of other taxes, the focus is now on the comprehensive re-structuring of parts of the tax system. In doing so, the social and environmental agendas have been linked, ecological tax reform can easily be interpreted and sold as a 'labour tax reform' (Weizsäcker and Jesinghaus, 1992, Görres et al, 1994). This idea appeals to many across party, or other interest, lines but not to the federal government. At the moment, there is almost no political momentum for an ecological tax reform since the opinion prevails that environmental protection and economic development are incompatible. Due to the severe problems Germany is faced with (recession, higher public expenditure related to unification, unemployment), priority is currently given to the traditional perception of economic growth as the motor for increasing or even maintaining welfare. There seems to be no confidence in the findings of studies on the double dividend of an ecological tax reform in terms of additional jobs in combination with environmental protection (Greenpeace, 1994, Ostertag and Schlegelmilch, 1996).

Green Accounting

In Germany, there is no long tradition of green accounting, although discussion about it began with a research project on the costs of environmental pollution by the BMU in 1986 (Hamilton et al, 1993). In 1989, the German

Bundestag held expert hearings on questions related to economic growth as one of the primary goals and conditions of development. Given that in the existing accounting system environmental costs are not internalised (such as measuring GDP), this is seen to be a distorted indicator of welfare. The debate was subsequently extended to ecologically adjusted indicators and the sustainability of economic growth. There was a consensus on the need to develop an environmental accounting system as a supplement to the existing accounting system: a so-called satellite system.

Subsequently, the Federal Statistical Office proposed a new system called Environment–Economic Comprehensive Accounting, established in 1990. A scientific advisory council was also created, consisting of economists to advise both the BMU and the Federal Statistical Office on methodological issues. However, the original impetus of that programme has disappeared since: 'of March 1993, all budgets are under review as the federal government comes to terms with the reunification in Germany' (Hamilton *et al*, 1993). Moreover, it has been suggested that the accounting program was not planned to support the sustainability discussion but was politically driven (Hamilton et al, 1994). Since the discussion of environmental accounting systems in Germany is of a theoretical nature, and given the short period of both discussion and research, it is not surprising that applications are prospective. Therefore, it: 'will require many more years before a consensus on its concepts and methods can be reached' (Serageldin and Steer, 1993).

A quicker and more operable method of valuing environmental impacts might be the use of labels for products, production processes or businesses. The latter method has been recently applied through the implementation of the European Commission's ecoauditing directive (directive 1863/93) which came into force in April 1995. In the early implementation phase, the majority of German businesses did not realise the need for, and opportunities of, integrated environmental protection. When discussing the EC directive both the BMZ and the traditional German industrial associations argued that ecoaudits would impose new additional obligations and administrative burdens on industry (Entsorga, 1994).[9] This lobbying weakened the directive (Friebel, 1994, p27). However, in the meantime the negative attitude changed into one of indifference or even enthusiasm. This is explained by the general acceptance of facts and the attempts to influence the implementation of the directive actively.[10] Another possible reason is the growing relevance of 'environmental friendliness' considerations for consumer decisions. At present, the number of enterprises using this instrument is steadily growing.

OBSTACLES FOR THE IMPLEMENTATION OF SUSTAINABILITY AND AGENDA 21 IN GERMANY

Having begun slowly and later than in other countries, at present sustainable development enjoys, rhetorically, a wide acceptance and consensus. However, the previous observations show that not many concrete steps have been taken towards implementing sustainable development. The reason is that consensus has been achieved only on an abstract level. The interpretations and motives of the different individuals and groups of actors often block or exclude each other (Steger, 1995). There is a lack of political will and pressure for the operation and realisation of sustainable development. The majority of government, industry and business representatives fear far-reaching consequences, such as the end to the paradigm of continuous economic growth. The following sections describe some obstacles and different arguments emerging from the above discussion that hinder implementation.

Political Obstacles

The main political obstacle to implementing sustainability is the unchanging nature of traditional political priorities. The federal government believes that German environment and development policy is quite successful, exemplary even by international comparison. Moreover, it is convinced that its environment policy is by now to a large extent identical with the aims and demands of the A21, particularly through the implementation of the principle of precaution in its environmental policy in 1971 (Wessel, 1995). These successes have reduced considerably the social and political pressure for further change (Steger, 1995).

Consequently, UNCED and A21 were not used as an opportunity for reorientating German environment and development policies, and there is no further strategy to implement A21. The concept of sustainable development is mostly ignored or interpreted in a curious manner: for example, the Federal Ministry of Food, Agriculture and Forestry holds the view that agriculture in Germany has been sustainable for a long time. The SRU feels that the concept of sustainability has not yet become a leading motive for the federal government's political practice. It is still predominantly understood as a theme that is only relevant for ecological or development politics. This was demonstrated in the coalition agreements after the federal election of 1994. It is also true for the federal states that ecological questions are not sufficiently connected with economic and social questions (Thones, 1996).

Organisational Obstacles

Government commitment to A21 did not result in the adjustment of institutional, or more precisely organisational, infrastructure at the federal level. There are no competent organisational units, in the government or in the ministries, which are explicitly responsible for the coordination and realisation of sustainable development and of A21, nationally or locally – except the departments that are responsible for the international environmental and developmental policies at the CSD level. Conceptional work at the national or regional level is mostly done by individual idealistic politicians and NGOs. Except for the National Committee for Sustainable Development, until recently there were no new discussion fora or round tables established at the national level to reflect the strong participatory elements of A21.

Ideological Obstacles

The fundamental conviction that economy and ecology exclude each other is still dominant and forms a massive barrier to implementing sustainability. While NGOs developed numerous initiatives and concepts, the large majority of business and industry offer little more than platitudes. If they speak at all, it is about improved energy and resource efficiency, which is to be achieved by technical innovations and entrepreneurial freedom rather than by state regulations or ecological taxes. Furthermore, it is claimed that customers are not prepared to pay higher prices for ecological products. It becomes obvious that not many economic interests are concerned about social-political dimensions. At best they are concerned with the reduction of emissions, but not about the necessary change of lifestyle and the future of society (Steger, 1995).

The Federal government's statements are still influenced by the paradigm of stable and sustained economic growth. Environmental policy is just another factor influencing the locational advantage of the industrial base. The influence of environmental policy ends when a negative impact on economy and industry is feared. In the opinion of the government, the concept of sustainability needs no fundamental social, political or economic change. Discussion on environmental policy was almost completely edged out by the economic recession, the financial burden after reunification, and fear about the shrinking locational advantages of German industries.

Instrumental Obstacles

Strategic decisions on the implementation of instruments, as recommended by the various expert councils, politicians and researchers, have still not been made. In its national strategy and also in its report *Environment 1994,* the Federal government favours voluntary 'self-commitments' as a primary means of establishing sustainable consumption and production patterns. Appealing to industry and households is quite important, but it is the responsibility of the government to establish a structural framework for the sustainable development of society. On the other hand, the government has made every effort to appeal to private households to adopt environmentally sound patterns of behaviour if only as compensation for its own political shortcomings. This prevailing economic growth paradigm is one of the main obstacles of implementing an ecological tax reform or other ecologically oriented instrumental boundary conditions at the federal level (Forum Umwelt und Entwicklung, 1995).

Behavioural Obstacles

The implementation of sustainability will depend to a large extent on the behaviour of individuals. Public awareness of environmental issues is generally good and there are several initiatives to expand awareness of the sustainability process. As studies such as *Sustainable Germany* show, there is a growing interest in, and discomfort with, the traditional development models. This is reflected in the rapidly expanding public debate about 'the future'. However, there exists a considerable discrepancy between knowledge and action. According to opinion polls, consciousness about environmental problems and the necessary consequences for one's own actions are often unrelated.

CONCLUSIONS

The previous observations show that German response to the sustainability discussion began late compared to other countries. At the moment, sustainability attracts a growing public interest, furthered by an atmosphere of general uncertainty concerning future economic and social developments in Germany. If this public interest in the issue is a stable and continuous phenomenon, it might be followed by a significant political reorientation, becoming the fourth global environment priority at the federal level after forest dieback, ozone depletion and climate change. However, this is speculative, since sustainability has not achieved real political priority. Because of its non-legally binding character, the influence of A21, as the internationally agreed interpretation of the sustainability concept, on domestic strategic policy-making is presently no more than rhetoric. However, there is now a dialogue process, where major groups have formed issue-specific working groups. The results will be used to prepare a national sustainable development strategy in 1998. This was recently announced by Mrs Merkl, the German environment minister.

Fuers (1997, p9) has produced a helpful summary of German responses to the A21 process. His summary table is reproduced as Table 9.1. Fuers's overriding conclusion (1997, p10) is that neither the BMU nor BMZ (the environmental and international development ministries) have managed to interest the 'hard' departmental sectors in sustainable development. There is no development of crucial governmental mechanisms, such as a high-level government policy coordination committee, departmental environmental auditing, or parliamentary surveillance. The NGOs are active but politically weak, and business prefers voluntary compliance to any formal responsibility.

The inevitable conclusion is that institutional reform has simply not taken place in Germany and that, given the German political dominance in the EU, this does not augur well for any significant shift in the European Union on the whole. Increasing recent public interest in the issue, and its link to other publicly discussed social issues, such as unemployment, imply that a significant impetus for future action may result from grassroots activities in a bottom-up process. At the moment, activities at the local and regional level are expected to have a stronger momentum than at the federal level, particularly if they feed into the proposed sustainability strategy.

Chapter 10

THE NORWEGIAN EXPERIENCE OF THE TRANSITION TO SUSTAINABILITY

Liv Astrid Sverdrup

INTRODUCTION

The first period of change following the launch of the Brundtland Commision report was marked by broad enthusiasm for the concept of sustainable development in Norway and led to the production of a national follow-up report, presented to parliament as early as 1989. Today few signs of a distinct national process for sustainable development can be found. The concept of sustainable development has turned into a slogan so frequently used that it has lost much of its sense and power. The weakening of this distinct process does not imply, however, that there have not been institutional changes towards sustainability. The development of interministerial cooperation, environmental legislation, environmental targets and data gathering, and the creation of green budgets and taxes, are some of the central institutional changes that have been made at state level. Moreover, these developments have been supplemented by a wide range of interventions at the local level, in the business and industry sector, and among non-governmental organisations. However, political interest in, and willingness to push for, a more specific and ambitious sustainable development process is missing. This lack of support stems from both the top and the bottom. In order to understand the Norwegian institutional response to sustainable development, this paper explores how it has evolved around the development of a specific national response *process*, as well as central *institutions*, to enhance sustainable development. The aim is to give an overview of the central measures initiated. A complete evaluation of the impacts of the various measures will not be given, but some aspects of the functioning of the measures are highlighted. To get a broader picture of the national response process, relevant attitudes and activities of environmental NGOs, the business community and local governments, in relation to sustainable development, are also identified.

The causal relationship between the UN process for sustainable development and the Norwegian response that we describe cannot easily be isolated and is often unclear. Of more than 150 international environmental agreements,

Norway has signed 60 (Skjærseth and Rosendal, 1995). The UN process for sustainable development and the A21 document with its 40 chapters covered a wide range of environmental policy issue areas; these are also partly covered in other international environmental policy processes. This relationship between environmental issue areas and regimes makes it difficult to identify what is caused by the international process for sustainable development and what is caused by other international environmental policy processes. One should, therefore, be aware that what may appear to be measures that are set out to respond to UNCED may in fact be measures initiated to respond to other international environmental regimes. Moreover, various national efforts identified as measures to respond to the recommendations of the Brundtland Commission and A21 may also have been part of national programmes and projects that would have been implemented independently of the international processes. The development of a Norwegian environmental policy started much earlier than 1987. Other explanations may therefore be found for the initiation of national measures. The timing of the formation and implementation of the measures may be a simple but useful indicator to reveal the causal relationship between the international process and the national initiatives.

INTERPRETING THE CONCEPT

The concept of combining growth and environmental protection was central to several government white papers in the 1960s and 1970s and during the establishment of the Ministry of the Environment (MoE) in 1972; it was also supported by several key NGOs. Therefore, when the idea of sustainable development and growth within environmental limits was launched in 1987 in the World Commission's report, it had already been established as an important concept for the environmental policy community in Norway.

On the basis of the Brundtland Commission's discussion of the concept and a variety of terms which had already been part of the national debate – such as the principles of endurance or nature's carrying capacity – the translation of the term 'sustainable' as *bærekraftig* (something capable of being upheld) was proposed. Both the MoE and the prime minister's office played an important role in choosing a suitable formulation. Alternative terms were proposed, such as *holdbar* (durable) and *varig* (permanent), *sjølbærende* (self-supportive) and *sjølbergende* (subsistence). Despite these alternative concepts, the translation *bærekraftig* gained broad acceptance. The term *bærekraftig* had earlier been used for describing farms where the soil is of such a character and is kept in such a manner that farming can be profitable. The term had not been in popular usage, however, and did not evoke very clear associations, opening it to multiple interpretations.

In order to launch a debate on the report and to mobilise popular participation, the Norwegian Campaign for Environment and Development was established in April 1987, funded by the government. More than 100 organisations took part in the campaign, involving cooperation between interest groups which did not normally meet or collaborate (Aasen, 1994). However, as discussions on developing specific measures for sustainable development progressed, the term itself became more politicised and this led to a less consensual NGO approach. The government's report *Programme for Norway's Follow-Up of the World Commission's Report on Environment and Development* (MoE, 1989) contained a theoretical discussion of sustainable development as a concept. Here both economic and developmental aspects of sustainable development were highlighted. The need for a mutual process of adjustment between economic and environmental policies was emphasised as important. The use of market forces and mechanisms were indicated as central to any process, but it was also underlined that market mechanisms alone cannot take environmental considerations into account in a satisfactory way (MoE, 1989, p7). The developmental and global aspects were also highlighted:

> ...*sustainable development is primarily meaningful in a global context. The sum of various countries' national efforts in accordance with united international goals will therefore be decisive.*[*ibid*, p15]

In spite of this early and broad process for interpreting and integrating the concept of sustainable development, enthusiasm for the concept has declined significantly over time. Yet the term has survived as a normative intention. The philosopher Arne Næss (1991) describes the concept's function:

> *Thanks to the Brundtland report, the eco-political argumentation has risen to a higher level. It is now possible to declare that a political decision is logically incompatible with the approved Brundtland report, that a logical contradiction is present, an inconsistency. Now that 'all' politicians pretend to be of a (moderate) shade of green, the debate may be effectivised. Who will admit to being out of step with themselves?* [*ibid*, p37]

A policy of sustainable development therefore provides an opportunity to put pressure on national governments and political parties to follow up on their international commitments concerning sustainable development (Lafferty and Langhelle, 1995). Yet the question is: who is willing to raise such criticism?

THE NATIONAL RESPONSE PROCESS

The Norwegian Government stated early on its intention to respond to the recommendations of the World Commission's report. To support its efforts, the State Secretary Committee for Environment and Development was created; led by the MoE, it recommended a broad public inquiry into the World Commission's report. In June 1987 a consultation process was initiated with both an internal hearing, including all ministries and directorates, and local and county authorities, and an external hearing including trade and labour organisations, political parties, voluntary organisations, and research communities.

It is interesting to note that the first initiative to induce various ministries to include the concept of sustainable development in parts of their policy areas came from the Ministry of Foreign Affairs. In August 1987, it established an environment–development section, which worked both to integrate the concept of sustainable development into Norway's foreign policy and to persuade various international organisations to incorporate the recommendations of the World Commission's report into various resolutions. An important result of the first objective was the development of a set of guidelines for Norway's foreign policy. These were made in cooperation with other relevant ministries, and included decisions concerning a wide range of issues, such as population growth, food security, biodiversity, energy, industry, urban development, oceans, and education. The output was presented in June 1988 in the Ministry of Foreign Affairs report *Norway's Contribution to International Efforts for Sustainable Development*, which also pointed out that Norway was in a good position to support and strengthen the international process.

In February 1988 a government environmental committee consisting of several ministers was established to discuss the political implications of the World Commission's report for the various sectors, the use of different political measures, and the initiation of research projects.[1] The committee proposed that a White Paper No 46 should be produced to follow up the Brundtland Commission's report. The work of the committee, led by the MoE, formed an important basis for the report. The MoE led the national process and each ministry was asked to define targets and measures for its own sector. Initial attitudes in the different ministries were rather optimistic and innovative; however, as it progressed many ministries found target setting and the selection of measures problematic. Questions of principle concerning ministerial responsibility for a national strategy on sustainable development were also raised. During the process several ministries became less willing to submit information to the MoE. The process was complex and difficult to coordinate for the MoE, which seemed to lack the necessary authority and support from a higher political level. *White Paper No 46: Environment and Development Programme for Norway's Follow-Up of the Report of the World Commission on Environment and Development* (MoE, 1989) was finally presented to parliament in April 1989.

The white paper introduced principles and measures to achieve sustainable development. It endorsed the main findings of the Brundtland Commission's report and declared that sustainable development was to be the overriding objective of the government's future policy. This was to be achieved by cross-sectoral policies at all levels of society. The white paper presented a range of national goals and measures to these ends.[2] Some of these were very specific, such as the quantitative CO_2, NO_x and SO_2 targets and those for reducing discharges of nutrient salts and toxic substances into vulnerable parts of the North Sea. The white paper was declared the framework and action plan for Norway's follow-up to the Brundtland Commission.[3] The ensuing parliamentary debate on the report was characterised by broad consensus, with the political parties attempting to outbid each other in a 'green beauty contest'. This resulted in the adoption of several ambitious environmental targets. The need for proper organisation and development of effective instruments for governance and control to handle sustainable development was also discussed in the report. It stressed that targets should be quantifiable and verifiable, and that routines for the evaluation of results, reporting and budgeting were important. The implementation of the measures was left to the relevant sectoral ministries under the MoE's coordination. It was also proposed that the government should prepare a status report on national and international progress to follow up the Brundtland Commission's recommendations in the next session of parliament, but several ministries opposed the idea and no report of this kind was made.

The government's attitude, portraying Norway as a frontrunner, both concerning its early response to the Brundtland Commission and to UNCED, combined with the perception that sustainable development is primarily meaningful in a global context, may have contributed to the lessening of the pressure for a further national follow-up. Indeed, the original A21 document was not translated into Norwegian and is still not available. After the Earth Summit in Rio the national response process changed character. The government chose to focus on the development of policies for specific environmental issues, rather than to develop a national sustainable development process any further. The government's reports to the CSD (Ministry of Foreign Affairs, 1993; 1995; 1996) are merely seen as communications so that the CSD's secretariat can be informed of, and synthesise, the national processes. The Ministry of Foreign Affairs coordinates and prepares the reports with the participation of other relevant ministries. The reports are not fed into the national policy process and are not used as instruments for monitoring the progress or integration of national policy.

After Rio, the government set up two coordinating bodies, with representatives from various ministries, local and regional governments, NGOs, and the business and industry sector: the *Committee for Sustainable Development* and the *National Committee for International Environmental Questions*. In Norway's reports to the CSD these two are presented as the key national coordination mechanisms for the Norwegian A21 process. The Committee for Sustainable Development supervises the follow-up to A21 with a special focus on national implementation, and the National Committee for International Environmental Questions meets to discuss international environmental issues.[4,5] However, neither meet regularly and appear to have purely information-gathering roles. Nevetheless, the lack of formal coordination meetings does not imply that government agencies and the various NGOs do not meet to discuss environmental policy. More informal contact and cooperation does take place with various NGOs, but often on more specific environment-related issues.

Since Rio, interest in developing a distinct national process for sustainable development has been small, both with the government and the political opposition. Instead, efforts are focused upon the MoE's promotion of sustainable consumption and production. Nevertheless, the Minister of Environment introduced a new white paper on sustainable development in the spring of 1997 (MoE, 1997). This led to some revitalisation of the process. The white paper provided a status report on Norwegian policy for sustainable development and specified the government's next long-term programme. The MoE coordinated the process, which was broad and involved various other ministries, local governments and non-governmental organisations.

INTERMINISTERIAL COOPERATION

In the government's 1989 follow-up report to the parliament on the World Commission, it underlined the need to integrate environmental considerations within all sectors in order to achieve sustainable development:

> *The government emphasises the integration of sustainable development into all societal planning and sectoral policy. The authorities of agriculture, fisheries, energy, and transport ... should all carry the responsibility to ensure that development and planning within these sectors are in accordance with sustainable development and that budgetary and other measures can be applied in such a manner that existing environmental problems can be reduced and new ones can be prevented. [MoE, 1989]*

Specific targets (preferably quantifiable) were to be set for all sectors. Both the implementation of measures and the control of achievements were to be the responsibility of each sector, with some reporting back to the MoE. The MoE was to coordinate the setting of the ministries' targets and to develop systems for supervision. To enhance interministerial cooperation the following four measures have been set out:

1) new planning and budget routines concerning the state budget;
2) the establishment of the State Secretary Committee for Environmental Issues;
3) the use of interministerial working groups; and
4) a new routine for environmental impact assessments within ministries.

For the first time in September 1988 the state budget proposal to parliament included an environmental profile. The purpose of the budget review was to establish a method by which all ministries were obliged to report to parliament, via the MoE, on the environmental effects of their allocations. The routine was meant to serve as an incentive to promote sustainable development and to provide greater transparency on the state's performance in each sector with regard to its environmental objectives. As from 1992 environment-related expenditure has been split into three categories: expenditure with primary environmental effects; expenditure with significant environmental effects; and expenditure with limited environmental effects. In the 1996 budget this routine has been further developed – all ministries present their efforts within 19 different categories.

The application of this new set of categories is intended to provide a more comprehensive overview and to form a better basis for evaluating ministerial environmental activities. All ministries are also responsible for reporting on their environmental achievements. These reports include a description of the environmental and resource problems in each ministry's respective sectors and the likely trends if no new measures are put into effect. Moreover, the reports include goals for meeting these challenges and proposals for long- and short-term measures to solve existing environmental and resource-management problems and to prevent problems from emerging. The impacts of the measures are, if possible, quantified. The quality of the ministries' reports and budgets has steadily improved and today most ministries report on all the issues listed above (Lindseth, 1995). As part of the reporting procedure, the corresponding units of the MoE may evaluate and comment upon each ministry's budget and report proposals. The procedure provides the MoE with early and extensive information on planning in the various ministries and enables the MoE to signal, at an early stage in the budget process, to other ministries or to the government if the specific or overall environmental profile is unsatisfactory. However, the MoE's ability to report back on possible inconsistencies in the other ministries' budgetary reporting is still limited, and the coordinating role of the MoE still lacks power and weight.

In 1989 the government developed a second coordinating measure, the establishment of the State Secretary Committee for Environmental Issues – a forum for interministerial cooperation and coordination on environmental policy, chaired by the state secretary for the environment. The committee is involved in developing methods to achieve better coordination of a comprehensive environmental policy, and provides a valuable function as a forum where interministerial conflicts may be solved at a lower political level before they reach cabinet level. The committee also discusses possible improvements in the total state budget's environmental profile each year. Discussions in the committee have several times led to changes in budget priorities, resulting in increased funding in some parts of the budget (Lindseth, 1995). Meetings are held monthly, enabling stable, operative and flexible cooperation between the ministries. Much effort has been put into the development of the committee's work to establish a smoothly functioning internal political process of coordination.

A third integrative measure is the formation of several interministerial working groups, representing an effort to promote better integration on cross-sectoral environmental issues. The government has mandated groups to report on issues such as environmental taxes, climate policy, environmental instruments and sustainable consumption. The method is based on consensus-building around a problem and the measures needed to solve it. However, the processes are often time consuming and can lead to conflicts and possible stalemates. Here, the role of the MoE is often to guide and influence rather than to direct the other ministries. The initiatives taken so far are seen as positive, reducing conflicts and increasing the basis for cooperation between ministries (NOU, 1995, p147). Nevertheless, the work partly depends upon the willingness of the ministries concerned to give priority to environmental issues over other sectoral interests, and the MoE exercises no absolute control in such issues and will therefore often have to negotiate with other ministries over environmental targets and strategies.

A fourth integrative mechanism is the development of environmental assessments within the ministries. Impact assessment involves reporting on the consequences of ministerial work through public reports, regulations, proposals and reports to parliament. Since December 1994 the routine has been extended to include environmental consequences. All ministries are now required to consult with the MoE concerning environmental impact assessments. The assessment is undertaken by the MoE, who provides it with the ability to direct the activities of other ministries according to environmental consequences.

Despite all these efforts at coordination the experience so far has been mixed. According to the OECD:

> *...integration does not operate in practice as satisfactorily as it should...These sectors do not always seem to work as closely with the Ministry of Environment as might have been expected in view of their role in environmental protection and degradation.* [OECD, 1993, p80]

The lack of interministerial cooperation has also been confirmed in statements by the environment minister, which highlight problems with establishing common interests and targets for sustainable development within the central administration.[6] Sustained political pressure to persuade sectoral ministries to accept and apply integrative mechanisms and procedures is therefore vital. Today the MoE seems to be fatigued with 'struggling' with other ministries in its attempts to create a sector-encompassing environmental policy, and the position of the environment ministry within the government is relatively weak. The State Secretary Committee for Environmental Issues may partly sustain pressure for an integrated environmental policy, but stalemates may occur due to interministerial disagreements. As far as political leadership and support from the prime minister is concerned, the situation also seems to have changed. In 1987 Gro Harlem Brundtland in her dual role as chairman of the World Commission and Norway's prime minister pressed for an ambitious environmental policy. In recent years she preferred to focus more on other issues, such as EU membership and oil and gas production; this has made cross-sectoral cooperation more difficult to achieve.

SETTING TARGETS, REPORTING ON ACHIEVEMENTS

The adoption of quantitative targets is one of the most distinctive features of Norwegian environmental policy (OECD, 1993). The setting of CO_2 and NO_x emission targets and targets for land-based ocean pollution are illustrative of Norway's situation regarding the ambitious environmental targets defined during the initial stage following the World Commission's report. Today the government faces problems in achieving many of the targets set at the end of the 1980s. Moreover, the economic cost of adopting the targets has become a more visible factor, changing the content of many of the environmental policy debates to focus more on meeting existing targets, rather than setting new ones.

Various documents present figures on targets and achievements, though no single document covers them all. The documentary process tends to be fragmented and is only connected to the policy process to a small extent.

An important reporting mechanism within parliament is the annual environmental statement by the environment minister, begun in 1987.[7] The content of the statements vary from year to year, depending upon what the minister would like to draw attention to or to downplay. Since 1991 an additional section of environmental background data accompanies the statement; this has gradually become more comprehensive. However, neither the statement nor the background data section give a complete overview of targets or trends based on a systematic use of indicators to monitor and report on status and progress. The statement is barely used as an instrument for control, but it does ensure an annual debate on the government's environmental policy in parliament, where criticism can be made. A further planning document is the government's long-term programme, issued every four years, prepared mainly by the Ministry of Finance. The two latest contained a separate chapter on sustainable development and the environment, but again failed to provide a systematic overview and evaluation of achieving established targets (MoE, 1994; 1995). As of 1994, the state of the environment in the Nordic counties is to be reported annually by means of environmental indicators. The indicators refer to different stages of the cause–effect change and are described as the pressure-state-response concept.[8] The work on the Nordic indicators closely follows the OECD's work on environmental indicators. Moreover, the Norwegian State Pollution Control Authority has started a pilot project to develop indicators for sustainable production and consumption.

ENVIRONMENTAL TAXES AND GREEN ACCOUNTING

Since 1989, a popularised version of the state budget has been issued annually as a *Green Book* containing a report on environment-related expenditure by all ministries and a short commentary on the overall green profile of the budget. The budgeting process is, however, a rather passive collection and reporting of pro-environmental efforts and does not contain the evaluation, reporting and control function that it was intended to have (NOU, 1995, p4).[9]

Nevertheless, Norway has taken the lead among OECD countries in terms of environmental taxation (OECD, 1993, p86). During 1989 to 1990 the use of environmental taxes and other economic instruments increased. On the government's initiative a Green Tax Commission was set up in December 1989 to study economic principles, strategies and measures for use as yardsticks in evaluating the various aspects of the environment. Three years later, the commission's work resulted in a comprehensive report and proposals for a more extensive use of economic instruments to promote a cost-effective environmental policy (NOU, 1992, p3). In its latest long-term programme (1994–97) the government signalled a further increase in the use of economic instruments; however, by 1996 no new environmental taxes were planned. Any further development of the CO_2 tax will, according to the government, due to Norway's small economy, depend upon the developments of taxation in Norway's neighbouring countries and the EU.

The Norwegian Green Tax Commission (1996, p55) concluded that the current tax regime is inefficient in that it penalises employment by making it financially burdensome to acquire additional labour, whereas higher taxes on environmental burdens, VAT and housing create efficiencies by removing these weighty distorting taxes. Therefore, the commission favoured an extension of carbon, sulphur and nitrogen taxes, including a wide variety of additional measures, partly for this macro-economic reason and not for sustainability reasons. This is another example of how institutional reform for any sustainability transition requires a 'leg up' from the heavyweight policy arenas of economic and business reform.

GREENING BUSINESS AND INDUSTRY

From playing an often defensive role, mainly adapting to state regulations and directives, surveys indicate that large sectors of business and industry in Norway are willing to recognise the environmental challenge and to take steps towards 'greening' business. The Confederation of Norwegian Business and Industry has urged its members to put environmental issues on the agenda and to prepare their own environmental reports. Approximately 100 companies have hitherto done so, but few businesses give quantitative environmental information. The information provided is often fragmentary and does not always suggest a good basis for evaluating companies' environmental status (Deloitte and Touche, 1995). The government plays a major role in promoting a greening of business and industry. In March 1991 it ordered all public and private activities to implement a documented internal control system for health, safety and the environment. A further reporting instrument is the obligation for all companies listed on the stock exchange to include in their annual report a paragraph on the pollution caused by the company and the mitigation measures initiated (Dahl, 1994).

The government gives special emphasis to promoting more sustainable patterns of consumption. In order to develop, pilot and promote methods of green management, the MoE, in 1991, established a green management programme involving business, trade unions, local authorities and environmental NGOs. In 1995 the programme was established permanently as the Norwegian Centre for Sustainable Production and Consumption; its remit was to motivate and facilitate sustainable development in Norwegian business and to focus on the market effects of environmental policy. So far there have been pilot projects for the sectors of: advertising, banking and finance, commercial buildings, information technology, local authorities, retailing, and tourism. Voluntary agreements have also been sought and developed with those parts of the industry sector that are exempt from the CO_2 tax. An environmentally sound public procurement policy has been introduced. This aims to steer public purchasing – amounting to 140 billion Norwegian krone in 1993 – towards more sustainable alternatives. No regulations exist in Norway to regulate the environmental labelling of goods (apart from prohibitions of certain chemicals which will be indicated pursuant to legislation). There are, however, some non-binding arrangements. Among these is the foundation called Environmental Labelling, organised by the Nordic Council, which has introduced the 'swan-mark' in Nordic countries.

A FUTURE SUSTAINABILITY PROCESS

The Norwegian national response process to sustainable development began early. In the period leading up to the Earth Summit in Rio much political energy was fed into the process, which gained broad support from the government and the political opposition, and among a wide range of NGOs. After Rio, political interest for the process waned. Five factors may explain this:

- the interpretation of the concept;
- the government's perception of Norway as an environmental frontrunner;
- the lack of political leadership and the absence of a strong political opposition;
- the perception of fewer environmental threats; and
- a perception within the government that it was more appropriate to focus on a wider set of specific environmental issues than to develop a process for sustainable development.

The Norwegian interpretation of the concept of sustainable development accorded well with the already prevailing ideology of combining economic growth and environmental protection. The incremental rather than radical approach to, and understanding of, the concept probably reduced the likelihood of achieving a more fundamental reorientation. However, the term sustainable development seems to have survived as a normative principle, providing an opportunity to put pressure on the national government to follow up on its commitments. Despite this, such criticism is not very strong.

The government's programmatic statements concerning Norway's frontrunner status, with regard to the recommendations in A21, may have eased internal pressure for continuing the national follow-up process. The image of being a frontrunner has, to some extent, been accepted by the public, diminishing a potential bottom-up pressure for action. The frontrunner role is, however, proving difficult to achieve due to high economic costs and the lack of political willingness to pursue an ambitious environmental policy.

The political opposition to the government is weak and no party is willing to take any green leadership role at the moment. The 'green beauty contest' among the political parties has definitely come to an end. A possible explanation for this reduced interest in environmental issues, in general, may be found in the changing environmental threats. When the Brundtland Commission presented its report, several international environmental problems posed a threat to Norway and led to broad interest and enthusiasm for the concept of sustainable development. Today, Norway's environmental situation seems to have undergone a transformation. Acid rain continues to cause problems but political solutions are in sight, and the Norwegian Government cooperates closely with Russia to reduce the risk of nuclear accidents. The lack of severe environmental threats to Norway, combined with the government's self-image of being a frontrunner in all senses, may have led to less attention being directed at environmental policy issues. The successful Olympic Winter Games at Lillehammer in 1994, the Oslo Channel in the Middle East peace process the same year, the debate and the result of the EU referendum in 1994, and Norway's economically strong position due to oil and natural gas exports – all these may have strengthened the Norwegian self-image of being an environmental frontrunner.

The government's weak interest in developing a distinct sustainable development process may, however, also be due to a perception that it is more appropriate to focus on a wider set of specific environmental policy issues, such as climate change, biodiversity, water pollution, waste management, and sustainable consumption, and to develop targets, policies and evaluations within each of these issue fields. Taken together, these form a complete environmental policy. A separate sustainable development process may therefore not be seen as necessary. This may partly explain why so little political energy has been fed into a specific sustainable development process after Rio.

As to the younger generations, increased interest in environmental education, both in schools and within environmental NGOs, may form the basis for a more long-term and stable environmental awareness among citizens. Nature conservation has been a compulsory subject taught in the Norwegian educational system since 1971. In 1991 the Ministry of Education, Research and Church Affairs formulated a national strategy for integrating education on environment and development throughout the school system and in the national curriculum guidelines. Environmental NGOs have also worked to increase children's environmental awareness. One of the most successful initiatives is *Blekkulf's Environmental Detectives*, established in 1989, under the auspices of the Norwegian Society for the Conservation of Nature. Through radio, television programmes and books children learn about Blekkulf, a cartoon octopus who needs help to clean up nature.

More recently, in December 1995 the Norwegian Research Council (1996) arranged a national hearing on sustainable development to discuss the content and role of the concept in public policy strategies. The panel recommended continuing the debate in a series of national hearings on more specific aspects related to sustainable development. These hearings may, if they are carried out, reestablish a broader debate on sustainable development. The outcome of the MoE's recently launched proposal for a new White Paper on sustainable development, by spring 1997, may also lead to a revitalisation of the process for sustainable development in Norway – but the final outcome of this process still remains to be seen.

CONCLUSION

The political process related to Norway's response to sustainable development has been characterised by shifting political interests. During the period of 1987 to 1992 a broad participatory, state-initiated process was carried out to follow up the World Commission's report and to prepare for UNCED, both at the national and international level. After UNCED, the interest in pursuing a distinct national process for sustainable development, both within the government and in the political opposition, has been limited. However, after Rio efforts to promote sustainable development practices continue, both at the state level and among NGOs, in the business and industry sector and at the local level. These structures and procedures continue to function relatively smoothly and more or less independently of fluctuations in the political interest for sustainable development. Many of the institutional developments described above started or were planned before the launch of the Brundtland Commission's report. This indicates that the Norwegian administrative and political system for environmental policy has developed partly independently of the international process for sustainable development. To get a total picture of the institutional developments for a more sustainable development in Norway, it is, therefore, vital to look beyond the specific national response process related to the World Commission's report and the UNCED.

Chapter 11

THE EVOLUTION OF SUSTAINABLE DEVELOPMENT STRATEGIES IN PORTUGAL

Teresa Ribeiro and Valdemar Rodrigues

INTRODUCTION: BEFORE RIO

In Portugal, the first official action concerning environmental matters was the establishment of the National Commission for the Environment (CNA) in 1971 to prepare for Portugal's participation in the UN Conference on Environment (held in Stockholm in 1972). The committee was initially established as part of the National Council for Scientific Research (JNICT), in charge of research programmes; this fostered the perception that the environment was a scientific rather than a policy or a political issue. The committee later became an autonomous body under the direct control of the prime minister and was responsible for the first efforts aimed at public information, awareness and training programmes with regard to the environment. Another early environmental institution, the National Parks Service, was established in 1974. Its objective was the creation of a framework for developing a network of natural protected areas. During the intervening years the service has assumed increased importance, and now has more than 500 people working all over the country in protected areas; these correspond to about 6 per cent of the national territory.

The 1974 revolution provided the conditions for the establishment of a State Department for the Environment (SEA) that later became the Ministry of Quality of Life (1979–1985). However, during this period nothing relevant or important was to happen. It was only in 1985 that a step forward was made with structural changes to the SEA and the creation of a new institution: the State's Secretariat for the Environment and Natural Resources (SEARN), now part of the new Ministry of Planning and Territory Administration (MPAT). The European Year of the Environment (1987) was a turning point concerning environmental policy and two main laws were approved: the Environmental Basic Act (EBA) and the Environmental Protection Associations Act (EPAA). These provided the legal framework for subsequent environmental action and public participation. The EBA also enabled the restructuring of SEARN, enlarging its competencies, doubling its budget, and resulted in the first serious initiatives towards defining a national environmental policy. This progress can be regarded as a convergence of three major factors: Portugal was finally recovering from the economic and political chaos evident since 1975; the process of joining the European Economic Community was finally completed in 1986; and, SEARN was a strong political leader, willing to fight for environmental causes.

The challenge became, then, the transposition of the copious European Community (EC) legislative body into national regulation, and the implementation of a demanding environmental policy in a country which had undergone a political and economic rupture. In fact, Portugal was adjusting to the exercise of democracy while, at the same time, trying to rebuild an economy which previously had been based on the exploitation of its colonies' natural resources and now had a considerably obsolete industrial base. Extensions were granted in complying with EC environmental legislation requirements in most areas, but a survey of the implementation of EC directives, undertaken in 1989, already indicated that in most areas the country was far from meeting its commitments.

Despite the opposition of many environmentalists – who preferred a strong secretary of state for the environment in a strong ministry rather than a weak ministry of the environment – in 1990 SEARN was transformed into a ministry: the Ministry of Environment and Natural Resources (MENR). Left out of its ministerial sphere were crucial areas for implementing environmental policy. An important portion of environmental competencies stayed with MPAT; this sometimes created a bicephalous policy with contradicting signals and a fragmentation of actions. Until the eve of UNCED, there was hardly any progress on implementing environmental policy, while at the same time consid erable investments were made in various sectors of economy supported by EC structural funds. The definition of a LA21 and governmental responses to the CSD were the most immediate consequences of UNCED in relation to Portugal's domestic sustainable development policy. However, a policy document was inspired by this momentum, the National Environmental Policy Plan (NEPP, 1995). Significantly for the success of any move towards greater sustainability, institutional debate did not start until 1992. However, this was not complemented by a wide scientific debate on what sustainability means and on how it could be operationalised in the context of the politically defined national priorities and development strategies. The first open scientific debate on sustainable development was held in Aveiro as recently as April 1996.[1]

Informing the A21 Process

Since public involvement in the decision-making process is a key issue for implementing sustainable development strategies, information represents a critical factor in their prosecution. This statement implies that information exists, that it is accessible, and that it is in a form that can be used by the general public. The message of A21 in this respect can be illustrated in Figure 11.1, where the oriented lines represent possible flows of information.

Political decision-making and public participation on development issues

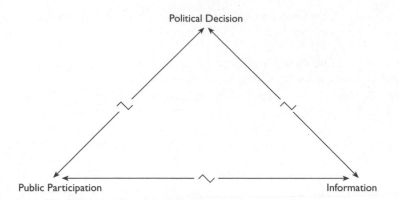

Figure 11.1 The information triangle: political decision, public participation and information – showing the possible ruptures on information flow

should ideally be determined by the information concerning each component of sustainable development, which means considering the social, environmental, institutional, and economic contexts of development (see Gouzee *et al*, 1995). It follows that whenever the existing information is scarce or insufficient, decision-making should be delayed while new elements are collected. This principle of political choice, when uncertainty is great, can also be termed the precautionary principle. On the other hand, public participation can be much more effective provided that information is good and available, with the same quality and quantity for both the decision-makers and the public. It has been observed in Portugal that sometimes the most relevant aspects underlying development options are unclear to the common citizen, or the NGOs. Whether deliberately or not, the options in the construction of the new bridge over the Tejo River in Lisbon is a paradigmatic example of this, as discussed by Clare Coffey in Chapter 7.

According to the message of A21, and in the context of a strategy towards sustainable development, it is also important to notice that none of the triangle's vertices in Figure 11.1 makes sense in the absence of the remaining two. Thus, for instance, the existence of a great amount of detailed information makes no sense when nobody uses it, or when decisions are made arbitrarily with no reference to public opinion. It also does not make any sense to have an inquiry into the public's opinion when the information available to the public on a given subject is not equivalent (quantitatively or qualitatively) to that available to the decision-maker.

Citizens' access to information is prescribed in Portugal's Constitution.[2] Also, the code of the administrative procedure (1991) regulates general relationships between citizens and state and focuses on questions of citizens' access to information – namely the terms by which information should be made accessible in public participation procedures. Environmental information is, however, scattered over a great number of governmental departments. Even mechanisms for evaluating the government's environmental performance, such as the

Annual Report on the State of the Environment or the *White Book* produced in 1991, have proved inadequate sources of accessible, consistent information or are ineffective as the basis of policy-making.

THE EVOLUTION OF NATIONAL STRATEGIES TOWARDS SUSTAINABLE DEVELOPMENT

The EBA, which constitutes the framework of national environmental policy, invokes the principle of public participation, establishing the requirement for the participation of various social groups when implementing environmental and landuse planning policies at local, regional and central levels.[3] It is often quoted internationally as one of the most interesting legal documents ever published in the field of environmental law. In the opinion of some experts (see Reis, 1992) the EBA has profoundly marked the juridical order in Portugal – probably not because of its immediate effects, but because of the new possibilities which legislators have had the courage to develop, and the general principles that were established as a result of its existence.

The term self-sustained development is introduced at the very beginning of EBA (article 2, number 2): '[T]he environmental policy aims at optimising and assuring the continuity of natural resources' utilisation, qualitatively and quantitatively, as a basic prerequisite for self-sustained development.' This article is of special importance since, for the first time, a legal document recognised the existence of a clear association between the environment and development. The concept of sustainable development underlying the article, although not explicit, is very similar to that of the Brundtland report, suggesting that it was probably a reference point for the legislator. Other parts in the EBA refer to the principles of environmental policy adopted by the EC when the first action programme was approved, for example article 4:

> *The existence of an environment adequate to population's health and welfare, and to social and cultural development of communities, presumes the adoption of measures towards the self-sustained social end economic development and the correct growth of urban areas, through landuse planning ... and the promotion of public participation in formulating and executing environmental and quality of life policies, as well as the establishment of continuous fluxes of information between the organs of the administration responsible for those policies and the citizens to which they are directed.*

In order to promote actions towards better environmental quality, and with special emphasis on providing information and training for citizens and NGOs, the EBA created a new institution, currently called IPAMB – the Institute of Environmental Protection. The structure adopted for this institution was unique in the context of Portuguese public administration, as most of the members of the directive council of IPAMB are from non-governmental sectors of society.

The EPAA defines the rights of environmental protection associations (EPAs) to participate in central, regional and local administrations.[4] EPAs are constituted in the terms of the general law, giving them juridical personality, and are non-profitable. Their objectives are: environmental protection, protection of the natural and architectural heritage, nature conservation, and the promotion of quality of life. The associations are further classified into local, regional or national, depending on the range of their actions. They must have a minimum number of members: 4000, 1000 and 200 for the national, regional and local associations, respectively. Article 3 declares all national EPAs, and some regional ones, as associations that are generically representative.[5] In practice this means that some political influence is attributed to EPAs, in the sense that they have specific rights, such as the statute of social partner for all legal effects and the right to use public TV and radio channels to broadcast their messages and ideas. They also have, according to their level of action, the right to participate in defining environmental policy and in its major legislative outcomes.[6] Consultation rights are also consigned to EPAs with regard to documents such as: regional landuse plans; municipal master plans; environmental impact assessment studies; agricultural and forest plans and projects; and the creation and management of protected areas.

Other aspects mentioned in the EPAA include the right to use administrative resources; the legitimacy of EPAs in making omissions public, or acts perpetrated by public or private bodies against the environment, and to act judicially when necessary; and the duty of cooperation between municipalities and EPAs concerning the protection and 'valuing' of nature and the environment. In article 9 EPAs were declared to have a right to the state's support through central, regional and local administration, for the prosecution of their objectives and for activities that develop citizens' information and training. The IPAMB should provide, according to the EBA, the technical or financial support to any EPAs applying for it. This aspect will be discussed further below.

A National A21

Immediately after UNCED, in August 1992, the Portuguese Government created a task force to implement the principles, programmes and actions arising from the Earth Summit conference in Rio. The result of the work undertaken by this ad hoc structure, a first draft version of a national A21 (CSD, 1994a), was presented to the Council of Ministers in January 1993. The final version of the document (MENR, 1994) was published after an internal debate at governmental level, and after consultation with other sectors of society. Five major impressions emerged from the public debate:

1) the urgent need for a national environmental policy plan;
2) the lack of consistency between the political rhetoric and Portuguese reality;
3) the need for the political commitment of all the ministries in relation to environmental questions;
4) the need to promote the participation of civil society; and

5) the necessity of mobilising multiple instruments.

However, this process appears to have had little effect on policy. Prepared during and after UNCED, the regional development plan shows no evidence of input either from the conference conclusions or from the national A21. In other words, it seems that the two processes were run in tandem by the government, with no intention of integrating them. On the one hand, the governmental departments were preparing the most important binding plan regarding development options until the turn of the century; on the other hand an ad-hoc commission was set up with the mandate of identifying the necessary action and of proposing political means in order to implement the Rio conclusions at national level.

Beyond the production of a national A21 strategy, other efforts are necessary to continue the process, such as the creation of a permanent institutional structure expressly concerned with sustainable development. Reports to the CSD submitted by the Portuguese Government (CSD, 1994a; CSD, 1994b) clearly show the absence of such a structure. The two ministries involved in reporting to the CSD were, as legally defined, the Ministry of Foreign Affairs and MENR. The role of the former ministry in this process has been quite worthless, and MENR has shifted the responsibility of CSD reporting onto IPAMB, which is somewhat inexperienced with such responsibilities.

IPAMB, in this role, came up against substantial reporting difficulties, mainly in those areas of A21 which require sectoral and cross-sectoral approaches. Since IPAMB had no legal mandate to legitimise its actions, the required information from other ministries and departments was difficult to obtain since they had no obligation to cooperate. The result is visible in the last CSD report (CSD, 1994a), both in the prolix character of the information presented for some areas and in the difficulty of disassociating areas and themes within the sphere of more than one ministry or department and, ultimately, in the number of non answered questions.[7] The lack of a national coordinating body with responsibility for sustainable development and A21 follow-up explains, in part, the absence of sustainable development indicators and criteria for their application at the domestic level (CSD, 1994a). In addition, the omission – until recently – of any broad debate involving experts from the different disciplines is also a factor.

INSTITUTIONAL RESPONSES TO SUSTAINABLE DEVELOPMENT: THE TOUCHSTONES

In this section we point out some particular institutional responses to sustainable development strategies observed at the level of the Ministry of the Environment, local and regional governments, environmental NGOs, and industrial sectors. With regard to public participation in issues concerning environment and development, we proceed with a detailed analysis of the EIA legislation and its practical outcomes.

Following the Rio conference and based on the targets established by the Fifth EC Environmental Programme, MENR underwent a process of reorganisation, apparently to adjust itself to implementing sustainable development strategies (Regulation 187/93):

> *...it is considered imperative an adjustment of the institutional structure, reflecting the recent, nevertheless significant, evolution of the concepts of action of the state within the environmental field, now centred on the main objective of promoting a sustainable development.*

At this time it was also emphasised that the main task of the ministry is 'to participate in the promotion of a sustainable development that respects the environment as its fundamental support'. Sustainable development requires all actors and all sectors to become involved, but a leader is required in order to guide the process and this is lacking. The concepts of shared and joint responsibility, policy integration and so forth allowed MENR to identify several areas where other bodies could be responsible; it subsequently abandoned its leading role, instead of using those concepts to develop a more coherent environmental policy (Ribeiro *et al*, 1996). In fact, MENR has been a very weak ministry; the most salient indicator of this is perhaps the Decree Law 186/90 on the process of EIA. Amongst the many technical failures of this law, the position of the ministry on a given project submitted to EIA is neither binding nor essential for a project's prosecution. In terms of decision capacity and influence on political decisions, MENR has today fewer powers than in 1987. Although some specific competencies have been transferred to MENR from other ministries (such as coastal planning and climate policy), MENR is often not consulted at all, or only invited to produce non-binding opinions in areas such as: landuse planning, forest management, agriculture, transport, and energy. With respect to MENR's actual competencies, there are two basic components which are clearly unbalanced: responsibility for sanitary and hydraulic works, which occupies most of MENR's budget; and environmental management, which is almost beyond the ministry's scope. This affects MENR's ability to take a strong lead on sustainability and represents a substantial institutional barrier to further progress at national level.

Environmental NGOs

Portugal, which is often considered a country in transition, was one of the nations included in a survey carried out on the environmental awareness of its citizens (Dunlap, 1994; Dunlap and Mertig, 1995). The results show that about 25 per cent of the Portuguese say that the environment is one of the most serious problems in the country; over 30 per cent believe in public participation to protect the environment and in the major role played by the NGOs; 85 per cent of respondents believe that the health of the next generation will be substantially affected by the degradation of the environment; and about 60 per cent say they are willing to pay higher prices to protect it. However, in Portugal

Table 11.1 Membership and resource base of environmental
NGOs in Portugal

Indicator	LPN	QUERCUS	GEOTA
Number of members (N)	6000	8000	900
Number of active members (AM)	na	na	40
Permanent staff (PS)	5	16	3
Ratio PS/N (%)	0.08	0.20	0.33
Ratio AM/N (%)	na	na	4.44
Basic maintenance costs/year (thousands of PTE)	900 *	5000	5000

* = the central administrative nucleus, located in Lisbon only
na = not available
PTE = Portuguese Escudos

people think of environmental problems as other people's problems and as having an external cause not related to their own activities (Schmidt, 1993). The EPAs could be important sources of information for the public if they had the technical capacity and the necessary staff to conduct independent studies on issues concerning sustainable development and environmental quality. Despite recent developments involving the major EPAs, most of them still have no permanent or technical staff, no technical resources such as (accredited) environmental labs, and survive with scarce or, at least, uncertain financial support. In 1995 about 140 environmental NGOs were registered with IPAMB. Table 11.1 gives some indicators of the dimensions and associative dynamics of the three most active national NGOs: LPN, QUERCUS, and GEOTA.[8,9,10]

The ratios of permanent staff to the number of affiliates are on average lower than 0.3 per cent for the three associations. This indicator of the association's professional activity is obviously very low and confirms the predominantly amateur nature of the Portuguese EPAs.

The support delivered by the IPAMB is project specific, and the EPAs have submitted funding requests every year since 1988. In 1995, for instance, 178 projects were presented to the IPAMB, of which 74 were approved (about 41 per cent). The 74 approved projects applied for a budget of 100,584,000 Portuguese escudos (PTE) (about 0.5 MECU), but the support provided by IPAMB was only 40 per cent of this (40,002,000 PTE).[11] Figure 11.2 depicts the variation in financial support delivered by the central administration to the Portuguese environmental EPAs between 1988 and 1995.

In April 1995, a public session sponsored by IPAMB was held in Aveiro with the objective of presenting the EPA projects supported by the government in 1993 – a total of 41 projects. The conclusions of the public session were:

- the work carried out by the EPAs is very important in terms of detection, data gathering, and public awareness, although this is dependent on the scope and execution capacity of each EPA;

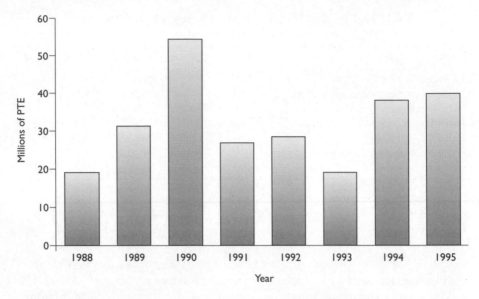

Figure 11.2 Financial support delivered by the central administration to the EPAs since 1988 (1995 constant prices)

- in view of the predominance of projects in areas such as nature conservation, environmental education and cultural and natural heritage, these areas should be considered by IPAMB as permanent priorities in terms of their financial support. The total budget allocated to EPA projects was felt to be clearly insufficient, and therefore other kinds of financial support should be implemented;
- institutions such as the Institute for the Protection of Archaeological and Architectonic Heritage, industry and other economic sectors, structural funds, and the municipalities, should be considered as forms of financial support;
- it was a noticeable problem for EPAs to execute their projects in the year corresponding to IPAMB support; therefore, more flexible funding forms should be examined; and
- the work of EPAs has a strong and almost exclusive component of voluntarism. This often causes variability in information accuracy and project structuring. Therefore the IPAMB, together with other institutions, should promote EPA training and help their staff to become more professional.[12]

The main problem for these organisations is perhaps the lack of independent information on the environment at the national level – besides the inability to produce it themselves. Since no alternative environmental data are produced, both citizens and NGOs have to rely upon governmental sources where information can be manipulated and distorted in order to serve political and other interests.

Voluntary Agreements in the Portuguese Industrial Sector

In November 1994, a global agreement on the environment and sustainable development (AGMADS, 1994) was signed between the government, the Confederation of Portuguese Industry, and the Confederation of Portuguese Land Farmers. The agreement involved MENR and other ministries and establishes major guidelines for institutional cooperation towards adjusting various industrial sectors in line with the environmental legislation in force. The leit-motif of the agreement was basically the recognition that environmental legislation was being transposed into the national context at a rate clearly unbalanced by the capacity of Portuguese industry to accommodate these requirements. In other words, companies felt that something should be done to permit a more progressive adjustment, to delay legal enforcement and to avoid the possible consequences. This general agreement should form the basis for more specific agreements, involving particular sectors of Portugese industry. The first sectoral voluntary agreement was signed in February 1995 between the governmental authorities and the national federation of swine-breeders' associations.

The lesson to learn from the process leading to these voluntary agreements can be synthesised in a few points. Firstly, companies and the industrial sector in general are more open to participation when they perceive some sectoral protection in the negotiation (or adjustment) processes. Secondly, the disconnection between the various governmental departments in issues concerning the environment causes distrust in environmental policy and tends to remove potential targets from the adjustment process. Thirdly, this process shows that, at the present, most of the industries in Portugal have problems other than environmental ones, and awareness about the environment still tends to be seen as a secondary question. In most Portuguese industries environmental management is still a misunderstood concept. The accomplishment of legislation, which seems to be the engine of these voluntary agreements, is part of a wider process that is now being learned for the first time by many of the economic leaders of Portuguese society.

Accommodating Sustainability within the Portuguese Democratic System

Despite the convergence achieved in economic, social and other fields within the EU, there are differences amongst the member states that cannot be ignored when analysing their institutional adjustments to sustainable development strategies. One of the major differences is due to the political structure of each member state, namely the structure and organisation of the various democratic systems. In the EU, democratic systems present marked differences and peculiarities (Laundy, 1989; Liebert and Cotta, 1990; PE, 1992). The Portuguese political system can be characterised by its very party-dependent nature. Citizens must vote for a party list and therefore cannot express their preferences by a given candidate, both in legislative and local elections. The lack of relationship between electors and the parliamentary candidates makes the elected deputies and candidates completely dependent upon the support of their party. This can subjugate the democratic system to what we refer to as a party logic – a major handicap of the Portuguese political system.

The most voted for party in the legislative elections has the opportunity to constitute government, alone or in cooperation with other parties (depending on the percentage of votes obtained). The prime minister is nominated by the president of the republic in view of the electoral results, and this usually coincides with the general secretariat of the most voted for party. The prime minister chooses the other members of the government, and therefore the ministerial composition and structure of the government often are a surprise to the common elector. Since it is essentially political power that is transferred after elections, the elected politicians must deal with interests previously established within their departments. And since these interests are indirectly protected by law, implementing a new policy may be a difficult task to accomplish during the limited period of a mandate.[13] The sustainability transition may also require a transition of technical – since sustainable development will involve new concepts and technical procedures not formerly known or experienced by the technicians that are still in charge in many governmental and para-governmental offices. Under these circumstances, even a strong political will can be sometimes hindered by the administrative machinery.

CONCLUSIONS

The concept of sustainable development is still unassimilated, which means that different institutions either base their judgements and viewpoints upon their own interpretations of sustainable development, through a more or less elaborated hermeneutic process, or simply introduce the term in their current speech without any concerns about its measurability. In the national context we cannot think about the existence of a real environmental conscience. This fact is related to the weak implantation of post-materialist values in Portugal, constrained by the relative immaturity of the existing democracy and by the still recent political and economic stability. On the other hand, there is a noticeable emergence of environmental awareness in almost every sector of Portuguese society. A sustainability transition in Portugal is hindered by several obstacles:

- the country's developmental stage, with regard to basic infrastructures, regional homogeneity and global efficiency in the use of resources and technology;
- the inertia or inability of the different institutions, which are, in general, poorly prepared to face the new challenges of sustainable development;
- the absence of an institutional cooperation model based on interdependence rather than on hierarchic relationships;
- the degree of democratic maturity; and
- the organisation and functioning of the political system.

A brief look into specific aspects or sectors shows little innovation or change. There is no novelty in key areas such as green accounting, ecological taxation, structural planning, and environmental analysis of regional development projects and programmes. The role of NGOs has been reinforced, but since public support for these organisations is still scarce and deficient, it certainly looks as if this is due to NGO efforts – probably aided by the effect of global environment trends. On the other hand, no permanent structures have been set up in order to define, follow up and evaluate the sustainability transition in Portugal – such as policy coordination mechanisms, interministerial committees, parliamentary committees, or any other discussion forums.

Chapter 12

ADJUSTING TO A CHANGING REALITY: THE GREEK RESPONSE

Panos Fousekis and Joseph Lekakis

THE PUBLIC AND POLITICAL CULTURE OF THE SUSTAINABILITY TRANSITION

Both social and natural sciences have extensively borrowed from the Greek vocabulary Christian concepts which are missing in other languages. 'Economics' and 'ecology', which typically represent the spectrum of these sciences, are truly composite Greek words. Despite the fact that the Greek language has been a goldmine of scientific terminology, a unique translation of sustainable development in Greek does not exist. While no absolute classifications can be made, the ecologist's label of sustainable development is *aieforiki anaptyksi*, from *aie* (always) and *faero* (bring, carry, produce). Sociologists, policy-makers and politicians appear to prefer the most popular label, *viosimi anaptyksi*, meaning viable, or capable of living. An alternative label, *ypostiriksimi anaptyksi*, meaning supportable, has been employed as well. The notion, however, of sustainable development has only recently become part of the scientific and political jargon in Greece.

Pyrovetsi (1994) uses the word *aieforiki*. According to her, societies should set the following priorities: to preserve life-support processes and biodiversity; to minimise the exhaustion of stock resources; and to function within the productive capacities of ecosystems. Pyrovetsi calls for a 'common responsibility' which necessitates a wide and active participation of governments, economic agents and the public in the form of citizens and consumers. All citizens ought to adopt an ethic of sustainable living, reconsider their values and alter their behaviour. Therefore, while advocating development which does not interfere with the productive capacity of ecosystems, Pyrovetsi calls for a change in personal values to reverse the present trend of environmental degradation.

Laskaris (1993) employs the label *viosimi anaptyksi*. For him, sustainable development occurs locally where societies are capable of integrating the concept within local conditions in the way they know best. Because local societies are economically, administratively and educationally dependent upon the government, sustainable development presupposes institutional freedom. The vehicle to gaining it is environmental education. Thus, Laskaris's view is also value-oriented, although he appears to understand the significance of political and economic factors.

Using *aieforiki, ypostiriksimi*, and *viosimi*, Kousis (1991; 1993; and 1994) adopts a political economy theorisation of sustainable development as a case of environmental conflict. Capitalist producers, assisted by the state, manage to transform ecosystems into 'exchange' values (profits), while consumers are interested in ecosystem use 'values' (recreation, aesthetics, public health). For Kousis, there are two sides to the sustainability issue: the social and the ecological one. When these two are compatible, then the process of sustainable development can be strengthened. Sakiotis (1995, pp20–22) adopts a political economy point of view as well. According to him, however, the main principles which ought to underlie a sustainable model of ecological management in Greece are:

- a balance between domestic consumption and production to ensure a dynamic equilibrium of the national economy;
- a decentralisation of resources, population, economic activities, and the promotion of economic organisation characterised by locality and diversity;
- the use of environmentally friendly methods of production and sources of energy; and
- upgrading the Greek citizen to become an active cell of the national political life.

For Sakiotis, the ultimate objective of a model of sustainable development must be the elimination of the 'new poverty', the establishment of social justice, and the improvement of quality of life. The main factor in this process cannot be the central government or the political parties but social mobilisation.

From the above discussion it follows that not only are there different domestic labels for sustainable development, but also a host of views regarding its interpretation and the means of achieving it. These views range from being value-oriented, emphasising the citizen–consumer responsibility and the role of environmental education, to more radical ones emphasising diversity, self-reliance, democracy and fairness. The majority of views, however, appear to recognise that local societies are bound to play a very important role in the shift towards sustainability. These conclusions are very much in the spirit of this book as a whole.

It is also necessary to mention that some influential figures of the Greek ecological movement appear to reject the concept of sustainable development altogether. In the words of Modinos (1995, p19):

> ... *the cunningly constructed notion of sustainable development, with the emphasis it places on the peaceful resolution of the ultimate conflict of our era (development vs environment), has played an instrumental role in assimilating the quest for political change into the market mechanisms...Sustainable development can only bring about small-scale changes through a negotiation process, which in spite of its*

'solemnity' will soon reach the limits of its own reasoning...The concept of sustainable development, in that sense, may be thought of as the most ambiguous plan of conflict resolution throughout history.

Official Labels and Views

The labels *viosimi* and *aieforiki* have found their way into official discourse only in the last four to five years. In official documents, both *viosimi* and *aieforiki* have been used. For example, as pointed out by Nigel Haigh in Chapter 3, the Greek editions of the Maastricht Treaty (1993), of the Treaty of the European Economic Area, and of the National Report to the CSD (YPEHODE, 1994 and 1995) all adopt the word *viosimi*, while the European Commission (1993) uses the label *aieforiki*. The three alternative domestic labels for sustainable development, however, have hardly found their way into vernacular discourse. The average Greek citizen has never heard of *viosimi*, *aieforiki*, or *ypostiriksimi anaptyksi*, let alone the ideas they embody, their goals or the implications of a sustainable development strategy. This is not only because the concept is rather new, but mainly because no organised effort has been undertaken to inform the public about these issues.

The Greek prime minister made no reference to sustainable development in his inauguration speech to the parliament on 23 October 1993. The only politician who referred, more or less systematically, to sustainable development was the minister for the environment, physical planning, and public works. In addressing the parliament two days after the prime minister, he defined the objectives of the government, in general, and his ministry in particular as:

*   the 'marriage' between ecology and *aieforiki (viosimi) anaptyksi*;
*   the preservation of balance, harmony and diversity in the natural environment;
*   the fight against pollution and improvement in the quality of life;
*   international cooperation on environmental problems; and
*   close cooperation between the government and ecological NGOs.

He went further to propose referendums on national and local environmental questions, and the establishment of an autonomous collective body which 'will organise and articulate the society's environmental concerns against the state's monologue'. Although these proposals are very novel, subsequent discussion will show that good intentions (if any) are not enough. In fact, Greece has, so far, made very few and only fragmentary steps towards meeting the obligations stemming from the Rio conference in 1992.

THE NATIONAL REPORTS TO UNCED AND THE CSD

The national report of Greece to the UNCED (1991), prepared in 1992, was assigned to a preparatory committee which consisted exclusively of representatives from several ministries and other governmental agencies. The preparation process was coordinated by the Ministry of Foreign Affairs and the Ministry for the Environment, Physical Planning and Public Works (YPEHODE). The final draft was approved by the two coordinating authorities and the Ministry of National Economy. Public participation in the document's preparation was meagre. The procedural note to the national report mentions that some ecological NGOs contributed through their ministries or through written views and publications. In essence, however, the preparation of the national report to UNCED was a purely bureaucratic process. Therefore, it is not surprising that public reaction to it was non-existent.

After Rio, Greece submitted two reports to the CSD, one in 1994 and one in 1995. Both were prepared by YPEHODE (in the Department of International Activities and EU Affairs), with the assistance of the sectoral departments of several other ministries. The 1994 report focused on both cross-sectoral and sectoral issues but was characterised by a tendency to overstate progress towards meeting the objectives of A21, and by vagueness and incoherence. The 1995 report also focused on cross-sectoral (national coordination of A21 follow-up, combating poverty, etc) and sectoral issues (land management, reforestation, sustainable agriculture and rural development, biodiversity, etc). Compared to the 1994 report, the latest report is much more informative. This is because the two documents have different formats; the 1995 national report is based on a very detailed questionnaire produced by the CSD secretariat. Therefore, there is little room for vagueness, incoherence and exaggeration, and the latest report provides a very clear picture of how far the country has gone in following up A21.

Although a signatory of the Rio convention, Greece has not yet produced any national plans on sustainable development. The Office of International and EU Affairs within YPEHODE asserts that the country's national strategy is the EU Fifth Action Plan on the Environment.[1] Despite the lack of a distinct national plan, one may still assess the country's commitment to sustainable development by examining whether there has been visible progress in establishing the mechanisms that are required for a sustainable development strategy – whether domestic or imported. These mechanisms include: policy coordination, targets, integration of environmental considerations into sector plans, structures of accountability, green accounting, information and public participation, and awareness raising.

Policy Coordination

A key national coordination mechanism to follow up A21 has not been established yet; until now this role has been performed by YPEHODE. It is worth noting that YPEHODE has not undergone any reorganisation to meet the requirements of its new role. The ability of the YPEHODE to coordinate environmental policies, in general, and sustainable development strategies, in particular, has been the focus of several studies (Vlassopoulou, 1991; Lekakis, 1995; Pridham *et al*, 1995). On the scientific front conclusions appear to be very similar. Sectoral fragmentation and absence of effective interministerial coordination are serious obstacles to implementing sustainable development strategies in Greece. This is further complicated by the dual role of YPEHODE. Vlassopoulou (1991) provides evidence that the merging of the housing and public works ministries in 1986 to give birth to YPEHODE has resulted in the subordination of environmental issues to developmental concerns.

The need for a distinct and strong coordinating mechanism for the environment appears to be gaining recognition on the political front as well. Presenting its programme on the quality of life, the leading opposition party has recently promised the establishment of a separate ministry and a National Council of Environmental Affairs chaired by the prime minister. Also, the latest *State of The Environment* report, which is about to be submitted to parliament, contains several innovative proposals, such as: conflict resolution among governmental departments through clarification and redefinition of the agencies responsible for the environment; establishment of an autonomous body to inspect the environmental performance of the sectoral departments; and the establishment of a new ministry for physical planning and the environment to initiate environmental policies which will be followed by the sectoral departments. Whether any of these promises will come to fruition remains to be seen. The accumulated experience is not very encouraging, since past attempts to break the vicious cycle of compartmentalisation and implementation deficits (eg Law 1650/86) have not been successful.

Targets and Accountability

The only targets which have been set up, so far, are related to CO_2 and CFC emissions. In April 1994, parliament ratified the Climate Change Convention and the country undertook to stabilise CO_2 emissions at 1990 levels by the year 2000. The follow-up plan was produced by YPEHODE and the Ministry of Industry, Energy, and Technology (YVET); it estimated that by the year 2000, if left unchecked, CO_2 emissions will increase by 27 per cent. Despite international obligations, the government decided that it would be more realistic to achieve a level of emissions 15 per cent higher than in 1990 because of: the limited time frame, the lack of resources, administrative weaknesses, and the inflexibility of the country's productive system. The response of Greece to the amended Montreal Protocol has been more satisfactory. Although EU Regulations 594/91 and 3252/92 allowed for production of CFCs at 15 per cent of the 1986 level, the government reached an agreement with SING (the main producer of CFCs in Greece) to reduce the quota to 7 per cent. Since January 1996 SING's production of these substances has been zero.

Given the absence of targets, in general, it is not surprising that accountability structures have been only partially developed. According to Law 1650/86, the government must bring to parliament an annual *State of the Environment* report. The first report was submitted in 1992 for 'acknowledgement'. The second report was published in November 1995 but has not been submitted to parliament (YPEHODE, 1995b). This latest report is a well-written document which largely subscribes to the concerns about institutional obstacles to pursuing sustainable development in Greece, as well as to specific proposals for change which have been long put forward by environmentalists. Overall, the document appears to have the potential to open up the discussion on sustainable development and the means to achieve it. Whether this will actually take place depends on how rigorously the leadership of YPEHODE pursues the objective stated in the report's introduction – that is, to make Greece the ecological and cultural envy of Europe.

Incorporating Environmental Considerations into Sectoral Plans

EIAs have been the main instrument to counter environmental degradation from economic activities, introduced by Law 1650/86 in compliance with EU Directive 85/377. However, the process of approving EIAs was determined only four years later in Joint Ministerial Decision 69269/5387/90. As if the delay was not enough, many problems have already been identified with its practical application in Greece (Bousbouras, 1992; Tsantilis, 1993; Papayiannakis, 1994). The most significant difficulties are:

* failure to perform comparative analysis of alternative solutions;
* failure to consider the cumulative effects of mega-projects – this was the case with two highly controversial projects, namely, the construction of the new international airport in Athens at Spata, and the diversion of the River Aheloos; with regard to the latter project, the Superior Administrative Court ruled in autumn 1994 that the plan constituted a violation of environmental legislation;
* often, projects have been implemented on the basis of preapproval and the EIA follows; and
* the environmental effects of many projects are evaluated at a local level where administrative personnel lack the necessary skills.

No regular inspection of compliance with environmental terms exists. Inspections take place when the authorities have information or a suspicion that a particular industrial policy pollutes the environment. Sometimes an advance warning precedes inspection. To address these issues the government is planning to create a body of inspectors which will be responsible for ensuring industrial compliance with environmental terms.

Green Accounting and Pollution Control Instruments

Decision-making for sustainable development requires the establishment of a 'green' accounting system capable of quantifying the interactions between environmental commodities and the economy (Pearce and Turner, 1990). Under the current national accounting system in Greece the environment does not constitute a separate category. Value added due to 'environmental services' is recorded as the product of 'other activities'. At the same time, the system does not account for 'environmental disservices'. From the latest national report to the CSD it appears that Greece has no immediate plan to establish a

219

green accounting system. In any case, such a step would be premature since green accounting systems are information-intensive, relative to conventional systems, and the country has a big gap to bridge in this respect. In the context of the Fifth Action Plan on the Environment, however, Greece has embarked on an effort to create the infrastructure for monitoring the state of the environment and for improving the availability of information. The most important measures to meet these objectives are: completion of the national networks for monitoring air and water quality; extension of the national network for environmental information to cover all 13 regions of the country; and drawing up the national cadastral.

Generally speaking, pollution control instruments can be classified into command-and-control and market-based instruments. According to economic theory, market-based instruments are preferable to command-and-control because they are more cost effective (Baumol and Oates, 1989). Greek governments appear to have no strategic approach with regard to any of these instruments for the simple reason that environmental protection has not been the focus but the by-product of even those national policies which have been termed as environmental. However, some command-and-control instruments have been introduced to cope with environmental crises. Investment grants for antipollution projects were employed in the 1980s to promote economic growth by strengthening aggregate demand. The only green tax instituted in Greece, so far, has been a five drachmas tax per unit of petrol sold in the metropolitan Athens area since 1992. A conflict, however, soon surfaced in the press between the Ministry of Finance and YPEHODE because the former withheld the revenues to fill 'black holes' in the budget. It was not until October 1994 that these tax revenues where finally transferred to YPEHODE to finance environmental projects.

Greek governments appear to consider green taxation as a threat to the manufacturing sector, an attitude evident in the reaction to the prospect of a carbon tax. Greece, in April 1994, requested an exemption from introducing such a tax from the EU Council of Ministers (Efthimiopoulos, 1994). A procedure exists to assess the potential usefulness of market-based instruments for pollution abatement in the country. Given that both economic theory and practical experience, at least in developed countries, have demonstrated the advantages of these instruments, this particular measure can be seen as nothing less than a pretext to avoid introducing green taxes in the near future.

Information and Public Participation

The right of the public to information and participation in environmental issues has its roots in Article 24 of the constitution: 'protection of the natural and cultural environment is the right and the obligation of every Greek citizen'. With regard to information, Law 1650/86 stipulates that citizens or their representatives can be acquainted with the content of EIAs and with the plans of central authorities to declare areas or resources as protected. Free access to environmental information is also dictated by the EU Directive 90/313 to which member states had to comply by the end of 1992. Greece has not implemented this directive, in spite of threats by the commission that the country will be arraigned by the European Court (Papayiannakis, 1994 and 1995). Although some institutional arrangements for access to information are in place (Papayiannakis, 1994 and 1995), those who seek information often encounter refusal. Papayiannakis (1995) cites the example of the EIAs concerning the port of Kalamata where access was denied on the grounds that an EIA is the intellectual property of the people who conducted it. No formal arrangement for public participation exists. Of course, informal consultation always take place, especially with those whose opinion is considered to matter; consulting the business community prior to taking any action, for example, seems to be part of the environmental authorities' routine.

Awareness Raising

Increased public awareness of environmental issues has been pursued by a variety of means including campaigns, the introduction of environmental courses into the curricula of the primary and secondary schools, and the establishment of Centres for Environmental Education (KPEs). Law 1892/90 provides for the establishment of KPEs in order to raise the awareness of the youth sector, to organise seminars for adult training, and to support local environmental education programmes. The first KPE has been operating in the prefecture of Achaia since 1993. It is expected that 20 more KPEs will be established in the country by the year 2000. Public awareness campaigns focus on specific issues such as recycling, protection of wetlands and coastal areas, prevention of forest fires, and the rational use of energy. Although no markers have been developed yet, it is generally accepted that public awareness is low (National Report to UNCED, 1991).

Environmental education was introduced to state schools by Law 1892/90. Since this institution is relatively new it is difficult to evaluate its influence over students' attitudes towards the environment. Some weaknesses, however, are becoming increasingly apparent. According to the Directorate of Environmental Education only 5 to 6 per cent of schools currently offer courses and student participation is low (10 to 15 students per school, on average). Furthermore, teachers are unwilling to get involved due to the lack of sufficient financial incentives. Environmental courses are offered at the later periods of the school day and this does not encourage students to participate. In addition, because the Greek bibliography is rather poor, translations of foreign books are used for the courses; as a result, students cannot associate the content of the courses with their personal experience (Kalaitzidis, 1994).

The Role of the Business Sector

With respect to sustainable development, environmental degradation by the industrial sector is a critical issue. However, Greek governments have traditionally viewed environmental protection as a threat to the country's economic growth – this attitude has hardly encouraged businesses to adopt pollution abatement measures. The behaviour of Greek industrialists until the early 1990s is illustrated by the results of a survey of 170 big businesses:[2]

- 65 businesses (38.3 per cent) had adopted some form of environmental standards;
- 70 businesses (41.2 per cent) believed that there was no need to take any measures because they considered their activities harmless to the environment; and
- 14 businesses (8.3 per cent) admitted that they had not established any standards.

From those businesses which already had an environmental programme in place, only 49.2 per cent had made concrete plans to improve their environmental performance in the near future. With regard to motivating factors in adopting environmental standards, 50.8 per cent cited the need to comply with European Community, national or international rules, 26.2 per cent to increase their competitiveness, 13.8 per cent to reduce production costs, and 21.5 per cent to improve the firm's public image. The evidence that only few firms have been actively involved in environmental protection is corroborated by other research; for example, Theohary (1995, pp21–22) finds that it is mainly the branches of multi-national companies which possess a coherent policy vis à vis the environment.

In November 1991, the Association of Greek Industrialists (SEB), declared 1992 as 'the industrial sector's year for the environment' in an attempt to raise environmental awareness in the business community. As part of this initiative it undertook several measures: meetings and seminars; joining the (international) Union of Businesses for Sustainable Development; establishing the Hellenic Etairia for Recycling to pursue, along with government agencies and other NGOs, a national strategy on product recycling; and currently, SEB operates a centre for information and advice on environmental issues and awards prizes to businesses with excellent environmental records. Another significant innovation, this time prompted by EU and international concern over ozone depletion, is the adoption of a voluntary protection scheme named the Responsible Care Plan by members of the Association of Greek Chemical Manufacturers (announced in May 1995), which is internationally acknowledged as the basis of chemical industries' environmental performance.

The process of transition, however, is likely to be very slow. Both the mentality of the government (environmental protection results in unemployment) and of business (the state rather than the private sector should care about the environment) impede the transition towards sustainable development.

The Role of Trade Unions

Environmental degradation in urban areas, and the ensuing deterioration of the quality of life for a large part of the working class in Greece, was bound to attract the attention of trade unions. In the last five years, protection of the environment has become an issue within the framework of industrial relations, along with the traditional issues such as wages and health and safety. Furthermore, the concept of sustainable development has been finding its way into the jargon of prominent workers' organisations, such as the Athens Centre for Workers (EKA) and the General Confederation of Greek Workers (GSEE).

Practical manifestations of the trade unions' interest in the environment are: the publication by EKA of a newsletter to raise workers' awareness; the organisation of seminars and meetings on the environment, industrial relations and sustainable development; and article 11 of the Annual National Contract 1994–95 which provides for the establishment of a joint committee by GSEE and SEB to investigate industrial pollution and to propose concrete abatement measures for the greater Athens area. Addressing a meeting on industrial relations and the environment, in November 1994, the president of EKA, however, recognised that there are obstacles to adopting sustainable development as a part of the trade unions' agenda. These obstacles are both subjective and objective. The former include the low level of awareness and the belief of several workers' organisations that striving for this new goal will weaken the efforts towards the 'basic' goal (to raise workers' standards of living). The objective interpretation is the general economic climate in the country and the sense of economic insecurity among Greek workers.

The Role of Ecological NGOs

The first ecological NGOs appeared in Greece in the early 1980s in response to the country's environmental problems and the influence of similar movements abroad. In October 1989, 46 ecological and 'alternative' organisations established a green political party named Ecologists–Alternatives, which managed to earn a seat in parliament. However, its lack of political organisation and experience, its inability to articulate a social-ecological alternative, and strife between the different factions led to the loss of its parliamentary representation in the 1993 elections. Although the attempt to establish a green party has failed, Greek ecological NGOs continue to coordinate their activities, especially at the local level. Coordination at the national level is more difficult since different NGOs have different interests; however, there is often international cooperation. Cooperation between the ecological NGOs and the state is limited since the former have not been considered by the state as 'equal partners'. Occasionally, some ecological NGOs are invited to participate in committees or events because of EU or international obligations (such as preparing the national report for the Earth Summit in Rio and establishing a board for awarding ecolabels). At the national level, however, no formal arrangement has been made to allow for the participation of ecological NGOs in the national sustainable development strategy.

A particular type of ecological NGO is the grassroots organisations. Tilly (1994) defines community and locally based grassroots movements as ad hoc social movements which are temporary, specialised and relatively successful at mobilising communities against a specific threat. Kousis (1995) discusses the causes as well as the bureaucratic organisation and the power centralisation of three such environmental mobilisations in rural Greece – namely, those in Milos, Kalamas and Astakos. In all cases local people were mobilised out of a concern for community health and for local environmental and economic resources. Also, the distrust of official documentation and technical reports by locals was reflected in their demands to participate in the decision-making process on environment and development matters in their region.

The Greek state has often given in to public demands for a cleaner environment. In the more industrialised nations, producers are more or less inclined to adopt environmental controls and to pass the costs on to the consumer, while in the less industrialised ones the state assumes the larger share of environmental investment costs. The semiperipheral state, however, appears closer to the core state in its will to legitimise its citizenry. The strong Greek civil society of the last two decades has been pressuring the state to maintain social harmony by satisfying public demands for a cleaner environment (Kousis, 1994, p133). The large variety of grassroots environmental mobilisations makes it difficult to conclude on the fate of these NGOs.

IMPEDIMENTS

In the light of the above discussion, Greece has shown a rather low degree of commitment to design and implement sustainable development strategies. Despite the politicians' rhetoric and the good intentions by the country's environmental authorities, the Greek experience is still far from a sustainable development strategy; in fact, it typically fits the picture painted by the literature on sectoral fragmentation and implementation deficits. The impediments to sustainable developments at the national level may be classified as strategic, structural and procedural.

At a strategic level, sustainable development has not been a national priority. Both the report to UNCED (prepared under the Conservative government), as well as the programme of the new Socialist government (presented to parliament in October 1993), can testify to the fact that rapid economic growth, as a means of converging with the northern EU member states, is the ultimate national policy objective. Official documents such as the national reports to the CSD and the reports to the parliament tend to highlight the establishment of new institutions (such as EIAs, EMAS and ecolabelling) and the creation of networks for monitoring environmental quality as indisputable evidence of the country's commitment to sustainable development. However, one should bear in mind that the new institutions were created under both the stick (European Court) and the carrot (money) of the EU. In addition, Greece is notorious for the gap between formality and reality. A better indicator of the country's commitment to sustainable development is the Regional Development Plan for the period of 1994–99. This plan places great emphasis on road construction (an increase in road density of 143 per cent), and the implementation of megaprojects such as the new international airport in Athens and the diversion of Acheloos, which are expected to incur huge and irreversible environmental damage. As such, it is strongly opposed by national and international NGOs, by local authorities and even by several Greek politicians. Clare Coffey explains the EU political context in Chapter 7.

On a structural level it is generally accepted that the holistic nature of sustainable development does not fit with fragmented and sectoral institutions established to deal with them. In Greece, there are about 50 agencies involved in the planning and implementation of environmental programmes and more than 150 pieces of legislation. Law 1650/86 has been an attempt to codify all the existing legislation and to assign the basic power of the public sector vis à vis the environment to a single agency, namely, the Executive Environmental Agency. This law, however, has not achieved its objective. The reason is that its implementation required a vast number of legislative acts (12 presidential degrees, four acts of the ministerial council, and 45 joint ministerial decisions), and most have not been issued yet. It is interesting to note that for six of the ten years since 1986, power was held by the same party (Socialist), which sponsored Law 1650/86. This is a clear indication that structural impediments are closely related to strategic ones, in the sense that the former stem from the low priority and lack of political will to implement sustainable development strategies. Structural blockages have been further aggravated by the lack of both administrative capacity and financial resources to implement environmental protection projects, especially at the regional and local level.

Finally, in procedural terms the level of environmental consciousness and the degree of public participation within the decision-making process remain low. The national report to UNCED recognises that 'environmental awareness is not highly developed in Greece'. A manifestation of this low level of environmental consciousness is the lack of a domestic green movement similar to those in western European and other developed countries. Political scientists and sociologists attribute the present state of environmental awareness to an articulate civil society. Statism and populism, together with a highly atomistic mentality and consumerism, discourage collective action over broader social goals such as sustainable development (Kousis, 1994; Pridham *et al*, 1995; Demertzis, 1995). Public participation in the decision-making process may take different forms. One way is to make formal arrangements for the participation of NGOs. Another is the organisation of public meetings and referendums over local and general environmental issues. Finally, public participation may take the form of greater involvement by parliament in environmental matters. As explained above, no formal arrangements have been made for the participation of NGOs. There are three reasons for this:

- the public sector in Greece is not accustomed to using external independent advice;
- the attitude of most NGOs (both ecological and trade unions) has been one of denunciation rather than cooperation; and
- in the absence of formal arrangements, governments may select for consultation only those NGOs which do not challenge their policies.

Participation in the form of public meetings or referendums has no tradition in Greece. During its first term in power (early 1980s) the Socialist Party encouraged public meetings over local issues. However, the process was soon discredited as the people realised that their decisions had a negligible impact on the policies of central government. The Conservative governments have been, in general, reluctant to introduce institutions of direct democracy.

The parliament's involvement in environmental issues is very limited. In the last two years YPEHODE was called upon only once in parliament to elaborate on its environmental policy. Harmonisation with EU directives has been taking place through joint ministerial decisions; as a result, parliament has been left out of this process. Parliament's rules and procedures provide for the establishment of special committees to investigate issues of national importance; their proposals, however, are rarely implemented. No special committee on the environment has been set up thus far.

CONCLUSIONS

The response of Greece to the challenge of sustainable development has been limited, partial and fragmented. Inertia at the national level is manifested in the absence of a domestically formulated A21 and of domestically initiated policy measures. O'Riordan and Jordan (1994) identified four stages of institutional adaptation to sustainable development, namely: acknowledgement by cosmetic compliance; adoption of new perspectives by social learning; formal realignment of position and influence; and second-order stability around new norms. The Greek experience suggests that the country has barely entered the first of these stages.

The economic and political climate in the country, together with administrative weaknesses (compartmentalisation and sectoral fragmentation), are major blockages to a sustainable development process. The drive for convergence with the wealthier EU member states has overridden any other priority. In the last ten years the capacity of governments has been, almost exclusively, judged on the grounds of how quickly they absorb community money for the purpose of economic growth. Integration of environmental considerations into sectoral policies is desirable only to the extent that it does not result in lower absorption rates. The political culture of the citizenry, having its roots in many years of 'controlled democracy', alternated with dictatorship regimes together with economic insecurity about the future, does not favour collective action on a broader agenda such as sustainable development.

Given the country's economic problems and the lack of a strong social movement for sustainable development, one may wonder what can possibly trigger the sustainability transition in Greece. Smith (1993) identified eight possible stimuli including change in external relations, emergence of new problems, introduction of new technologies, and cultural shift. In the case of Greece, changes in external relations and, in particular, developments within the EU can play an important role in the short run. In contrast with other international organisations, the EU possesses the means to enforce institutional innovations. Furthermore, the reorganisation of DG XI (as discussed by David Wilkinson in Chapter 6) can serve as a model for national coordination mechanisms. In the longer run, the emergence of new problems, such as economic interests threatened by environmental degradation (eg the tourism industry), water shortages, floods due to deforestation; and the introduction of new technologies, may stimulate the sustainability transition. Cultural shift, however, is unlikely to influence the process in the near future.

Part IV

Local Agenda 21 and the Sustainability Transition

Significantly, local authorities have been addressing the issues involved in implementing sustainable development before most national governments. Based on their growing reputation in this area, an international alliance of local government bodies lobbied to have access to the Earth Summit in Rio and were successful. John Chatfield of the UK Association of County Councils, and chairperson of the International Union of Local Authorities explains:

> Our message to world leaders is this: listen to local people; recognise the role of local government in environmental action; work with local communities and empower and enable them to guide their own destinies; and involve us as your essential partners in defining what is meant by 'sustainable development', and – most importantly of all – in putting it into practice. We are ready to work with you. [LGMB, 1992a]

The outcome of this concerted effort and cooperation was recognition of the role of local government in international environmental action and the achievement of a practical local action agenda. Many of the topics included in A21 were of direct relevance to the daily functions of local government; an estimated two-thirds for UK local authorities (LGMB, 1992b). Chapter 28 of A21, entitled 'Local Authorities' Initiatives in Support of Agenda 21', was formulated and essentially written by the international local government representatives at UNCED. It set out the specific actions of this sector, emphasising the significance of their role in attaining the objectives of A21:

> Because so many of the problems and solutions being addressed by Agenda 21 have their roots in local activities, the participation and cooperation of local authorities will be a determining factor in fulfilling its objectives. Local authorities construct, operate and maintain economic, social and environmental infrastructure, oversee planning processes, establish local environmental policies and regulations, and assist in implementing national and sub-national environmental policies. As the level of governance closest to the people, they play a vital role in educating, mobilising and responding to the public to promote sustainable development. [UNCED, 1992]

Chapter 28's main objective is for local authorities to 'have undertaken a consultative process with their populations and [to have] achieved a consensus on "a local Agenda 21" for the community' by 1996 (UNCED, 1992, para 28.2a). LA21 is not legally binding for nation states or local authorities. However, the involvement of international local government organisations indicates a commitment to implement LA21 at this level. The reason why is linked to this central objective.

In order to undertake an LA21 process a form of local government is required that is far more autonomous and locally responsive than is the case in most countries; therefore, implicit in LA21 is the directive from the local government sector itself that it should readdress its power and legitimacy in relation to national governments and local communities.

> *The requirement is for more democratic and holistic local authorities which integrate a concern for environmental issues across the whole area of policy making, and which can reach out both to educate and to learn from their citizens.*
> [Patterson and Theobald, 1996, p10]

At the third session of the CSD in May 1995, a day was devoted to presenting LA21 experiences. ICLEI reported that around 2000 local authorities are implementing specific LA21 programmes in 26 countries. Evidence from different local authorities supported the need for a consensus-based approach that enters into consultation with local residents and organisations, and for a decentralised, participatory and democratic model of local decision-making. A presentation from Peru indicated that an expansion of local leadership and self-determination has improved democratic processes, urban–rural communications, conservation and the recovery of natural resources (Earth Negotiations Bulletin, 1995). Based on evidence such as this which points to the success so far of LA21, it was emphasised at the second United Nations Conference on Human Settlements (otherwise known as Habitat II, held in Istanbul, June 1996) as the delivery mechanism for achieving local action plans designed to provide adequate shelter for all and to move towards sustainable settlements within the context of an urbanising world.

In 1997 UNGASS reviewed the whole A21 process. In preparation, the international local authority associations compiled details on the successes and failures of LA21 in order to inform discussions on the future of A21. Assessment by ICLEI in collaboration with the UN Department for Policy Coordination and Sustainable Development reinforced earlier figures indicating a huge response to LA21 (ICLEI, 1997). However, most municipalities were still at the very early stages of implementation. Five key elements characterised the LA21 response between 1992 and 1996, and are reflected in the three chapters that follow:

- *multisectoral engagement* in the preparation of long-term sustainable development strategies;
- *consultation* with local people to create a shared vision and to identify problems, opportunities and ideas;
- *participatory assessment* of local social, economic and environmental conditions and needs;
- *participatory target setting;* and,
- *monitoring and reporting procedures.*

Local efforts at implementing A21 proved to be one of the rare success stories of UNGASS. The future timetable for LA21 remains unclear, but the CSD has been asked to devise targets over the next two years to focus efforts.

The following chapters look at the implementation of LA21 in the UK, Norway and Germany. In these countries there is a troubled relationship, both politically and financially, between local and central governments. This is especially noticeable in the UK, where devolution in Scotland will create further fissures between the unitary Scottish local authorities and a London-based Treasury. Even without devolution, the connections between local and central government are complex, ambiguous, contradictory and constantly shifting in somewhat unpredictable ways.

In each country this central–local relationship combines with different political cultures to produce unique responses to LA21. For example, as Chapter 15 shows, Norwegian local authorities have long been active in the 'old' green agenda of recycling, energy management and nature conservation and biodiversity. In this they have been supported by central government. But for the deeper and wider arenas of social, educational and cultural integration for the sustainability transition, they are ill prepared. Ironically, this is partly because the commitment to ecotechnology and administrative efficiency at national and local level has so captured the local administrative polity that there is little political capacity for the much more complicated and sensitive empowerment and revelatory arenas.

Here it is also worth mentioning the situations in Portugal and Greece which are not discussed in separate chapters. In these two countries local governments are being reorganised and democratised. This follows 20 years or more of dictatorships which crushed local autonomy and effective political institutions. Nowadays, not only are municipalities and rural areas carefully but tardily being given some voice, but tiers of electorally driven regional governments are also beginning to appear. This rather messy, but understandable, arrangement will take quite a while to settle down. The sustainability transition is awkward enough without the trials and tribulations of political, fiscal and administrative reorganisation at the local level. Arguably, of course, this is precisely the time to experiment with new, sustainability-sensitive local government institutions.

In both Portugal and Greece the current structure of local government is driven primarily by reasons of administrative convenience, namely as a vehicle to enable central government to apply policy to the regions. But, to date, these arrangements are insensitive to local political, cultural and economic considerations. In both countries, hamlets of less than 200 souls are commonplace. This is why an element of political regionalisation is beginning to take place, and hence some scope for more integrated local action may become possible. The new-style regional councils should be more democratic, more bureaucratically coordinated, and armed, via regional funds from the EC, with the financial muscle to address economic and social investments more strategically. Whether they will do so depends on the pull of the old 'parish pump' political networks, often based on family ties, that for the most part characterise local politics in these areas.

The international LA21 networks, such as those of ICLEI or the UN Centre for Human Settlements and the UN Environment Sustainable Cities Programme, are likely to become more important for these nations in the years to come. Even the more go-ahead countries such as the UK and Germany will be strongly influenced by these institutions and their dissemination of best practice. This information exchange will grow in significance in the years to come as money is pumped internationally and nationally into local electronic nerve centres precisely for such purposes.

The evolution of LA21, therefore, will depend in part on the willingness and enthusiasm of central government politicians to pick up the trends in local autonomy and constructive community activism. In the introductory chapter we emphasised how empowerment was made possible through a politically and economically more self-reliant society. To this we can add the scope for innovation and accessing information. This scope for responding to LA21 will in part depend on changes in education, democracy and in responsiveness to leadership and local participatory initiatives.

This last point, namely the revelatory qualities of the transition, remains the stumbling block for the political accommodation of LA21. In all the studies that follow, the harsh truth is that local political institutions are least able to cope with a more representative and participatory culture. The desire to hold onto the old local political order is a powerful one since there is potentially a lot to lose. Nevertheless, huge efforts are being made to adapt to new democratic demands to ensure the future of local government. Efforts are also being made to improve equity, introducing LA21 to the socially disadvantaged members of local communities. This is a sensitive task that demands preparation and local leadership. There is no blueprint for such initiatives since every set of circumstances will be unique. But the fact that the interests of those normally alienated from the political scene are now being incorporated into empowerment and revelatory efforts is a sign the LA21 is far more attuned to the sustainability transition than to the environmentalist agendas of a generation ago.

Chapter 13

LOCAL AGENDA 21 IN THE UK

Heather Voisey

INTRODUCTION

This chapter looks at the local level response to A21 in the UK. The 471 local authorities in the UK differ enormously in capacity, management structure, political commitment and leadership.[1] Local diversity is one of the strengths of locally based A21s, and many of the initiatives are being developed at present under this banner. LA21 indicates a responsiveness to local needs and preferences now and in the future. However, there are more constraints on implementing LA21 than just local factors, such as political will and resources; it appears that national factors pose the biggest challenge. In order to look at the capacity of local government to undertake A21, now and in the future, it is necessary to examine the constraints and opportunities experienced by local authorities so far, as well as their achievements.

Local government in the UK has no power of general competence under which it can act on behalf of its communities. A creature of national government statute, it is only able to act under specific direction from parliament (Elcock, 1994). Absolute power lies with the centre, but tensions between the centre and the locality exist. Local government is not merely the agent of central government, but 'central–local relations are nowhere defined and are hence a perennial subject of controversy' (Elcock, 1994, p6). As the level of elected government closest to the people, it is locally responsive and this causes conflict when its values and actions differ from those held by central government, generally or relating to a specific policy area. As discussed later, this has led to problems in recent years where the centre has sought to control local government in order follow its own political agenda. This conflict between central and local government has implications for the success of any local response to A21. Therefore, the context set for implementing LA21 by central–local relations and the framework of national sustainability policies shall be discussed first.

CENTRAL–LOCAL RELATIONS

1979 saw the election of a Conservative government bent on loosening the market from the ties of the state and in doing so, redefining the role of government as one of an enabler. The policies of this and successive Conservative governments, particularly under Mrs Thatcher, have curbed the power of local government, transferring it to the centre, and imposed strict financial constraints. This process has been reinforced by the deregulation and contracting out of many local authority functions, and the rise in the number of quangos taking over these responsibilities, fragmenting remaining power. This has reduced local autonomy, accountability and status. As the resources of local government have become severely restricted, local authorities have taken up a residual enabler role rather than a service-delivery role; this may have removed the ability for long-term planning, a process crucial to implementing LA21. The result of these multiple processes is the reduced ability of local government, in general, to respond positively to LA21 because of the lack of resources and the powers to do so. Although it has been suggested that the Conservatives were following a master plan, the reality of the last 18 years indicates a series of ad hoc policies designed to constrict the activities of local government, removing it as an obstacle to the free market and enhancing its role as an agent for central government (Duncan and Goodwin, 1988; Rhodes, 1991). These were imposed by central government rapidly and often reactively and have served only to cause confusion and instability in this policy arena.

1987 to 1997 saw central government, still under the Conservatives, enter a period of innovation in its approach to local government. The programme became one of accountability, competition, consumerism, managerialism and reorganisation – two of which are particularly significant (Rhodes, 1991, p99).

Compulsory competitive tendering (CCT) was introduced in 1988 and requires local authorities to put an increasing range of their services out to tender. Previously, they provided services through their own direct service organisations, carrying the property, equipment and staff to do so. These now have to compete with private sector tenders for contracts, with the local authority obliged to accept the lowest tender. However, it is questionable whether CCT has fulfilled its stated rationale of widening competition, efficiency and accountability in local service provision: 62 per cent of contracts have been awarded in-house; there is little evidence of cost savings or improved quality of service delivery; administrative complexity has been increased; and customer involvement is limited. Despite the potential for environmental performance requirements to be built into contracts, it appears that this is not occurring, particularly as they could be perceived to restrict or distort competition.

This requirement to take the lowest bid reduces the power of the local state to act in support of the local or regional economy by purchasing goods and services from local firms with local purchasing agreements, which could provide a contribution to environmentally sustainable local economic development. [Patterson and Theobald, 1996, p14]

Local policy-making as a result of CCT is being reduced to a series of contracts which have limited flexibility, discretion and innovation, and fragmented policy planning and accountability, as discretionary power increasingly lies with ministers rather than with local councillors (Patterson and Theobald, 1996, p18).

Local government reorganisation is another challenge facing local government, drawing again on scarce resources. The government's aim was to review whether unitary authorities should replace the two-tier system of district and county authorities that largely exists at present, creating a more effective form of government. The review was carried out in an arbitrary and inconsistent fashion (Johnston and Pattie, 1996). However, in England fewer changes were recommended than feared, with most rural areas remaining two tier, but many urban areas gained unitary status, as did all authorities in Scotland and Wales. This process of change will continue over the next two years as previous decisions take affect. But this is not the only legacy. Rivalry and tension between levels of local government were exacerbated, and vast amounts of resources and political energy were expended as local authorities attempted to defend themselves against, or influence the manner of, change.

The experience so far of unitary authorities indicates that there is a lack of strategic planning and a fragmentation of service provision, which leads to the proliferation of coordinating organisations responsible for vast amounts of resources but a step away from local accountability. There also appears to be a reduction in the ability of local communities to influence decision-making and a general weakening of local government's relationship with the people it represents (Rookwood, 1994). Reorganisation could have been an opportunity to address the problems of local responsiveness and the faults of the two-tier system, but instead only the structural dimension has been examined, ignoring those of: powers and responsibilities; finance; and management (Wilson, 1993; Chisholm, 1995).[2] In new unitary authorities LA21 is likely to be given a very low priority. There will be discontinuity in existing environmental programmes, practices and expertise, and in links between local government and the wider community which are necessary for implementation and public participation. Unitary councils will be smaller in terms of resources, and their ability to take a strategic view will be lessened. Furthermore, additional changes in the political makeup of councils will disrupt effective power coalitions and therefore implementation (Fourth National Environmental Coordinators Forum, 1994).

THE FRAMEWORK SET BY CENTRAL GOVERNMENT

Chapter 8 illustrates that there has been a lack of political will on the part of central government in addressing sustainable development. This reluctance has extended to the local level were there is a lack of coherence in the government's approach to local environmental protection and sustainability. Local authorities have a long tradition in the field of environmental protection, with foundations in health and safety, the prevention of water and air pollution, housing and waste management, and the protection of the physical environment, usually for recreation purposes. This role was marginally expanded in the 1990 White Paper (HM Government, 1990) to promoting awareness of the environment and encouraging action at local level, but presented no specific policy initiatives or resources. Since 1990 other responsibilities have been given incrementally to local government, such as new duties in local air quality management and domestic energy conservation. But in areas such as waste disposal, which were transferred to the national regulatory body – the Environment Agency – responsibilities have been fragmented, further muddying the waters of accountability at a local level. Overall, local government's ability to undertake local environmental management policies is being recognised. Although this might be an attempt to transfer expenditure burdens down to the local level, it is a spur to environmental awareness among councils and should provide greater information on which to base future policies.

In terms of sustainable development, the 1990 White Paper heralded a key potential mechanism for its implementation. Under the 1991 Planning and Compensation Act all local authorities have to produce local landuse plans, taking account of environmental considerations. A number of planning policy guidance documents, produced by the DoE, structure local planning policy. In recent years these have been reformulated around the principles of sustainable development. The indication, therefore, is that there is guidance from central government on implementing sustainable development, at least in the area of planning. But in reality this guidance has very little substance as a basis for action and in places is inconsistent and unclear; nevertheless, its existence provides an impetus for policy and environmental awareness within decision-making (Royal Town Planning Institute, 1993; Parker, 1995). *Sustainable Development: The UK Strategy* (HM Government, 1994) placed LA21 officially within the remit of local government, but has provided no clearer direction. Despite its emphasis on the importance of partnership between local and central government, there is no discussion of the crucial issues of funding and powers for local government. The annual reviews, however, do illustrate a growing recognition of the efforts of local government through LA21, but offer few supporting actions (see HM Government, 1996, pp13–31; and 1997, p7).

So far the DoE has concentrated on promoting the technical exercises of LA21, through guidance on: ecoauditing, environmental management systems, sustainable development indicators, and sustainability reporting. There was a consultative mechanism established through the white paper process in 1990, the Central–Local Government Environment Forum. Introduced to improve communications between central and local government, it had high-level representation but a low profile and appears to have had little real effect other than information sharing. This has now been superceded by the new concordat agreement between the Local Government Association (LGA) and the new Labour Government. The pinnacle of this new agreement is thrice yearly meetings between the deputy prime minister and the chairman of the LGA. Under the agreement it is proposed that there will be a series of meetings between local government members and individual ministers on issues of joint concern, but the structure of these is still fluid. LA21 as an organising principle appears to have a high status in this new relationship, which is likely to be reflected in a series of meetings addressing the themes of sustainable development, the environment and regeneration.

There is increasing recognition of LA21 within central government in the light of its success, experimentation and high international profile; therefore, greater national-level support in terms of resources and powers may be more forthcoming. However, there are indications that, increasingly, political support has not translated so far into changing attitudes in central government towards local government's role in achieving sustainable development. In 1997 the Audit Commission published *It's a Small World – Local Government's Role as a Steward of the Environment*. Despite setting the context for the report as UNCED and the LA21 initiative, the report stuck resolutely to the traditional environmental services of local government, such as waste management, water and energy conservation, and car commuting. There was little integration with other council duties, such as social services or housing management, and it had little to recommend on topics such as biodiversity, transport, planning, economic development and social exclusion, all central to LA21. It urged local authorities to take up a leadership role in their localities, to aid communication of the principles of sustainable development, to act as a link between global issues and people – but it presented no new ideas on how that was to be done. Its main message was to encourage authorities to do better within their existing resources in traditional areas before attempting anything more ambitious, or asking central government to help them do so with improved resources or powers.

LOCAL AUTHORITIES AND LA21

Internationally, local government has seen a role for itself in the sustainability transition and this has been taken up by local government in the UK, partly as a response to emerging global environmental issues but also as a result of several domestic factors: the success of the Green Party in the European elections in 1989; NGO lobbying; and the desire of local authorities to reassert and develop their role in this area when many of the responsibilities have been removed from local government control to quangos and agencies (Christie, 1994; Cope and Atkinson, 1994).

Despite the constraints resulting from the last 18 years of central government policies on implementing LA21, opportunities have also been presented. Local government's management and administrative structures are now more open to change and are more flexible than previously. Therefore, it is easier for LA21 to be addressed with its emphasis on further cooperation and integration between policy sectors, particularly with the new institutional structures created in the wake of reorganisation. As a result of this process and the loss of traditional functions and powers, local government is very open to undertaking LA21, particularly the public participation aspects of it, and to legitimise its role since it now has the policy space, although not the resources, available to do so. By providing more information on authorities' activities, and the limits to their powers, as well as developing mechanisms for public involvement and feedback, the process of policy-making can become more responsive to people's real, rather than expertly perceived, needs. The early evidence from some local authorities, such as Mendip District Council and Lancaster County Council, is that given the chance to express their ideas and local knowledge, and with information on the constraints and choices available to local authorities, people can engage in new relationships with local government. This may go some way to countering people's disillusionment with local government and what it can achieve, and with traditional mechanisms of communication between government, experts and the public (Young, 1995; Macnaghten *et al*, 1995; Selman and Parker, 1997). Local authorities who face a crisis concerning their democratic role, as manifested in low and falling voters at local elections (Stewart, 1993; 1994; 1996), are using the environment as an issue to defend their democratic position:

> *Environmental concern has the dual advantage of being able to provide some justification for the defence of some locally provided services, whilst simultaneously allowing a demonstration of a new enabling role. It provides an opportunity to prove to a sceptical local electorate and an unsympathetic central government that they have a useful, popular role in a democratic society. Developing and promoting environmental policies is therefore a way of creating new political space for local authorities through the concept of local guardians of the environment, and equally a way of defending their traditional service role.* [Ward, 1993a, p466]

This move towards participatory democracy represents a significant shift from the 'mix of weak representative democracy and bureaucratic paternalism' which has characterised local government in the past (Wilks and Hall, 1995, p39).

Local government nationally and internationally has been increasingly active in the area of the environment, undertaking initiatives and moving towards cooperation and experience sharing. For local government in the UK, UNCED precipitated an unprecedented level of cooperation on several levels: internationally through their principal international associations; nationally with central government – the official UK delegation included a representative from local government; and within the UK local government system, which itself produced a document setting out its strategy for attaining sustainable development locally (LGMB, 1993a). The momentum continued after UNCED.

Responsibility for coordinating the LA21 initiative lies with the local government management board (LGMB), under guidance from a steering group made up of NGOs and groups representing many of the other stakeholders in the Rio process. This structure has been set up by the local UK government associations who are the main agents driving this initiative.[3] The LGMB's role in relation to LA21 is to support local authorities, other sectors and community groups by providing information, guidance and training. Beginning before UNCED and continuing since, it has produced a number of documents setting out the position of local government concerning sustainable development and has attempted to provide an explicit, non-prescriptive

---

BOX 13.1 THE PILLARS OF LA21

I   Principles of the policy making process:
- partnership;
- policy integration;
- appropriate scale and the 'partnership of responsibility';
- freedom of information and open government.

II   Principles of policy choice:
- precautionary principle;
- demand management;
- continuous environmental improvement;
- polluter pays principle.

III Tools for policy-making:
- state of the environment reporting, sustainability indicators and resource accounting;
- strategic environmental assessment;
- environmental management systems;
- investment appraisal;
- environmental information, education and training.

Source: LGMB, 1993a, p31

---

framework for action in the future (see Figure 13.1). In setting out the rationale for action, a definition of sustainable development is outlined which includes a sense of the social and ethical dimensions of human welfare, and as such is stronger than the definition central government has adopted (see Box 13.1).

The LGMB has also been active in lobbying the government for funding; essentially, this has been modest for coordination and promotion work within the LGMB. However, it does provide funding through the Environmental Action Fund or regeneration programmes for projects with an LA21 rationale, for which millions of Sterling are available. The key challenge for the LGMB as the coordinating body is to establish some minimal baseline of competence, while allowing each local authority to establish its individual programme responsive to local needs and circumstances. Although each LA21 should be tailored to the individual authority, a broad consensus is emerging that they should include:

- the involvement of all sectors of society;
- a commitment to the process throughout the local authority;
- an environmental strategy for the local authority;
- an environmental management scheme for the local authority;
- a state of the environment report;
- the collection of data on environmental indicators and the setting of targets; and

241

6 **Measuring, monitoring and reporting on progress towards sustainability**
Environmental monitoring, state of the environment reporting, sustainability indicators, targets, environmental impact assessment, strategic environmental assessment

5 **Partnerships**
Meetings, workshops and conferences, working and advisory groups, round tables, partnership initiatives, developing-world partnerships and support

4 **Consulting and involving the general public**
Public consultation processes, forums, focus groups, 'planning for real', parish maps, feedback mechanisms

3 **Awareness raising and education**
Support for environmental education, events, visits and talks, support for voluntary groups, publication of local information, press releases, initiatives to encourage behaviour change and practical action

2 **Integrating sustainable development aims into the local authority's policies and activities**
Green housekeeping, landuse planning, transport policies and programmes, economic development, CCT, housing, tourism, health strategies, welfare and poverty strategies, environmental services

1 **Managing and improving the local authority's own environmental performance**
Corporate commitment, staff training and awareness raising, environmental management systems, environmental budgeting, policy integration across sectors

Figure 13.1 Steps in the LA21 process

• a continuous review of the whole process. [Morris, 1993]

LA21 is continuing to develop, with the steering group looking at the areas of health, housing, poverty, ethical investment and environmental education, and translating their efforts into a growing resource of guidance, seminars, conferences, best practice, initiatives and partnerships with NGOs and businesses. There are also efforts to deepen LA21 down to the level of parish councils and up to the regional tier through the efforts of the government's regional offices.

ANALYSING THE LOCAL RESPONSE TO A21

While some local authorities have pioneered LA21's development and continue to do so, others have done nothing except perform their traditional environmental protection role as instructed by central government. A survey of local authority responses to LA21, commissioned by the LGMB (Tuxworth and Carpenter, 1995) in 1994–95, showed that 71.5 per cent of respondent authorities were committed to participating in LA21, with 42 per cent having agreed an action plan (41 per cent and 23 per cent respectively of all authorities). A repeat survey in 1996 (Tuxworth and Thomas, 1996) indicated that now 91 per cent of respondent authorities are committed to participating in a LA21 process, with

40 per cent committed to producing a strategy document by the end of 1996.[4] These surveys also showed that although many authorities were tackling LA21 within existing institutional arrangements, and progress was generally slow, there was considerable evidence of new administrative mechanisms; policy integration; public participation mechanisms; partnerships with other stakeholders; the development of environmental management systems; state of the environment reporting; environmental audits; and sustainability indicators (Tuxworth and Carpenter, 1995). In 1996 Tuxworth and Thomas found:

- 36 per cent of authorities had created new liaison groups to integrate LA21 at officer level;
- 88 per cent of authorities' committees had discussed LA21;
- 61 per cent of authorities had organised seminars, workshops, or training days to raise LA21 awareness internally;
- 30 authorities had registered under new environmental management systems EMAS and BS7750;
- 63.5 per cent of authorities had held public LA21 awareness events;
- 45 per cent of local authorities had created new LA21 forums, 25 per cent had conducted focus groups, and 39 per cent had set up working groups or roundtables on LA21 themes;
- 48 authorities had completed state of the environment reports and 14 had already reviewed or updated them;
- 37 per cent of authorities were developing sustainability indicators; and
- over 200 LA21 strategies were sent to the LGMB in the run-up to UNGASS.

However, despite the very positive picture so far, this and other research points to the importance of examining the quality of response and the reasons why this differs, rather than the quantity of response. Some problems are particularly evident from this survey alone:

- LA21 responsibilities are most commonly added to the work of existing officers rather than appointing or seconding new staff dedicated to LA21;
- LA21 is not commonly discussed in health, environmental health, buildings and works, or community services committees;
- integration of sustainable development is poor and it has little or no influence in areas of health, economic development, housing, tourism, anti-poverty, welfare, social services or investment strategies;
- few local authorities have set up effective partnerships with other sectors, such as business;
- 45 per cent of respondent authorities have either rejected or not undertaken a state of the environment report, and many of those that have been undertaken are only partial, so the development of workable targets is problematic;
- it is too soon to say if all this innovation is having a positive or negative effect on the environment; and

- there is no information on the 44 per cent of authorities who did not respond to the survey.

Research into the implementation of environmental auditing and assessment, and the integration of sustainable development objectives into unitary development plans, indicates that response is variable with some authorities quicker to act than others (Leu *et al*, 1995; Bruff, 1996). The institutional structure of local authorities appears to be a significant factor in the willingness to undertake new initiatives. This evidence also indicates that deeper institutional change by professionals and in administrative procedures still has to occur. It is all very well to add on environment forums and policy integration committees to the machinery of local government, but a harder task is changing what already exists and the institutional cultures that support it.

In recent years some work has been undertaken to formulate a typology of LA21 response in the UK, such as that by Ward (1993a), Peattie and Hall (1994), and Wilks and Hall (1995). In essence, they all compare authorities in terms of progress along various stages of LA21, from no response, through purely internal adjustment, to action within the wider community, and the level of innovation with regard to these stages. For Ward (1993a), pioneer authorities are leading and developing the original concept of LA21 into real policies and strategies. Authorities such as Lancashire, Sutton, Kirklees and Leicester come under this banner and are pioneering ideas such as environmental charters, forums and audits, as well as state of the environment reports and sustainability indicators.[5] However, they number perhaps 20 of all local authorities; the rest fall into the less responsive categories. Adapter authorities are those that incorporate the general principles of LA21, altering the ideas and polices developed in other authorities to complement their locality and resources; this constitutes most of the authorities. Register authorities are those that have yet to produce any environmental plan, audit or assessment for their area or their organisation – although they may have environment programmes in action, they have yet to look at their policies in the light of LA21.

Building on Ward's work, it is possible to analyse the characteristics of local authorities to identify some of the local factors which are necessary for a successful move towards LA21. The presence of a policy entrepreneur or enthusiastic political party is crucial, with Conservative-dominated councils being less progressive. It does, however, appear not to be a specific party group but a committed group of individuals who develops policies in this area – the policy entrepreneurs – and these have a better chance of becoming policy if the party in control is not Conservative. Significantly, after the 1996 local elections the Conservatives control only 13 councils in England, Wales and Scotland.[6]

Empirical research in five authorities indicates that the presence of a well-motivated and trained coordinator for LA21 is also important in bringing together work done by different departments under one banner, as a focal point for information, and to continue the pressure for change once initial impetus has been dissipated by other priorities.[7] It also appears to be important that the initiative resides within the chief executive's office; if it develops within a particular department (such as planning or environmental health) it can all too easily be subsumed into the priorities and institutional culture of that department. A rolling programme of training for all officers is often neglected but is crucial in providing information, skills and confidence. All these factors enable the institutional capacity of local authorities to be increased with regard to LA21. However, resources are vital in turning this capacity into effective action, especially guaranteed funding for a time period in order to put long-term

Table 13.1 Factors in the existence and survival of an LA21 initiative

Negative	*Positive*
• uneasy relationship between central and local government	• coordination with other local authorities in the area
• uneasy relationship between local authorities, ie district and county councils	• support and information from other local authorities, the LGMB and NGOs
• poor coordination between national policies	• national guidance, such as policy planning guidance notes, which have orientated policy-makers who integrate sustainable development principles
• lack of guaranteed financial resources	
• lack of an officer as a focus for information and liaison with the community	• ring-fenced, pump-priming funds
• inadequate staff training on sustainable development, LA21 and communication with the wider community	• staff that can act as a focus for the organisation of LA21 and liaise with the community
• only junior staff are given responsibility for producing an LA21 for the whole council	• staff trained in sustainable development, LA21 and how to approach the community to engage them
• only one department has responsibility for implementing LA21	• support from senior officers
• no support from political parties or individual members	• a corporate approach that is either created by a team or is based in the chief executive's office to enable LA21 to be considered in all departments and policies
• no support from senior officers	
• retain traditional community consultation procedures	• cross-party support
• poor relationships with NGOs, businesses and other stakeholders	• mechanisms for public participation
	• partnerships with NGOs, businesses etc
• a political agenda dominated by economic issues, where employment is a priority at any environmental cost	• a political agenda that links LA21 to issues of economic prosperity, social wellbeing and environmental protection and enhancement, usually through the concept of a quality of life
• local government reorganisation	
• CCT	• peer pressure

projects into effect; this enables other funds to be tapped into and local people to feel confident about committing their energies to the projects. These and other factors are summarised in Table 13.1.

Other factors in the successful development of an LA21 response have been the ability and willingness of a local authority to engage in networks and partnerships with other stakeholders such as NGOs or with the EU. Networking channels appear to be highly significant in disseminating knowledge and best practice, enabling authorities to see what can be achieved and making the whole process more feasible. These channels are present between authorities, between authorities and local government organisations, and between authorities and the professional organisations and international networks, such as those facilitated by the ICLEI. A number of authorities have also developed formal partnerships in the context of specific projects with NGOs, businesses and academic institutions in order to benefit from a more intensive form of networking and resource sharing, and in order to have greater trust between different sectors at a local level. However, there are problems with networks and partnerships that are often ignored. Activities are focused within the network at the expense of other non-network actors; networks are often highly dependant on voluntary effort; different members have different financial or other resource capabilities or contributions to make; members have conflicting objectives in the long term; there is complexity as membership expands; and often there is ossification of the network.[8]

It is estimated that 40 per cent of *Towards Sustainability* (CEC, 1992) necessitates action at the local level, in the areas of: spatial planning, economic development, infrastructure development, control of industrial pollution, waste management, transport, public information, education and training, and internal auditing (LGMB, 1993a, and 1993b). The EU's environmental policies do provide a role for local authorities; however, in the case of UK local government, they do not have powers in all the above areas to take action as in other member states.[9] Nevertheless, the current moves towards increased regional representation via the committee of regions are an opportunity for local government to bypass central government in constructing its own policy responses (Ward, 1993b). The EC is also a possible source of resources for implementing sustainable development, particularly with the greening of the structural funds. Nevertheless, details as to how the Fifth Action Plan can be translated into a practical programme for policy action are unclear. Research by Ward and Lowe (1994) and Gibbs (1997) indicates that although there are benefits for both local government and the EU in working together in the environmental field, partnership, integration and cooperation is very patchy and difficult, with central government still holding the funding reigns in many cases. Local authorities have a limited understanding of the relevance of the Fifth Action Programme, in particular regarding their activities. This is possibly a result of central government's reticence in involving local government in implementing earlier action programmes, its own lack of reference to it as the basis of environmental policies, and because the scale of the programme is generally beyond the remit of UK local authorities.

Tabe 13.2 The resources of central and local government

Central Government	Local Government
• control over legislation and delegated powers	• employs all personnel in local services, far out numbering civil servants
• provides and controls the largest proportion of local authorities' current expenditure through the Revenue Support Grant	• has, through both councillors and officers, detailed local knowledge and expertise
• controls individual authorities' total expenditure and taxation levels by 'capping'	• controls the implementation of policy
• controls the largest proportion of local capital expenditure	• has limited powers to raise own taxes and set own service charges
• sets standards for, and inspects some, services	• can decide own political priorities and most service standards, and how money should be distributed among services
• has national electoral mandate	• has local electoral mandate

Source: Wilson et al, 1994

Despite the interventionist style of the Conservative government's policies towards local government in the last 17 years, local government is still required in order to take into account local circumstances when formulating and implementing policy, and elections continue to provide political legitimacy to this level of government. Therefore, as Duncan and Goodwin (1988, p59) state: 'local government cannot simply be formed into a mere agent of central government', and it has not been to date. It is possible to show that local government does have resources to deploy in the battle with central government that have helped it to survive thus far (Elcock, 1994; see Table 13.2).

The model of an enabling local government which emphasises its strategic and public participatory role, such as LA21, is seen as something of an opportunity that local government must take. However, commentators such as Williamson (1995) suggest that already local government is too far emasculated to fulfil this new role or to protect itself further because of the wider social and economic changes which it continues to face. This is one reason for the response to LA21 in the UK, as a strategy deployed by local government to maximise its resources. The environment is a good political issue; no one wants to be seen as destroying the air, water and land which we need in order to survive – as such, local government support and action on the environment generally, and local environmental issues in particular, is one way of gathering support amongst the electorate. The participatory element that is being developed as the new pillar of such moves is a further boon to this element, although such an emphasis on democratic innovation is not new by any means (see Committee on Public Participation in Planning, 1969; Elcock, 1994). Developing a project such as LA21, often by providing pump-priming funds from general accounts, is also a way of drawing in funds from elsewhere. Much of LA21 is about developing information about the local environment that is required if national environmental policies are to work. The result is that central government, committed as it is to LA21, is increasingly predisposed to support such issues because of their political salience and to meet international agreements – so far, UK local authorities are some of the world leaders on this initiative.

Therefore, developing LA21 could be seen as a way of fighting off further encroachment by central government on the responsibilities and policy-making powers of local government. Initially, the opportunity was sighted by the local authority associations and international bodies, eager to protect local government. Wilson *et al* (1994) indicate that the power of the local government associations was on the wane in the 1980s, compared to their earlier insider position when they were valued consultees; therefore, it was in their interests to develop LA21 in order to adopt some role in the consultation process, since they would now hold knowledge and expertise that the government required. It was also in the interest of the professional associations that make up the wider local government system to be amenable to such moves in an attempt to circumvent the impacts of managerialism and CCT.

CONCLUSION

In conclusion, there is a lot of potential and enthusiasm amongst local authorities and their associations, but most of this is dissipated in the face of considerable multiple barriers to policy-making in this area from central government. However, central government appears to have recognised recently the breadth of initiative at local level and wants to be associated with it.

At UNGASS, the new prime minister expressed his support for the LA21 initiative in the UK. The deputy prime minister, the LGA and the LGMB will have launched a document in January 1998 setting out clear, practical guidelines for councils on why LA21 strategies are needed and how to create and implement them. Local authorities will also be asked to give a copy of their strategies to the chairman of the LGA by 15 December 2000 (HC Debates, 1997a). However, the new government has made clear that it does not want a coordinating role – other bodies already fulfil this task (HC Debates, 1997b). This begs the question: what sort of role will it undertake?.

Whether this will help break down barriers to local action in the real terms of resources and powers, or just mimic the guidance provided elsewhere remains to be seen. We can see local sustainability as part of a drive towards greater local self-determinism that is the result of increasing central constraints. This has created policy space and political will, more so than in other countries, that has coincided with UNCED and the call to develop LA21. It appears so far that there is great potential for implementing sustainable development at this level, and that institutional change is occurring – but at this early stage there are local and national constraints that need to be overcome, and deeper institutional change needs to occur if greater policy integration and behavioural change is to result.

Appendix 13.1 Structure of local government in the UK (post April 1997)

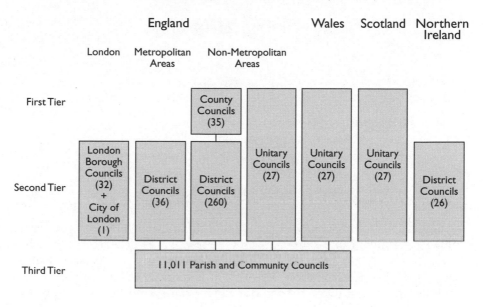

Chapter 14

LOCAL AGENDA 21 IN GERMANY

Christiane Beuermann

INTRODUCTION

From preliminary observations, we can conclude that LA21, four years after UNCED, is still a low priority issue in Germany. Exact data are not available, but it appears that less than 30 of Germany's more than 16,000 municipalities have initiated an LA21 process. This lack of response justifies a more detailed analysis of the institutional conditions and political obstacles that prevent German local authorities from initiating new forms of policy-making processes, as required by A21.

This highlights two questions, namely the nature of central–local relations and the local authorities' competence and responsibilities regarding environmental policy. The right of political autonomy for the German municipalities is an important determining factor. However, in recent years there have been strong shifts of power from the local to central authorities. As noted in the editorial introduction, this has proven to be a complicating backdrop to the evolution of LA21 generally.

Central–Local Relations

The German political system has a federal structure. After the unification of former East and West Germany on 3 October 1990, it now consists of 16 federal states (*Länder*) with a total of 16,121 municipalities. The general distribution of policy responsibilities between the different governmental levels is set out in the German basic law. The complicated rules of responsibility are defined according to the subsidiarity principle, with the municipalities in principle having the right of autonomy (Wehling, 1985). Article 28 (2) of the constitution (*Grundgesetz*–GG) states that:

> *As to the municipalities the right is to be guaranteed to decide on all affairs of the local community in their own responsibility according to the laws.*[1] [article 28 (2) GG]

Generally, the municipalities are responsible for all tasks and decisions that have impacts at the local and municipal level (Ebert, 1994; Joseph, 1995). The municipalities are part of the federal states, and as such can implement laws or measures where regulation is the responsibility of the federal states, where there is an absence of regulation at the federal level or by the federal states, or where the specific task has been delegated to the municipalities. These municipal tasks are undertaken on the following basis (Ebert, 1994):

- voluntary tasks (eg museums, theatres, parks, townhalls);
- compulsory tasks without directives (municipalities have to do them but can decide on how they are managed, eg schools);
- compulsory tasks with directives (municipalities must apply passed instruments or device, eg municipal elections, social security); and
- state or government tasks (eg police).

The room for municipal decision-making, of course, decreases from point 1 to point 4. Municipal autonomy, with respect to administration, comprises sovereign decisions with regard to the following categories (Gisevius, 1991):

- *personnel:* the right to select, employ, promote and dismiss administration staff;
- *organisation:* the right to develop the organizational structure of its administration;
- *planning:* the right to develop planning guidelines to organise the municipal territory;
- *laws:* the right to enact municipal statutes;
- *finances:* the right to manage revenue and expenditure; and
- *taxes:* the right to impose taxes (unless this right is not annulled by higher laws on financial adjustment).

As to sectoral policies, the most important tasks of municipalities are (Bormann and Stietzel, 1993):

- road infrastructure, transport policy;
- public security (eg fire prevention, trade supervision);
- social security (public welfare, homes for the elderly , shelter for the homeless);
- education and culture (schools, kindergarten, adult education programmes, libraries, theatres, orchestras, museums):
- utilities and housing (water, electricity, gas, house-building, urban planning);
- environmental management and health, and youthcare (waste management, canalisation, public greens, cemeteries, hospitals, playgrounds, sport arenas); and
- state tasks (eg registry office, food quality control, resident registration, statistics).

As a result, German municipalities have traditionally enjoyed a relatively large scope for the development of their own local policy strategies in the sectors most relevant to LA21, such as energy, transport, waste, sewage, air quality, and urban planning (Ebert, 1994). Furthermore, participatory rights for citizens, with different legal qualities, exist as follows (Gisevius 1991):

- *constitutional rights* concerning municipal elections, right of assembly, participation of political parties, legal protection;
- *other participation rights* with a legal basis: several forms of citizen participation in municipal decision-making processes of right to appeal, and matters in the construction sector;
- *non-statutory participation:* information, inquiries, hearings, planning forums, citizens' opinions, honorary posts, etc; and
- *organized participation:* citizens' action groups, political parties, citizen experts committee membership, district or local councillor.

On this basis, applying existing participation patterns to the regular involvement of local actor groups, such as business groups, environment and development NGOs, and churches, in LA21 processes should be feasible.

However, despite the room for local action, the capacity of municipalities to fulfill even their compulsory tasks is shrinking due to several factors (Witte, 1992; Pohl, 1994; Karrenberg and Münstermann, 1995). In particular, municipal finances are detoriating. There are three principal sources of revenue, each accounting for approximately one third of the total tax revenue (eg land tax, trade tax, second home tax); financial assignments from federation and *Länder*; and charges for municipal services (eg waste disposal). Since 1990 there have been significant and increasing financial deficits (Bundestagsdrucksache, 1994a). According to the Federal Ministry of Finance, the debts of German municipalities will exceed 250 billion Deutschmarks (DEM) by 1997. (Bundestagsdrucksache 1994b). In its *Report on the Municipal Finances (Gemeindefinanzbericht) 1995*, the Association of German Cities, Deutscher Städtetag (DSt, 1995), identifies three main reasons for the financial crisis (see also Figure 14.1): declining revenue from trade taxes; growing expenditure for income support; and financial transfer to the former East Germany.

In particular, tax revenue is forecast to be lower than expected because of the recent recession and as a result of amendments to the tax basis by the federal government (Pohl, 1994; Fiedler, 1994; DSt, 1995). Other authors, however, assign some responsibility for the present situation to the municipalities themselves with regard to excessive expenditure during the economic boom (Bonsen, 1993). As shown in Figure 14.1, municipal expenditure is longer controllable by local governments, largely because they have to pay for income support as part of the German social security system. Income support is paid for several reasons and is expected to grow steadily in the future. An important factor is the growing number of long-term unemployed people who, after receiving two kinds of unemployment aid at higher levels (*Arbeitslosengeld, Arbeitslosenhilfe*), in the end are reduced to locally financed income support. The

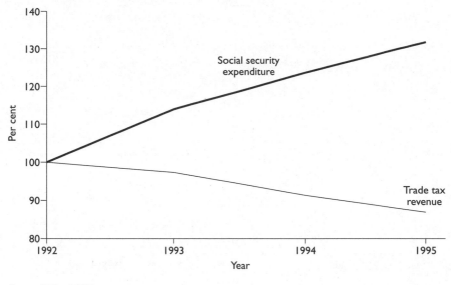

Source: DSt, 1995

Figure 14.1 The municipal financial crisis in Germany

development of unemployment and, in particular, long-term unemployment is shown in Figures 14.2 and 14.3.

Another important process with regard to LA21 is the aim of the federal government to privatise state-owned enterprises (such as postal services and railway) and to transfer and promote such a process at the local level. The idea is that this would improve efficiency in the enterprises that municipally owned (utilities and services, credit institutes, etc) and reduce costs. The revenue of the 'sell out' (*Ausverkauf*) as critics call this process is supposed to consolidate municipal finances (Handelsblatt, 1994a). However, the privatisation of utilities reduces municipal influence and opportunities to develop sustainable local energy policies.

These tendencies are seen as a fundamental attempt to undermine the municipalities' right of autonomy, aiming to shift responsibility and power from local to federal government, and have been harshly criticised by the DSt but also by the labour union for civil services and transport (ÖTV). The federal government denies all this (Bundestagsdrucksache, 1994a). As a matter of fact, many municipalities are simply forced to privatise enterprises although they realise this reduces their administrative responsibilities (*Kommunale Briefe für Ökologie*, no 1994).

Local Environmental Policy

As a major consequence of the growing green political movement in Germany, the federal environment policy has progressively shifted to the *Länder* and to the municipalities. During the 1970s, implementation of the federal environmental

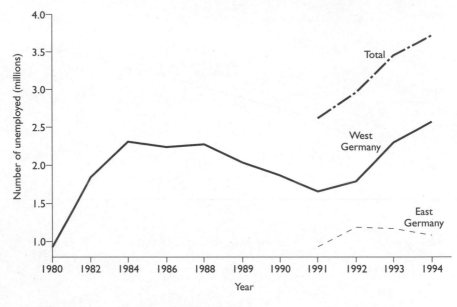

Source: Statistisches Budesamt,1992–1995

Figure 14.2 Unemployment in Germany 1980–1994 (average)

laws was often insufficient. In fact, municipalities had little interest in taking responsibility for environment policy (Quante and Schwartz, 1996).

This response changed as public environmental awareness steadily grew at the local and regional level. Norms and expectations regarding municipal environmental policies were changing (Schuster and Dill, 1992; Joseph, 1995), particularly because the environmental problems then evident had mostly regional or even local impacts. Pollution levels in the municipalities were generally high and, therefore, urban quality of life was perceived to be low (Quante and Schwartz, 1996). In the meantime, in a number of local governments, environmental concerns were integrated into strategic decision-making within existing municipal competences (Ebert, 1994) and some *Länder* and municipal authorities appeared to enjoy experimenting with environment policy (Weidner, 1995). However, the majority of German municipalities are still not judged to be forerunners in environmental policy, since they continue to implement reactive measures that do not address the causes of the environment problems (Quante and Schwartz, 1996).

Despite the fiscal crisis, a new push in favour of precautionary environment policy was introduced when the global problem of climate change emerged on the political agenda. Clearly, climate change is an issue without a direct cause and effect relationship at the local level. But, surprisingly, it was enthusiastically addressed at the local level, supported by an immense public reaction. About 400 German municipalities are organised within the Climate Alliance of the Cities, having adopted a target of 50 per cent CO_2 reduction by

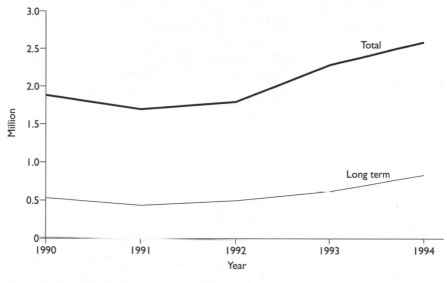

Source: Statisisches Budesamt, 1992–1995

Figure 14.3 Total and long-term unemployment (>one year) in
West Germany 1990–1994

the year 2010 compared to 1990 levels (Klinabündnis and Alliance del Clima, 1993). To some extent, strategies developed as climate protection initiatives are similar in content to an LA21 response covering some of the same policy fields, but they lack the social dimension that is particularly important in LA21.

THE LOCAL RESPONSE TO AGENDA 21

It is high time for action! There are only few municipalities known for adopting a decision to develop a LA21 … The English, Danes and Dutch have impressively demonstrated to us how this process is to be implemented by administration, policy and citizens. [Fiedler, 1996]

This statement made by a representative of the German Association of Cities summarises the dilemma of the German LA21 'process'. Four years after A21 had been signed, the LA21 process in Germany was judged to be only at the beginning (Unmüßig, 1996). At present, only 20 to 30 municipalities have voluntarily initiated LA21.[2] These LA21 processes are experimental and vary widely in structure and content. The initiatives are rooted in responses to the issue of climate change, the engagement of churches, environmental NGOs, developing world groups, as well as individual local authorities. Due to the early involvement of all or some of these actors in bottom-up LA21 processes, the participatory element is often strongly developed and the process is often more accepted in the municipality. One of the best-known examples is given in Box 14.1.

Box 14.1 LA21 in Berlin-Köpenick

City: District Berlin–Köpenick
Name: Local Agenda 21 Berlin–Köpenick
Date of Start: 1993
Initiated by: P Wazlawik
- church background
- employee of Federal Environment Ministry

Goal: Development and implementation of a LA21
What has been achieved?

- 'one world' initiative
- sustainability projects drop-in centre in the municipal and the environment department
- economic forum
- forum on environment and development
- four working groups of the forum on:
  - transport/urban planning
  - energy/resources/waste
  - conservation/water/tourism
  - economy/social affairs/north–south/ education
- decision of the district government to develop an LA21
- LA21 office
- LA21 project proposal, feasibility study, status report,10-point agenda

Source: Clearing-house for Applied Futures, 1995

Generally, LA21 has been a reorganisation task, which means that the structures considered to be necessary have been established. The content of the LA21s, however, remains somewhat vague or has not yet been comprehensively developed, though there are some interesting projects connecting LA21 criteria with local sectoral policies. Box 14.2 gives an example of one of those projects in the transport policy sector in Bremen. Implementation is highly improbable at the moment as the prospective residents refuse to sign legally binding commitments which stipulate that they must never own a car.

Information on existing LA21 initiatives is increasingly disseminated as new networks compile examples of good practice and coordinate the activities of their members. The established municipal associations have started focusing on LA21 and the LA21 coordinators, communicating their experiences, and attracting the media's interest to the issue (Alternative Kommunalpolitik, 1996, Politische Ökologie, 1995). Finally, in contrast to other countries – for example, The Netherlands where the implementation of LA21 is subsidised by the

---

BOX 14.2 LA21 IN BREMEN

City:	Bremen
Name:	Sustainable mobility – housing without cars
Date of start:	1993
Initiated by:	Environment department (Ecological urban design)
Objectives:	• reduce impacts associated with individual car use by:
	– providing practical and sustainable alternatives to car owning, and
	– creating an urban environment where not having a car has distinct advantages
Achievements:	• house-building company has agreed to project (partially municipally owned)
	• project details developed in roundtables
	• start of construction was scheduled for autumn 1995, but implementation problems

Source: International Council for Local Environmental Initiatives (ICLEI), 1995a

---

government (Coenen, 1996) – the German Federal Government is not very involved in LA21 and provides almost no support (Wessel, 1995). A short summary of the status quo is provided in Box 14.3.

As a matter of fact, the small number of existing LA21 initiatives have been mainly induced by highly devoted individuals forming focal points for action. The following obstacles appear to have been the most important:

- lack of information on A21;
- focus on other issues;
- lack of information on the consequences of introducing a LA21 process regarding implementation steps, costs and impacts;

BOX 14.3 STATUS QUO OF THE GERMAN LOCAL AGENDA 21 PROCESS (MID 1996)

Active municipalities	very few
Commitment	voluntary
Approaches	manifold
Coordination of existing LA21 initiatives	in parts systematic
Dissemination of information on LA21	increasing
Support by federal government	none
Dynamics	increasing interest

process has been characterised as being at the
embryonic stage

- insufficient support by other actors; and
- organisation of the local environmental administration.

Lack of Information on A21

Generally, the German public remember UNCED in Rio de Janeiro in 1992 as the Environment Summit. Moreover, the first Conference of the Parties to the Framework Convention on Climate Change (FCCC) was always referred to as the Rio follow-up conference. Information on the climate change issue and, in particular, on the FCCC is good while the non-legally binding document Agenda 21, dealing with the connection of environment and development, is almost unknown to the general public (Fiedler, 1996). An explanation might be that in contrast to other countries, the Brundtland report *Our Common Future* was little discussed by the German public even though environmental NGOs and other groups stressed the general importance of A21 very early on. One reason for this may be the late and inappropriate translation of the document into the German language. As a result, the discussion on sustainable development began later than in other countries. At present, the situation is changing and A21 seems to outstrip the issue of climate change in the public discussion.

A Focus on Other Issues

LA21 is seen to compete with other pressing local political issues. Due to the recent municipal financial crisis, environment policy is often limited to reactive measures (Fiedler, 1996). This view demonstrates that the integration aspect of LA21 often has not been recognised or is not perceived to be feasible. In a survey on the problems of urban development and municipal policy, local authorities consider the following three issues as most important (Deutscher Institut für Urbanistik, 1995):

1) consolidation of municipal finances;
2) economic development, employment, economic structural change; and
3) transport.

Moreover, the response is to a large extent dependent on local policy traditions. Municipalities with a stronger environmental consciousness do not see the necessity of developing an LA21 as they are convinced that they have already implemented a sustainability policy with a long-term orientation (ICLEI, 1995b). Furthermore, municipalities interested in the UNCED follow-up are often members of climate protection initiatives (ICLEI, 1993). In both cases, characteristic elements of LA21 are covered and introduced by conscious local authorities. At least some of these authorities seem less interested in going further and applying a new concept. Doing so is considered to be a renaming of activities that have already existed for years (old wine in new bottles).[3]

Insufficient Support from other Actors

Early information deficits significantly delayed the German LA21 process compared to other European countries since no one knew who should provide the information needed and why this did not happen. A21 was the result of an international negotiation process. Although municipalities participated in the German National Committee, which was the preparatory committee prior to UNCED, outcomes of UNCED seem to have been insufficiently communicated to the subordinate federal levels.

The Federal Ministry for the Environment (BMU) is responsible for the organisation and coordination of the UNCED follow-up. As such, it could be considered the contact for municipalities with regard to LA21. The responsible authorities rhetorically acknowledge the importance of LA21, but they do not provide the necessary resources. Reservation and absence of support is justified with reference to the municipalities' right of autonomy (BMU, 1994; Wessel, 1995). Consequently, there is no development of a general guiding, steering or funding mechanism at the federal level (Wessel, 1995). Significantly, in only one LA21 initiative (Berlin Köpenick) is there a relationship between a municipality and the BMU as a result of personal contacts (Clearing house for Applied Futures, 1995; Schiller-Dickhut, 1996). This might be a point of departure for the future engagement of the BMU in the German LA21 process. In addition, there is some funding for research into LA21.

The Federal Ministry for Urban Development (BMBau) states the central aims of sustainable cities namely, the promotion of an urban development, taking care of resources, and being environmentally friendly – as being of major importance in Germany. In doing so the Charter of the European Sustainable Cities (the Aalborg Charter), referring to municipal day-to-day policies, can be considered as a helpful guideline (BMBau, 1996). Furthermore, the report refers in several chapters to the importance of LA21 but remains very vague. At the moment it is not foreseeable whether or not the BMBau will further engage in the LA21 process, but there are some informal talks between it and actors involved in LA21 concerning financial support for capacity-building projects.

There are several NGOs who deal with LA21-related questions. Most prominent is the Forum for Environment and Development, an umbrella organisation for NGOs dealing with UNCED-related issues. One of its standing working groups deals with urban development. However, this working group was established in autumn 1994 and has not yet been very effective in influencing discussions or providing support. In the long run, these groups aim to strengthen the cooperation of German NGOs on LA21 (Sibum, 1995; Dodds, 1995). Moreover, they see themselves mainly as a counterpart to the federal government.

In contrast to the UK where the local government associations focused very early on LA21, German municipal associations did not respond for a long time (Hoffmann, 1996). Recently, LA21 has become an issue. For example, the DSt has adopted a resolution that establishes LA21 as a priority on its agenda. Consequently, it has developed an LA21 guideline identifying 19 sectors for projects (DSt, 1995). Furthermore, DSt has urged its almost 6400 member cities to develop and implement LA21. Other associations have started similar LA21 initiatives (such as DStGb, 1995). It is not clear whether there will be programmes established for furthering the LA21 idea.

Given that the municipal associations have only produced vague guidelines or recommendations, lack of orderly information has been a vital obstacle for the majority of municipalities. In effect only the ICLEI network has been effective.[4] But these networks mainly assist municipalities that are already interested in LA21, climate protection or global issues in general. In order to further the diffusion of the LA21 idea among the municipalities, and to convince them that it increases the opportunities for local policy-making with beneficial side effects for other local problem areas, LA21 has to be promoted by the established traditional municipal associations.

Organisation of Environment Administration

As environmental issues emerged on the municipal political agenda, the traditional administrative sectors crowded them out. Consequently, environmental responsibilities have been established as a sector apart. Implementing an LA21 means restructuring policy and decision-making processes, and this requires not only cross-sectoral cooperation between the existing structures but also the establishment of new structures (for instance, for public participation). However, many local authorities are simply not interested in such a development and want to continue their policies in a business-as-usual way. Because of its relative success as a reactive local policy, and in the light of a 'natural' tendency of administrations to resist change, municipal environmental administration adapts only slowly to calls for policy integration.

CONCLUSION

Implementing A21 at the local level in Germany has been characterised so far by the initiatives of a few lead municipalities. The huge majority of the 16,121 municipalities have not yet discovered LA21 as a policy concept that suits specific municipal conditions and enlarges the municipalities' capacity to develop individual political strategies within the existing bounds of municipal competence. Given constitutionally guaranteed municipal competence, along with a more than 25-year environmental policy tradition and a strongly environmentally aware population, one should expect that LA21 would have attracted more interest and response by local actors. Comparatively large successes in reducing pollution at the local level should have been good preconditions for broadening local LA21 activities.

However, the margin for developing individual local policies has been shrinking in recent years due to worsening municipal finances, an increase in statutory tasks and a general tendency to weaken local government. Only because of the emerging strong environmental consciousness of the public has local government demonstrated its ability to integrate new issues flexibly. But apart from a minority of municipalities, the integration of environmental concerns into day-to-day politics has not taken place. Today, municipal environment policy is still dominated by reactive measures. Compared internationally, the enforcement of these policies has made Germany a forerunner in environmental policy implementation. Nevertheless, the persistence of the reactive approach reflects an implementation gap concerning the proper role of the precautionary principle adopted as the general basis of German environment policy in 1971. The recent broad municipal response to the issue of climate change may be seen as a decisive push to establish a common understanding at the local level to reorganise environmental policy in order to promote sustainable development.

The analysis of obstacles to LA21 showed mainly two arguments explaining the initial lack of response. For many local authorities, LA21 is only a new description of what they have already been doing for years. They have developed structures and procedures for local environmental policies and do not agree on the necessity of applying a new concept. Others need more information on what to do when initiating and developing an LA21. Coordination and support have so far only insufficiently been provided by existing municipal associations or institutions at the federal level. In particular, the federal government should have a strong interest in doing this since LA21 should be a significant instrument at the local level to achieve other federal environmental goals, such as the reduction of CO_2 emissions.

The few existing LA21 processes are due to personal commitment and the enthusiasm of some local authorities or other interested persons who recognise the potential of LA21 for implementing an integrated, environmentally conscious, long-term policy according to the precautionary principle. When initiating and developing their LA21s, success depended to a large extent on new coalitions which have been formed on different levels:

- among interested individuals in the respective municipality (first-mover coalitions), forming a network to establish LA21 on the local agenda;
- among interested individuals in the local government and administration across departmental borders (local authority coalitions), forming networks to promote local government commitment to LA21 and to make way for integration across policy sectors;
- among different local actor groups to further acceptance and to establish structures for participation (local actor coalitions); and
- among municipalities developing LA21s to exchange information, via membership in umbrella networks, to do more effective lobbying and public relations, but also to increase and secure motivation by some kind of creative competition (LA21 coalitions).

These coalitions have so far been effective; in a number of local governments formal decisions have been made to develop and implement LA21. Most of these municipalities have established institutions for participation according to the comments-based character of LA21. Furthermore, these participation structures work by focusing local public attention on the issue of LA21. Since no municipality has finished the development of an LA21 (no documented strategies) so far, it is an open question as to how effective these coalitions will prove to be in the LA21 implementation phase. These coalitions should be broadened but this process will result in much resistance. Regarding information exchange, pioneering municipalities have been increasingly successful in attracting public and media attention. This diffusion of examples of good practice is expected to push the issue of LA21. This will be followed by the establishment of new networks to develop databases on LA21 in Germany. Moreover, an increasing number of research activities focus on LA21, in part financed by the federal government. This might be an initial sign for a future engagement of the federal government in LA21. From these observations, we can conclude that the German LA21 process is still underdeveloped, but recently there has been some promising movement. LA21 has the potential to become a priority issue in the public and municipal discussion of sustainable development, a discussion that is unavoidable in the coming decade.

Chapter 15

LOCAL AGENDA 21 IN NORWAY

Liv Astrid Sverdrup

INTRODUCTION

Until recently, the issue of Local Agenda 21 (LA21) has not been discussed very much in Norway. However, this does not imply that local environmental policy and the idea of 'thinking globally – acting locally' has not been a subject for local and central government discussion and action. In 1987 the government launched a comprehensive programme for environmental protection at the local level (EPLL). The aim of this chapter is to study existing Norwegian local environmental policy efforts in relation to the recommendations of LA21 plans. In the summer of 1994 the notion of Norway as the 'cleverest girl in the LA21 class' was presented by Prime Minister Gro Harlem Brundtland in a newspaper article:

> *As a result of EPLL approximately 150 municipalities have made local resource and environmental programmes, and about the same number are about to make such programmes. The work with resource and environmental issues has therefore come further in Norway than the development of Local Agenda 21.* [Nationen, 1994]

NORWEGIAN LOCALISM

Local government has a long tradition of autonomy in Norway. The general distribution of competence between central and local government allows local government to carry out all functions that are not explicitly defined as county or state government tasks (Ramsdal, 1995). Local authorities execute a variety of environmental functions, ranging from purely administrative ones to planning and information. Landuse planning, sewage, waste, open air activities, local road-building, hunting and fisheries administration, water supply, charting, and public areas are all the responsibility of the municipalities. Local authorities also impose taxes on services related to water supply, sewage and waste disposal. The planning system grants local authorities a central position with regard to local environmental policy. The Norwegian Planning and Building Act of 1985 regulates landuse and regional planning in Norway and ensures a comprehensive planning process where all affected parties are included. Guidelines on the coordination of physical and transport planning and environmental impact assessments for major projects are also included in the legislation. The act is administered by the Ministry of Environment (MoE) and is meant to facilitate the relations and coordination between national, county and municipal activities.

A brief glance at the historical development of municipal environmental policy shows how the responsibility for local environmental policy has shifted back and forth between the central, county and local levels (Aall and Høyer, 1995). In the mid 1960s nature conservation and regional policy were coupled. In 1965 the decision was made to transfer issues related to nature conservation from the Ministry of Church and Education to the Ministry of Local Government and Labour, which already bore responsibility for regional policy and planning. This coupling of environmental policy and regional planning can be seen as an expression of the perception that environmental protection policy had to be the result of a continuous balancing act between the use or consumption of, versus the protection of, environmental resources (Aall and Høyer, 1995). Underlying this was the belief that the local community should play an important role by carrying out this balancing. In the same period the building act was introduced, underlining the need for general planning at the local level. This act was an important instrument for local authorities, enabling them to develop their own policies for resource management.

In the 1970s and the first half of the 1980s central government increased its environmental policy activity – partly at the expense of the regional and local levels. The MoE was established in 1972. This led to a discussion about the coupling of environmental policy and regional planning and resulted in the transfer of the responsibility for regional planning to the MoE. During the next ten years environmental protection at the county level and partly also at the local level was first and foremost defined as a task for central government.

At the end of the 1980s the trend began to shift towards a more locally governed environmental policy. Since then environmental policy administration has been decentralised. This is partly a result of the EPLL programme. Furthermore, a general decentralisation can be found in the relationship between central and local government during this period. This decentralisation has been characterised by the following three traits:

1) the municipalities have been assigned a stronger degree of self-determination as to the application of state rules;
2) a general delegation of tasks from the central to the local level has been carried out; and
3) municipalities have gained more responsibility for cross-sectoral coordination, for instance with regard to local planning (Naustdalslid and Hovik, 1994).

In 1987 a locally initiated pilot project was started in three municipalities, which led to the employment of environmental protection officers. Neither the MoE nor the Association of Local and Regional Authorities were particularly interested in the project to begin with. However, with the launching of the Brundtland report, the MoE began changing its attitude. The Brundtland report stressed the need to include local government in order to achieve sustainable development. In a white paper on open air activities (White Paper No 40, 1986–1987) the government recommended the establishment of a joint committee for environmental protection in the municipalities. In 1987 the MoE initiated the three-year EPLL (1988–1991) programme. The aim of EPLL was to develop and strengthen local environmental policy and its organisation. Early experience from the independent local level environmental initiatives formed the background to MoE's launching of the programme. In 1992 the programme was reshaped into one for all local authorities.

The relatively high level of local autonomy, local government's right to execute a variety of functions, and its central position concerning local planning form a firm basis for the shaping of a local policy in correspondence with the recommendations from the Earth Summit in Rio. The policy defined three targets, reflecting the need for global concerns at the local level. Firstly, local authorities would have to take their share of the responsibility in implementing international commitments with regard to the reduction of various emissions. Secondly, local environmental protection should be strengthened and local authorities should be delegated more power. Thirdly, county authorities should include environmental considerations in their responsibility areas. Early Norwegian experience from EPLL, together with the recommendations from the International Union of Local Authorities conference on Environment, Health and Lifestyle held in Oslo 1991, constituted a central input and gave special emphasis to local authorities' role in promoting sustainable development (Holtane and Grann, 1995). However, no local governments participated at UNCED, nor did they participate in the making of the Government's White Paper on UNCED in 1992 (MoE, 1992).

In a statement by the MoE three years later, in February 1995, it was stated that the environmental plans created under EPLL formed a firm basis for securing public support for a LA21 process by 1996 (MoE, 1995). In the autumn of 1995 the report *Local Agenda 21 – Norwegian Municipalities' Environmental Work after Rio*, by the research institute Project for an Alternative Future/ProSus in cooperation with the Idea Bank, triggered discussion on LA21. The report concluded that non-local government had started work on a LA21 plan (Armann et al., 1995). The report received much attention both from central and local government. The minister of the environment responded to the criticism by arguing that the EPLL programme was of relevance to LA21 and that the actual activities carried out in the municipalities should not be brushed aside as irrelevant to LA21.

EPLL – A Forerunner to Local Agenda 21?

The purpose of the EPLL programme was to test and develop political and administrative organisational models at the local level and to strengthen municipal competence-building and management of environmental protection. Increased local participation and mobilisation of local-level responsibility for environmental policy to reach national targets were important factors in establishing the programme. It was also aimed at achieving a more integrated approach to environmental problems at the local level. Local authorities and the Norwegian Association of Local and Regional Authorities (KS) were invited to participate actively in the formation of the programme in close cooperation with the MoE. Interest in participating was considerable: 220 local governments applied, of which 91 were invited to participate in the first period. An important incentive for participation was the available funding earmarked for the participants. EPLL included projects on the following three aspects:

- political and administrative organisation of local environmental policy and the appointment of environmental protection officers;
- delegation of environmental tasks from central government to local authorities; and
- the making of local environment and natural resource programmes.

EPLL has introduced and integrated environmental considerations into municipal planning and policy, and has also contributed to raising general environmental awareness among the local population.

Environmental Protection Officers

Traditionally, in nearly all municipalities, environmental protection officers have had a place on the staff of the chief municipal executive. Today this is slowly changing due to an increased variation in the general political and administrative organisation of local authorities. Environmental protection officers play different roles, some working as autonomous experts who focus on specific environmental issues, while others play a more politicising or bureaucratic role. Environmental officers combining an expert role with a planning function, supported by local groups, has proved to be a successful combination (Jansen, 1991). As of February 1995, 420 out of 435 municipalities had appointed an environmental protection officer. So far about 700 million Norwegian krone has been provided for EPLL from the central government budget. The earmarked transfers and grants have primarily funded the employment of local environmental protection officers. As of 1997 these funds form part of the ordinary block of grants to the local authorities. Central government hopes that local governments will subsequently consider environmental policy, and the role of the environmental protection officer, important enough to fund it themselves. Today approximately 60 per cent of all environmental protection officers have permanent appointments, and in densely populated areas the percentage is much higher. In small municipalities where the funding for the environmental protection officer has covered only half a man-labour year, the authorities have often financed the second part of the man-labour year. Both these trends signal that local authorities regard environmental protection as a permanent task and that they are willing to finance it themselves.

Environment and Natural Resource Programmes

As part of both the initial EPLL and its follow-up, all participating municipalities were asked to draw up an environment and natural resource programme. It was to be both a sector-encompassing status quo document and an environmental protection action plan containing targets, strategies and measures. Previously very few municipalities had produced integrated local environmental plans. This was, therefore, crucial, serving as an important trigger and learning process for the first generation of environmental plans. Today several local authorities have started the development of a second or third generation environmental plan. The MoE established some very comprehensive guidelines. The local authorities were encouraged to develop an action plan around the most locally important environmental problems requiring solutions.

In May 1993 the MoE issued the circular *Think Globally – Act Locally: national priorities for local-level environmental protection to improve the planning process.* The circular pointed out how local authorities, through already existing routines, may realise a binding LA21. The circular was also designed to ensure improved correspondence between national and local priorities. Five national priority areas for the 1990s were listed – namely, environment- and resource-friendly development in towns and urban areas; waste management and recycling; biological diversity; coastal and freshwater environments; and cultural heritage, cultural landscapes and other cultural environments. A year later, KS presented a similar document setting out priority areas for environmental protection at the local level, underlining the need to develop LA21s and for a precautionary health and environmental policy.

Many local authorities saw the environmental plan process as very comprehensive and time consuming. By April 1994, two-thirds of the local authorities in Norway had prepared or were preparing plans for environmental protection. However, some local authorities do not intend to make separate environmental plans, instead preferring to integrate environmental planning into the general local planning process. There is no systematic reporting procedure for local authorities to submit their plans to the MoE, and the plans are not used as a control instrument by central government. However, several county environment departments have partially collected and evaluated the plans. Also, the KS has attempted stringently to collect the plans, in order to obtain an overview of the local efforts made.

However, the MoE and the directorates have established different systems for collection, systematisation and control of selected environmental data. The existing system was rather fragmented. (Aall, 1995). It appears that local governments have developed a more coordinated structure for their environmental policy process than has the state. One effort to improve this situation is the development of a research programme on environmental auditing and strategic environmental assessment as tools for long-term planning.

The Focus on Local and National rather than Global Problems

Local environmental plans reflect local problems and only seldom global concerns. In a survey in 1993 into which issues are given highest priority in environmental plans, water supply, sewage and waste had top priority in 42 per cent of the municipalities, and together with the management of natural resources and outdoor recreation these three issues ranked highest (Hovik and Johnsen, 1994). Traffic, nature conservation, biodiversity, energy consumption and energy saving, however, are all issues with a global aspect that have not been given priority.[1] Another study of 19 environmental plans concludes that discussions on global challenges and local contributions belong to the exceptions (Armann et al, 1995). Global environmental problems have not been decisive for local priorities, and links between international agreements and local action are few. The same attitudes can also be observed among municipal councillors. A recent study by Hovik and Harsheim (1996) concludes that many councillors are willing to give priority to environmental concerns but are mainly preoccupied with local environmental problems and are less interested in global ones. They are also hesitant to take responsibility for national tasks founded on international environmental agreements.

The lack of interest in, and focus on, global problems may partly be explained by the fact that most environmental tasks delegated to, and fulfilled by, local authorities are based upon national or local problems and priorities. Local authorities were encouraged by the MoE to develop an action plan around the most important environmental problems requiring solutions. Most of the environmental protection officers also work independently, with little external input concerning the priority of issues. Many environmental problems are generated locally and the consequences also seem to be felt locally. However, the means to solve the problems are often taken care of at the state level. Local governments have also been given few competencies within policy fields of relevance to global problems such as for instance energy consumption or transport. This lack of both competence and the potential of influencing these policy fields can partly explain local governments' priorities.

The environmental plans made under EPLL often lack any long-term perspective as most plans are made for a four-year period (Armann et al, 1995). Most plans lack quantifiable targets and specific timetables for reaching the targets. However, local governments are also obliged to set out a general municipal plan with a 12-year perspective, alternating every four years. An approved municipal plan has the status of law while the environmental plan does not. A common notion is therefore about to be established that the municipality's general plan is the most central planning document (Aall, 1996). Several local governments are therefore working to integrate their environmental plans into their general plan. The state has also recognised this notion and recommends in the Pollution Control Act that plans for the management of waste should be included in the general plan. But so far this integration and the environmental planning has been difficult to achieve.

Experience of Participation

Broad participation from different social groups is crucial to the development of LA21s. Following the World Commission's report, several local authorities established local gro-commissions to discuss specific ideas for sustainable development at the local level. The commissions consisted of representatives from local authorities, business and industry, various NGOs and local inhabitants. The commissions were active in the period from 1987 to 1989. Then, after Rio, most of the commissions were dissolved due to reduced interest and capacity. The EPLL programme has refocused attention on public participation in environmental policy-making.

The Planning and Building Act formally allows broad public participation in local policy-making. Yet the range of different actors who participate in the making of environmental plans varies and a more active broadening of the range of participants at the local level seems crucial. A study by Hovik and Johnsen (1994) in which actors participate, deliver information or give statements in the making of local environmental plans in 105 municipalities, concludes that it is mainly local government units that participate in the making of plans. Environmental NGOs, other voluntary organisations and local business interests do not participate very actively in the explicit making of such plans. If they do participate they usually deliver information or give statements. Many municipalities have strict administrative processes for the drawing up of plans. In only 15 per cent of the municipalities asked did environmental NGOs participate in the making of plans (Hovik and Johnsen, 1994). When it comes to cooperation with voluntary organisations on specific environmental activities, the tendency is somewhat different. A study by Taugebøl (1994) explains that 93 per cent of the 125 local authorities asked have cooperated with various voluntary organisations in their environmental activities. The cooperation is mainly limited to specific projects.

More recently, environmental NGOs have contributed to putting LA21 on the political agenda, which is a new trend. Participation from environmental NGOs was weak during the first years of EPLL; in the years following Rio very few efforts were made by the NGOs to initiate LA21. Until recently, most NGO initiatives have focused on some aspects of sustainable development such as sustainable consumption, and not on the process as a whole.

An interesting initiative that works towards broader cooperation is the Environmental Home Guard, a broad-based NGO movement established in October 1991. The Home Guard strives for a reduction in the level of consumption and tries to make consumption more sustainable by providing information on how to make more environmentally friendly choices. Norway's largest environmental NGO, the Norwegian Society for the Conservation of Nature, provides the Home Guard with environmental expertise. The Environmental Home Guard currently has 15,000 individual members.

Moreover, it has established regional offices in six counties and works within approximately 60 to 70 municipalities. The Home Guard cooperates with local voluntary organisations and local governments and develops local networks for sustainable consumption based upon already existing local voluntary organisations. The Environmental Home Guard's project on sustainable consumption is supported by the MoE. Since 1992, funding has more than doubled, currently amounting to 5.4 million Norwegian krone annually.

With regard to public opinion's support for an ambitious environmental policy, the results from the latest local elections show that this cannot be taken for granted. In September 1995 immigration policy proved to be the most central issue. The elections resulted in a turn towards a more conservative policy at the local level. The Socialist Left party, with the reputation of being active in environmental policy, lost voters while the right-wing Progress party gained strong, increased support.

FURTHER PROGRAMMES TO DEVELOP LOCAL ENVIRONMENTAL POLICY

EPLL is the most comprehensive programme on local environmental policy, but other programmes of relevance to LA21 have also been developed. The oldest is the ecomunicipality pilot programme, established as early as 1985, including five rural local authorities. The programme was established to promote a bottom-up initiative for local environmental policy.[2] The programme has been run by the Forum for Norwegian Ecomunicipalities (FONE), where the representatives have been local politicians. The interest and participation of local politicians is a central aspect of the ecomunicipality programme. The ecomunicipalities have all committed themselves to work for sustainable development and to adopt the so-called FONE declaration, an ecopolitical manifesto in which the municipality commits itself to working towards sustainable development. The members are supposed to integrate environmental considerations into local policy mechanisms and to promote local action on global problems. Members also aim at involving people and improving local governance. Aall (1995) presents the following five aspects as being characteristic of the ecomunicipalities:

1) a bottom-up perspective in which the initiative has been taken up by the municipality itself;
2) a district perspective in which local problems and the challenges related to the relationship between centre – periphery have been an important aspect;
3) representatives from the environmental and various alternative movements have participated in local government's policy process;
4) a sustainability perspective – the municipalities apply a wider perspective than the traditional environmental-protection perspective; and
5) efforts are made to develop an alternative professional expertise – the municipalities have cooperated closely with various expert research groups and institutions.

Vital for the ecomunicipality programme are research and development programmes. Most of the programmes have been undertaken by the Western Norway Research Institute and have been supported by the MoE and the KS. The programmes include projects on environmental education for politicians, environmental auditing, local environmental planning, and greening of business projects.

There are only nine ecomunicipalities while eight others also participate in the various research and development programmes developed within the ecomunicipality programme (Ramsdal, 1995a, 1995b). The programme is financed by the MoE and KS. The idea has been to use the funding to develop expertise and experience in a small set of local governments and later to distribute this to a broader audience (Lund, 1995).

Another relevant programme is the MoE initiative Environmentally Friendly Towns and Cities, involving five urban areas. The programme was set up in 1993 and over a four to six year period the participants, together with the county government and the ministry, will develop strategies and measures to create a model for comprehensive sustainable development in towns and cities. The number of local authorities participating in the project is rather small. Although the participants include many of Norway's largest cities and towns, the MoE seems to have developed models rather than comprehensive programmes. These five cities have also signed the Aalborg Charter for sustainable cities and towns. The Norwegian programme consists of six issue areas: area and transport planning; urban development; living local communities; green structure and nature and open-air leisure activities; recycling of waste; landuse planning, and protection of cultural sites. The selection of issue areas has some relevance to global environmental problems and also presupposes a long-term perspective and the inclusion of a wide range of participants. To handle each issue area, groups consisting of representatives from local authorities, ministries and directorates have been formed. An analysis of the project in relation to LA21 concludes that the projects set out are comprehensive and often maintain a long-term perspective (Armann *et al*, 1995). However, most projects are dominated by administrative actors. Other groups tend to come into the process only at a late stage when much of the planning is done. Due to the financing situation, many of the efforts set out are based upon national rather than local priorities. Some of the participants have developed scenarios and long-term perspectives and visions, but when it comes to the setting of specific and quantitative targets, these are only in place until the year 2000.

In 1993, an interesting local business initiative was set up called the Green City Foundation in Stavanger. The main idea of the foundation is to make the business sector integrate environmental considerations within their activities, independently of public authorities' policies. The participants must adopt and report on at least one voluntary environmental measure, in addition to fulfilling general environmental requirements. The environmental protection officer in Stavanger and the information director of AMOCO, an oil company located in Stavanger, took the initiative to set up the foundation. By spring of 1996 about 100 companies were participating in the Green City Foundation, which provides information and practical support. Moreover six Green councils have been established to discuss ideas and specific projects on the following topics: resource management, waste disposal and recycling, transport, landuse planning, oil and energy, and overall environmental planning. Representatives from business and industry, environmental NGOs and local government participate in the groups. Cooperation on the development and use of electric cars and a project on waste disposal are two specific results of the Green City Foundation. The experience gained will also be an important aspect of Stavanger's participation within the MoE's programme for sustainable consumption at the local level, which is still under development. Six municipalities will participate in the project which also aims to increase public participation in the making of local environmental policy.

In May 1995, a new cooperative relationship was established between the Norwegian Society for the Conservation of Nature and the trade union Norwegian Union of Municipal Employees: The Trade Unions' Environmental Responsibility. The agreement signals the birth of an interesting alliance. The parties intend to cooperate in fields such as waste treatment, transport, energy, landuse planning, public purchasing and health and nature conservation. More specifically, a handbook entitled The Small Green One for the Local Authority has been compiled and distributed to the trade union's 220,000 members. Furthermore, a high-level think tank has been set up, with participants from both the environmental NGOs and the trade unions, to discuss, on the basis of A21, quality and standard of life, growth and consumption and the role of trade unions in the development of a sustainable society. The trade union is providing the funding of 750,000 Norwegian krone.

Taken together, these projects provide valuable experience within fields highly relevant to a LA21 process. The ecomunicipality programme provides important experience of political participation. The programme has also generated interesting research on issues highly relevant for the LA21 process, such as environmental education for politicians, local environmental planning and environmental auditing. While the ecomunicipality project focuses upon rural district municipalities, the MoE's project on sustainable cities and towns develops models for sustainable urban municipalities. The latter project has also been quite successful in adopting global problems and a long-term approach. These projects are complemented by various NGO and business initiatives. The Environmental Home Guard's work for more sustainable consumption is a central initiative in this respect. Efforts have been made to establish a dialogue between local NGOs and local government authorities. As previously discussed, the Environmental Home Guard also works to develop a nationwide network of NGOs to promote more sustainable consumption. More recently, environmental NGOs have put LA21 on the political agenda. The Idea Bank, together with the project for an Alternative Future (since January 1996 called Prosus) and the Environmental Home Guard maintain an important function in pushing for, and providing information on, the LA21 issue.

COMMENTARY

Until recently Norway has had no specific LA21 process. So far only one LA21 plan has been prepared, by the municipality of Sogndal. The late start of a specific LA21 process may be explained by the general perception held by the government that EPLL, initiated in 1987, was of such a character that the Norwegian experience was in accordance with the development of LA21. The MoE has therefore begun to promote the making of LA21 plans. But recently the minister of the environment has signalled the need to develop specific LA21 plans in Norway. This characterises a change in the MoE's understanding of what a LA21 process should be about, and hence what is missing in the case of Norway.

This chapter argues that the experience of the EPLL programme has led to improved local environmental policy. It will, however, be necessary to promote a broader participatory process, the inclusion of more global environmental issues and the application of a longer-term perspective. Combined with the experience gained from various other programmes and projects already initiated, Norway has a wide and valuable basis for the further development of a more specific LA21 process. Both top-down and bottom-up initiatives have been established and broad experience has been built up during a ten-year period with the ecomunicipality programme, starting as early as 1985, followed by EPLL in 1987.

The emphasis on developing models to guide local decision-making indicates the level of freedom given to the local level in deciding the form of sustainability.[3] The MoE draws up some general guidelines but leaves implementation to the local level. This use of models and pilot studies may, however, limit a potentially broader process with more participants. As long as the MoE chooses the model approach, it will be vital to establish a comprehensive information system where other local governments may learn from the experience gained. What is important is to compile all the experience gained and distribute this knowledge to local governments.

Knowledge about the relationship between global problems and local solutions and of the structure and content of an LA21 process should also be improved. Environmental NGOs, together with the MoE, could play an important role in providing this kind of information. More active Norwegian participation in international organisations could certainly also provide local governments with useful input.

In spite of the shortcomings identified, it is maintained that the existing portfolio of projects forms a firm basis for the further development of an LA21 process. To avoid a situation in which LA21 is perceived as just another reform or planning process initiated by the state, it will be important to develop an LA21 process based upon existing experience. The launch of a more ambitious LA21 policy process with a wider participatory aspect, including a broader local society and a more active participation from NGOs, could be a useful continuation of the Norwegian process after the EPLL and ecomunicipality programme. To support such a process more coordinated and comprehensive support from central government is vital.

Table 15.1 Overview of the most central local environment-initiatives

Project	Date	Objectives	Scale	Coalitions
Programme for environmental protection at the local level	1987–91 1992–96	To test and develop models for local environmental policy: • appointment of environmental protection officers; • delegation of tasks from the central to the local level; • making of local environment and natural resource programmes; • development of a network of competence between the environmental protection officers.	91 municipalities; since 1992 all municipalities	Funded by the MoE, carried out in cooperation with the Norwegian Association of Local and Regional Authorities.
The Ecomunicipality programme	1985–96	To develop a bottom-up initiative for local environmental policy: • rural-district approach; • commitment to work for sustainable development; • development of alternative professional expertise in cooperation with research institutions.	9+(8) municipalities	Cooperation among local governments, local politicians and research institutions; funded by the MoE and the Norwegian Association of Local and Regional Authorities.
The Environmental Home Guard	1991	To work for a general reduction in the level of consumption and to make consumption more sustainable. • development of local networks.	15,000 individual members; projects in 60–70 municipalities	Cooperation between environmental NGOs, other voluntary organizations and the local governments; funded by the MoE.
Environmentally Friendly Towns and	1993–97/ 99	To develop a model for sustainable development in towns and cities:		Cooperation between local and county

Cities		• working groups on six issue areas of relevance to LA21	5 municipalities	governments, ministries and directorates; funded by the MoE
The Green City Foundation	1993	Make the business sector integrate environmental considerations into their activities.	100 companies	Cooperation within Green councils between business, industry, NGOs and the local government of Stavanger
The Trade Union's Environmental Responsibility	1995-	To develop cooperation between an environmental NGO and a trade union on various environmental issues	One trade union and one environmental NGO	Cooperation between the Norwegian Society for the Conservation of Nature and the Norwegian Union of Municipal Employees; the project is funded by the trade union

Chapter 16

CONTINUING THE TRANSITION

Tim O'Riordan and Heather Voisey

The transition towards sustainability is definitely underway. In discourse terms, the goal of sustainable development has a language, a shared meaning and identifiable responses. The concept of sustainable development may not be on everybody's lips, but the principle of planetary stewardship, linked to social and political equity through quality of life, is implanted in cultures and politics worldwide. This may not appear to be much, given the paucity of responses in programmatic institutional terms. But the fact that sustainable development has become incorporated within international agreements, the Amsterdam Treaty, international business and NGO networks, and in the environmental rhetoric of almost every decision-making body around the globe, indicates that the notion has staying power and some organisational focus.

The sustainability transition will progress more by stealth than by design. Its best bet is to jump on bandwagons already rolling along than to alter their direction and reinforce their staying power. The principal trends are summarised in Figure 1.1 in Chapter 1. These include the release of innovative effort around clean technology, ecoefficiency, holistic management, and more comprehensive regulation. This package is assisted by huge and rapid advances in information technology, making it possible to add wealth by manipulating knowledge itself. It is thus possible to visualise an economy with far less dependence on primary materials production and linear waste discharges. Add to this the emergence of a civil society full of pluralistic pressure groups, do-it-yourself 'street-level' politics and greater openness generally, and there is a propulsion that provides the basis for sustainability.

This rosy picture must, however, be tempered by a failure to assist the poor everywhere, the developing world generally, and the terms of trade, aid and capacity-building amongst those less able to assist themselves. The trends noted above will help the wealthy to become more sustainable but at the expense, as always, of the poor. A lower primary materials-using economy will hurt those developing economies still utterly dependent on such products. Ecotaxes on carbon and phosphorous will affect those economies still reliant on coal and phosphate rock for a quarter of their employment and a fifth of foreign revenues. In the short term at least, the poor will suffer in the name of sustainability.

Another primary difficulty with the transition, from a political vantage point, is that it does not conform clearly to any ideal for the spin doctors and image-makers. The concept is woolly, ill-understood, inextricable from other unresolved policy arenas such as poverty, debt, unbalanced trade and aid, and enormously politicised in the North–South debate. Furthermore, it has no popular currency, no identity for a leader to illuminate, and cannot be delivered by any single level of political or economic institution. For the politically ambitious it is graveyard territory. No wonder the big names such as Clinton, Blair, Kohl and even Brundtland herself confine the notion to set speeches in international arenas, where promises trip comfortably off the lips and a pliant press reports with disbelieving sympathy.

An additional difficulty facing the sustainability transition is the current ambivalence over environmentalism. Polls in Europe generally show signs of fatigue and resignation over the apparent inability to rid ourselves of environmental scares and ecological crises. Yet contrarians pop up everywhere to assure us that environmentalists are misguided doomsdayers, and that all is well with economics and the availability of fuel and raw materials (see especially *The Economist*, 20 December 1997, pp21–24). So policy-makers are put off their guard, lobbyists for the status quo gain strength and credence, and environmental and social disruption continues apace under the veil of scientific ignorance and impotence. There is no easy answer here. Environmentalism is subtly changing into a post modern agenda which is adjunct to sustainability but which is not properly connected. It is frustrating, but this is real politics.

THE US EXPERIENCE

One cannot therefore look to any identifiable leadership to push the sustainability transition forward. For example, in the US, arguably the most influential nation – economically and politically – in the world, leadership is absent. The President's Council on Sustainable Development (PCSD) (1996) produced a 186-page report. Its secretariat (Olson, 1996, p10) made it clear that the federal government could not on its own deliver the transition to sustainability, and implied that only coordinated partnerships at a host of levels of formal and informal institutions could do the job (PCSD, 1996, p52). Arguably, a more sombre conclusion could be reached, namely that American constitutional arrangements, designed by the founding fathers to ensure checks and balances at all points of decision-making and policy formulation, are trapped by an inextricable democratic paradox. In short, the US simply cannot do it without a wholesale transformation in the culture of the governed and the governing. As the distinguished US environmental commentator Kai Lee commented (1996, pp33–34), the US will have to undergo three kinds of learning:

1) a fundamental change in outlook so that 'rich' means wanting little rather than having much;
2) the hardwiring of sustainability into daily decision-making against a pattern,

today, that mostly does the opposite; and

3) knowing more about ecosystem responses to human intervention in order to incorporate adaptive, sequential and responsive management into strategies and actions.

Each of these three nodes of learning requires a combination of government, private caution and individual endeavour. This is the mixture of markets, regulation and justice that we pointed out in Table 2.1, but nowhere is there a clear analysis in the President's Council report on empowerment or revelation. The reasons for that are reasonably obvious:

1) The American public has little understanding or information about the complexities of the sustainability transition. They have not been exposed to the many drivers or the trade-offs (sacrifices) necessary to put this transition firmly on the political map. Lee's first learning node, namely a shift in attitudes to consumption, is nowhere near first base. More to the point, there is no political or educational initiative in this direction, nor are the NGOs active on this level of discourse.

2) The post PCSD effort to publicise the findings of the report, and its follow-through, have been minimal. These are not ideas that attract the media, to industrial efficiency, tax reform, social justice, information quality, or revitalised communities. They simply do not convert to a soundbite or a newsworthy story, let alone a catchy headline. Even *The New York Times* on its dullest day would look lively by comparison.

3) The 1996 presidential campaign, like all electoral struggles, stuck to safe ground, manageable topics, and centrist, conservative philosophies. No presidential aspirant would run on a sustainability platform, for the reason cited above. Nobody would understand him or her, even if the message was in plain English. It is significant that the Democratic party presidential aspirant for the 2000 election, Vice President Al Gore, a noted environmentalist in the early 1990s (Gore, 1992), is positively *distancing* himself from his environmental credentials in the long, long run-up to the next campaign. More to the point, President Clinton, as a rare example of a second-term president, and hence free to focus on moral and horizontal themes for his departing electorate, is bedevilled by scandal. His shattered political credibility would hardly be enhanced by a crusade in favour of the sustainability transition. A minority would consider him ready for the psychiatrist's chair, following the court decisions on his sex and electoral misdemeanour charges.

4) Nevertheless, the actual report of the PCSD remains sound, well argued and pragmatic. The new generation of PCSD efforts are directed particularly at city initiatives; here is where the life blood of American community activism can be tapped. Seattle, Chattanooga, Austin, Chicago, Denver and many more have embarked on a host of citizens' initiatives involving self-help schemes, community-support programmes and joint private–public sector initiatives of enormous variety and energy. Watch out for a burst of

indicator studies and internet-connected learning experiences. It may not generate actual results in the near future, but it is the most appropriate zone for American activism because it connects to a host of other community programmes relating to poverty alleviation, job training, educational uplift, caring for the disadvantaged, and ecojustice initiatives that transcend the multi-ethic boundaries that criss-cross urban America.

CHARTING THE NEXT STEPS

Let us return to the seven themes we selected as possible organising foci for any further move along the pathway to sustainable development.

The language of sustainability (*theme 1*) remains deliberately obscure and contradictory. Terms such as stewardship and empowerment are rich in meaning but devoid of reality. The task ahead is to incorporate these within cabinets, parliaments, boardrooms, community centres, classrooms and living rooms to the point where they enable and encourage response, rather than highlight moral discomfort. Community activism of the kind well summarised by Diane Warburton (1998) adds to a sense that education and capacity-building will take place beyond the school and university gate and outside of formal learning structures, and provides one ray of light. This is a pattern that should be encouraged for its own sake, and in doing so, should take the sustainability transition along with it.

Policy integration (*theme 2*) will always be difficult, even in a world of programme budgeting, performance indicators and adaptive scenario management of the kind Kai Lee advocates. There have to be common understandings across units of decision and action, where – at present – institutional balkanisation and budgetary jealousy dictate fragmentation and duplication. One school of thought advocates more professional and specialised administrators. But there is still a need for the strategic generalist who is also a charismatic diplomat generously imbued with patience.

Interdepartmental coordination (*theme 3*) is beginning to take place. The rise of partnerships and institutional forms that link departmental effort means that administrators and policy advisors will increasingly interact in decision-making. John McNeil's notions of Aristotelian consensus is beginning to appear in the alluring language of precaution, civic science, ecoauditing and ethical weighting. Interdepartmental coordination is likely to be spurred on by green accounting, which in turn will promote the cause of ecological tax reform. It is an arena of enormous ferment that is more significant than it appears. Because it is difficult to pinpoint and to measure, it is given partial attention but deserves more in the years to come.

Green accounting (*theme 4*) is here to stay and will become the beneficiary of international comparison and cooperation, and knowledge management. The breakthrough will come as the 'indicator revolution' shifts from established environmental items, such as air and water quality and the costs of transport, to social auditing and the patterns of alienation and deprivation that coalesce into disadvantage on a comprehensive scale. The analysts are not there yet because much work and innovation is needed for definable measurement. In any case, it requires civic science approaches and community empowerment techniques for its manifestation and validation. These remain embryonic, but are very much the focus of attention in the next generation of LA21. Therefore, we feel sure that the green accounting revolution will transcend to the 'soft' social indices of empowerment and revelation, where the gains associated with improving community and personal wellbeing can be translated into real cost savings on possible crime and drugs offences, and into measures of democratic support that any aspiring politician should cherish.

Tax reform (*theme 5*) is more than in the air. Every western government is at it, and research abounds. But tax reform, though not widely recognised as a matter of fiscal prudence and efficiency, remains a sluggish policy arena. This is partly a matter of the sheer complexity of tax rules, which are so intermuddled as to be virtually inextricable, even with political will. It is also an outcome of a network of interests, many of which are politically powerful, whose gains in the reform may not appear evident at the outset. Therefore, political warring will always accompany tax reforms, no matter how well presented. In addition, the really interesting sustainability fiscal changes are in arenas where international action is required. This weakens the resolve of even the most ardent government if competitiveness is stifled by well-meaning sustainability objectives. This is especially the case in relation to climate change and biodiversity, where any national action could be painful for a modest global gain in a world of uncertain science. So we do not anticipate any dramatic revolution in ecological tax reform, simply because both the mechanics and the use of the revenue are deeply politicised in structures that owe their origin and survival to nonsustainability. The best hope lies in the general drift in tax policy from income to consumption.

Business (*theme 6*) will continue to inch its way forward towards what it defines as profitable sustainability. How far companies can profit by making the economy a fitter and leaner place is anyone's guess. In the early stages of the transition, there are definite gains to be made; ecoefficiency and clean technology are good selling images, and regulations promote their cause. But the late–early stages of the transition generate a more problematic picture. If progressive ecological tax reform was in place, then it might be possible to see further profitable enterprises surrounding the late–early stages of the transition. In the absence of these reforms, one has to be sanguine. Few businesses today embark on full-cost accounting beyond a casual paper exercise.

Product stewardship, ethical audits, social responsibility and fair trade are all likely to progress over the remainder of this decade and beyond. These initiatives will benefit from improvements in green accounting and in sustainability indicator innovation. But it is still difficult to see how this will prove successful beyond the package of voluntaristic compliance that we introduced in Chapter 2. Frankly, we do not feel a great optimism for significant development along the pathways for business and sustainability until the boardrooms contain genuine and knowledgeable advocates who can communicate in the language of 'what is in it for me'; until the consumer openly demands product stewardship at the point of purchase, we are a long, long way from that. Yet that is probably the best one can do in the controversial realm of sustainable consumption.

So we look to LA21 (*theme 7*) for our most promising arena of future change. We are not widely optimistic even here for the reasons already stated in the introduction to Part III of this book. Nevertheless, the local level is the point of activity and identity, so we remain hopeful that the transition to sustainability will continue to be most active where everyone lives, works, plays, prays and dreams.

We leave you with a vision of a society that has the capacity to be fairer, more compassionate and more secure in livelihood than any society before it. The information revolution could just provide greater wealth with less effort than the predecessor agricultural and industrial revolutions. It is too early to tell, but we can see a misty image of a sustainability transition where more people gain than lose, linking the emerging information revolution to the patterns of change, nascent though they are, that we have described in this book. If the long-term gains can be popularly appreciated over the short-term losses, we may just overcome the democratic paradox that, to date, has held the transition to sustainability close to the starting gun. It is an image at least worth contemplating and acting upon, because the prospect of prolonged sacrifice in the face of a promise of a more sustainable world, somewhere around the mythical corner, simply will not wash in any democracy of which we are aware.

ENDNOTES

NOTES TO CHAPTER 2

1 The authors would like to thank Martin Hession for his valuable comments on this chapter.
2 Of course, as sustainable development is now part of the task of the EU it is also hard law, but the question remains as to whether interpretation of this principle will give rise to operational rules.
3 The Departments of the Environment and of Transport merged in 1997 to form this super-ministry.

NOTES TO CHAPTER 3

1 Court of Justice Case 240/83, *Procureur de la République v Association de Défense des Bruleurs d'Huiles Usagées.*
2 Lord Avebury, President of the Conservation Society in a letter to *The Times*, 20 January 1975.
3 See, for a cross-section of opinion: *The 1996 Intergovernmental Conference: Integrating the Environment into other EU Policies*, Institute for European Environmental Policy London, April 1995; *Greening the Treaty II: Sustainable Development in a Democratic Union – Proposals for the 1996 Intergovernmental Conference*, European Environmental Bureau et al, May 1995.

NOTES TO CHAPTER 4

1 This paper will refer to the European Union as the political entity and the European Community as the legal entity (consequently European Community Law) as under Maastricht these elements are distinct and the Provisions Governing the Union are not recognisable by the European Court. European policy in so far as it exists may appertain to the Union, the community or member states.
2 See Les Verts v The European Parliament 1986 ECR 1339.
3 291/69 Stauder v Ulm 1969 ECR 419, 11/70 International Handelsgessellschafft 1970 ECR 1125, 4/73 Nold II 1974 ECR 491, 44/79 Liselotte Hauer v Rheinlandpfalz 1979 ECR 3727. More recently German Maastricht decision BVerfGE 89, p155.
4 See Article 2.
5 Most famously in the Van Genden Loos Case (26/62 (1963) ECR 1).
6 See the Wallonia Waste Case (1993 Common Market Law Review, p356).
7 Case 120/78 Cassis de Dijon 1979 ECR 649; Case 8/74 Dassonville 1974 ECR 837 (National Measures and the Single Market).
8 Van Genden Loos Case 26/62 (1963) ECR 1 (Direct Effect), Case 106/77 Simmenthal (1978) ECR 629 (Supremacy of EC Law).

9   Case c-300/89 Re Titanium Dioxide: Commission vs Council 1991 ECR 5545; Case 155/91 Commission vs Council 17 March 1993; Case c-62/88 Greece vs Council 29 March 1990 (Choice of Legal Basis). See Wallonia Waste Case for interaction of market and environmental rules. Re Wallonia Waste Ban; Commission vs Belgium 1993 *Common Market Law Review.*

10 C-461/93 An Taisce and WWF-UK v Commission 23 September 1994, Case T-585/93 Stichting Greenpeace Council et al v Commission Judgement of 12.2.94. Reported in Journal of Environmental Law 8(1).

11 In broad terms internal tariffs and customs duties, discriminatory taxes, quantitative restrictions broadly defined, restrictions on the free movement of workers and on the self employed, or on the freedom to provide services, state subsidy and anti-competitive behaviour by economic enterprises, are either automatically invalid or subject to Commission approval in accordance with defined principles. There are special provisions on state undertakings and provisions on the equal treatment of men and women at work.

12 In a degree of activism, the court confirmed environment as such a ground prior to its formal introduction into the treaty text in Case 240/83 Procuruer de la République v Association de Défense des brûleurs d'huiles usagées (ADBHU) (1985) ECR 531.

13 Case 174/82 Sandoz BV 1983 ECR 2445.

14 73 Nold II 1974 ECR 491, 44/79 Liselotte Hauer v Rheinlandpfalz 1979 ECR 3727.

NOTES TO CHAPTER 5

1   Referred to in the rest of this chapter as the Amsterdam Treaty amendments. At the time of writing (August 1997) the Conclusions of the Presidency had still not been formally agreed upon and signed by the parties. Formal amendment of the treaty (which requires referenda in some countries) is probably still several years away. Under the Amsterdam amendments, the integration duty would be repositioned as a new article 3d at the head of the treaty.

2   Council resolution endorsing the Third Action on the Environment (1982–86) established the integration of an environmental dimension into other community policies as a priority, and in 1985 the European Council 'affirmed its determination' to give community environmental protection policy 'the dimension of an essential component of the economic, industrial, agricultural and social policies implemented by the community and by its member states'.

3   A number of expert commentators soon noted the potential significance of the provision. Ludwig Krämer (1990) that it 'must be considered the most important provision in the entire section on the environment' : Nigel Haigh (1987) also commented that it is 'potentially the most important new provision'.

4   See, in particular, C 13/83 European Parliament v EC Council [1985] ECR 1513.

5   For example, case C–62/88 Greece v EC Council [1990] 1 ECR 1527.

6   The rule of law underlies the operation of the community in that any legal measures taken by the community (such as legislation) must expressly be founded on a specific provisions of the treaty (such as those concerning agriculture, transport, the environment, etc). Ultimately the European Court has the power to determine whether a particular measures falls within the remit of the provision claimed. Since different procedural consequences can flow from the choice of treaty provision, there have been frequent legal disputes between the European Council, the European Commission, the European Parliament and member states over the correct legal base.

7   For example, case Greece v EC Council [1990], ECR 1527.

8   This was said of the constitution of the German Democratic Republic, which

included a mandate to the legislature and a fundamental duty to protect nature (Brandl and Bungert, 1992).

9   There is an important fourth objective of promoting measures at international level to deal with regional or worldwide environmental problems, but this relates more to geographical competence than to substantive content.

10 Hallo draws an analogy with the subsidiarity principle which 'underwent a similar migration in the Treaty of Maastricht, moving from the environment article to a new separate article at the beginning of the treaty'. He notes how following that move, serious political attention was given to refining and developing the principle into workable criteria.

11 See case c–13/83 European Parliament v EC Council [1985] ECR 1513.

12 Part 3 of the treaty, for example, is entitled *Community Policies* and includes competition policy, economic policies, and free movement of goods, and includes sections entitled 'economic policy' and 'monetary policy'.

13 This approach is reinforced by the historical background to the proposal and the declaration at the Maastricht Conference that the commission undertakes to take full account of the environmental impact and the principle of sustainable growth in implementing its proposals – no qualification confining the scope of those proposals is provided in the declaration.

14 Both the Council of Ministers and the committees of the European Parliament have been organised along traditional functional lines (transport, agriculture, environment, etc) which does not necessarily assist the integration process. The council has occasionally held joint meetings (energy and environment) but the European Parliament has yet to establish any 'cross-cutting' committee structure.

15 UK case law has held that the precautionary principle as expressed in article 130r binds member states only when developing a community policy and does not apply to other fields unencompassed by community legislation: R v Secretary of State for Trade and Industry ex parte Duddridge (Court of Appeal 6 October 1995; see case note by Hughes (1995) *Journal of Environmental Law*, 7 (2) 224,226).

16 See case T–194/94 Carvel and *Guardian* Newspapers v Council [1995] ECR II–2765 and case T–105/95 WWF UK v Commission 5 March 1977. Here the Court concluded that although the commission's decision to adopt the code of practice was 'in effect, a series of obligations which the Commission has voluntarily assumed for itself as a measure of internal organisation, it is nevertheless capable of conferring on third parties legal rights which the Commission is obliged to respect'.

17 Whether the conservative interpretation was correct was at the heart of the Mullaghmore case, case T–461/93 An Taisce and WWF (UK) v Commission [1994] ECR II–733. The applicants challenged the commission's narrow interpretation of the structural funds regulation that measures financed by such funds must be in keeping with 'Community policy on environmental protection'. Unfortunately, the substance of the argument was not considered since the case was ruled inadmissible on procedural grounds, a decision confirmed on appeal, case C–325/94 [1996] ECR 1–3727.

18 In a slightly different context, in the Danish Bottles Case, Commission v Denmark [1989] 1 CMLR 619, the European Court was called upon to define an objective standard of environmental protection which was reasonable for a member state to pursue, where this would inhibit the free movement of goods. The court studiously avoided providing an answer, and refused to interfere with the judgement of the member state on the issue. Posing the question of what is a reasonable degree of environmental protection, Kramer (1993) succinctly replies, 'the answer is relatively simple: we do not know'.

19 For example, the right to procedural protection can include cases where the only evidence of a breach of procedures is the evidence of an inadequate substantive result which would not have occurred if adequate procedural protection had been given.

20 In the general scheme of rights, individual human rights tend to have the character of substantive rights which are guaranteed exclusively to them, whereas collective rights, such as those relating to the environment, do not. The only sense in which a collective right may be ensured is by way of a guarantee in individual participation.

21 See, for example, case 5/73 Balkan–Import–Export GmbH v Hauptzollamt Berlin-Packhof [1973] ECR 1091.

22 Member states may also initiate enforcement actions under article 169 against other member states but are highly reluctant to do so, again for the fairly cynical reason of mutual reassurance.

23 See case 26/62 Van Gend en Loos [1963] ECR 1, where the Court commenced its extensive jurisprudence on this doctrine.

24 Case 25/62 Plaumann v Commission [1963] ECR 95 established the key test and has been consistently applied in subsequent cases.

25 Stichting Greenpeace Council and others v Commission, case T–585/93 12 February 1994; 1996 *Journal of Environmental Law* vol 8, no 1; Danielsson and others v Commission, case T–219/95R 22 December 1995.

26 In WWF UK v Commission, case T–105/95 Court of First Instance 5 March 1997, the court argued that article 190 served two purposes – first, to permit interested parties to know the justification of a measure in order to enable them to protect their rights; and second, to enable the community courts to exercise their power to review the legality of decisions.

27 Case 5/67 Baus [1968] ECR 83. See also case C–350/88 Delacre v Commission [1990] ECR 1–395.

28 In the Wallonia waste case, EC Commission v Belgium [1992] 1 ECR 4431, the court was prepared to invoke the principle of community environmental action that damage should be rectified at source to justify a local ban on the import of wastes. Although the reasoning in the decision has been much criticised, the court in essence recognised that member states could claim the benefit of the principles of community environmental policy in the face of preemptive community rules concerning free movement.

29 Under the Declaration to the Final Act of the 1997 Amsterdam Conference, the conference noted that 'the commission undertakes to prepare environmental impact assessment studies when making proposals which may have significant environmental implications'.

NOTES TO CHAPTER 6

1 The classic discussion of integration within organisations is P Lawrence and J Lorsch (1969).

2 SEA is the ex-ante assessment of proposed sectoral policies, plans and programmes.

3 EEC Fourth Environmental Action Programme 1987–1992, *Official Journal* C328, 7 December 1987.

4 Commission of the European Communities, *Towards Sustainability: A European Community Programme of Policy and Action in Relation to the Environment and Sustainable Development*. COM (2) 23, 27 March 1992.

5 Commission of the European Communities, *Progress Report from the Commission on the Implementation of the European Community Programme of Policy and Action in Relation to the Environment and Sustainable Development Towards Sustainability*, COM (95) 624 10 January 1996.

6 Council Resolution on a community programme of policy and action in relation to the environment and sustainable development, *Official Journal* C 138, 17 May 1995.

7 Commission of the European Communities, *Report from the European Community to the Commission on Sustainable Development on Progress towards Implementation of Agenda 21. The*

Third Session, April 1995, p 2.

8   Unpublished review by IEEP London.

9   Department of the Environment (1994) *EC Fifth Environmental Action Programme Towards Sustainability: Government Action in the UK*, December 1994.

10   *Op cit* Annex 2.

11   Speech by Mrs Bjerregaard to ERM/Green Alliance Forum, London, 2 November 1995.

12   Commission of the European Communities, internal communication: *Integration by the Commission of the Environment into other Policies*, SEC (93) 785/5, 28 May 1993.

13   Commission of the European Communities, *Manual of Operational Procedures*, 7th Edition, September 1994.

14   Information obtained from interviews with commission officials.

15   Personal communication with author.

16   Internal Commission Information Note: *Implementation by the Commission of the Measures of 2 June 1993 on the Integration of the Environment into its other Policies*, December 1994.

17   *Op cit.*

18   Commission of the European Communities, *General Report on the Activities of the European Union,* 1994, 1995.

19   Commission of the European Communities, *Progress Report on Implementation of the European Community Programme of Policy and Action in Relation to the Environment and Sustainable Development, 'Towards Sustainability'*, COM (95) 624, 10 January 1996, p 104.

20   European Parliament, *Report from the Committee on Budgets on the Draft General Budget of the European Communities for the Financial Year 1996*, A4 -0235/95/Part D.

21   *Official Journal,* C109 1 May 1995, p 46.

22   European Parliament, *Report from the Committee on Budgets on the Draft General Budget of the European Communities for the Financial Year 1996*, A4 -0235/95/Part D.

23   Commission of the European Communities, *Cohesion Policy and the Environment*, COM (95)509, 22 November 1995.

24   Unpublished.

25   European Parliament, *Report from the Committee on Budgets on the 1996 Draft Budget, as Modified by the Council*, A4-0305/95. 11 December 1995.

26   Final adoption of the general budget of the European Union for the financial year 1996, *Official Journal* L22, 29 January 1996, subsection B2, pp 689–794.

27   European Parliament, *Report of the Committee on Budgets on the Draft General Budget of the European Union for the 1997 Financial Year*, 1996, A4-0310-11/96 October 1996.

28   European Environment Agency, *Environment in the European Union 1995 – Report for the Review of the Fifth Environmental Action Programme*, Office for Official Publications of the European Communities, Luxembourg, 1995.

29   Commission of the European Communities, *Progress Report on Implementation of the European Community Programme of Policy and Action in Relation to the Environment and Sustainable Development 'Towards Sustainability'*, COM (95) 624, 10 January 1996.

30   Commission of the European Communities, *Proposal for a European Parliament and Council Decision on the Review of the European Community Programme of Policy and Action in Relation to the Environment and Sustainable Development, 'Towards Sustainability'*, COM (95) 647, 29 February 1996, OJ C 140, 11 May 1996.

31   European Parliament, Committee on Environment, Public Health and Consumer Protection, *Report on the Proposal for a European Parliament and Council Decision on the Review of the European Community Programme of Policy and Action in Relation to the Environment and Sustainable Development, 'Towards Sustainability'*, A4-0300/96, Rapporteur Mrs Lone Dybkjaer.

32   Department of the Environment, *Explanatory Memorandum* 5641/96 on COM (95) 647, 7 May 1996.

33   See, for example, Council Regulation 2083/93 on the Regional Development Fund, Article 1f, OJ, L193, 31 July 1993.
34   Commission of the European Communities (1996) *Reinforcing Political Union and Preparing for Enlargement,* COM (96) 90.
35   Speech to conference on the Intergovernmental Conference organised by BUND, Berlin, 4 October 1996.

NOTES TO CHAPTER 7

1   Material produced by project participants on Greece and Portugal was used as the basis for the analysis on cohesion fund spending in these countries. Additional material on Ireland and Spain was largely derived from a number of recent studies.

NOTES TO CHAPTER 8

1   The authors would like to thank Andy Jordan and the members of the project group for their comments and assistance in the writing of this paper.
2   The *Blueprint* series published by Earthscan Publications Ltd, provides an accessible summary of this debate (Pearce, Barbier and Markandya, 1989).
3   Local Agenda 21 is the name for initiatives that are being undertaken under Chapter 28 of A21.
4   In addition, *A Guide to Risk Assessment and Risk Management for Environmental Protection* (DoE, 1995a) has been published. This contributes to the practices of the previous documents by setting out a more structured approach to risk assessment. Significantly, this document clarifies government ideas on the precautionary principle, accepting perceptions of risk as the basis for policy-making in conditions of uncertainty, and the role of monitoring in determining the accuracy of risk assessments.
5   The new Labour Government has recently made the deputy prime minister the president of the round table, with Sir Richard Southwood as sole chair. Previously they co-chaired it, a rather larger role than most of the respondents to the consultation process for the strategy had wanted. This indicates a distancing of the government from the process.
6   £1 million of which is subject to obtaining matching private sector funding.
7   The March budget of 1993 announced the government's intention to put VAT, at an initial rate of 8 per cent, on domestic fuel prices, rising to 17.5 per cent in the following year. However, when the government came to increase VAT in a second stage move from 8 per cent to the full 17.5 per cent, it failed. Initially introduced as an environmental measure, this rationale was not sustained and the compensation package for the 'nearly' poor was not in place. The new government reduced VAT down to 5 per cent in September 1997 in an attempt to illustrate its good intentions with respect to people on low incomes. However, they did not decrease VAT with respect to energy-saving materials to the same level.
8   This was set at a tame 6 per cent by the Labour Government in July 1997.
9   The Labour Government's abolishment of the gas levy, announced in the July 1997 pre-budget statement, will make domestic and industrial energy prices cheaper, and the accomplishment of climate change emissions targets harder.
10 The results of deliberations by an interdepartmental working group, published by the DoE and the Government Statistical Service, indicating a notable coordination effort on the part of the government and Whitehall.

11   These showed that since 1970 travel by car had almost doubled, becoming the dominant form of transport even on short trips, and that fuel use for road transport had risen by nearly 90 per cent, to account for a quarter of all energy consumption now (DoE and Government Statistical Service, 1996).

12   It was established on 7 July 1997.

NOTES TO CHAPTER 9

1   An Enquete Commission is an advisory body to the federal government. One half of the members are politicians the other are scientists appointed by the parties represented in parliament. Enquete commissions are established to give policy advice on complex political issues.

2   This was defined in the law on stability and growth in 1967 (*Stabilitäts und Wachstumsgesetz*). According to this law, stable price levels, a high employment rate, balanced foreign trade as well as continuous and appropriate economic growth are the goals of German economic and fiscal policy.

3   It had the following mandate(Deutscher Bundestag, 1992b):
   •   describe the most important problems of industrial material flows and work out possible strategies to solve these problems;
   •   develop scientifically reasonable criteria for the valuation of ecobalances on which a consensus might be reached among all groups of society;
   •   describe alternative scenarios for the extraction, processing and disposal of materials, taking into account technical, economic, ecological and social parameters;
   •   support consensus-building processes by intensifying dialogues in the chemical and industrial political arenas; and
   •   give recommendations for political action to the German Bundestag.

4   BUND is Bund für Umwelt und Naturschutz Deutschland (German section for Friends of the Earth); DNR is Deutscher Naturschutzring (umbrella group of German environmental organisations); WWF is the Worldwide Fund for Nature.

5   DGB is Deutscher Gewerkschaftsbund (German Trade Union Federation); BUKO is Bundeskongress Agrarkoordination (agriculture and development NGO); WEED is world economy, ecology and development (NGO).

6   Minister Töpfer was responsibile for the strong positions and political leadership of Germany in climate change politics during the end of the 1980s and the early 1990s.

7   Furthermore, the federal government supports activities of international NGOs and NGO-networks like Centre for Our Common Future, International Institute for Environment and Development (IIED), and European Environmental Bureau (EEB). As part of its development cooperation the federal government increased the funds for assistance to international NGOs since 1993 by about 5 million Deutschmarks a year.

8   The National Committee was set up in 1991 to prepare for UNCED and to advise the federal government on the follow-up process. It was a multisectoral NGO group chaired by the environmental minister. It was to be disbanded but discussions are still taking place on how to make it more effective in the future, so it looks likely to continue.

9   In 1996, even a municipality (Bad Dürkheim) produced an ecoaudit.

10   Apart from consideration of the traditional industry associations, the traditional auditors expect new economic impulses as a result of the directive because a new job-profile was created. See, for example, Förschle, 1994.

Notes to Chapter 10

1   At the same time, the work of the first State Secretary Committee for Environment and Development was terminated.
2   National sectors for which goals and measures were presented were energy, transport, industry, genetic resources, agriculture, fisheries, education, health and consumption patterns, local government, and development aid. International issues were climate change; depletion of the ozone layer; other long-range pollution; pollution in the North Sea/Skagerrak; industrial discharges; hazardous wastes; chemicals and oil pollution control; and the natural resource base.
3   Concerning the fulfilment of the targets, some ministries have put a lot of effort into it, while others have at best shown a slow internal process to implement the goals.
4   The committee is chaired by the prime minister and consists of the following members: the ministers of the environment, transport and communications, industry and energy, representatives from the Norwegian Society for the Conservation of Nature, Norwegian Confederation of Trade Unions, Confederation of Norwegian Business and Industry, and Norwegian Association of Local and Regional Authorities.
5   Seats are held by the Office of the Prime Minister; the ministries of foreign affairs, environment, industry and energy, finance, fisheries, agriculture, transport and communications, together with representatives from various NGOs such as the Norwegian Society for Conservation of Nature; the Confederation of Norwegian Business and Industry; the Research Council of Norway; the Norwegian Confederation of Trade Unions; the Norwegian Association of Local and Regional Authorities; and the Norwegian Forum for Environment and Development.
6   Thorbjørn Berntsen in the parliamentary environmental debate, 13 May 1993, and in interview in *Aftenposten*, 17 April 1994.
7   Environmental statement to parliament by the minister of the environment, 27 May 1987. See MoE, 1987; 1994; 1995.
8   Human activities exert pressure on the environment in different ways, for instance through emissions – this is reflected in changes in the quality and quantity of natural resources. Society's response in order to prevent these changes or to repair environmental damage is the third step of the concept.
9   An exception was found in 1989, when Gro Harlem Brundtland – then in political opposition – proposed an alternative budget to that presented in the *Green Book*; parliamentary support for her proposal led to an increase in the environmental budget of approximately 100 million Norwegian krone.

Notes to Chapter 11

1   The Fifth National Conference on Environmental Quality was held in Aveiro, 10–12 April 1996.
2   Articles 20, 37, 66, and 268 of the constitution were regulated by the recent Law 65/93 (22 August 1993) as a consequence of transposing the EC Directive 90/313/CEE (on citizens' access to environmental information) into Portuguese legislation.
3   Law 11/87 of 7 April 1987.
4   Law 10/87 of April 1987.
5   These were compared by IPAMB to national EPAs.
6   NGOs have a seat in the Social and Economic Council, Directive Council of IPAMB, Consultative Council for the Attribution of Ecolabels, general or consultative councils for protected areas, National Water Council, river catchment councils, and general

councils of the Commission for Air Management. However, their participation is also granted by some specific diplomas, such as the EIA legislation and the diploma on serious industrial risks.

7   This is explicit in the report (CSD, 1994b, p 57), where it is stated that 'Chapters 11 through 14 (of the A21) must be regarded as sectors of this chapter (Chapter 10)'.

8   League for the Protection of Nature.

9   National Association for Nature Conservation.

10   Group for Studies on Landuse Planning and the Environment

11   1 ECU = 200 PTE; 1 MEcu = 1,000,000 ECU.

12   This is currently being done by IPAMB, and an inquiry was sent to the Portuguese EPAs for the elaboration of a training programme.

13   Public administration and public institutions in general still provide the most stable technical careers in Portugal. Public administration (central and local) had 654,494 employees in 1994 (Barreto and Preto, 1996), which represents about 15 per cent of the total active population.

NOTES TO CHAPTER 12

1   Personal communication with Ms Kritikou, YPEHODE, Athens.

2   Published in the newspaper *To Vima* on 8 October 1992.

NOTES TO CHAPTER 13

1   This number is calculated after the local government reorganisation in April 1997 in Scotland, Wales and parts of the UK, which has reduced the number of local authorities. Previously there were 538. This also does not take into account parish or community councils which have little powers and authority (*Municipal Year Book*, 1997). See Appendix 13.1 for details of the current structure of local government in the UK (this diagram does not include the Isle of Man or the Isles of Scilly).

2   Local government finance and management have been the subjects of two separate review and consultation processes, which are not discussed in the same depth because they have not created the same interauthority problems of cooperation as the structural review. Together, these three processes appear to have failed to create a coherent review of local government.

3   In 1996 the three associations merged to form the Local Government Association (LGA).

4   The response rate was 56 per cent (identical to that of the previous survey in 1994–95), although reorganisation makes it difficult to determine this figure exactly as responses came in both sides of the reorganisation, reducing the number of authorities.

5   The LGMB coordinates the Sustainability Indicators Research Project (LGMB, 1995). This is an attempt to develop work that has been carried out internationally into a framework that can be used in a national context for measuring sustainable development at a local level; the second phase of the project involves the testing of these indicators in six pilot authorities and four shadow authorities. Hopefully this initiative will inform the development of national indicators and research in other countries. Many of the pioneer authorities work in partnership with NGOs so that they may benefit from other experiences and resources; this shall be examined in more detail later.

6   The 1996 recent local council elections, where a third of councils were up for reelection, continued to see the decline of the Conservative party in local elections from 12,143 councillors in 1979 to 4400. To summarise: the Labour party controls 212 councils,

Liberal Democrats control 55, and councils under no overall control (where no party has more than 49 per cent of the seats) account for another 185 (*The Times*, 1996).

7   These authorities are: Mendip District Council, Oxfordshire County Council, Oxford City Council, Plymouth City Council, and Devon County Council.

8   Summarised neatly in Parker and Selman, 1996.

9   This occurs especially in Northern Ireland, where local government deals mainly with environmental health, refuse collection and disposal, and leisure.

NOTES TO CHAPTER 14

1   This and the following translations from German sources are unauthorised.

2   At the time of writing, there are no comprehensive surveys or other databases on LA21 and, generally, on municipal environmental programmes in Germany. As long as municipalities do not publish or otherwise distribute information on their initiatives, they are only locally or regionally known. Therefore, the present general description and analysis of the status quo of the German response to LA21 is based on available literature on LA21 case studies (in particular from ICLEI), on publicly discussed pioneering municipalities (Berlin Köpenick, Munich) as well as on field work on the LA21 process in Güstrow and Berlin-Köpenick.

3   This interpretation is somehow ambiguous and probably only true for an early stage of LA21. It might later become an argument for some municipal authorities to start a LA21. Observations made with regard to climate policy at the local level show that as soon as an issue has gained some public attention and priority, a renaming is suggested as useful for giving new incentives to policies that otherwise would not sell any longer.

4   ICLEI has a network of more than 80 European municipalities, of which about 16 are German. The objective is to promote LA21 by providing support, coordination, technical advice and information (Hewitt, 1995).

NOTES TO CHAPTER 15

1   Concerning biodiversity, the situation has changed in the period after the survey was carried out. The MoE is now working on a national action plan for biodiversity. Much of the responsibility for biological diversity will be left to the local governments. Municipalities may play a central role, in cooperation with voluntary organisations, to collect and make local overviews of the biodiversity situation.

2   The idea of ecomunicipalities was first launched in Finland in 1980. The initiative stressed the opportunities that a local environmental policy could provide; local development should be based on the safe use of local resources and the depletion of local resources could counteract the general trends of centralisation and urbanisation. In 1983 Swedish municipalities also adopted the concept.

3   Due to the delegation of power to the local level, the state will often have to use soft instruments to induce local authorities to follow up on national targets. One soft instrument applied by central government is the making of national directives. In August 1993 the government issued national guidelines for the coordination of landuse and transport planning. The purpose was to improve the coordination of planning at different administrative levels and sectors. The contents of many of the national guidelines are often vague and usually provide recommendations rather than prohibitions. Furthermore, they are often marked by compromises between the interests of the transport and road sectors (Kleven, 1994).

REFERENCES

REFERENCES TO PREFACE

O'Riordan, T and Jäger, J (eds) (1996) *Politics of Climate Change: A European Perspective*, Routledge, London

REFERENCES TO CHAPTER 1

Adams, W R (1990) *Green Development: Environment and Sustainability in the Third World*, Routledge, London

Banuri, T, Maler, K G, Grubb, M, Jacobson, H A and Yamin, F (1996) 'Equity and social considerations' in J P Bruce, H Lee and E F Haites (eds) *Climate Change 1995: Economic and Social Dimensions*, Cambridge University Press, Cambridge, pp 79–124

Basiago, A (1995) 'Methods of defining sustainability', *Sustainable Development*, 3(3), pp 109–129

Bateman, I (1995) 'Environment and economic appraisal' in T O'Riordan (ed) *Environmental Science for Environmental Management*, Longman, Harlow, pp 45–64

Beck, U (1992) *Risk Society: Towards a New Modernity*, Sage Publications, London

Bichsel, A (1996) 'NGOs as agents of public sustainability and democratisation in inter-governmental forums' in W M Lafferty and J Meadowcroft (eds) *Democracy and the Environment: Problems and Prospects*, Edward Edgar, London, pp 234–256

Bigg, T (1997) *Report on Earth Summit II, the UN General Assembly Special Session to review outcomes from the Rio Summit*, UNED-UK, London

Bramble, B (1997) 'Financing resources for the transition to sustainable development' in F Dodds (ed) *The Way Forward: Beyond Agenda 21*, Earthscan Publications Ltd, London, pp 190–205

Brown-Weiss, E (1989) *In Fairness to Future Generations: International Law, Common Patrimony and Intergenerational Enquiry*, Dobbs Ferry, New York

Brundtland Commission (1987) *Our Common Future: Report of The World Commission on Environment and Development*, Oxford University Press, Oxford

Burch, W R (1971) *Daydreams and Nightmares: A Sociological Essay on the American Environment*, Prentice Hall, Englewood Cliffs, New Jersey

Clayton, A N H and Radcliffe, N J (1996) *Sustainability: A Systems Approach*, Earthscan Publications Ltd, London

Costanza, R et al (1997) 'The value of the world's ecosystem services and natural capital', *Nature*, 387(15 May), pp 253–260

Dalton, T (1994) *The Green Rainbow: Environmental Groups in Western Europe*, Yale University Press, New Haven, Connecticut

Dobson, A (1996) 'Environmental sustainabilities: an analysis and a typology', *Environmental Politics* vol 5, no 3, pp 401–428

Dodds, F (ed) (1997) *The Way Forward: Beyond Agenda 21*, Earthscan Publications Ltd, London

Dowdeswell, E (1997) 'Building sustainable production and consumption patterns' in F Dodds (ed) *The Way Forward: Beyond Agenda 21*, Earthscan Publications Ltd, London, pp 206–214

Dryzek, J S (1996) 'Strategies of ecological democratisation' in W M Lafferty and J Meadowcroft (eds) *Democracy and the Environment: Problems and Prospects*, Edward Elgar, London, pp 108–123

Earth First! (1997) *Do or Die: Earth my Body, Fire my Spirit*, South Downs E S I, Brighton, pp 1–59

Ekins, P (1997) *Business, Trade and the Environment: Prospects for a Steady Playing Field*, Environmental Policy Unit, University of Keele, Keele

Giddens, A (1990) *The Consequences of Modernity*, Polity Press, Cambridge

Giddens, A (1992) *Modernity and Self Identity: Self and Society in Late Modern Age*, Polity Press, Cambridge

Goldsmith, E (ed) (1992) *A Blueprint for Survival, The Ecologist*, reprinted by Penguin, Hamondsworth

Grove, R (1990) 'Threatened islands, threatened earth: early professional science and the historical origins of global environmental concerns' in D J R Angell, J D Gomer and M L N Wilkinson (eds) *Sustaining Earth: Response to the Environmental Threats*, Macmillan, Basingstoke, pp 15–32

Hajer, M (1995) *The Politics of Environmental Discourse*, Oxford University Press, Oxford

Hays, S P (1959) *Conservation and the Gospel of Efficiency: The Progressive Conservation Movement, 1890–1920*, Harvard University Press, Cambridge, MA

Hildyard, N (ed) (1992) 'Whose Common Future'? *The Ecologist* vol 22, no 4, pp 122–206

Irwin, A (1995) *Citizen Science: A Study of People, Expertise and Sustainable Development*, Routledge, London

Jacobson, H K and Brown Weiss, E (1997) 'Strengthening compliance with international environmental accords' in P F Diehl (ed) *The Politics of Global Governance: International Organizations in an Interdependent World*, Lynne Rienner Publishers, London, pp 305–334

Jordan, G and Maloney, W (1996) *The Protest Business?* Manchester University Press, Manchester

Jordan, A J and O'Riordan, T (1993) 'Sustainable Development: measuring the political and institutional challenge' in D Pearce (ed) *Blueprint 3: Measuring Sustainable Development*, Earthscan Publications Ltd, London, pp 183–202

Lee, K (1983) *Compass and Gyroscope: Integrating Science and Politics for the Environment*, Island Press, New York

Lemon, J (ed) (1996) *Scientific Uncertainty and Environmental Problem Solving*, Blackwell, Oxford

Lindner, C (1997) 'Agenda 21' in F Dodds (ed) *The Way Forward: Beyond Agenda 21*, Earthscan Publications Ltd, London, pp 3–14

Lovelock, J (1992) *Gaia: The Practical Guide to Planetary Medicine*, Gail Bowles, London

Mannion, P (1992) *Global Environmental Change*, Longman Harlow, London

McGarvin, L (1994) 'Precaution, science and the sin of Hubris' in T O'Riordan and J Cameron (eds) *Interpreting the Precautionary Principle*, Earthscan Publications Ltd, London, pp 69–101

Meadows, D M, Meadows, D L, Randers, J and Behrens, T (1992) *Limits to Growth*, Pan Books, London

Milton, K (1996) *Environmentalism and Cultural Theory: Exploring the Role of Anthropology in Environmental Discourse*, Routledge, London

Moffatt, I (1996) *Sustainable Development: Principles, Analysis and Policies*, The Parthenon Publishing Group, London

O'Hara, S (1996) 'Discursive ethics in ecosystems valuation and environmental policy', *Ecological Economics*, vol 16, no 2, pp 95–107

O'Keefe, P, Middleton, N and Moao, S (1993) *Tears of the Crocodile*, Pluto Press, London

O'Mahoney, P and Skillington, T (1996) 'Sustainable development as an organising principle for discursive democracy', *Sustainable Development*, vol 4, no 1, pp 42–81

O'Neill, J (1993) *Ecology, Policy and Politics: Human Wellbeing in a Natural World*, Routledge, London

O'Riordan, T (1993) 'The politics of sustainability' in R K Turner (ed) *Sustainable Environmental Economics and Management: Principles and Practice*, Wiley, Chichester, pp 37–69

O'Riordan, T (1996) 'Democracy and the sustainability transition' in W M Lafferty and J Meadowcroft (eds) *Democracy and the Environment: Problems and Prospects*, Edward Elgar, London, pp 140–156

O'Riordan, T (1997) 'Valuation as revelation and reconciliation', *Environmental Values* vol 6, no 2, pp 169–183

O'Riordan, T and Cameron, T (eds) (1994) *Interpreting the Precautionary Principle*, Earthscan Publications Ltd, London

O'Riordan, T and Jäger, J (eds) (1996) *Politics of Climate Change: A European Perspective*, Routledge, London

O'Riordan, T and Voisey, H K (eds) (1997) *Sustainable Development in Western Europe: Coming to Terms with Agenda 21*, Frank Cass, London

Paelke, P (1996) 'Environmental challenges to democratic practice' in W Lafferty and J Meadowcroft (eds) *Democracy and Environment: Problems and Prospects*, Edward Elgar, London, pp 18–38

Patterson, M (1997) 'Sovereignty', *Global Environmental Change* vol 7, no 2, pp 175–178

Pearce, D W (1993) 'Sustainable development and developing country economics' in R K Turner (ed) *Sustainable Environmental Economics and Management: Principles and Practice*, John Wiley, Chichester, pp 70–105

Pearce, D W (1996) 'Biodiversity: economic valuation procedures' in T O'Riordan (ed) *Economics of Biological Resources and Biodiversity: Summary of a Seminar*, CSERGE, Norwich

Pezzoli, K (1997) 'Sustainable development: a transdisciplinary overview of the literature', *Journal of Environmental Planning and Management* vol 40, no 5, pp 507–575

Pigou, A (1926) *The Problem of Social Cost*, Macmillan, London

Posey, D A (1997) 'Protecting indigenous peoples' rights to biodiversity', *Environment* vol 38, no 8, pp 6–9 and 37–42

Rangecroft, D (1997) 'Protest action', *Police Review*, 21 March, pp 22–23

Redclift, M (1996) *Wasted: Counting the Cost of Global Consumption*, Earthscan Publications Ltd, London

Renn, O, Webler, T O and Wiedermann, P (eds) (1955) *Fairness and Competence in Citizen Participation: Evaluating Models of Environmental Discourse*, Kluwer, Dorderecht, The Netherlands

Sachs, W (ed) (1993) *Global Ecology: A New Agenda for Political Conflict*, Zed Books, London

Sachs, W (1994) 'Introduction' in W Sachs (ed) *Global Ecology: A New Arena of Political Conflict*, Zed Books, London, pp xv–xvii

Schwerin, E W (1995) *Mediation, Citizen Empowerment and Transformational Politics*, Praeger Publishers, New York

Shiva, V (1992) 'Recovering the real meaning of sustainability' in D E Cooper and J E Palmer (eds) *The Environment in Question*, Routledge, London, pp 187–191

Simmons, I (1989) *Changing the Face of the Earth: Culture, Environment and History*, Blackwell, Oxford

Street, P (1997) 'Scenario workshops: a participatory approach to sustainable urban living' *Futures* vol 29, no 2, pp 135–158

Therivel, R, Wilson, E, Thompson, S, Heaney, D and Pritchard, D (1992) *Strategic Environmental Assessment*, Earthscan Publications Ltd, London

Toulmin, C (1997) 'The Desertification Convention' in F Dodds (ed) *The Way Forward: Beyond Local Agenda 21*, Earthscan Publications Ltd, London, pp 55–64

Turner, R K (1993) 'Sustainability: principles and practice' in R K Turner (ed) *Sustainable Environmental Economics and Management: Principles and Practice*, Wiley, Chichester, pp 3–36

Turner, R K, Pearce, D W and Bateman, I (1994) *Environmental Economics: An Elementary Introduction*, Harvester Wheatsheaf, Hemel Hempstead

UN Development Programme (1996) *Human Development Report*, Oxford University Press, Oxford

Watkinson, A (1997) 'Biodiversity: an ecological perspective' in T O'Riordan (ed) *Economics of Biological Resources and Biodiversity: Summary of a Seminar*, CSERGE, University of East Anglia, Norwich, pp 7–12

Welford, R (ed) (1997) *Hijacking Environmentalism: Corporate Responses to Sustainable Development*, Earthscan Publications Ltd, London

Wilson, E O (1994) 'An interview with the father of biodiversity', *Nature Conservation* July–August, pp 24–29

REFERENCES TO CHAPTER 2

Beardsley, D, Davies, T and Hersh, R (1997) 'Improving environmental management: what works, what doesn't', *Environment* vol 39, no 7, pp 6–8 and 28–35

Bhargava, S and Welford, R (1996) 'Corporate strategy and the environment: the theory' in R Welford (ed) *Corporate Environmental Management: Systems and Strategies*, Earthscan Publications Ltd, London, pp 13–34

Biggs, T and Dodds, F (1997) 'The UN Commission on Sustainable Development' in F Dodds (ed) *The Way Forward: Beyond Agenda 21*, Earthscan Publications Ltd, pp 15–36

Brugman, J (1997) 'Local authorities and Local Agenda 21' in F Dodds, (ed) *The Way Forward: Beyond Agenda 21*, Earthscan Publications Ltd, London, pp 101–112

Brundtland Commission (1987) *Our Common Future: Report of the World Commission on Environment and Development*, Oxford University Press, Oxford

Davis, G A, Wilt, C A and Barkenbus, J N (1997) 'Extended product responsibility: a tool for a sustainable economy', *Environment* vol 39, no 7, pp 10–15 and 36–38

Department of the Environment (1996) *Indicators of Sustainable Development for the UK*, HMSO, London

Easterbrook, G (1996) *A Moment on the Earth: The Coming Age of Environmental Optimism*, Penguin Books, Harmondsworth, Middlesex

Environmental Data Services Ltd (1997) 'Photovoltaics – paving the way for the technology of innovation', *ENDS Report*, 270, pp 16–21

European Commission (1993) *Growth, Competitiveness, Employment: the Challenges and Way Forward into the 21st Century*, White Paper, Bulletin of the European Communities Supplement 6/93, European Commission, Brussels

Friends of the Earth and New Economics Foundation (1997) *More Isn't Always Better: Quality of Life Briefing*, NEF, London

Fussler, C and James, P (1996) *Driving Eco-Innovation: A Breakthrough Discipline for Innovation and Sustainability*, Pitman Publishing, London

Giddens, A (1984) *The Constitution of Society*, Polity Press, Cambridge

Jordan, A and O'Riordan, T (1997) 'Social institutions and climate change: applying cultural theory to practice', *CSERGE Working Paper*, 97–14, University of East Anglia, Norwich

Labour Party (1997) *New Labour: Because Britain Deserves Better*, Labour Party, London

Leek, K (1993) *Compass and Gyroscope: Integrating Science and Politics for the Environment*, Island Press, New York

Lenton, M (1997) *For the People, By the People: Report of the Citizens Enquiry*, Charter 88, London

Lindner, C (1997) 'Agenda 21' in F Dodds (ed) *The Way Forward: Beyond Agenda 21*, Earthscan Publications Ltd, London

Local Government Management Board (1995) *Indicators for Local Agenda 21 – A Summary*, LGMB, Luton

Mullaney, A (1997) 'Auditing equity', *Town and Country Planning* vol 66, no 6, pp 162–163

Norwegian Tax Commission (1996) *Policies for a Better Environment and High Employment*, Ministry of Finance, Oslo

O'Neill, J (1993) *Ecology, Policy and Politics: Human Well-Being and the Natural World*, Routledge, London

O'Neill, J (1996) 'Cost benefit analysis, rationality and the plurality of values', *The Ecologist* vol 26, no 3, pp 98–103

Organization for Economic Cooperation and Development (1997) *Environmental Taxes and Green Tax Reform*, OECD, Paris

O'Riordan, T (ed) (1997a) *Ecotaxation*, Earthscan Publications Ltd, London

O'Riordan, T (1997b) 'Sustainability and the new Labour radicalism,' *Ecos* vol 18, no 1, pp 12–14

O'Riordan, T and Jäger, J (eds) (1996) *Politics of Climate Change: A European Perspective*, Routledge, London

O'Riordan, T and Jordan, A (1996) 'Social institutions and climate change' in T O'Riordan and J Jäger (eds) *Politics of Climate Change: A European Perspective*, Routledge, London, pp 106–154

O'Riordan, T and Voisey, H (1997) 'The political economy of sustainable development' in T O'Riordan and H Voisey (eds) *Sustainable Development in Western Europe: Coming to Terms with Agenda 21*, Frank Cass, London, pp 1–23

Prescott, J (1997) *Speech to UNED-UK Conference*, 5 June, Department of Environment, Transport and the Regions, London

President's Council on Sustainable Development (1996) *Sustainable America: A New Consensus*, Government Printing Office, Washington, DC

Schrader-Freschette, K (1996) 'Methodological rules for four classes of scientific uncertainty' in J Lemons (ed) *Scientific Uncertainty and Environmental Problem Solving*, Blackwell, Oxford, pp 12–39

Vaze, P And Balchin, S (1996) *The Pilot UK Environmental Accounts*, Office of National Statistics, London

Von Weizsacker, E, Lovins, A B and Lovins, L (1997) *Factor 4: Doubling Wealth: Halving Resource Use*, Earthscan Publications Ltd, London

Welford, R (1996) *Corporate Environmental Management: Systems and Strategies*, Earthscan Publications Ltd, London

REFERENCES TO EDITORIAL INTRODUCTION, PART II

Haigh, N and Lanigan, C (1996) 'Impact of the European Union on UK environmental policy making' in T S Gray (ed) *UK Environmental Policy in the 1990s*, Macmillan, London, pp 18–37

Hession and Macrory (1996) 'Balancing trade freedom with the requirements of Sustainable Development' in N Emiliou and D O'Keefe (eds) *The European Union and World Trade Law: After the GATT Uruguay Round and Beyond,* Wiley, Chichester and New York

REFERENCES TO CHAPTER 3

Civic Trust (1974) 'Limit to Growth and the Treaty of Rome', *Civic Trust Newsletter*, Civic Trust, London

Commission of the European Communities (CEC) (1984) *Bulletin of the EC* vol 17, no 2, Office for Official Publication of the EC, Luxembourg

European Environment Bureau (1977) *One Europe–One Environment: A Manifeso*, European Environment Bureau, Brussels (republished 1979)

European Parliament (1983) *European Parliament Document PE 83/32 G/A* 22 March 1983

Haigh, N (1992) *Manual of Environmental Policy: the EC and Britain*, (regularly updated), Longmans, Harlow

Haigh, N (1996) 'Sustainable development in the European Union Treaties', *International Environmental Affairs* vol 18, no 1, pp 87–91

Haigh, N and Kraemer, R A (1996) 'Sustainable development in den Verträgen der Europäischen Union Zeitschrift', *Umweltrecht* vol 5, no 7, pp 239–242

House of Lords Select Committee on the European Communities (1977/78) *Approximation of Laws under Article 100 of the European Treaty*, HL 131, HMSO, London

House of Lords Select Committee on the European Communities (1979/80) *Environmental Problems and the Treaty of Rome*, HL 68, HMSO, London

OJC (1973) *Official Journal of the EC*, C112, 20 December 1973

OJC (1993) *Official Journal of the EC*, C 138, 17 May 1993

Von Motke, K (1977) 'European Community: the legal basis for environmental protection', *Environmental Policy and Law* vol 3, pp 15–21

Wilkinson, D (1992) 'Maastricht and the environment: the implications of the EC's environmental policy on the Treaty on European Union' *Journal of Environmental Law*, vol 4, no 2, pp 211–239

REFERENCES TO CHAPTER 4

Armstrong, K (1995) 'Regulating the free movement of goods: institutions and institutional change' in J Shaw and J More (eds) *New Legal Dynamics of the European Union*, Clarendon Press, Oxford

Axelrod, R (1994) 'Subsidiarity and the environmental policy of the European Community' in *International Environmental Affairs* vol 6, no 2, p115

Barents, R (1990) 'The Community and the unity of the Common Market: some reflections on the economic constitution of the Community' in *German Yearbook of International Law*, vol 33, Dunker and Hamblot, Germany, pp 9–36

Bellassa, B (1994) 'The theory of economic integration' in B Nelson and A Stubb (eds) *The European Union: Readings on the Theory and Practice of European Integration* Lynne Rienner, Colorado, USA

Bulmer, S (1983) 'Domestic politics and european policy making', *Journal of Common Market Studies* vol 21, no 4, pp 349–363

Cappelletti, M (1987) 'Is the European Court of Justice running wild?' in *European Law Review* vol 12, p 3

CEC (1993) *Towards Sustainability: A European Community Programme of Policy and Action in Relation to Environment and Sustainable Development,* Office for Official Publications of the European Community, Luxembourg

Chalmers, D (1995) 'The Single Market: from prima donna to journeyman' in J Shaw and J More (eds) *New Legal Dynamics of the European Union* Clarendon Press, Oxford; and Chalmers, D (1995) 'Environmental protection and the single market' *Legal Issues Of European Integration* vol 1, p 65–82

Climatic Network Europe *et al* (1995) *Greening the Treaty II: Sustainable Development in a Democratic Union – Proposals for the 1996 Intergovernmental Conference* Climate Network Europe, European Environmental Bureau, European Federation for Transport and Environment, Friends of the Earth Europe, Greenpeace International, European Unit Worldwide Fund for Nature; WWF, 1 May

Closa, C (1992) 'The concept of citizenship in the Treaty of the European Union' *Common Market Law Review* vol 29, no 6, pp 1137–1170

Coffey, C (1996) 'Introduction to the Common Fisheries Policy: An environmental perspective', *International Environmental Affairs*, vol 8, no 4, pp 287–308

Cohen, J and J Rogers (eds) (1995) *Associations and Democracy,* Verso, London and New York

Conrad, J (1993) 'Agriculture and environment in Western Europe', *International Environmental Affairs* vol 5, no 2, pp 79–95

Dahl, A (1995) 'Environmental actors and European integration', *International Environmental Affairs* vol 7, no 4, p 299

de Búrca, G (1993) 'The principle of proportionality and its application in EC law', *Yearbook of European Law* vol 12, (annual), Clarendon Press, Oxford, p 105

de Búrca, G (1995) 'The language of rights and European integration' in J Shaw and J More (eds) *The New Legal Dynamics of European Union,* Clarendon Press, Oxford

De Witte, B (1991) 'Community law and national constitutional values' *Year Book of European Law* vol 10 (annual), Clarendon Press, Oxford, p 221

Du Bois, F (1996) 'Social justice and judicial enforcement of environmental rights and duties' in A Boyle and D Anderson (eds) *Human Rights Approaches to Environmental Protection,* Clarendon Press, Oxford

Ely, R (1980) *Democracy and Distrust: A Theory of Judicial Review,* Harvard University Press, Cambridge, USA

Etzioni, A (1996) 'A moderate communitarian proposal', *Political Theory* vol 24, no 2, pp 155–171

Eurobarometer (1998) *The Eurobarometer Series* no 48, Office for Official Publications of the European Commission, Luxembourg, March

Falke, J and Winter, G (1996) 'Management and regulatory committees in executive rule making' in G Winter (ed) *Sources and Categories of European Union Law: A Comparative and Reform Perspective,* Nomos Verlag, Baden-Baden, pp 541–582

Gellner, E (1994) *Conditions of Liberty: Civil Society and its Rivals,* Penguin, London

Giddens, A (1990) *The Consequences of Modernity*, Polity Press, Cambridge

Graubard (1994) 'Europe through a glass darkly – preface', *Daedulus*, vol 123, no 2, R pp 5–15

Habermas, J (1996) 'The European nation state – Its achievements and its limits on past and future sovereignty and citizenship' in G Balakrishnan (ed) *Mapping the Nation* Verso, London and New York, pp 281–294

Hession, M and R Macrory (1996) 'balancing trade freedom with the requirements of sustainable development' in N Emiliou and D O'Keefe (eds) *The European Union and World Trade Law: After the GATT Uruguay Round and Beyond* Wiley, Chichester and New York, pp 181–217

Hoffman, S (1964) 'Europe's identity crisis', *Daedelus* vol 93, no 4, p 1

Hoffman, S (1994) 'Europe's identity crisis revisited', *Daedelus* vol 123, no 2, pp 1–23

Krämer, L (1991) 'The implementation of community environmental directives within member states: some implications of the direct effect doctrine', *Journal of Environmental Law* vol 3, no 1, pp 39–56

Krämer, L (1996) 'Public interest litigation in environmental matters before the European Courts', *Journal of Environmental Law* vol 8, no 1, pp 1–18

Ladeur, K (1996) 'Environmental constitutional law' in G Winter (ed) *European*

Environmental Law: A Comparative Perspective, Dartmouth, Aldershot and Brookfield (US), pp 15–35

Liberatore, A (1997) 'The integration of sustainable development objectives into EU policy making; barriers and prospects' in S Baker, M Kousis, R Richardson and S Young (eds) *The Politics of Sustainable Development – Theory Policy and Practice in the European Union,* Routledge, London and New York, pp 107–126

Midgely, M (1995) 'Duties concerning islands' in R Elliott (ed) *Environmental Ethics: Oxford Readings in Philosophy,* Oxford University Press, Oxford, pp 89–104

Monnet, A (1962) 'A ferment of change', *Journal of Common Market Studies* vol 1, no 1, pp 203–211

Nelson, B and Stubb, A (1994) (eds) *The European Union: Readings on the Theory and Practice of European Integration,* Lynne Rienner, Colorado, USA

Petersmann, U (1995) 'National constitutions, foreign trade policy and European Community law', *European Journal of International Law,* vol 4, no 1, p 1

Rasmussen, H (1986) *On Law And Policy Of The European Court Of Justice,* Martinus Nijhoff, Dordrecht

Sagoff, K (1995) 'Can environmentalists be liberals?' in R Elliot (ed) *Environmental Ethics: Oxford Readings in Philosophy,* Oxford University Press, Oxford

Schmitter, P and Streeck, W (1994) 'Organized interests and the European Union of 1992' in B Nelson and A Stubb (eds) *The European Union: Readings on the Theory and Practice of European Integration,* Lynne Rienner, Colorado, USA

Schnaiberg, A (1997) 'Sustainable development and the treadmill of production' in S Baker, M Kousis, R Richardson and S Young (eds) *The Politics of Sustainable Development – Theory Policy and Practice in the European Union,* Routledge, London and New York, pp 72–88

Scott, J (1997a) 'Environmental compatibility and the Community's Structural Funds: A legal analysis', *Journal of Environmental Law,* vol 8, no 1, pp 99–114

Scott, J (1997b) 'From Rio to Inverness: Environment and development in the Highland and Islands Objective 1 Enterprise Area' in J Holder (ed) *The Impact of EC Environmental Law in the United Kingdom,* Wiley, Chichester and New York, pp 318–333

Scott, J (1997c) *Law Legitimacy and the and the Governance of the EU: Subsidiarity, Partnership and the Communities Structural Funds,* Queen Mary and Westfield College, London (unpublished)

Sedemund, J (1988) 'Statement on the concept of free movement of goods and the respect for national action under Article 36 of the EEC Treaty' in J Schwarze (ed) *Discretionary Powers of the Member States in the Field of Economic Policies and their limits under the EEC Treaty,* Nomos Velag, Baden-Baden

Slater, M (1982) 'Political elites and popular indifference and community building' *Journal of Common Market Studies* vol 21, no 1/2, pp 62–69

Smith, A (1997) 'National identity and the idea of European unity' in P Gowan and P Anderson (eds) *The Question of Europe,* Verso, London

Streeck, W (1995) 'Inclusion and succession: Questions of the boundaries of associative democracy' in J Cohen and J Rogers (eds) *Associations and Democracy* Verso, London, pp 184–193

Temple Lang, J (1991) 'The Sphere in which Member States are obliged to comply with general principles of Law and Community fundamental rights principles' *Legal Issues of European Integration,* vol 1, p 23

Weiler, J (1994) 'Fin de siécle Europe: On ideals and ideology in post Maastricht Europe' in D Curtin and J Heukels (eds) *Institutional dynamics of European Integration: Essays in honour of Henry Schermer* vol 2, Matrtinius-Nijhoff, Dordrecht p 23

Weiler, J, Haltern, U and Mayer, F (1995) 'European democracy and its critique – Five uneasy pieces', *Jean Monnet Working Paper* Harvard, September

Wiener, A and Della Sala, V (1997) 'Constitution-making and citizenship practice –
    Bridging the democracy gap in the EU?' *Journal Of Common Market Studies* vol 35, no 4,
    pp 595–614
Winacott, K (1995) 'Political theory, law and the European Union' in J Shaw and J More
    (eds) *New Legal Dynamics of the European Union* Clarendon Press, Oxford
World Commission on Environment and Development (WCED) (1987) *Our Common
    Future – The Brundtland Report,* Oxford University Press, Oxford

REFERENCES TO CHAPTER 5

Brandt, E and Bungert, H (1992) 'Constitutional entrenchment of environmental protec-
    tion: comparative analysis of experiences abroad', *Harvard Environmental Law Review*
    vol 16, no 1, pp 1–89
Cotterrell, R (1984) *The Sociology of Law: An Introduction,* Butterworths, London, p 142
Edelman, M (1964) *The Symbolic Use of Politics,* University of Illinois Press, Chicago and
    London
Haigh, N (1987) *EEC Environmental Policy and Britain,* Longmans, Harlow
Hallo, R (1997) *Sustainable development and integration of the environment into other policies,*
    Conference Paper: IGC and the Environment, Brussels, 27 January
Krämer, L (1990) *EC Treaty and Environmental Protection,* Sweet and Maxwell, London
Krämer, L (1993) *European Law Casebook,* Sweet and Maxwell, London
Krämer, L (1994) 'Public interest litigation in environmental matters before European
    Courts' *Journal of Environmental Law* vol 1, no 1, pp 1–18
Macrory, R (1996) 'Environmental citizenship and the law', *Journal of Environmental Law* vol
    8, no 2, pp 219–236
Wilkinson, D (1992) 'Maastricht and the environment', *Journal of Environmental Law*
    vol 4, no 2, pp 221–229

REFERENCES TO CHAPTER 6

Lawrence, P and Lorsch, J (1969) *Organisations and Environment: Managing Differentiation and
    Integration,* University of Illinois Press, Illinois
Wilkinson, D (1992) 'Maastricht and the Environment: The Implications for the EC's
    Environment Policy of the Treaty on the European Union' *Journal of Environmental
    Law* vol 4, no 2
Wilkinson, D (1994) 'Using the European Union's Structural and Cohesion Funds for the
    Protection of the Environment', *Review of European Community and International
    Environmental Law* vol 3, issue 2/3, pp 119–126

REFERENCES TO CHAPTER 7

BirdLife International (1995) *The Structural Funds and Biodiversity Conservation,* BirdLife
    International, Brussels
CEC (1991) *Improve your Environment – Using the Financial Instruments of the European
    Community,* Commission of the European Communities, Brussels
CEC (1992) *Towards Sustainability: A European Community Programme of Policy and Action in
    Relation to the Environment and Sustainable Development,* COM(92)23, Commission of the
    European Communities, Brussels

CEC (1995a) *Annual Report Cohesion Financial Instrument 1993/1994*, COM(95)1, Commission of the European Communities, Brussels

CEC (1995b) *Cohesion Policy and the Environment*, COM(95)509, Commission of the European Communities, Brussels

CEC (1997a) *Annual Report on the Cohesion Fund 1996*, COM(97)302, Commission of the European Communities, Brussels

CEC (1997b) *Agenda 2000: For a Stronger and Wider Union*, COM(97)2000, Commission of the European Communities, Brussels

CEEETA (1995a) *Institutional Adjustments to Sustainable Development Strategies: Implementation in Portugal*, Centro de Estudos em Economia da Energia dos Transportes e do Ambiente, Lisbon

CEEETA (1995b) *Institutional Tensions and Conflicts: 3 Case Studies*, Centro de Estudos em Economia da Energia, dos Transportes e do Ambiente, Lisbon

Council Directive 79/409 on the conservation of wild birds, OJ L103, 25.4.79

Council Directive 85/337 on the assessment of the effects of certain public and private projects on the environment, OJ L175, 5 July 1985

Council Directive 91/271 concerning urban waste water treatment, OJ L135, 30 May 1991

Council Regulation 1973/92 establishing a financial instrument for the environment, OJ L206, 22 July 1992

Council Regulation 792/93 establishing a Cohesion Financial Instrument, OJ L79, 25 May 1994

Council Regulation 1164/94 establishing a Cohesion Fund, OJ L139, 25 May 1994

Council Regulation 1404/96 amending Regulation 1973/92 establishing a Financial Instrument for the Environment, OJ L181, 20 July 1996

Court of Auditors (1995) Special Report No 1/95 on the cohesion financial instrument together with the commission's replies, Court of Auditors, OJ C59, 8 March 1995

European Parliament (1995) *European Parliament Resolution on the Annual Report of the Commission on the Cohesion Financial Instrument (1993/94)*, OJ C183, 17 July 1995

Fousekis, P and Lekakis, J (1996) 'Sustainable Development in Greece' in T O'Riordan and H Voisey (eds) *Sustainable Development in Weston-Europe: Coming to Terms with Agenda 21*, Frank Cass, London

Hey, C and Tiltcher, R (1993) *Transport and the Structural Fund/Cohesion Fund*, Draft report for Greenpeace International, Amsterdam

IER (1996) 'Portugal must boost environment protection or lose Commission funding for Tagus bridge', *International Environment Reporter*, Bureau of National Affairs, Washington

Karas, J (1995) *New Directions for the Structural Funds*, New Economics Foundation, London

Wilkinson, D (1994) 'Using the European Union's Structural Funds and Cohesion Funds for the Protection of the Environment', RECIEL, *Review of Community and International Environmental Law* vol 3, no 2/3, pp 64–75

REFERENCES TO CHAPTER 8

DETR (1997) *Experience with the 'Policy Appraisal and the Environment' initiative*, DETR, London

DoE (1989) *Sustaining Our Common Future*, HMSO, London

DoE (1991) *Policy Appraisal and the Environment: A Guide for Government Departments*, HMSO, London

DoE (1994) *Environmental Appraisal in Government Departments*, HMSO, London

DoE (1995a) *A Guide to Risk Assessment and Risk Management for Environmental Protection*, HMSO, London

DoE (1995b) *News Release: UK Round Table on Sustainable Development*, 19/02/95

DoE (1995c) *News Release: Going For Green*, 6/02/95

DoE and Government Statistical Service (1996) *Indicators of Sustainable Development for the United Kingdom*, HMSO, London

Department of Transport (1995) *The Transport Report 1995: The Government's Expenditure Plans 1995–96 to 1997–98*, HMSO, London

Environmental Data Services Ltd (1995a) 'Sticky Start for Round Table with Rebuff on Energy Policy', *ENDS Report* 245, p 3

Environmental Data Services Ltd (1995b) 'Business Almost as Usual on Sustainable Development' *ENDS Report* 249, pp 28–29

Environmental Data Services Ltd (1995c) 'Department of Transport Backs M-Way Tolls, Stalls on Urban Road Pricing', *ENDS Report* 247, pp 13–14

Environmental Data Services Ltd (1995d) 'Treasury put to test over sustainable development', *ENDS Report* 242, pp 29–30

Environmental Data Services Ltd (1996a) 'Round Table responds to ineffectiveness charges', *ENDS Report* 255, pp 9–10

Environmental Data Services Ltd (1996b) 'Energy saving on back burner as gas competition looms', *ENDS Report* 253, pp 7–8

Environmental Data Services Ltd (1997a) 'Government's fresh attempt at greening of Whitehall', *ENDS Report* 271, pp 3–4

Environmental Data Services Ltd (1997b) 'Whitehall go-slow on energy efficiency', *ENDS Report* 264, p 27

Environmental Data Services Ltd (1997c) 'Gummer leaves Labour a legacy on greening of Whitehall', *ENDS Report* 267, p 3

Environmental Data Services Ltd (1997d) 'Sustainable development strategy promised for late next year', *ENDS Report* 272, pp 35–36

Environmental Data Services Ltd (1997e) 'In Trust for Tomorrow, or Somewhat Later', *ENDS Report* 271, p 2

Environmental Data Services Ltd (1997f) '"Green Book" promised for next year's Budget', *ENDS Report* 270, pp 28–29

The Financial Times (1996) 'Car emerges as villain in 'green' survey', *The Financial Times*, 13 March

The Government's Panel on Sustainable Development (1995) *First Report*, HMSO, London

The Government's Panel on Sustainable Development (1996) *Second Report*, DoE, London

The Government's Panel on Sustainable Development (1997) *Third Report*, DETR, London

Green Alliance (1991) *Greening Government: the failure of the Departmental Annual Reports to reflect integrated policy making*, Green Alliance, London

Green Alliance (1992) *Greening Government 2: update to the 1991 report*, Green Alliance, London

Green Alliance (1993) *The Parliamentary Newsletter*, w/e 4 June, p 1

Green Alliance (1995) 'Memorandum to HOLSCSD', *Report from the Select Committee on Sustainable Development* vol 2, HL paper 72, session 1994–95, HMSO, London, pp 539–541

Green Alliance (1996a) *The Green Alliance Report*, 96/1 March, Green Alliance, London

Green Alliance (1996b) 'Money Talks', *Parliamentary Newsletter*, w/e 24 May 1997, Green Alliance, London, p 1

Green Alliance (1997) 'Super news for the environment?', *Parliamentary Newsletter*, 6 May 1997, Green Alliance, London

The Guardian (1996a) 'British Gas fury at price control', London, 7 June, p 4

The Guardian (1996b) 'Car-bound Britain is wasting its fuel', *The Guardian*, London, 13 March

HC Debates (1996a) *Weekly Hansard, House of Commons Parliamentary Debates*, Written Answers, 16 February, vol 271, col 626–627

HC Debates (1996b) *Weekly Hansard, House of Commons Parliamentary Debates*, Written Answers, 26 April, vol 275, col 497

HC Debates (1996c) *Weekly Hansard, House of Commons Parliamentary Debates*, Written Answers, 8 November, vol 285, col 600–601

HM Government(1990) *This Common Inheritance*, Cmnd 1200, HMSO, London

HM Government (1991) *This Common Inheritance: the first year report*, Cmnd 1655, HMSO, London

HM Government (1992) *This Common Inheritance: the second year report*, Cmnd 2068, HMSO, London

HM Government (1994a) *Sustainable Development: The UK Strategy*, Cmnd 2426, HMSO, London

HM Government (1994b) *This Common Inheritance: the third year report*, Cmnd 2549, HMSO, London

HM Government (1995a) *Government Response to the First Annual Report of the Government's Panel on Sustainable Development*, 29 March, DoE, London

HM Government (1995b) *This Common Inheritance: UK Annual Report*, Cm 2822, HMSO, London

HM Government (1996a) *Government Response to the Second Annual Report of the Government's Panel on Sustainable Development*, 30 March, DoE, London

HM Government (1996b) *This Common Inheritance: UK Annual Report*, Cm 3188, HMSO, London

HM Government (1997) *This Common Inheritance: UK Annual Report*, Cm 3556, HMSO, London

HM Treasury (1995) 'Memorandum and Oral Evidence to HOLSCSD', *Report from the Select Committee on Sustainable Development* vol 2, HL paper 72, session 1994–5, HMSO, London, pp 669–683

House of Lords Select Committee on Sustainable Development (HOLSCSD) (1995) *Report from the Select Committee on Sustainable Development*, vols 1 and 2, HL paper 72, session 1994–95, HMSO, London

Hill, J (1996) personal communication, March 1996

Hill, J and Jordan, A (1993) 'The Greening of Government: lessons from the White Paper process', *ECOS* vol 14, no 3/4, pp 3–9

The Independent (1996) 'Gummer admits to "green" failure', *The Independent*, 13 March

Pearce, D W, Barbier, E and Markandya, A (1985) *Blueprint for a Green Economy*, Earthscan Publications Ltd, London

Powell, J C, and Craighill, A, (1996) 'The Landfill Tax' in T O'Riordan (ed) *Eco-Taxation*, Earthscan Publications Ltd, London, pp 304–320

Sachs, W (ed) (1993) *Global Ecology: A New Arena of Political Conflict*, Zed Books, London

Sills, R (1997) *The Status of Entrust*, IBC UK Conference, 2.12.1997

UK Round Table on Sustainable Development (1996) *First Annual Report*, DoE, London

UK Round Table on Sustainable Development (1997) *Second Annual Report*, DoE, London

World Commission on Environment and Development (1987) *Our Common Future*, Oxford University Press, Oxford

REFERENCES TO CHAPTER 9

Beuermann, C and Jäger, J (1996) 'Climate change politics in Germany: how long will any double dividend last?' in T O'Riordan, and J Jäger (eds) *Politics of Climate Change*, Routledge, London

Bleischwitz, R (1995) (pers comm)

BMU (ed) (1994a) *Umwelt 1994 – Politik für eine nachhaltige, umweltgerechte Entwicklung*,

Bundestagsdrucksache 12/8451, BMU, Bonn

BMU (ed) (1994b) *Environment 1994: German Strategy for Sustainable Development – Summary*, BMU, Bonn

BMU (ed) (1996) *Protokoll der Sitzung des nationalen Komitees für nachhaltige Entwicklung am 7 Februar 1996*, unpublished

BMU/BMZ (ed) (1994) *German Report to the 3rd CSD-Session 1995*, BMU, Bonn

BMU/BMZ (ed) (1995) *CSD 96 Guidelines for National Information, Part 1: Cross Sectoral Issues*, BMU/BMZ, Bonn

Brundtland, G and Hanff, U (1987) *Unsere Gemeinsame Zukunft: Der Brundtland-Bericht der Weltkommission für Umwelt und Entwicklung*, Eggenkamp, Grevan

BUND (ed) (1995) *Ökologische Steuerreform: Ein Beitrag zu einem Zukunftsfähigen Deutschland*, BUND, Bonn

BUND and MISEREOR (eds) (1995) *Zukunftsfäluges Deutschland: Ein Beitrag zu einer Global Nachhaltiger Entwicklung*, Birkhäuser, Basel, Boston, Berlin

Deutscher Bundestag (ed) (1989a) *Bundestags–Drucksache 11/5175, Kritik am 7: Entwicklungspolitischen Bericht der Bundesregierung*, Deutscher Bundestag, Bonn

Deutscher Bundestag (ed) (1989b) *Bundestags–Drucksache 11/4863, Erfolgskontrolle in der Entwicklungspolitik*, Deutscher Bundestag, Bonn

Deutscher Bundestag (ed) (1992a) *Bundestags–Drucksache 12/2286, Umwelt und Entwicklung: Politik für eine Nachhaltige Entwicklung*, Deutscher Bundestag, Bonn

Deutscher Bundestag (ed) (1992b) *Bundestags–Drucksache 12/1951*, Deutscher Bundestag, Bonn

Entsorga (ed) (1994) 'Vorsorgender Denkansatz Öko-Audits im Unternehmen Gewinnen an Bedeutung', *Entsorga* vol 13, no 5, pp 146–156

European Commission (1995) *Progress Report on Implementation of the European Community Programme of Policy and Action in Relation to the Environment and Sustainable Development 'Towards Sustainability'*, EU Commission, Brussels

Feus, T (1997) *Rio Plus 10: The German Contribution to Sustainable Development*, Development and Real Foundation, Bonn

Förschle, G (1994) 'Umwelt-Audit als Betätigungsfeld für Wirtschaftsprüfer', *Wirtschaftsprüferkammer Mitteilungen* vol 33, no 1, pp 1–8

Forum Umwelt und Entwicklung (1995) *Drei Jahre nach Rio*, Forum Umwelt und Entwicklung, Bonn

Friebel, M (1994) 'Weg von den Inselloesunden', *Politische Okologie* vol 3/4, pp 26–9

Geschäftsstelle Eine Welt für Alle (ed) (1991) *Plattform*, Eine Welt für alle, Köln

Görres, A, Ehringhaus, H and v Weizsäcker, E U (1994) *Der Weg zur Ökologischen Steuerreform: Weniger Umweltbelastung und mehr Beschäftigung Das Memorandum des Fördervereins Ökologische Steuerreform*, Olzog, München

Greenpeace (ed) (1994) *Ökosteuer – Königsweg oder Sackgasse?* Greenpeace, Berlin

Hamilton, K, Pearce, D, Atkinson, G, Gomez-Lobo, A and Young, C (1994) *The Policy Implications of Natural Resource and Environmental Accounting*, CSERGE Working Paper GEC 94–18, Norwich, UK

Leitschuh-Fecht, H and Burmeister, K (1994) 'Das Leitbild sustainabilitymuß klarer gefaßt werden – eine Bilanz der bisherigen Diskussion', *Ökologische Briefe* no 46, pp 7–11

Loske, R (1995) pers comm

Ostertag, K and Schlegelmilch, K (1996) *Saving the Climate – That's My Job. Mögliche Beschäftigungseffekte von Klimaschutzmaßnahmen durch die Realisierung des Toronto-Ziels einer 20-prozentigen Reduktion von CO_2-Emissionen bis zum Jahre 2005 gegenüber dem Jahre 1988 Literaturstudie: Deutschland*, Wuppertal Paper no 54, 3/1996, Wuppertal Institut, Wuppertal

Sachs, W, Loske, R and Linz, M (eds) *Greening the North: A Post Industrial Blueprint for Ecology and Equity*, Zed Books, London

Serageldin, I and Steer, A (eds) (1993) *Valuing the Environment,* proceedings of the First
    Annual International Conference on Environmentally Sustainable Development held
    at the World Bank Washington, DC 30 September–1October, 1993, World Bank,
    Washington, DC
Simonis, U E (1991) 'Globale Umwelttprobleme und zuk unftsfähige Entwicklung', *Aus
    Politik und Zeitgeschichte* vol 41, no 10, pp 3–10
Spangenberg, J (1995) (pers comm)
Steger, U (1995), 'Konsens ohne Worte', *Die Zeit* vol 50, no 37, 8 September, p 26
Thones, H W (1994) *Umwelt-Gutachten 1994: Für eine Dauerhaft-Unweltgerachte Entwicklung,*
    Metzler-Poeschel, Stuttgart
Thones, H W (1996) *Umweltgutachten 1996: Zur Umsetzung einer Danerhaft-Umweltgerachten
    Entwicklung,* Metzler-Poeschel, Stuttgart
Unmüßig, B (1995) *Vortrag zur Entstehung und Arbeit des Forums Umwelt und Entwicklung
    anläßlich des Strategieseminars des Forums Umwelt und Entwicklung am 10/11 Februar 1995 in
    Mülheim/Ruhr,* unpublished
WBGU (1993) *Welt im Wandel: Grundstucktur Globaler Mensch-Umwelt Bezielungen.
    Jahrensgutachten 1993,* Economica, Bonn
Weizsächer, E U V and Jesinghaus, J (1992) *Ecological Tax Reform: a Policy Proposal for
    Sustainable Development,* Zed Books, London
Wessel (BMU) (1995) pers comm
Wuppertal Bulletin (1995) 'Young entrepreneurs and friends of the Earth: dialogue, not
    polemics!', *Wuppertal Bulletin for an Ecological Tax Reform,* vol 1, no 3/4, pp 24–25,
    Wuppertal Institut, Wuppertal

REFERENCES TO CHAPTER 10

Aasen, B (1994) *Strategic Review of the Norwegian Campaign for Environment and Development,*
    Norsk Institutt for By-og Regionsforsking/NIBR, Working Paper 1994, p 104, Oslo
Dahl, A (1994) *EUs og Norges miljolovgivning – Likheter og forskjeller (EU's and Norway's
    Environmental Legislation – Similarities and Differences),* Fridtjof Nansen Institute Report,
    p 5, Oslo
Deloitte and Touche (1995) *Miljøinformasjon i norske selskapers årsrapporter (Environmental
    Information in Norwegian Companies' Annual Reports),* Oslo
Lafferty, W and Langhelle, O (eds) (1995) *Bærekraftig utvikling – Om utviklingens mål og
    bærekraftens betingelser (Sustainable Development – The Development and Preconditions of
    Sustainability),* Ad Notam Gyldendal, Oslo
Lindseth, A (1995) pers comm
Ministry of Environment (1987) *Environmental Statement to Parliament by the Minister of the
    Environment,* 27 May, Oslo
Ministry of Environment (1989) *Report to the Storting No 46 (1988–1989) Environment and
    Development Programme for Norway's Follow-Up of the Report of the World Commission on
    Environment and Development,* Oslo
Ministry of Environment (1992) *Norges nasjonalrapport til FN-konferansen om miljø og utvikling,
    Brasil 1992 (Norway's National Report to UNCED Brasil 1992),* Oslo
Ministry of the Environment (1994) *Environmental Policy Statement: Minister of Environment
    Thorbjørn Berntsen's Policy Statement to the Storting,* 11 April, Oslo
Ministry of the Environment (1995) *Environmental Policy Statement (1994): Minister of
    Environment Torbjørn Berntsen's Policy Statement to the Storting,* 11 May, Oslo
Ministry of the Environment (1997) *Report to the Storting No 58 (1996–97) Environment Policy
    for a Sustainable Development,* Oslo
Ministry of Foreign Affairs (1988) *Miljø og Utvikling, Norges bidrag til det internasjonale arbeid*

for en bærekraftig utvikling (Environment and Development, Norway's Contribution to the International Work for Sustainable Development), Aktuelle utenrikspolitiske spørsmål, no 45, Oslo

Ministry of Foreign Affairs (1993) *Norway's Follow-Up to the United Nations Conference on Environment and Development, National Report to the UN Commission on Sustainable Development*, Oslo

Ministry of Foreign Affairs (1995) *National Report of Norway to the United Nations' Commission on Sustainable Development*, Oslo

Ministry of Foreign Affairs (1996) *National Report of Norway to the United Nations' Commission on Sustainable Development*, Oslo

Næss, A (1991) 'Den dypøkologiske bevegelse: aktivisme ut fra et helhetssyn' ('The Deep-Ecological Movement: Activism in an Overall View') in S Gjerdåker, L Gule, and B Hagtvet (eds) *Tanke og handling i miljøkampen (The Insurmountable Boundary: Thought and Action in the Battle for the Environment)*, Chr Michelsens Institutt/J W Cappelens Forlag, pp 21–43

Norwegian Green Tax Commission (1996) *Policies for a Better Environment and High Employment*, Arnesen, Oslo

NOU (1992) *Mot en mer kostnadseffektiv miljøpolitikk (Towards a More Cost-Efficient Environmental Policy)*, Norges Offentlige utredninger/NOU 1992, p 3, Oslo

NOU (1995) *Virkemidler i miljøpolitikken (Environmental Policy Instruments)*, Norges Offentlige utredninger/NOU 1995, p 4, Oslo

OECD (1993) *OECD Environmental Performance Review Norway*, Organisation of Economic Cooperation and Development, Paris

Skjærseth, J B and Rosendal, K (ed) (1995) 'Norges miljøutenrikspolitikk' ('Norway's International Environmental Policy') in T Knutsen, G Sørbø and S Gjerdåker, *i Norges Utenrikspolitikk (Norwegian Foreign Policy)*, C Michelsens Institutt/J W Cappelens Forlag, pp 21–43

The Norwegian Research Council (1996) *Report from the Consensus Conference on the Management of Biological Diversity in Norway*, 23 May, Oslo

World Commission on Environment and Development (1987) *Our Common Future*, Oxford University Press, Oxford

REFERENCES TO CHAPTER 11

AGMADS (1994) *Acordo global em matéria de ambiente e desenvolvimento sustentável celebrado entre os Ministérios do Ambiente e Recursos Naturais, da Indústria e Energia, da Agricultura e as Confederações dos Agricultores de Portugal (CAP) e da Indústria Portuguesa (CIP)*, November, Lisbon

CSD (1994a) *Implementation of Agenda 21 in Portugal* (UNCED follow-up), annual report submitted to the CSD, Lisbon

CSD (1994b) *Follow-up Report (Portugal)*, submitted to the CSD, January, Lisbon

Dunlap, R E (1994) 'International attitudes towards environment and development' in H O Bergesen and G Parmann (eds) *Green Globe Yearbook 1994*, Oxford University Press, Oxford, pp 115–126

Dunlap, R E and Mertig, A G (1995) 'Global environmental concern: a challenge to the post-materialism thesis' in P Ester and W Schluchter (eds) *Social Dimensions of Contemporary Environmental Issues: International Perspectives*, The Netherlands, Tilburg University Press, pp 71–92

Gouzee, N, Mazijn, B and Billharz, S (1995) *Indicators of Sustainable Development for Decision-Making*, Report of the Workshop of Ghent (Belgium), 9–11 January 1995, submitted to the UN Commission on Sustainable Development, Federal Planning Office of Belgium, Brussels

Kuik, O and Verbruggen, H (eds) (1991) *In Search of Indicators of Sustainable Development*, Kluwer Academic Publishers, Dordrecht, The Netherlands

Laundy, P (1989) *Parliaments in the Modern World*, Dartmouth Publishing, Andover, Hants

Liebert, U and Cotta, M (1990) *Parliament and Democratic Consolidations in Southern Europe: Greece, Italy, Portugal, Spain and Turkey*, Pinter Publishers, London

MENR (1994) *Síntese Estratégica: Aspectos mais relevantes para o seguimento em Portugal das conclusões da CNUAD*, MENR, Lisbon

NEPP(1995) *Plano nacional de política de ambiente*, Lisboa, Ministério do Ambiente e Recursos Naturais, Lisbon

PE (1992) *Os sistemas eleitorais para os parlamentos nacionais nos países da comunidade europeia*, Parlamento Europeu, Direcção-General de Estudos, Colecção de Estudos e Documentação, Série Política, W–16, Lisbon

Reis, J P (1992) *Lei de Bases do Ambiente, anotada e comentada e legislação complementar sobre ambiente*, Almedina, Coimbra

Ribeiro, T, Rodrigues, V and O'Riordan, T (1996) 'Ajustamentos institucionais às estraté-gias de desenvolvimento sustentável: o caso português' in C Borrego, C Coelho, L Arroja, C Boia and E Figueiredo (eds) *Proceedings of the 5ª Conferência Nacional sobre a Qualidade do Ambiente* vol 1, pp 43–56

Schmidt, L (1993) *O verde preto no branco*, Gradiva, Lisbon

REFERENCES TO CHAPTER 12

Baumol, W and Oates, W (1989) *The Theory of Environmental Policy*, Cambridge University Press, Cambridge

Bousbouras, D (1992) 'The institution of environmental impact assessment in Greece', *Nea Oikologia*, June (in Greek), pp 17–26

Demertzis, N (1995) 'Greece: Greens at the Periphery' in D Richardson and C Rootes (eds) *The Development of Green Parties in Europe*, Routledge, London, pp 61–74

Efthimiopoulos, H (1994) 'The energy tax: potential and deadlock of a policy', *Nea Oikologia*, September (in Greek), pp 41–52

Kalaitzidis, D (1994) 'Upgrading environmental education in Greece', *Nea Oikologia*, September (in Greek), pp 79–84

Kousis, M (1991) 'Development, environment and social mobilisation: a micro-level analysis', *The Greek Review of Social Research* vol 80, no 1, pp 161–172

Kousis, M (1993) 'Collective resistance and sustainable development in rural Greece: the case of geothermal energy on the Island of Milos', *Sociologia Ruralis* vol 33, no 1, pp 3–34

Kousis, M (1994) 'Environment and the state in the EU periphery: the case of Greece', *Regional Politics and Policy* vol 4, no 1, pp 118–135

Laskaris, C (1993) 'Environmental crisis: a world social and educational problem' in *Environmental Crisis: Theory Methodology and Special Perspectives*, Athens, Synchroni Epoche (in Greek), pp 17–31

Lekakis, J (1995) 'Environmental management in Greece and the challenge of sustainable development', *The Environmentalist* vol 15, no 1, pp 16–26

Modinos, M (1995) 'Conflict resolution', *Nea Oikologia*, May (in Greek), pp 7–2

National Report of Greece (1991) *UN Conference on Environment and Development* (held in Brazil, June 1992), YPEHODE, Athens

O'Riordan, T and Jordan, A (1996) 'Social Institutions and Climate Change' in T O'Riordan and J Jäger (eds) *Politics of Climate Change: A European Perspective*, Routledge, London

Papayiannakis, M (1994) 'Evro-oikologika', *Nea Oikologia*, March (in Greek), pp 3–10

Papayiannakis, M (1995) 'Evro-oikologika', *Nea Oikologia*, January (in Greek), pp 12–17
Pearce, D and Turner, R (1990) *Economics of National Resources and the Environment*, The John Hopkins University Press, Baltimore
Pridham, G, Verney, S and Konstandakopulos, D (1995) 'Environmental policy in Greece: evolution, structures and process', *Environmental Politics* vol 5, no 2, pp 17–25
Pyrovetsi, M (1994) 'Our future? sustainability' in *Modern World Problems and the Responsibility of the Scientist*, Salonika Aristotelian University and Institute for Education and Peace (in Greek), pp 35–42
Sakiotis, J (1993) 'Greek economy: ten principles for a sustainable model of economic management', *Nea Oikologia*, April (in Greek), pp 17–21
Smith, M (1993) *Pressure, Power and Policy: State Autonomy and Policy Networks in Britain and the United States*, Harvester Wheatsheaf, London
Theohary, C (1995) 'Industrial relations and environment in Greece' in *Environment and Labour in Greece*, EKA, Athens (in Greek), pp 32–47
Tilly, C (1994) 'Social movements as historically specific clusters of political performances', *Berkeley Journal of Sociology* vol 38, no 1, pp 1–30
Tsantilis, D (1994) 'Dreams and miracles in environmental performance', *Nea Oikologia*, December (in Greek), pp 17–21
Vlassopoulou, C (1991) *La Politique de l'Environment: le cas de la Pollution Atmosphérique à Athens*, DPhil Thesis, University of Picardie (in French)
YPEHODE (1992) *Annual Report on the State of the Environment*, Athens (in Greek)
YPEHODE (1994) *National Report to the UNCSD*, Athens
YPEHODE (1995a) *National Report to the UNCSD*, Athens
YPEHODE (1995b) *Greece: Ecological and Cultural Stock. Data, Actions, Programmes for the Protection of the Environment*, Athens (in Greek)

REFERENCES TO EDITORIAL INTRODUCTION TO PART IV

Earth Negotiations Bulletin (1995) *Day of Local Authorities* vol 5, no 42, IISD
ICLEI (1997) *Local Agenda 21 Survey: a Study of Response by Local Authorities and Their National and International Associations to Agenda 21*, ICLEI in Co-operation with the UN Department for Policy Co-ordination and Sustainable Development, Toronto
LGMB (1992a) *Earth Summit Rio '92 Information Pack for Local Authorities*, LGMB, Luton
LGMB (1992b) *Agenda 21: A Guide for Local Authorities in the UK*, LGMB, Luton
Patterson, A and Theobald, K S (1996) 'Local Agenda 21, Compulsory Competitive Tendering and Local Environmental Practices', *Local Environment* vol 1, no 1, pp 7–20
UNCED (1992) *Agenda 21*, UNCED (available on the internet at <http://www.unep unep.no/uneo/partners/un/unced/agenda21.htm>)

REFERENCES TO CHAPTER 13

Audit Commission (1997) *It's A Small World: Local Government's Role as a Steward of the Environment*, Audit Commission for Local Authorities and the National Health Service in England and Wales, London
Bruff, G (1996) *Sustainable Development and Unitary Development Plans: a comparison of the two agendas*, conference paper: ERP Environment international Sustainable Development Research Conference, Manchester, UK, March
Chisholm, M (1995) 'Some Lessons from the Review of Local Government in England', *Regional Studies* vol 29, no 6, pp 563–580

Christie I (1994) 'Britain's Sustainable Development Strategy: Environmental Quality and Policy Change', *Policy Studies* vol 15, no 3, pp 4–20

CEC (1992) *Towards Sustainability, The EC's Fifth Action Programme on the Environment*, CEC, Brussels

Committee on Public Participation in Planning (1969) *People and Planning*, Ministry of Housing and Local Government, Scottish Development Department and Welsh Office, HMSO, London

Cope, S and Atkinson, R (1994) 'The Structures in Governance in Britain' in S P Savage, R Atkinson and L Robins (1994) *Public Policy in Britain*, Macmillan, London

Duncan, S and Goodwin, M (1988) 'Removing Local Government Autonomy: Political Centralisation and Financial Control', *Local Government Studies*, November/December, pp 49–65

Elcock, H (1994) *Local Government: Policy and Management in Local Authorities*, third edition, Routledge, London

Fourth National Environmental Coordinators Forum (1994) *Conference Report*, July

Gibbs, D (1997) 'On Course for a Sustainable Future? European environmental policy and local economic development', *Local Environment* vol 1, no 3, pp 247–258

HC Debates (1997a) *Weekly Hansard, House of Commons Parliamentary Debates*, Written Answers, 25 November vol 301, col 463

HC Debates (1997b) *Weekly Hansard, House of Commons Parliamentary Debates*, Written Answers, 9 July vol 297, col 498

HM Government (1990) *This Common Inheritance*, Cmnd 1200, HMSO, London

HM Government (1994) *Sustainable Development: The UK Strategy*, Cmnd 2426, HMSO, London

HM Government (1996) *This Common Inheritance: UK Annual Report*, Cm 2822, HMSO, London

HM Government (1997) *This Common Inheritance: UK Annual Report*, Cm 3556, HMSO, London

Johnston, R J and Pattie, C J (1996) 'Local Government in Local Governance: the 1994–95 Restructuring of Local Government in England', *International Journal of Urban and Regional Research* vol 20, no 4, pp 671–696

Leu, W-S, Williams, P W, and Bark, A W (1995) 'An Evaluation of the Implementation of Environmental Assessment by UK Local Authorities', *Project Appraisal* vol 10, no 2, pp 91–102

LGMB (1993a) *A Framework for Local Sustainability*, LGMB, Luton

LGMB (1993b) *Towards Sustainability: the EC's Fifth Action Programme on the Environment, a Guide to Local Authorities*, LGMB, Luton

LGMB (1994) *Local Agenda 21 Principles and Process: A Step by Step Guide*, LGMB, Luton

LGMB (1995) *The Sustainability Indicators Research Project*, LGMB, Luton

Macnaghten, P, Grove-White, R, Jacobs, M, and Wynne, B (1995) *Public Perceptions and Sustainability in Lancashire – Indicators, institutions, Participation*, Lancashire County Council, Preston

Morris, J (1993) 'LA21 in the UK: the first steps', *ECOS* vol 14, no 3/4, pp 27–29

Municipal Yearbook and Public Services Directory (1997) Municipal Journal Ltd, London

Parker, B (1995) 'Better practice, partial success', *Town and Country Planning* vol 64, no 11, pp 304–305

Parker, J And Selman, P (1996) *Policy Process and Product in Local Agenda 21 – Working Paper no 1: Background to the Research: Case Studies and Methodology*, Countryside and Community Research Unit, Cheltenham and Gloucester College of Higher Education, Cheltenham

Patterson, A, and Theobald, K S (1996) 'Local Agenda 21, Compulsory Competitive Tendering and Local Environmental Practices', *Local Environment* vol 1, no 1, pp 7–20

Peattie, K And Hall, G (1994) 'The Greening of Local Government: A Survey', *Local Government Studies* vol 20, no 3, pp 458–485

Rhodes, R A W (1991) 'Now Nobody Understands the System; The Changing Face of Local Government' in P Norton *New Directions in British Politics?: Essays on the Evolving Constitution*, Aldershot, Edward Elgar

Rookwood, R (1994) 'Danger to Democracy', *Town and Country Planning*, January, pp 5–7

Royal Commission on Environmental Pollution (1994) *Eighteenth Report: Transport and the Environment*, Cm 2674, HMSO, London

Royal Town Planning Institute (1993) *Sustainable Development: a discussion paper*, unpublished

Selman, P and Parker, J (1997) 'Citizenship, Civicness, and Social Capital in Local Agenda 21', *Local Environment* vol 2, no 2, pp 170–184

Stewart, J (1993) 'Reinventing Local Democracy', *Parliamentary Brief*, July

Stewart, J (1994) 'Returning Government to the Community', *Parliamentary Brief*, June/July

Stewart, J (1996) 'Innovation in Democratic Practice in Local Government', *Policy and Politics* vol 24, no 1 pp 29–41

The Times (1996) 'Local election results: Town hall disaster will sap Tories' campaign strength', 4 May, pp 8–9

Tuxworth, B and Carpenter, C (1995) *Local Agenda 21 Survey 1994/5: Results*, LGMB, Luton

Tuxworth, B, and Thomas, E (1996) *Local Agenda 21 Survey 1996*, LGMB, Luton

Ward, S (1993a) 'Thinking Global, Acting Local? British Local Authorities and Their Environmental Plans', *Environmental Politics* vol 2, no 3, pp 453–478

Ward, S (1993b) *The Politics of Mutual Attraction? UK Local Government and the Europeanisation of Environmental Policy*, draft paper to the Colloquium on UK Environmental Policy, December

Ward, S and Lowe, P (1994) *Adaptation, Participation and Reaction: British Local Government – EU Environmental Relations*, Centre for Rural Economy, Reset Report, Newcastle

Wilks, S and Hall, P N (1995) 'Think Globally, Act Locally: Implementing Agenda 21 in Britain', *Policy Studies* vol 16, no 3, pp 37–33

Williamson, J (1995) 'Local Government as a Context for Policy' in Mullard, M, *Policy Making in Britain: An Introduction*, Routledge, London

Wilson, D J and Game, C with Leach, S and Stoker, G (1994) *Local Government in the UK*, Macmillan, Basingstoke

Wilson, J G (1993) 'British Local Government Finance under the Conservatives' in Gibson, J and Batley, R (eds) *Financing European Local Governments*, Frank Cass, London, pp 55–78

Young, S (1995) 'Participation – out with the old, in with the new?', *Town and Country Planning* vol 64, no 4

REFERENCES TO CHAPTER 14

Alternative Kommunalpolitik (1996) *Heft* 2/1996

BMBau (ed) (1996) *Siedlungsentwicklung und Siedlungspolitik Nationalbericht Deutschland zur Konferenz Habitat II*, BMBau, Bonn

BMU (ed) (1994) *Umwelt 1994. Politik für eine Nachhaltige Umweltgerechte Entwicklung*, Bundestagsdrucksache 12/8451, BMU, Bonn

Bonsen, E Z (1993) 'Die Klagen der Städte', *Süddeutsche Zeitung*, 17 December

Bormann, M and Stietzel, C (1993) *Stadt und Gemeinde. Kommunalpolitik in den Neuen Ländern*, Bundeszentrale für politische Bildung, Bonn

Bundestagsdrucksache (1994a) 12/6815, (publications of the German parliament) 9 February

Bundestagsdrucksache (1994b) 12/213, (publications of the German parliament) 3 March
Clearing House for Applied Futures (1995) *Kommunale Strategien für eine Zukunftsfähige Entwicklung. Eine Analyse der Einflußfaktoren der Strategie-Entwicklung und Umsetzung am Beispiel von Berlin-Köpenick und Güstrow*, unpublished
Coenen, F (1996) *Local Agenda 21 in The Netherlands*, unpublished
Deutsches Institut für Urbanistik (ed) (1995) *Aktuelle Probleme der Stadtentwicklung und der Kommunalpolitik. Umfrageergebnisse 1995*, Difu, Berlin
Dodds, F (1995) 'Habitat II. Der Nationale Vorbereitungsprozeß', *Rundbrief 4/1995*, (Forum Umwelt und Entwicklung), Bonn
DSt (1993) *Rede des Präsidenten des Deutschen Städtetages Anläßlich der Außerordentlichen Hauptversammlung 'Städte in Not' des Deutschen Städtetages am 18 Oktober 1993*, Bonn, unpublished
.DSt (ed) (1995) 'Städte für eine Umweltgerechte Entwicklung. Materialien für eine Lokale Agenda 21', *DST-Beiträge zur Stadtentwicklung und zum Umweltschutz*, Reihe E Heft 24, Köln
DStGb – Deutscher Städte und Gemeindebund, Kommunale Umwelt-AktioN (UAN) (ed) (1995) *Rathaus und Klimaschutz Hinweise für die Pommunale Praxis (Lokale Agenda 21)*, DStGb, Hanover
Ebert, T (1994) *Möglichkeiten Kommunaler Umweltpolitik. Umweltpolitische Kompetenzen im Föderalen System der Bundesrepublik Deutschland*, Diplomarbeit, GHK, Kassel
Fiedler, K (1996) 'Eine "Lokale Agenda 21" für Deutschland', *dh-Info*, January 1996
Gisevius, W (1991) *Leitfaden durch die Kommunalpolitik*, Dietz, Bonn
Hewitt, N (1995) *European Local Agenda 21 Planning Guide. How to Engage in Long-Term Environmental Action Planning towards Sustainability*, European Sustainable Cities and Towns Campaign, Brussels
ICLEI (ed) (1993) *Klima Schützen heißt Städte schützen*, ICLEI, Freiburg
ICLEI (1995a) *Local Initiatives. ICLEI Members in Action 1993–1995*, ICLEI, Freiburg
ICLEI (1995b) *Erläuterungen zu Recherche: Kommunen auf dem Weg zu 'Nachhaltiger Entwicklung'*, unpublished
Joseph, M (1995) *Die Analyse Kommunaler Umweltpolitik aus Sicht der Neuen Politischen Ökonomie*, Lang, Frankfurt
Karrenberg, H and Münstermann, E (1995) 'Gemeindefinanzbericht 1995. Städtische Finanzen '95 – unter Staatlichem Druck', *Der Städtetag*, March
Klimabündnis, Alliance and del Clima E V (eds) (1993) *Klima – lokal geschützt. Aktivitäten europäischer Kommunen*, Raben–Verlag, München
Kommunale Briefe für Ökologie (1994) 'Privatisierung: Gewetz zum Verkauf des kommunalen Tafelsilbers' no 8
Kommunale Briefe für Ökologie (1996) 'Zukunftsfähiges Deutschland Bedeutet "Sustainable Cities" no 1/2, 17 January, pp 3–4
Pohl, W (1994) 'Den Gemeinden Geht die Luft aus. Zum Gemeindefinanzbericht 1994', *Alternative Kommunalpolitik*, March, pp 32–35
Politische Ökologie (1995) no 44, Schwerpunkt Nachhaltige Stadtentwicklung
Quante, M, and Schwartz, T (1996) *Kommunale Umeltschutzpolitik*, Hans Böckler Stiftung, Düsseldorf
Schiller-Dickhut, R (1996) 'Machen wir einen Plan! Lokale Agendas 21 in Deutschland', *Alternative Kommunalpolitik*, 2, pp 59–60
Schuster, F and Dill, G W (eds) (1992) *Aufgaben der Kommunalpolitik in den 90er Jahren Band 4: Wohnungsbau, Städtebau, Umwelt*, Dt Gemeindeverlag, Köln
Sibum, D (1995) 'Pläne der AG Stadt und Regionalentwicklung', *Rundbrief No 4*, Forum Umwelt und Entwicklung, Bonn
Statistisches Bundesamt (ed) (1992–1995) *Statistische Jahrbücher 1992–1995 für die Bundesrepublik Deutschland*, Metzler-Poeschel, Wiesbaden

Unmüßig, B (1996) 'Mehr als TransFair. Die Rolle der Kommunen für ein Zukunftsfähiges Deutschland', *Alternative Kommunalpolitik* no 2, pp 57–58

Wehling, H G (1985) 'Kommunalpolitik in der Bundesrepublik Deutschland' in P von Haungs and E Jesse (eds) *Beiträge zur Zeitgeschite* 17, Volker Speiss, Berlin

Weidner, H (1995) *25 Years of Modern Environmental Policy in Germany. Treading a Well-Worn Path to the Top of the International Field*, WZB, FS II, pp 95–301, Berlin

Wessel (1995) (Federal Ministry for Environment, Nature Conservation and Reactor Safety) pers comm

Witte, G (1992) 'Mit dem Grundgesetz die Städte Stärken. Die Vorschläge des Deutschen Städtetages in der Verfassungsdiskussion', *Der Städtetag*, no 3

REFERENCES TO CHAPTER 15

Aall, C and Høyer, K G (1995) 'Kommuneøkologi og miljøproblemer' ('Municipal ecology and environmental problems'), *Plan* no 6, pp 13–19

Aall, C (1995 and 1996) 'Økokommuneprogrammet' ('The Ecomunicipality Programme'), *Plan* no 6, pp 2–6

Armann, K A, Hille, J, and Kasin, O (1995) *Lokal Agenda 21: Norske kommuners miljøarbeid etter Rio (Local Agenda 21: Norwegian municipalities' environmental work after Rio*, Alternative Future and the Idea Bank, no 5, p 95, Oslo

Hovik, S and Harsheim, J (1996) *Miljøvernets plass i kommunepolitikken* (Environmental Policy in Local Politics) Norwegian Institute for Urban and Regional Research/NIBR Report 1996, p 5, Oslo

Hovik, S and Johnsen, V (1994) *Fra forsøk til reform Evaluering av MIK–programmet (From experiment to reform – an evaluation of the EPLL programme)*, Norwegian Institute for Urban and Regional Research/NIBR Rapport 1994, p 23, Oslo

Holtane, E and Grann, O J (1995) 'Att ta Rio på alvor ('Taking Rio seriously')', *Nord Revy* No 2 14–18

Jansen, A I (1991) *Reform og resultater – Evaluering av forsøksprogrammet miljøvern i kommunene (Reform and Results. Evaluation of the Programme for Environmental Protection in the Municipalities)*, Noras, Oslo

Kleven, T (1994) 'Miljøvern og planlegging – norm og virkelighet' ('Environmental protection and planning – norm and reality') in J Naustdalslid, and S Hovik (eds) *Lokalt Miljøvern (Local Environmental Protection)*, Tano, Oslo, pp 129–154

Nationen (1994) 'Lokal Agenda 21 følges opp' ('Local Agenda 21 is followed up') *Nationen*, 1 November

Naustdalslid, J and Hovik, S (eds) (1994) *Lokalt Miljøvern (Local Environmental Protection)*, Tano, Oslo

Lund, E (1995) 'Hva nå med FONØ?' ('What now with FONE?') *Plan* no 6, pp 7–8

Ramsdal, H (1995) 'Ute på prøve. Evaluering av Økokommuneprogrammet som miljøpolitisk strategi' ('Out on parole. Evaluation of the Ecomunicipality Programme as an Environmental Policy Strategy') *Plan* no 6, pp 9–13

Ministry of Environment (1989) *Report to the Storting No 46 (1988–1989): Environment and Development Programme for Norway's Follow-Up of the Report of the World Commission on Environment and Development*, Oslo

Ministry of Environment (1986) *Report to the Storting No 4 (1986–1987): Open Air Activities*, Oslo

Ministry of Environment (1992) *White Paper No 13 on the UN Conference on Environment and Development, Rio de Janeiro (1992–1993)*, Oslo

Ministry of Environment (1995) *Two-thirds of Norwegian Local Authorities Have Adopted Action Plans for Environmental Protection*, leaflet prepared for the Oslo Roundtable Conference, 6–10 February 1995

Ramsdal, H (1996) 'Økokommune som miljøpolitisk strategi' ('Ecomunicipality as environmental policy strategy') *Plan* no 6, pp 13–17

Taugebøl, T (1994) *Miljøvernsamarbeid mellom kommune og frivillige organisasjoner (Environmental protection cooperation between muncipalities and voluntary organisations)*, KS Research, Oslo

REFERENCES TO CHAPTER 16

Lee, K (1996) 'Charting a course', *Environment* vol 38, no 4, pp 33–34

Olsen, M H (1996) 'Charting a course for sustainability', *Environment* vol 38, no 4, pp 16–15 and 30–36

President's Council on Sustainable Development (1996) *Sustainable America: a New Consensus*, Government Printing Office, Washington, DC

Warburton, D (ed) (1998) *Community and Sustainable Development: Participation for the Future*, Earthscan Publications Ltd, London

INDEX